CH00449580

House of Commons

Welsh Affairs Committee

Inward Investment in Wales

Eighth Report of Session 2010–12

Volume II

Oral and written evidence

Additional written evidence is contained in Volume III, available on the Committee website at www.parliament.uk/welshcom

Ordered by the House of Commons to be printed 31 January 2012

HC 854-II
Published on 21 February 2012
by authority of the House of Commons
London: The Stationery Office Limited
£23.00

The Welsh Affairs Committee

The Welsh Affairs Committee is appointed by the House of Commons to examine the expenditure, administration, and policy of the Office of the Secretary of State for Wales (including relations with the National Assembly for Wales).

Current membership

David T.C. Davies MP *(Conservative, Monmouth) (Chair)*
Stuart Andrew MP *(Conservative, Pudsey)*
Guto Bebb MP *(Conservative, Aberconwy)*
Geraint Davies MP *(Labour, Swansea West)*
Jonathan Edwards MP *(Plaid Cymru, Carmarthen East and Dinefwr)*
Nia Griffith MP *(Labour, Llanelli)*
Mrs Siân C. James MP *(Labour, Swansea East)*
Susan Elan Jones MP *(Labour, Clwyd South)*
Karen Lumley MP *(Conservative, Redditch)*
Jessica Morden MP *(Labour, Newport East)*
Mr Robin Walker MP *(Conservative, Worcester)*
Mr Mark Williams MP *(Liberal Democrat, Ceredigion)*

The following Members were members of the Committee during the Parliament:

Alun Cairns MP *(Conservative, Vale of Glamorgan)*
Glyn Davies MP *(Conservative, Montgomeryshire)*
Owen Smith MP *(Labour, Pontypridd)*

Powers

The Committee is one of the departmental select committees, the powers of which are set out in House of Commons Standing Orders, principally in SO No 152. These are available on the internet via www.parliament.uk

Publications

The Reports and evidence of the Committee are published by The Stationery Office by Order of the House. All publications of the Committee (including press notices) are on the internet at www.parliament.uk/welshcom

The Reports of the Committee, the formal minutes relating to that report, oral evidence taken and some or all written evidence are available in printed volumes.

Additional written evidence may be published on the internet only.

Committee staff

The current staff of the Committee is Adrian Jenner (Clerk), Anwen Rees (Inquiry Manager), Jenny Nelson (Senior Committee Assistant), Dabinder Rai (Committee Assistant), Edward Bolton (Committee Support Assistant) and Jessica Bridges-Palmer (Media Officer).

Contacts

All correspondence should be addressed to the Clerk of the Welsh Affairs Committee, House of Commons, 7 Millbank, London SW1P 3JA. The telephone number for general enquiries is 020 7219 3264; and the Committee's email address is welshcom@parliament.uk

Witnesses

Professor Michael Scott, Vice-Chancellor and Chief Executive, **Mr Tony Hawkins**, Managing Director, Glyndŵr Innovations and **Mr Andrew Parry**, Executive Adviser to the Vice-Chancellor and Head of Corporate Communications, Glyndŵr University, **Ms Karen Padmore**, Business Development Manager and **Mr James Goodman**, Programme Development Manager, Bangor University

Ev 74

Thursday 15 September 2011

Professor Mark Drakeford AM, Welsh Labour Party, **Eluned Parrott AM**, Welsh Liberal Democrat Shadow Minister for Enterprise, Transport, Europe and Business, and **Nick Ramsay AM**, Welsh Conservatives, Shadow Minister for Business, Enterprise and Technology, National Assembly for Wales

Ev 78

Mr David Stevens, Chief Operating Officer, Admiral Group plc

Ev 86

Tuesday 8 November 2011

Mr Nick Baird, Chief Executive, **Mr Martin Phelan**, Director, Investment Projects and FDI Transition, and **Ms Kirstyn Boyle**, Head of Strategy and Business Partnerships, UK Trade & Investment

Ev 91

Monday 5 December 2011

Rt Hon Dr Vince Cable MP, Secretary of State for Business, Innovation and Skills, **Lord Green of Hurstpierpoint**, Minister for Trade and Investment, Department for Business, Innovation and Skills, and **Rt Hon Mrs Cheryl Gillan MP**, Secretary of State for Wales, Wales Office

Ev 99

List of printed written evidence

Oral evidence

Taken before the Welsh Affairs Committee

on Tuesday 8 March 2011

Members present:

David T.C. Davies (Chair)

Stuart Andrew   Mrs Siân C. James
Guto Bebb   Susan Elan Jones
Geraint Davies   Mr Mark Williams
Jonathan Edwards

_____

Examination of Witnesses

Witnesses: **Dr John Ball**, Swansea University, **Professor David Pickernell**, University of Glamorgan, and **Professor Emeritus Peter Gripaios**, University of Plymouth, gave evidence.

Q1 Chair: A very good morning to you. Thank you for coming today to give evidence to the Committee. Perhaps I could introduce myself. I am David Davies, the Chairman of the Committee, and these are my colleagues. I wonder whether for the record you would just introduce yourselves and we will begin.
Professor Gripaios: I am Peter Gripaios, emeritus professor at the University of Plymouth.
Dr Ball: I am Dr John Ball. I am a lecturer in economics at Swansea University.
Professor Pickernell: I am David Pickernell. I am a professor of economic development policy at the Centre for Enterprise at the University of Glamorgan.

Q2 Chair: Thank you very much. Could I begin by asking all or any of you to give a brief history of inward investment into Wales? Perhaps you could elaborate on why it seems to have fallen in relation to the rest of the United Kingdom and make any comments you might have on the success or otherwise of the WDA, which appear to be very successful in bringing in inward investment.
Dr Ball: "Success" is a term that has been bandied about to some extent unwisely. As I have said in my paper, to some extent inward investment undoubtedly made a difference to employment. There is no question that without inward investment the employment situation in Wales would be much worse. As I have said in my submission, the problem with inward investment in the past is that, although it addressed the first issue in terms of regional policy, it failed to address self-sustaining growth. I think on that basis it was a relative failure, and that is the position even as we speak now. Clearly, past policies on inward investment can be counted as a fail, in my view.
I would, however, with your permission, Chair, comment on the Welsh Development Agency. I had the most frustrating 10 years working for the Welsh Development Agency. I still take the view that the WDA talked a good fight. It was not at arm's length from government; it did not have appropriate policies; it was poorly managed and led; it did not have clear objectives; and it certainly did not have good management. Dare I say, with great respect, that if one of the recommendations here is that WDA be reborn,

then I very much hope that it will be reborn in an entirely different guise?

Q3 Chair: Those are strong words, and we like that on the Committee. Looking at the statistics—I do not have them exactly to hand—it was very clear that Wales was getting a much greater share of inward investment into the UK when the WDA was in existence than it does now. I think it was somewhere in the region of 20% or 25% at the time as opposed to about 6% now, so why are you so harsh on the WDA?
Dr Ball: Because at the end of the day it was any employment. I remember my former Welsh Office colleagues saying that at the end of the day inward investment would provide, at a stroke, 200 or 300 jobs, which did matter—of course it mattered—but the reality of it was and is that it was employment at any price. It was low skilled and relatively low wage. I remember that in the days of the WDA I was on a plane coming from New York and there was a screen running advertisements. Basically, the advertisement said, "Come to Wales because it's cheap labour." We are paying a price for that, because cheap labour is now the policy elsewhere. Essentially, it was based on cheap labour. It is as simple as that.
Professor Gripaios: I think hindsight is a very easy thing. There is no question that Wales did go for FDI in a big way. It was seen almost as a one-trick pony; it was the solution to the problems of the decline of traditional industries. It was extraordinarily successful in getting a lot of manufacturing branch plant operations and later also lower level back office jobs in services. You asked two questions. Why was it? One thing is that it went for it very hard; secondly, it had a lot of money, which some English regions in particular did not have to chase it down.

Q4 Chair: But should they not be going at it very hard? We like it when civil servants go at it hard.
Professor Gripaios: When I say that hindsight is an easy thing, looking back you can see the deficiencies in the policy, but it seemed at least to give a breathing space at the time to replace the jobs in heavy industry which had gone. We all know that not a lot of coal miners and so on were employed in these new branch plant operations. There is much more female labour;

a lot of it is unskilled and not nearly as well paid. You also asked why it is going now. The reason is that the kinds of operations which Wales had on the basis of low labour costs are no longer competitive because you can get lower wage costs elsewhere. It is okay being the cheapest in the UK. The same argument has been applied to Cornwall, Plymouth, the north-east and so on, but that does not help you very much if you are in a big European market where Hungary is a lot cheaper and if you are in a world market where China is a lot cheaper.

Q5 Chair: Finally from me, so that I do not hog it, in your submissions one of you said that one of the issues you had was that these were low-paid jobs brought in in the 1990s and were not a good replacement for the relatively high wages received by people in the mining and steel industries. I thought it was interesting. Historically, there is a tendency to think that the people who worked in the mines and steel industries were very low paid and just scratched a living, but now, all of a sudden, history seems to be being rewritten, they were very well paid and their jobs were replaced by relatively low-wage jobs on production lines.
Professor Gripaios: I think that is to do with time scale. If you went back to the time before the second world war they certainly were very poorly paid jobs, but that changed with nationalisation.

Q6 Chair: I do not go that far back, but I can go back to the 1970s or 1980s. What did it look like then?
Professor Gripaios: Sadly, I can go back a little further. In the 1970s and 1980s, they were very well-paid jobs in the steelworks.
Chair: But they were always on strike. Anyway, there we are. I would like to bring in some of my colleagues.
Professor Gripaios: We are going along party political lines, then.

Q7 Mrs James: I am from the Valleys as well. During the 1980s they were well-paid jobs, and we fought for well-paid, meaningful jobs in the Valleys. We saw what inward investment—Mickey Mouse jobs, as we called them—did to the Valleys, so I am very interested in this issue. Going back to the discussion, does attracting foreign direct investment still remain a valid policy goal for Wales?
Professor Pickernell: I think it depends on what you want the inward investment for. I do not think that with the previous policy, which was very much employment based, you can solve that problem any more, because those jobs have gone to central and eastern Europe and China. As to the way in which we attracted investment in the 1970s, 1980s and early 1990s with grants and relatively low-cost labour, that advantage does not exist any more.
If you are talking about very specific areas where you might be able to build indigenous development, that is possible. In my submission, I have suggested that it must be much more co-ordinated with other policies. I got the impression from talking to people at the WDA at about the time of the change from a foreign direct investment focus to a more indigenous development focus that there was not a co-ordination of policy in the way there should have been.
I have done work with colleagues to compare the situation with Ireland, where during the 1990s and early 2000s there was much more of a co-ordination, and two policies working together seemed to have a more beneficial effect. At the end of the 1990s and early 2000s, I got the impression that it was almost like two legs bad, four legs good, and there was a flip-over of policy about which one was good and which one was bad. I think the reality is that it depends on what you want from the policies and how you integrate them. That will determine whether you should attract certain types of inward investment. You need to be very much more focused than we probably were in the 1980s and 1990s, but at the time it was about attracting jobs; now it is not in the same way.

Q8 Mrs James: Is there a conflict in a way? Here we are talking about inward investment, foreign investment, and so on, and we know that as a small, clever country we need to grow indigenous businesses and support them. Are we ever going to manage that? Is it going to be complementary? Will we always have that conflict?
Professor Pickernell: In terms of the work I was doing 10 years ago, at the time the policies were switching over there seemed to be a lot of conflict between them because of resources. At the time a lot of money was still being given to inward investors to stay, essentially, and to a lesser degree there still is, and that was taking resource away from indigenous development entrepreneurship policies. I think that now it has to be a situation where people look at those resources together and look at them collectively. Therefore, I suppose my answer is: they can be complementary. They were to an extent in Ireland; I think they have been less complementary in Wales in the past. That does not mean they could not be more complementary in the future.
Professor Gripaios: I think that the problem in Wales is the same problem you have in other parts of the UK. You have had very large employers who have always provided. It is the same in Plymouth where the dockyard and the Navy have always provided. In those situations—south Wales is particularly bad at this—there has always been a culture where some big employers come in and provide it, so there is not a tradition of entrepreneurship. I suspect there is a difference there with Ireland where you did not have that situation. There were other disadvantages, and there still are, obviously, in the Irish case, but there is a particular problem not just in Wales but most of the periphery of the UK, where the big firms provided. There just was not the tradition of entrepreneurship and there is not the aspiration either to set up your own business and perhaps get on with it in that way, other than by moving up through big firms. I think there is a very important cultural issue to address.
In some ways, it is the same answer to the problem of FDI. The things that would be attractive to the types of FDI you want are the same things that perhaps would make people more entrepreneurial—as you said, the clever economy, the bright economy and so on—and somehow you have to change people's

aspirations. They have to be hungrier and better educated; they have to be more go-getting than in the past, rather than relying on Hoover, say, for a management job in Merthyr Tydfil.

Q9 Mrs James: Coming back to the dependency we may have had, in my constituency it was the docks, the steelworks and the collieries, but now when I talk to people about the current job situation more and more of them say, "Why can't we have manufacturing back? When will we get manufacturing jobs?" It is very difficult for me to explain that those big companies no longer think or operate in the way they did before and smaller companies are telling me that we are losing out to FDI. So what should we be saying?

Professor Gripaios: There is no question that you have to change attitudes. You are right and they are wrong. I do not think there is a future in the low-level manufacturing jobs that we used to do. The whole of society, by which I mean the whole of the UK outside London and the south-east, has to change attitudes in the manner I have suggested.

Q10 Susan Elan Jones: On the point you made about inward investment, is there any correlation between this and the decline of the Japanese economy in the early 1990s? In the 1980s and 1990s, there was a big move to get Japanese companies across Wales. What I am interested in is this. When their own economy declined, there was massive pressure for employment in that country, not least because they saw in many of their companies the end of the jobs for life scheme. Would you say there has been any correlation with that, and has that affected Wales disproportionately?

Dr Ball: I would like to answer that, if I may. To tell you the honest truth, I had not thought about that as a correlation, because I take a different view. I have said in my submission that the Japanese firms in south Wales were producing products which were at the end of their life cycle. I gave evidence to this Committee in 2004 and 1998, and I am repeating it again. The inward investors who came were at the end of the life cycle. The Japanese left when the life cycle ended. We made wonderful televisions in Bridgend. Along came flat screen televisions, which were produced elsewhere. Nobody has big fat televisions any more. It is an interesting correlation, Mrs Jones. I had not thought of that. But there is no question in my view that it was because the products were at the end of their life cycle.

If I may comment on something Professor Gripaios said, I think there is a future in manufacturing. It may be a different kind of manufacturing. Again, I have said in my submission that if we are to be looking for inward investment—because it is inward investment with which we are concerned here, though I take the point about enterprise—then there has to be inward investment based on the skills we have. There has to be inward investment based on the skills and the multiplier effect of those skills. I do not think the days of manufacturing are over by any stretch of the imagination. What we need to do is to build on the skills we have got. We have significant manufacturing

skills in Wales and south Wales. What we do not have are the inward investors with products at the beginning of their life cycle, with high margins and so forth, which people really want to buy. That is where we should be going. I am not one of those who says we are at the funeral of manufacturing by any stretch of the imagination.

Chair: Thank you. I think we will come back to the issue of skills and training fairly shortly.

Q11 Geraint Davies: Thinking now about the kind of inward investment we want, how important are skills and infrastructure in terms of doing that? What is the relationship between those?

Dr Ball: Again, I have said in my submission that there are areas that are a matter for the Assembly, not this House, but at the end of the day there is no question but that the skill levels in Wales are appalling, the education system leaves a great deal to be desired, and the skill is simply not there for inward investors. At the end of the day, the risk we still run is inward investment for its own sake on low skills and low pay. We need to do something very serious about education.

Chair: That is a strong comment, Dr Ball. I wonder whether the other two witnesses agree.

Dr Ball: With your permission, Chair, I will repeat a story. I was at a debate where the chief executive of Northern Foods—I forget his name—said that its most successful factory was one north of Dublin. He smiled and said, "Well, I would say that, wouldn't I, because I'm an Irishman? But the fact is that Ireland has a multi-skilled education system. They are sound in mathematics and in science, and they are capable of learning new skills and driving forward the business." We don't have that in Wales.

Q12 Chair: Is that something the other panellists would agree with broadly?

Professor Gripaios: Absolutely.

Professor Pickernell: Broadly. There has, however, been some recent work done—there is a reference to it in my submission—to show that one of the key reasons they have stayed is that they perceive the skills levels are there for their particular businesses. I do not know whether that is something they have done themselves, but that is an area on which we need to focus in future.

Q13 Geraint Davies: We went to GE Aviation in Nantgarw, of which you will be aware. They are a very successful inward investor and for a long period of time they have had some grants. They argued they were taking local people and then adding value through apprenticeships, and so on. So it can be done, but it did not seem to be that reliant on the indigenous skills provided, although there were partnerships. Tell us what should be happening to get the quality and flexibility of skills. Is this unique to Wales, or are we talking about a UK problem?

Dr Ball: If we look at the evidence, it is probably a UK problem. It is worse in Wales. From what I see around me, I do not think we are, frankly, pushing the schools in the way we should be pushing them. My wife has a PGCE in mathematics; she did this later in life. I won't mention the school because that simply is not fair, but she was asked to explain fractions and decimals to fourth year comprehensive school pupils. I was absolutely appalled. There are students at certain universities—I hasten to add, not my university— taking degrees in business studies who can totally avoid doing accountancy. How the hell you can have a degree in business studies and avoid understanding accounts is entirely beyond me.

Professor Gripaios: Even less economics.

Dr Ball: But there are serious issues here. At the end of the day, it is not about choice; it is to some extent about the three Rs, and schools have to do something. There was an interesting article in *The Economist* last week, strangely enough, about the number of French citizens who now live and work in London. There was a lovely paragraph saying that one of the reasons is that French schools are so strong in mathematics, and apparently we have a disproportionate number of investors and so forth in London because of their skills in mathematics. But at the end of the day the schools have to do something about the level of good generic skills: mathematics, science and English.

Q14 Geraint Davies: Do people agree with this across the piece?

Professor Gripaios: Absolutely. You have to start by asking the question: what is going to bring investors into the UK, or what is going to make UK investors more competitive than they are now? How are we going to compete with other parts of the world? How are we going to compete with newly industrialising countries? How are we going to compete with locations which employ very, very cheap labour? There is only one answer to that: we have to be better educated, more focused on research and development right at the top end, not necessarily manufacturing, but the design of manufactured products. That is the only way the UK will compete, and that is why the south-east and London are more competitive than other parts of the country, because they attract those kinds of people, some of whom are possibly educated in Wales and other parts of the UK. They gravitate to London because that is where the jobs are, and because they have gravitated to London the jobs also come there.

Q15 Geraint Davies: In terms of what should happen—maybe David Pickernell could answer this— if our ambition is to get more added value, more HQ, and so on, I guess the issue is: what should happen? We are aware now from the PISA results that inward investors can go down a graph and see that Wales and England, in particular Wales, are slipping down the league, and they will move over here. As a country, you can compete for inward investment by increasing your rankings. One of the issues is: should we do that? How should we perform? David, I do not know whether you have a particular view on that.

Professor Pickernell: That is going into the level of education rather than other policies. Broadly speaking, it would be interesting to look in more depth at exactly why the figures are so low. Certainly, in a survey done a couple of years ago, when inward investors were asked where potentially they would

relocate, over one third talked of areas in other parts of the UK, and the issue that came back was related to skills. That highlights the fact that, even within the UK, a lot of these companies were not talking about going to China or central or eastern Europe but about other parts of the UK. One of the key reasons for them remaining was related to ongoing grant support. It highlights the fact that there is an issue, because that will become less and less viable in the future.

When we are looking at inward investment there are two sides to it. You have attracting in new inward investment and you also have keeping and developing what you already have. There are going to be two sets of policies. They are going to be interrelated and linked to that. In terms of the ones you already have, the ones that have not gone and are long-lasting and have been there 14, 15, 20 years are the ones that are more likely to be embedded and the ones to which you can link other policies via the supply chain, entrepreneurship and developing indigenous businesses out of and through linkages with universities and so on. One of the key questions is: to what extent should we be focusing on keeping and developing those we already have, because they are also more likely to be doing things like research and development and being innovative? To what extent will we be focusing on attracting in new inward investors in specific areas? Clearly, over the last couple of years the trend has moved away from manufacturing towards services and distribution, which are lower value added in terms of their multiplier effects on the economy.

Chair: I am going to cut this a little short because we have so many questions to ask and it is fascinating.

Q16 Mrs James: I just want to come in on research and development. When we talked to overseas companies and looked at these things in the past, it is really clear that the end of life of a product is significant, but if we do not attract those companies and their R and D bases into Wales and the UK, it is a bit like the chicken and egg: you have to have one to get all of the process. How successful are we in Wales in attracting companies with R and D?

Professor Gripaios: Not at all, really. If you look at the statistics, they rather suggest there has been an increase in R and D, but it would be interesting to note whether that is due to foreign companies taking over indigenous companies. I have not worked on this for a while, but about 10 years ago I did a study that compared Plymouth, Cardiff and Bristol. It seemed that Bristol had been much more successful in getting the research end. For example, it had Hewlett Packard, which has either gone or is a much smaller operation than it used to be, but it also had the regional headquarters of Canon and all kinds of digital people, whereas Wales certainly struggled. It is not that far away; we are not talking huge distances between Bristol and Cardiff.

Geraint Davies: We need an electrified rail line to Swansea. That is what I want.

Chair: We'll not even go there, Stuart Andrew.

Q17 Stuart Andrew: Do you accept the analysis that the falling levels of manufacturing inward investment could have a rebound effect on the Welsh economy and its relative GDP per capita?

Professor Gripaios: I said so in my submission. I can't prove it, but I think it would be quite difficult to suggest otherwise. It's bound to, isn't it? Wales has put so much resource into that. There was great resentment in other parts of the UK, particularly perhaps in the south-west—or I picked it up in the south-west—about businesses being attracted to Wales, or pinching them, actually. There were some that closed in Plymouth but kept their Welsh operation, but in some ways you may have done us a favour, because what you don't have you don't lose—or it is not all going in a rush.

Q18 Stuart Andrew: Professor Pickernell just touched on that. Has it been compensated in any way in other sectors like the service industry?

Professor Pickernell: There has been an increase in foreign direct investment in services and distribution. It has not totally compensated; the amount of employment has gone down. If you look at where the location of a lot of the foreign direct investment has been, the lower-skilled and lower-paid jobs are in places in the Valleys, but more particularly in the south-east and north-east of Wales. If you were looking to develop higher-level, higher-skill jobs, innovation and that side of things, then the issue of the attractiveness of place—Florida's idea of the creative class and the attractiveness of certain locations—is likely to mean that you would be promoting areas closer to the larger cities than probably you would have been doing in the past when it was about manufacturing and assembly. That is another issue about thinking about what exactly you want to do and why you want the inward investment.

Professor Gripaios: If you were to look at the developing prosperity of parts of the UK, two things stand out. One is the growing importance of London and the south-east, and the other is the concentration of GVA in a few provincial capitals. Leeds, in particular, has become the business centre of the north of England; Manchester to a lesser extent; Birmingham and Bristol; and to a much lesser extent Cardiff. These seem to be the places where the jobs are and where you can compete. They are in the financial services and in the media, where there is some success in Cardiff, and so on. It seems to me that they are the knowledge-based jobs which you really have to go for, but you have to take a long view. It is no good thinking that you will get them quickly. You have to put the foundations in place and, quite frankly, some of those will take 20 years.

Q19 Stuart Andrew: Are the policy levers the same for attracting manufacturing inward investment as the service industry?

Professor Gripaios: I think they are. They come back to Dr Ball's comment about the quality of education, but as I said, there are two other things. One is aspiration. It is not just what you offer; you have to get the kids to take it up. There is another issue which we have not talked about and which is particularly serious in Wales, which is welfare dependency. You cannot hope to have a high level of GVA per head if

a high percentage of your population is dependent on welfare benefits.

Q20 Chair: Professor Pickernell, you said in one of your earlier answers that we needed to change legislation and Government policy anyway to keep companies in Wales.

Professor Pickernell: No, I did not say that. I think that is something to look at.

Q21 Chair: But what policies would you change to keep companies in Wales if you were the First Minister?

Professor Pickernell: I have not done an analysis of how much grant assistance has gone in over the last 10 years. I looked at it 10 years ago and it was clearly an issue then. In the more recent studies I have read, it is still an issue. There is resource going in there to keep them. I do not think that is a long-term policy. The issue is the skills area. It is linkages with institutions such as universities; it is creating that, if you like, stickiness of place. We have done it in the past with low labour costs. That is always a relative issue, and there is always somebody cheaper than you are. There is the grants issue, and that has compensated for some companies for a while. That is likely to become more difficult in the future. You are left with education, skills, innovation and that kind of activity, and that links in with the institutions that you already have.

It is also to do with thinking clearly about what key infrastructures you can develop to make places more attractive. A couple of days ago, I read a study which talked about companies that had gone to Dublin, and one of the key reasons was linked to the airport, for example. A lot of work is being done in places like Australia on the development of their airports as hubs around which they are building a lot of inward investment attraction activities in both manufacturing and services. Clearly, we have a disadvantage at the moment. I am just saying that that is an issue. It is either about making sure we have a good link to a major airport, for example, Heathrow, or to what extent you can develop other infrastructures as well.

Q22 Jonathan Edwards: Previous FDI strategies in Wales were based on grants and allowances. Would a tax-based investment policy be more appropriate for the poorer parts of the United Kingdom, and if so, what taxes?

Dr Ball: May I respond to this? I have said this in my submission. It is perfectly clear that there are a million things we could do to improve inward investment, many of which are not the duties of this House, but at the end of the day we have to learn lessons from what is happening elsewhere. There is no question in my mind that corporation tax-based incentives are working. They have worked very well in Ireland. Although there are sovereign debt problems in Ireland, the level of inward investment has not fallen away, because low levels of corporation tax, by definition, attract organisations that are making profits. If organisations are making profits, the chances are they are at the beginning of life cycles, they are innovative and are global, and it is a policy that works.

By the way, this is not some kind of underhanded nationalist agenda. This could apply to other parts of the UK as well. I should make that point quite clear. But I think we have to be realistic about what works. What works are not grant-based but tax-based incentives. I have set out one or two ideas in my submission.

Q23 Chair: Would the same principle apply to higher levels of income tax in terms of persuading the leaders or owners of those companies to come and live in the countries in which their companies are investing?
Dr Ball: Why not?

Q24 Chair: What we are getting into is the Laffer curve and whether we accept that at a certain level it is a good idea to lower tax rates because in that way you get in more income.
Dr Ball: I have also said, with respect, in my submission, that this idea of a national UK tax base is a myth anyway. To some extent, there are different tax levels. For example, SET in the 1960s was, by definition, a regional tax. So I think this idea of an overall UK tax is a myth anyway.
Chair: We come to a few questions on skills and education.

Q25 Mr Williams: Before that, and still on the theme of conditions required to attract inward investment, I direct these questions to Dr Ball. In your submission you use the phrase a "race to the bottom" and the risk of a "race to the bottom". First, I want to ask about the extent to which current policy, such as exists, runs that risk. Secondly, could you explain a little more about the concept you elaborate in your submission entitled "The Production Mandate"?
Dr Ball: Thank you for that. The first response is that we are at the bottom. Of that there is no question. How do you compete against the far eastern low-wage economies? The answer is that you can't, so you don't. We are at the bottom; there are no two ways about that. I was coming up on the train yesterday and in my mind I was ticking through all of the manufacturers I remembered, in some of which I worked. They have now largely disappeared, so we are at the bottom. If you are trying to compete on price, you will end up being knocked out, and that is what has happened to the Welsh economy.

The production mandate is an idea that had its roots in Canada. I elucidated on this the last time I was privileged to give evidence to the Committee about five years ago. The idea is straightforward enough. Inward investors are offered inducements of various kinds, but they are dependent upon the amount of mandate that local management has. For example, if company X came to, say, Swansea, then the assistance in terms of skills, tax allowances or whatever was on offer would vary according to the amount of research and development they had the mandate to do, or the amount of product development they had the mandate to do. It has been used in the provinces of Canada with some considerable success. Black & Decker is an example that leaps out, which I looked at a little

while ago. At the end of the day, we need to start using some imagination. The race to the bottom, as I have called it, has to stop. We have to start being innovative and push the curve; we have to get on with it. Aside from tax-raising powers, or rather tax-varying powers—I am sorry; that was a Freudian slip there—which we have got to look at, we have to consider other measures. At the end of the day, the production mandate would provide attraction.

The problem then is that, if there is no mandate, we say, "No, thank you." That takes the kind of courage WDA did not have. To some extent there is a great risk here of flying this kite and still ending up with the same problem. Anyway, the problem is the amount of mandate to do R and D, through product development, to produce local management and to develop local supply chains. All the incentives, which could be an extra package, would depend on the amount of mandate that inward investor has. It has worked in Canada and elsewhere; to some extent it has worked in Ireland, though they do not call it the production mandate. I think it is something we should be looking at very seriously.

Q26 Mr Williams: You have flown that kite. What has the reaction been to that kite when you have raised this before?
Dr Ball: No response. I have raised this idea twice, and in a book about Welsh affairs. I am still waiting for a response, but there we are.

Q27 Mr Williams: Keep going. We talked earlier at length about the skills agenda. I would be interested in why you feel we are failing in terms of those basic skills. Some of us would argue that it is a political question; some of us would argue it is about resources available for education from primary level right the way through. Inevitably, people will ask about the professionalism of teachers, the nature of the curriculum and whether we are pursuing too generalist an approach in terms of our curriculum. The seed is there. I am going to an exhibition later this week of the Engineering Council, constituents of mine, who are delivering excellence. You wonder what the next step will be for them in the engineering projects on which they are working. Where does the fault lie in terms of education and the lack of those basic core skills?
Professor Gripaios: Thanks for looking at me. It would be simplistic to say there is any one fault. There is no question that we have to up our game to be competitive with other countries. Parts of the Indian work force are very highly educated. Parts of the Chinese work force are very highly educated and rigorous in pursuing skills and qualifications. The level of aspiration, what is offered and what is acceptable in terms of pass rates are very important. You can get a GCSE in maths with a very low level of mathematical attainment.

Q28 Chair: Do you think that the standards required to get the basic pass level have gone down over the last 20 years, Professor Gripaios?
Professor Gripaios: Yes, I do.

Chair: What about the other witnesses? Yes or no on that one?

Dr Ball: Yes.

Professor Pickernell: I do not have any evidence on which to base this, but my gut answer would be yes.

Q29 Mr Williams: I want to turn to the specific role of higher education. Various submissions have alluded to that essential role. I think we are potentially well placed in Wales, at least geographically, to pursue that role. How would you advance the ability of higher education institutions to attract inward investment? Are we talking about hubs or the development of centres of excellence? How can we advance that? That is a question to all of you.

Professor Gripaios: I don't know why everyone looks at me on these difficult questions. I think it would be very wrong simply to blame the schools for the deterioration in educational standards. I think higher education also has some blame. What is provided? At the end of the day, students are very important to keep universities going. They offer what students want, but it is not necessarily what is sensible for the country, or indeed, their long-term careers, as we are now finding out. I do not think we can say that we are there at that level of the pyramid and just concentrate on the rest. All parts of the pyramid need to up their game. There needs to be a change in the kinds of courses offered, and to go with that there has to be a change in attitudes of students to take more rigorous subjects—the sciences, medicine and such things—maybe more than others.

Q30 Mrs James: When we have travelled abroad we have looked at these issues. There seems to be a lot more specialising at a younger age, for instance, in industry, engineering and the sciences. Young people are encouraged to look at them at a much younger age, and businesses in Swansea are constantly telling me about this deficit of training and skills. I was speaking to somebody who is very involved in the call centre industry where letters have to go out. They have to sit their trainees down first of all and teach them to write letters.

Professor Gripaios: Sadly, this is not just trainees in the call centre industry. You should see some of the essays that I have marked.

Mrs James: I have had the applications from Oxbridge students, yes.

Professor Gripaios: When my son was about 12, I was marking final-year scripts and putting them down as I finished. He picked one up and said, "God, this isn't very good, is it?" He was right.

Professor Pickernell: I teach students from a variety of different backgrounds and countries. Probably the strongest students I find in terms of application, attitude and overall work level, on average, come from Germany. They are already in jobs. Basically, they do one term in their work and one term at a university either in Germany or, they come over to us for one term. The difference there is incredible, because the attitude is so different. I do not know to what extent the background in terms of what they have been taught before has given them this, but certainly in terms of their attitude and application it is

very different. I used to notice that when we had more sandwich students who between their second and final years, went out into industry for a year, when they came back their attitude was different, because they felt that what they were doing was not "academic" academic; they could see the actual point of it. So the way we structure our education at the higher level is of importance.

Q31 Geraint Davies: This is anecdotal, but my older daughter, who is now 17, got an A in additional maths at GCSE. My daughter below her is now being told that you cannot get an A any more in additional maths at GCSE because they are getting rid of it; you just get a pass. I wonder whether you, as people in universities, have any evidence that the different examining boards are competing against each other in a race towards the bottom to get more people in higher grades, to get them into university, and the incentives are in the wrong direction.

Professor Pickernell: I do not have any evidence on that. That is not a field I deal with.

Dr Ball: At the end of the day, dare I say there are simply too many universities of 20,000 or 30,000 students? In my view, and it's only a personal view, I hasten to add, that is simply too big.

Professor Gripaios: I have not had any dealings with admissions, so I have not looked at that issue.

Q32 Mr Williams: I am not knocking primary education in particular, where I served for some years as a primary school teacher. I think there is still an appropriate emphasis on skills at that level. What concerns me—I suspect it may concern you, and it is certainly Siân James's point—is the extent to which later on people are not encouraged to develop those specialisms academically and, critically, practically, which, as David Pickernell indicated, is really important.

I am interested that there has been some success in the higher education sector in developing quite meaningful partnerships between developing economies. For instance, I think of the relationship between Aberystwyth University and China. We see a flow of activity between Wales and China and less of a flow back, and I think those are the relationships that we need to be pursuing in terms of developing a more innovative spirit sometimes in our higher education institutions. Are there any reflections on that?

Chair: Very briefly, gentlemen. I am afraid we are almost out of time.

Professor Pickernell: It is important to do that. Again, it is about looking at this holistically, because developing universities which are developing innovations, which can then be put out into the marketplace more quickly—it is a project that I am working on at the moment, in collaboration with others—is not focused specifically on inward investors. In that case, it is about trying to get business angels to come in and help develop the products more quickly to get them to market. It could be that that is picked up by a local firm; it could be that it is picked up by academics or students who spin out a company. The point is that it is the starting point—generating that innovation—which is of importance. When it is picked up, it could be a range of factors and you do not just decide the outcome before you start. You have to think about what it is you want to do, which is to encourage innovation, and then try to develop the structures around that to support it.

Q33 Stuart Andrew: It has been really good listening to your candid answers. I just wonder whether, after everything you have said, you think the target of getting 50% of school leavers to university is the right focus, Dr Ball.

Dr Ball: No.

Chair: Thank you for that. We like these short answers. Professor Gripaios?

Professor Gripaios: No.

Chair: Professor Pickernell?

Professor Pickernell: I don't know how to answer that, to be honest.

Chair: Your silence is instructive.

Professor Gripaios: If I may give a very quick answer to the previous point raised by Mark Williams, I think an awful lot could be done to make British universities and the people within them much more entrepreneurial than they are.

Mr Williams: And the schools as well.

Professor Gripaios: And the schools as well.

Chair: Let me bring in Susan Elan Jones for a very quick last question, if I may.

Q34 Susan Elan Jones: There are a lot of questions I could ask. What recommendations would you make for improving the level of inward investment? Also, is the concentration on the six sectors under WAG's economic renewal policies the right approach?

Professor Pickernell: From a general point of view, while it is useful to have sectors you would like to target, it can be detrimental in the sense that you can find fast growth, and high-growth new firms, in ranges of different sectors. If it is eliminating resources from a general area, then you really have to think about that.

Professor Gripaios: I think the public sector has been terrible at picking winners and saying that is what we should go for. I am much happier with the idea that you should be helping them do, within whatever activity or sector they are, the sort of things you want them to do. I think you ought to look at the production mandate and get them to bring in R and D, and pay them if they do that sort of thing.

Professor Pickernell: I would add that when you look at trying to develop entrepreneurial skills, etcetera, that does not necessarily mean people have to be setting up their own businesses. They could be more entrepreneurial or "intrapreneurial" within existing or larger organisations so the skill sets can be transferable at least to a degree so it would be beneficial across the board.

Dr Ball: Very quickly, frankly, the identification of the six sectors is a nonsense.

Chair: Come off the fence.

Susan Elan Jones: Get in there, John.

Dr Ball: It is perfectly clear that the public sector is not good at identifying winners. I said that five or six years ago to this Committee. The Welsh Assembly Government has this fixation with certain sectors that are not growing but declining. A lot of nonsense is talked about financial services and the number of people who work in it. They are call centres; they are not financial services. The automotive industry is producing products at the end of their life cycle. It is a complete nonsense.

As far as recommendations are concerned, I would certainly hang my hat very much on tax incentives. I think this House and the Government should be looking at that. I think we should be looking at sectors that fit into the existing skills we have, because you cannot talk about financial services, R and D and so forth with the levels of education that we have. That is cloud cuckoo land.

The first question you asked, Chair, was about the WDA. What I would dearly love is for somebody to crunch some sensible numbers. When I gave evidence in 1998, I produced evidence that the then Welsh Development Agency was making up numbers on the number of successful inward investments. I had nothing better to do this morning but go for a cup of coffee. I had a quick look at two of the submissions. According to the Welsh Assembly Government, there are exactly 1,045 overseas-owned companies, however defined. According to the same paper produced at the same time by UWIC, there are 513, except that when you add up the UWIC numbers there are 592. So you can take your pick, ladies and gentlemen, as to which of these is correct. So I think my last plea is: can somebody please crunch some sensible numbers?

Chair: Thank you very much indeed, Dr Ball. We really enjoyed those direct, frank and sometimes very short answers. We look forward to seeing you again.

Witnesses: **Mr David Rosser,** Regional Director, CBI Wales, **Mr Roy Thomas,** Director, Cardiff Business Partnership, and **Mr Graham Morgan,** Director, South Wales Chamber of Commerce, gave evidence.

Q35 Chair: Gentlemen, thank you very much indeed for coming along today. Would you like to introduce yourselves for our record and then we can start?

Graham Morgan: I am Graham Morgan, director of South Wales Chamber of Commerce.

Roy Thomas: I am Roy Thomas, director of Cardiff Business Partnership.

David Rosser: I am David Rosser, director of CBI Wales.

Q36 Chair: Thank you very much indeed for coming along. I saw your eyebrows rise at a few of the comments made by our previous panel, so feel free to comment on anything you heard at some point in the questions. Perhaps I could kick off by asking in broad terms whether you think that foreign direct investment is still something on which we should be concentrating very hard in Wales, and are we getting it right? I put that question to all or any of you. Graham Morgan, perhaps you would start.

8 March 2011 Mr David Rosser, Mr Roy Thomas and Mr Graham Morgan

Graham Morgan: I am happy to kick off. I think it has to be a combined effort. You have to focus on the opportunities that foreign direct investment brings, particularly in relation to some of the resources in Wales and the ability to develop some of them. At the same time, we have to use that investment to provide impetus for local businesses and also look at how we develop those businesses. From a chamber of commerce perspective, we feel that perhaps the ambition within some of the businesses in Wales to look at markets beyond Wales is not where it needs to be and there needs to be some form of mechanism introduced to encourage those businesses with good products and good services to raise their game and look at other opportunities. It is very much a combination.

Roy Thomas: In context, I would like to look at the figures for the UK which I have been researching. Every day the UK attracts nearly five inward investment projects; every day 146 new jobs are created by inward investment; and every day 258 jobs are created or safeguarded. Every week the UK attracts 31 projects. I would like to see more of them coming to Wales.

Q37 Chair: Do we get proportionally what one would expect to get?

Roy Thomas: Last year we did okay, but we then scrapped the department that actually performed, which was a big surprise to a number of businesses.

David Rosser: I think the attraction of FDI continues to play a meaningful role in the economic development of Wales going forward, certainly for the reasons Roy has just explained, but, equally, because we have an extensive installed base of inward investment companies already in Wales. I am reluctant to quote figures after the previous contributions, but according to the ONS we have over 1,000 companies in Wales providing about 12.5% of employment, which is about 20% of private sector employment. We have an installed base, which means that, if we decide, today, we no longer want to do FDI as an economic policy, we will see greater disinvestment in that operation than we would otherwise see.

Q38 Mr Williams: Gentlemen, why did Wales lose its competitive advantage in terms of attracting inward investment? If we start with a gloomy prognosis, in your view what constitutes a successful inward investment policy? Why, and then what is the next step?

Roy Thomas: I think we have just become uncompetitive. I have looked at figures for Scotland, for example. I notice from the last session that Scotland was not mentioned. In the 1990s we competed very well with Scotland. I had an opportunity yesterday to talk to Jack McConnell, Scotland's First Minister, at the time the WDA was scrapped. His line to me yesterday—I spent an hour and a half with him looking at Scotland—was that they reinforced their inward investment team when Wales lost its team. Indeed, last December they appointed a new chief executive to look at Scottish Development International. The evaluation coming out of Scotland—I would ask you, Chair, perhaps to look at and take evidence from Scotland—is that inward investment is alive and kicking in Scotland, whereas it is not in Wales. I think we have lost our edge. When the Ryder Cup came to Wales, there was an early-day motion tabled by 50-odd Scottish MPs saying it should not go to Wales because Scotland is the home of golf. That was the competitive framework we had during that period. We seem to have backed off now.

Q39 Mr Williams: How would you characterise the Assembly's stance strategically, starting with the WDA over the past 12 years?

Roy Thomas: I do not want to go backwards and say whether or not we should have a WDA. I think that will run. Going forward, we leave a lot to be desired in terms of internationalisation. Again, Scotland has embraced that and it has a plan for internationalisation. The evaluation of SDI last May by an independent firm showed that inward investment was a key driver of the Scottish economy. Indeed, if you look at where Scotland is in the league tables compared with where we are, it is up there. I suppose the anti-dividend for devolution has been that we have been inward and not outward-looking, particularly on trade and investment.

Q40 Mr Williams: But there are opportunities there for the Welsh Assembly Government, of whatever political complexion, and the question some of us ask after our trip to Berlin is whether they have risen robustly enough to the challenge over the past 12 years.

Graham Morgan: My observation is that, perhaps as a result of devolution, it has been an inward-looking regime, and, as Roy said, what has not been done is international connectivity. There is certainly an element of "siloism" in terms of both the private sector and public sector in Wales. If we are to have a true international proposition, we need to encourage greater interaction between public and private. There has been a blame culture where the private sector has pointed its finger at International Business Wales for not delivering. I do not think International Business Wales profiled some of the good things it did and some of the good people it had, and as a result there was not a joined-up approach which made Wales as attractive.

To come back to your point on competition, it is not that Wales has lost its competitive edge; it has not framed what its competitive offering is. That is a slightly different thing. The earlier debate about low labour costs and all that is a thing of the past. The WDA thrived at a time when that was the competitive opportunity. What we have not done is joined up the public and private sector and academia to talk about what Wales has to offer competitively in the new market.

Q41 Chair: Very briefly, using a yes and no format if I may, do you agree with the comments of one member of the previous panel who was very critical of the WDA? Do you think that was a fair criticism, Mr Thomas?

Roy Thomas: We both worked for the WDA at the time, and Dr Ball, whose views were well known at time, criticised us.

Q42 Chair: You worked for the WDA?
Roy Thomas: Yes; I was legal director for nine years, so I had a declaration of interest. Indeed, we listened to Dr Ball quite a lot during that period and also to the likes of Professor Kevin Morgan, for example, who was a harsh critic of the WDA in 1994, but if you read his work now he is a supporter in academia of the WDA. You will always have that debate.

Q43 Chair: What about you, Mr Morgan, if you were not involved at the time?
Graham Morgan: I had nothing to do with the WDA, to be honest. All I have picked up is that, clearly, certain folks have seen certain positive things about the WDA. One fairly critical thing was that it was fleet of foot. It was operating at a distance from the public sector and as a result it developed a reputation of its own. One difference we have currently is that that freedom to move quickly has been removed.

Q44 Jonathan Edwards: To build on the theme about Wales losing its edge, to what extent do you think that is down to the fact there is no UKTI presence in Wales, whereas there is in Scotland, along the lines they have done in English regions?
Graham Morgan: I guess that, from the perspective of the chamber, UKTI in many locations across the UK has worked with us. The bottom line in Wales is that the chamber has been fairly parochial and fragmented for a number of years, and it is only now that we have created a scale and size where we are in a position where perhaps we can work more closely with a number of organisations. Certainly, the model of chamber/UKTI/Enterprise Europe working in harmony for the common good is a tried and tested one in Birmingham, Bristol and Manchester, so it demonstrates that that physical opportunity exists. Certainly, UKTI or the ability to access it would give us a bigger opportunity.

Q45 Chair: Would you both like to see UKTI have a representative in Wales?
David Rosser: Yes. I would certainly like to see much closer working between the UKTI and the Welsh Assembly Government. All I see at the moment is that they are trying to instil that, and that is encouraging.
Graham Morgan: If I may add to this very good question, we were always pushing at the envelope with UKTI because there is a remit across the UK. I think we have lost that connection. We always pushed. They would have floating inward investment coming to the UK, and to push Wales one would have to lobby very hard in UKTI to get our fair share.

Q46 Geraint Davies: Anecdotally, I am aware of a chap who heads up a company called British Biocell International that was linked to technology related to pregnancy tests and that sort of thing. It wanted to set up a plant in Wales with a couple of hundred people and cutting edge R and D. He went to the Welsh Assembly and ended up in Scotland, even though he is from Swansea. How can that kind of thing happen? What kind of support packages and flexibility in your mind are happening in Scotland? I know you said we should take evidence, and I agree with you, but, anecdotally, how does this Welsh offer differ from the Scottish offer now for those kinds of people? In my example, someone from Swansea wanted to stay in Wales and has now ended up in Scotland.
Roy Thomas: I have done some research and I have some graphs for the Clerk. I am very happy to hand it round, but that is probably not what should happen. I have some graphs showing the R and D investment in Wales compared with Scotland, and it is pretty startling. We have Scotland at 19% and Wales at 6% of UK R and D projects. Perhaps the Committee would like to see those. If you look at that graph, it is pretty startling. You are right to concentrate on R and D because that is where you get value added. We maintained that Panasonic, Sony and companies we had in the past—David was at the forefront of this— should bring in R and D facilities. If you look at Panasonic, its European R and D facility is in north Cardiff.

Q47 Geraint Davies: Is that integrated into the universities, or is it part of the answer?
Roy Thomas: It is. I would say that, university-wise, in life sciences, Swansea is doing a fantastic job. If you look at life sciences, it is a growing field of inward investment. Last year 23% of inward investment in the UK was in life sciences, so again that is a key area.

Q48 Jonathan Edwards: What priorities do your members give to promoting inward investment in general?
David Rosser: I think CBI members remain convinced that FDI has a key role to play in our economy going forward. Our SME members see international businesses as customers, and for larger Welsh businesses they see them as welcome contributors to a healthy, thriving economy, contributing to work with universities and developing skills. The bigger companies in Wales tend to be inward investors, if not from overseas, certainly from other parts of the UK. The larger companies have a capacity to work with universities and colleges to provide training that sometimes smaller companies find difficult, so they contribute to the wider business community in a range of ways.
Roy Thomas: We have Admiral as a member. If you look at Admiral—we had a discussion on financial services earlier—that is now a £1 billion company. It started by grant in the mid-1990s and its history is well known. It is the only FTSE100 company in Wales, which we are very proud of. It opened in Cardiff and then went to Newport and Swansea. That company has grown to 3,000 people, with an average age of 30. You have young people going there and, hopefully, we will get young versions of Henry Engelhardt, David Stevens and the like coming out of that company, because their practices are doing something that we have not seen in Wales before. They are kind of indigenous with a foreign feel, because Henry, of course, is from North America.

Q49 Jonathan Edwards: I want to put a question specifically to the CBI. You recently held a six-month dialogue with your members across the UK. What did that reveal?

David Rosser: I was taken by one of the comments by Professor Gripaios earlier. It is the same factors that underpin the attractiveness of this environment for UK businesses, Welsh businesses and overseas businesses, and we certainly believe that is the case. We sought to talk to a range of companies across the UK and a range of companies not present in the UK, about what the key factors were which would encourage them to invest here more—what are the key parameters of an intrinsically attractive business environment?

I have listed some in the evidence we have given today. We score very well on some factors already: labour and employment flexibility; culture; quality of life; English language. There are some key enablers that we believe could contribute to a step change in investment performance and some key barriers that need to be taken down, and I can expand on any of those I have listed if that is of interest.

Q50 Jonathan Edwards: Perhaps I may finish by raising a question I asked of the earlier witnesses. What is your view on a tax-based incentive policy and regional taxation across the UK?

David Rosser: The CBI has not formulated an organisational policy position on this. Clearly, tax competitiveness is key to the intrinsic attractiveness of a business environment, and we are strong supporters. We listed as one of the barriers to investment current business taxation levels in the UK. That needs to be set against the value that companies place in a clear, stable and unified tax system across the UK. For inward investment, it might be a highly attractive opportunity. In my previous life, to which Roy has referred, working in inward investment for the WDA, I can remember having discussions about tax with prospective investors. To take an economy-wide view, that needs to be set against other consequences that might flow from breaking up the current unified system. It is a complex area but it is certainly one that bears investigation.

Graham Morgan: If I may add to that, the interesting thing that we certainly picked up from interaction with chambers overseas, and I attended a meeting with a delegation from Brazil, is that the question they asked immediately was: what are the tax incentives? Certainly, when you look at what chambers in other countries are doing within their kitbag to attract people, tax is one of those aspects. I do not think it is the be-all and end-all, but it is certainly a component that probably needs to be considered within the kitbag.

Roy Thomas: I concur with that.

Q51 Geraint Davies: David Rosser made a point about the common currency of taxation so people know what they are doing. On a parallel line, if Wales embarked on a completely different education system, so that instead of GCSEs at 16, or whatever they are at a different age, and all that kind of stuff, would that negatively influence inward investment? Obviously, companies that come in want a common currency for education as well in terms of moving their children around. Do you think those kinds of thing have any influence?

David Rosser: We do not have that now. For overseas companies coming in we have the UK education system, which is different from those elsewhere.

Geraint Davies: It is just a thought. I was supposed to be asking something about infrastructure.

David Rosser: I talk to the Assembly Government a lot about areas where they wish to create a different system in Wales, in whatever policy field it might be. The view I express and I hold quite strongly is that Wales is quite a small place, with quite a small market. No company will come to Wales just to serve the Welsh market. Pretty much all Welsh companies need to serve markets outside. If we make Wales different, whether it is in the education or tax system or in environmental regulation, it has to be better. We cannot afford, because of the size of our home market, to make Wales different and worse.

Q52 Geraint Davies: On the environmental costs to business, do you think that is an issue? Is that part of the criteria for inward investment?

David Rosser: That is a very broad question. You need to look at examples. We stand a real chance in the next year or two of making it more expensive to construct properties in Wales than in the rest of the UK. That will have a consequence because building regulations are being devolved; we will have mandatory sprinklers; our waste policies will be different; and so on. We wish to apply higher carbon energy efficiency standards. Those have consequences. They could be costs, and in some areas they could be benefits. If they are costs, they may not be the tipping point, but when we choose in other areas to make Wales different in a policy environment we need to be fully aware of the consequences on competitiveness issues.

Chair: I am going to have to suggest that you ask a last brief question, because we have to come on to skills.

Q53 Geraint Davies: In general, what should the Welsh Assembly Government, and indeed the UK Government, be doing to improve the infrastructure of Wales to attract inward investment? I know that people talk about railways.

Roy Thomas: The key thing is that the planning process needs to be a little swifter. The 22 local authorities we have in Wales have different ways of working on planning and it is pretty much disastrous. Most businesses will tell you.

I will give you a live example. SEGRO owned Treforest Industrial estate, which is one of the oldest industrial estates in Wales, with employment and 30 acres. SEGRO bought that estate—it is well publicised—for £68 million; they sold it for £28 million last year. SEGRO have said to me personally that they will not go further than Avonmouth any more. That is a FTSE100 property company. Treforest goes back to the Conservative intervention policy in the 1930s when employment was needed then, as it is now. That industrial estate is in a very poor state and Rhondda Cynon Taf declined planning permission for SEGRO.

Q54 Chair: On what grounds?

Roy Thomas: On transport grounds. That turned them off. Investors need to have an able and willing planning authority for investment, particularly in job creation. I think we are lacking that in Wales.

David Rosser: We heard earlier that the success of Wales in inward investment in the past was all down to big grants. That was part of it, but the Welsh Development Agency made it really easy to invest in Wales and to set up plants. The report that the CBI is about to produce on encouraging investment contains the following quote: "One high tech company told us how it had been courted by the Lower Saxony government, which had co-ordinated planning, utilities, links into the local university and access to regional and Federal grants to secure its investment in a new manufacturing facility." That is what the WDA did; it used to do all of that. It can still do it. The Amazon example of planning is one that I find frustrating because it is continually trotted out as Wales's best practice in planning. The problem is that it is a wholly exceptional situation. We have opportunities now. The Assembly has just acquired loads of new powers. It could introduce a law to simplify the planning system in Wales. It could start to use the new powers it has acquired in a highly productive way to facilitate inward investment and make it easier.

Q55 Geraint Davies: Do you mean the imposition of a unified planning system without all these different local authorities interfering?

David Rosser: No, that is not what I meant; that is a gross simplification. We can make it easier for companies. We can make the system better. We can introduce presumed consent. We can require local authorities to deal with planning applications within a set time frame. There are a number of ways in which we can make it easier while respecting local authorities' roles.

Chair: We look forward to seeing it all in the wonderful Wales now being built with the new powers.

Q56 Mrs James: Going to skills, we have had lots of evidence sent to us about the importance of the higher education sector in Wales and its role in attracting foreign inward investment. How do you think the higher education institutions might encourage new inward investment? You talked about Lower Saxony and how they were plugged in immediately to the university.

David Rosser: There are probably two ways in which universities could be plugged in and play a meaningful role in this. The first quite specialist way is where a company is attracted in because of some pretty specialist expertise that we have. I do recall at the end of my period working on inward investment for the WDA that we were taking International Rectifier into Swansea university because they had particular expertise in power electronics. It is very narrow and highly specialist. That was expertise

which that company found really quite attractive and it made a difference in their investment location decisions. I suspect that we will have relatively few of those within our Welsh HE sector, but we should know what they are and which companies would value them, and we should try to put the two together. More generally, there is perhaps not the high level specialism but the broader ability of universities to produce a pipeline of qualified graduates, particularly postgraduates, in materials science or chemical engineering, not power electronics. If companies come in and they know that a university is willing to tailor a course and ensure that that course will run for the next five years, producing graduates or postgraduates that that company will at least look at for employment, if not guarantee, you can start to build good interactions there. That is happening. Companies like General Dynamics and Cassidian and EADS in Newport are working with Cardiff and Swansea universities in those kinds of areas. I think that is a welcome, growing and developing field. We just need to make sure it continues to develop.

Roy Thomas: The same goes for universities with financial services. We heard about financial services earlier. 30,000 people work in financial services in Cardiff, but if you are Legal & General you train people up so they may get their first job as a graduate. They may then go to Admiral; they may then go to Principality. So you are creating clusters. They have career advancement. In my day we used to go to the City in London to have that training, but now that is here in Cardiff or Swansea with Admiral, which is near you.

Q57 Guto Bebb: You mentioned that the relationship between universities and business was starting to develop. Is that not in itself a damning comment? For as long as I have been aware of the Welsh Assembly's efforts to develop business support in Wales, they have always argued that there is a need to build on these specialisms that are developing in our universities, and yet we have seen the Technium experiments and your comment just now about this starting to work. Has it therefore not been a success in the past?

David Rosser: I do not want to damn progress. Equally, it should not be a surprise to you if I say there is further to go and more to be developed. We are making good progress on this. I worked on inward investment for the Welsh Development Agency between 1995 and 2000, which was between 10 and 15 years ago. At the start of my period there I was wandering around haulage companies asking for freight rates to Stuttgart and Düsseldorf to support inward investment inquiries.

Towards the end of my period there I was wandering around universities, talking to professors and departments about the expertise that they had which could be deployed for inward investment. I have no doubt that has continued to develop over the last decade, and I see more and more companies now working with universities, some very successfully and some with less deep links, but I see it moving forward. One could, if one wished, criticise the pace but I choose not to.

8 March 2011 Mr David Rosser, Mr Roy Thomas and Mr Graham Morgan

Graham Morgan: In this preoccupation with skills, it is important to understand what skills businesses are looking for. One of the feedbacks we get from our members is that it is very difficult to employ a reliable unskilled person. At one end of the spectrum those gaps are filled. You also find that the interaction with universities is particularly strong with those businesses that employ large numbers of people, and that works exceptionally well. I guess, on a wider skill basis, you still have constant feedback around maths and English, which you debated earlier, and lack of language skills, which is consistent across Wales.

If you look at the international agenda, it is very difficult to drive that when very few people come out with anything other than English and Welsh and IT skills. Again, every modern business needs IT skills and many youngsters don't even choose to take that as a subject. I guess there is an element of delivering the right skills for the future, but the link between the universities and some of the bigger employers historically has been big. The challenge with the smaller businesses and those looking to grow is the actual resource available to give somebody a day or two days off a week to go and develop those skills. I think that is the misconnection. Another factor is that, at times over the last few years, there has been European funding pushed out to training companies and colleges and they are delivering courses as opposed to delivering the right skills. That is a significantly bigger area to look at.

Q58 Guto Bebb: Just to follow up on that, in terms of the university relationship with business, one of the arguments that has been made in the past is that that is a means by which we can create a more innovative economy in Wales. First, in terms of developing innovation, is there any evidence that that is happening as a result of links with universities? Secondly, is there any way in which we can link the universities into inward investment in relation to the issue of a more innovative Welsh approach? The argument has been made that in the past we have depended on a competitive low-wage economy, whereas now we need to compete in a more innovative way. Is that happening in our universities?
Roy Thomas: As to innovation and universities, academics don't really get business. You have to realise that, Mr Bebb. From the work we have done with them, you need to get a businessman to take a product to market and then make a profit. Academics do not do that. It is important that the academics stop and then the guys who know how to make a product take over. That is what has happened. Entrepreneurs, indeed, are people who probably have not been to university. The make-up of a modern-day entrepreneur is somebody who is prepared to take risks, does not intellectualise too much and will make a business plan work.

Q59 Chair: Just going back to the comments made earlier by the academics on the numbers of people going to university and the kinds of things they are doing, what did you make of that? In simple terms, do you agree that there are too many going to

university and they are doing the wrong things? You cleared your throat first.
Graham Morgan: It is a very difficult one to answer. A lot of the folks currently in the university system prepared to go to university four or five years ago when perhaps some of the skills they were preparing for were in a different marketplace. What you have to look at is a dynamic skill base whereby people have got the basics and can adapt to whatever the next few years hold. Perhaps one of our preoccupations for the last 10 years is that we are trying to channel people in particular directions and they do not physically get there.

Q60 Chair: Come on. What do you think? Do you think that 50% is too high?
Graham Morgan: I guess that in any pyramid system—I think these words were used earlier—the best people will gravitate to the top, if that makes sense. If you come back to the situation where you force people to go to university because it ticks a box, then nobody will be a winner out of that, to be perfectly blunt. I think a bigger aspect is that, if you look at Wales as having 8% of its population from overseas, that is quite an influx of students. I hate to think what percentage of Welsh students are currently studying overseas, but I could probably guess it will be sub-1%. I would prefer to see a process whereby you encourage more Welsh people to go beyond Wales so that there is outward connectivity and study overseas. David and I were at a meeting with Indonesians. They were looking at how they could get more of their students to come to the UK to open their minds. I think that is a bigger piece than forcing 50% of people to take degrees in Wales, to be perfectly honest, because there is nothing wider.

Q61 Chair: Are there any other comments on that?
David Rosser: I think that is a ridiculously simplistic comment and argument that I hear from a lot of people, including business people. We are now moving to a situation where more of the costs of going into higher education fall on the student. We need to move to a situation where businesses who desperately need certain specialisms, and can offer meaningful careers on the back of those, will start to contribute toward the costs of higher education themselves and will absolutely take more effort in explaining what career opportunities are available, depending on the skills and university degree you have got. We will start to see a market developing where young people, if they get the right quality advice, will make up their own minds about whether a university degree is the right, sensible course for them, whether a vocational qualification is the right way to go or whether they should go straight into the work force. Under the previous as well as the current system, sufficient quality advice has not been given to young people on outcomes and the value of different qualifications and institutions to enable them to make those decisions.

Q62 Geraint Davies: On this particular point, when we made a trip to Germany to take evidence in Düsseldorf and Berlin, one of the things that emerged was that, as you may know, any company in Germany is required to be a member of the chamber of commerce both locally and regionally. Those chambers of commerce are required to provide training and apprenticeships on a regional basis that fit the needs of those businesses. In Germany, there is an institutional framework for the delivery of high-value apprenticeships alongside the university system. If it is being suggested in some sense that we are being too ambitious with 50% on the university side, what we need is something that fills the gap. We do not want to jump between university and very low skills on the assembly line. What is the direction of travel in that? Would you agree with the German approach?

Roy Thomas: I think there is a lot of merit in that, but on the issue of universities you cannot force people to go to university. You have to give somebody an opportunity. My family were miners; my father and grandfather just did not have the opportunity to do that. You have to give somebody the opportunity if they want to do that, but, again, where are they going to go with it? Are you going to scrap all history departments across the UK, which would be absolutely ridiculous, or are you just going to promote just physics or mathematics? You need that balance in life, and a graduate certainly brings that. It is not only learning at university; you learn life skills. For lots of people it is perhaps the first time they have been away from home and they see that as a different world.

Q63 Mrs James: To come back to the skills agenda, businesses in my constituency are constantly telling me that it costs money to train people to get a good skills base. Many of these are small entrepreneurial companies which do not really have the basis. So they rely heavily on the advice of business organisations funded by the Assembly on what is needed and what level of skills needs to be taught in colleges, universities, etcetera. Do you think there is a good enough link-up at that point? I am seeing a real misunderstanding. Businesses feel frustrated. I will give you an example. Lots of students go to university to study Italian; they study Dante. Is that what is needed today? Of course it is important to study Dante, but business-wise you may not use that kind of Italian. Is there a match there? I am sensing that there isn't.

Graham Morgan: Feedback from our members is that, yes, there is always a need for training, but there is quite a significant amount provided, and there is this dichotomy between physically releasing people to do the training and that investment in time. To take your point, I think that anybody who learns Italian, regardless of what it is, is in a better position than somebody who does not. So you have to look at what is positive in terms of how that can be used in the wider marketplace.

Q64 Mrs James: But are they listening?

Roy Thomas: To come here, of course, you need to study Aristotle.

Mrs James: I did not study Aristotle, actually.

Roy Thomas: I think it is horses for courses. You have to listen to what the employer needs, and what happens is that the bigger companies train people up.

You have the Admirals in Swansea training people up and then they filter down to maybe smaller companies. Typically, that is what happens. If you look at the training programme at Legal & General, one of our members, it is second to none. Again, it is a FTSE100 company. People are sent away for weeks to training courses in Brighton. They come back in a different way, and are able to further a career, perhaps somewhere else. Of course, Legal & General don't like that; they have invested a lot of money in that individual, who may go off and work in the Principality in Cwmllynfell—if there is one in Cwmllynfell.

Mrs James: I don't think there is.

Roy Thomas: I don't think there is, actually.

Q65 Mrs James: But surely, a smaller company just cannot rely on that, if you are an individual entrepreneur with three employees.

Roy Thomas: Those are the facts of life more than anything else; that is the market.

Q66 Mrs James: To come back to the decline in manufacturing and inward investment, how does it affect us in innovative terms? We have seen the decline in manufacturing. Inward investment is getting tougher and tougher. Is it suppressing innovation or is it still alive and well there?

Roy Thomas: We had, and still have, an excellent automotive sector in Wales and we had a supply chain which worked with indigenous companies. So you have got the Visteons, the Bosches and the Fords. Thank goodness we still have Ford in Bridgend. Supply chain issues should be looked at a little more. For example, food is a big sector. If you look at Tesco in Wales, it is supplied with £100 million worth of food for Welsh stores. That is the biggest private sector employer in Wales with 18,000. Mark Grant in Llantrisant does that single-handedly. He is a Llantrisant boy and he procures for Tesco in Birmingham and the south-west. For Asda, it is about £30 million. If you look at those industries, SMEs can live off that. If you are doing Penclawdd cockles or water, which we do for Penderyn whisky, you are selling product outside Wales.

Mrs James: Or Tomos Watkin's beer in my constituency.

Chair: I must appeal for very short questions and answers with no supplementaries, because we have already run out of time.

Q67 Guto Bebb: Mr Rosser mentioned the fact that there was an issue in terms of vocational education, which I was very glad to hear. We tend to talk about HE, but I think there is a role for FE as well. Certainly, in my part of north-west Wales we have seen a partnership between Coleg Menai and Coleg Llandrillo, trying to train up young people to be ready for the opportunities that will arise, possibly with a second nuclear power station. To what extent do you see an interaction between business and FE in Wales and certainly with potential inward investors as well? To what extent do you see the FE sector taking their responsibilities seriously?

David Rosser: To a very great extent. Over a longer period, FE colleges have tended to work more closely, especially with local businesses, than higher education has. Both sets of institutions understand their responsibilities in this area. I see many examples of both sets of institutions advancing that agenda.

Q68 Guto Bebb: Is that relationship being encouraged in the same way as it was encouraged in the past, ensuring that people are aware of the training and support that is available for potential inward investors, which is an important aspect, and the co-ordination of all this that you mentioned WDA used to do? Is that still available? In other words, are we selling Wales properly in terms of the FE sector we have?
David Rosser: I am not sure of the quality of skills and training advice that is given to businesses generally and inward investors. I think it is patchy; it does depend on the quality of the particular account manager you might have.
Graham Morgan: I would quickly add that I visit a number of FE colleges across the whole of south Wales. I think that, generally speaking, there is a fairly good interaction with the local community. If you take Pembrokeshire, there is a huge interaction with the petrochemical industry, which is big inward investment, and the care sectors. Consistently where you have that need, it is addressed, generally speaking, whether that is facilitated by the Welsh Assembly or by people just coming together and doing the right thing. It is a combination of both.

Q69 Chair: I will demonstrate what I think is a quick question with no supplementary and a short answer. At the moment are employment regulations too strict, not strict enough or about right to encourage companies to come here and grow?
Roy Thomas: I think they are too strict.
David Rosser: I would agree.

Q70 Stuart Andrew: We heard some interesting observations on how well Cardiff has performed in terms of attracting inward investment compared to other areas. What are your thoughts on how well it is doing perhaps in comparison with Bristol and Swindon? But, also, do you think that the ambition should be a bit wider than just cities that are close by and one should look to compete with major cities in the country and on the continent?
Roy Thomas: That is a very good question. We have to compete first of all with UK core cities, so you are looking at cities like Manchester, Leeds and Edinburgh, and then you look far away into Europe and cities like Helsinki and Oslo. Cardiff is doing that. I think we can do more. Cardiff is like some kind of Rolls-Royce; it has been kept in the garage too long, as Dublin was in the 1990s. The Irish got behind Dublin and pushed it. I think we are now sensing that Cardiff is the capital and we are losing parochialism. We have more North Walians in the media in Cardiff than I have ever seen. They speak Welsh in Pontcanna where I live. It is great to see the combination of the dialects coming together.

There is no doubt that Cardiff is important as a shop window and the Assembly has neglected a bit of it in the past. We constantly push the fact—that is why we formed the Cardiff Business Partnership—that Cardiff is a great location. People will come to your capital city. If they are going to invest in your country, they will come to your capital city. As they come to London when they come to the UK, they land here and then you take them to Swansea, north Wales or Ammanford. You then take them elsewhere. That was exactly what the WDA did. It tried to take them out of the M4 corridor as we then had targets, but you have to get your capital city right, otherwise you have real problems.

Q71 Guto Bebb: On that point, is the success of Cardiff good news for the economy of north Wales?
Roy Thomas: I think so.

Q72 Guto Bebb: On what basis?
Roy Thomas: Because I think people enjoy going to north Wales. They have a flight now, which is well publicised, and more people should be encouraged to use it. North Wales is part of Wales and we are one, as the vote showed last week, and it is important for us to see that. Unfortunately, you have north Wales looking east towards Liverpool and Manchester, and I would like it to look a little more south than vice versa. I think Merthyr is a kind of Watford Gap. People do not go up to north Wales and see what an amazing place it is, but that should be encouraged.
Chair: We won't mention Monmouth and Tenby.
David Rosser: I think the success of Cardiff is good for all of Wales. People come to Cardiff and say, "Gosh! Isn't Wales a great place?" That impression is important.
Chair: Can I bring in some very brief questions?

Q73 Geraint Davies: On the back of this, what do people think about Brand Wales and marketing Wales generally and, in terms of public investment, how should that be focused? There is already half an answer in some sense by using the window of Cardiff, but does anyone want to say anything about Wales the brand?
Graham Morgan: The feedback I have had from four different countries is that our biggest brand is our flag in terms of an icon. I think we need to put a whole raft of support behind that flag, to be perfectly honest. We need to look at our connectivity and be picky, because Wales is a small place. In the overall context, we cannot be all things to all parts of the world. We need to be far more specific and target perhaps 12, maybe 24, locations and push on that with an open door-type approach rather than try to be broad based. So we should be very much more focused on where we are going to aim our approach.

Q74 Geraint Davies: Are you referring to trade fairs and those kinds of things as well, or what?
Roy Thomas: We keep reinventing the brand. Again, a bit of an anti-dividend was logos which at the beginning of the Assembly were prevalent and there were dragons that looked like swans, for example.

People played around with these things. For me, the brand in business is the value. The brand is your people. That is what a brand is. The brand for a corporation is the values within the organisation and how they are espoused. It is not just about logos. People think that brands are just dragons, leeks, daffodils and goodness knows what.

Q75 Mr Williams: Referring to the role of trade fairs and how important they are, we received that message very strongly in Germany. How much do we do? How much should we be doing? How can that be encouraged to promote Wales at those fairs?
Graham Morgan: Personally, I think a lot more can be done and it needs to be very focused. As I said earlier, it is no good going to a different trade fair every year; you have to create your bridgehead and then move from that. There will be a number of trade fairs around the world that focus on the six sectors. We can agree or disagree on the sectors. That gives you a principle. It is then a matter of looking at what else you physically want to target but having a very robust approach over a three to five-year period.

Q76 Susan Elan Jones: I was very interested in what you said, Mr Thomas, about brand. It is not symbols; it is primarily relational and value driven. In view of that, would you say that probably Wales may need even more and not fewer overseas offices if we are building links between people, preferably perhaps even people who can speak the languages of the countries where they are located?
Roy Thomas: Absolutely. I think we should have an office in London, for example. Cardiff is two hours away from one of the biggest markets in the world. We should be talking about that. We should have an embassy here where we should be talking to the Indian, Chinese and US ambassadors on an everyday basis. We should have offices in major economies.
Chair: That brings us neatly to a question that has been suggested to me. Do you want to ask it very briefly, Geraint Davies?

Q77 Geraint Davies: I just wanted to comment on the movement from the WDA to a different Department and changes that have been occurring. When we spoke to UKTI in Germany, they said they had not really heard much for 18 months because of structural changes in the economic, transport department or whatever. What is your perception of what is happening in terms of WAG's role following the WDA in terms of a focused approach to attract inward investment?
Roy Thomas: Businesses are up in the air about it; they do not really know what is going on. The international director was suspended last year. We read about that in the *Western Mail.* He was quite a high profile figure. In the days of the WDA we would

have been summoned to this Committee to answer on that, or perhaps to something called the Public Accounts Committee, perhaps, to say what was going on. There is a need for more scrutiny and I welcome this morning's session. I think it is important that we talk about these things openly.

Q78 Chair: Mr Rosser, would you say that WAG has been good at getting FDI into Wales?
David Rosser: In the last five years we have still attracted into Wales between 6% and 9% of FDI. We have consistently ranked somewhere between fourth and sixth in the UK regions over that period. I would say it is an average performance.

Q79 Mrs James: I want to ask about the paper you submitted, Graham. In it you mention a one-stop shop for international trade. Would you like to tell us a little more about that?
Graham Morgan: We launched the South Wales Chamber brand and we work closely with the North Wales Chamber which links into Cheshire, and they submitted some views to support me today. We spent a fair bit of time last year trying to understand exactly what happens in the international trade arena. We went out to businesses and a whole range of people which are included in my document. I think the general feeling was that there was not an actual gateway through which there could be focus and from which it could be spun out. We believe at the moment that is missing very much on a joined-up basis between the public sector, private sector and academia to draw on the strengths and connectivity of all those different operations. We can cite chambers like the Dubai chamber and other chambers throughout the world which have these kinds of portals that make a difference to those economies. What we are doing is to replicate the wheel in some respects.
Mrs James: It is a good idea; it is worth doing.
Graham Morgan: Yes. It is a proven mechanism through which things move.
Roy Thomas: Chairman, perhaps I may say that on inward investment we have been very poor compared with Scotland. Again, I urge you to look at the Scottish example comparative to what we are up to and look where they are in terms of the Scottish economy and what they are doing. On trade, they are far ahead of us with offices across the world. Susan Elan Jones mentioned offices. They have offices and brand; they are out there competing.
Graham Morgan: I have looked at the Edinburgh chamber in particular, and certainly the actual model that the chamber has been moving in in Scotland has added to some of the stuff that has been going on. It is very proactive.
Chair: Thank you very much indeed for that. We have kept you here far beyond the agreed time. Thank you for answering the questions so well.

Tuesday 15 March 2011

Members present:

David T. C. Davies (Chair)

Stuart Andrew   Mrs Siân C. James
Guto Bebb   Susan Elan Jones
Geraint Davies   Karen Lumley
Jonathan Edwards   Jessica Morden

Examination of Witnesses

Witnesses: **Sir Terry Matthews OBE**, Chairman, and **Mr Simon Gibson OBE**, Chief Executive Officer, Wesley Clover, gave evidence.

Q80 Chair: Could I thank both of you very much indeed? Sir Terry, I think you have come over from Canada this week. Simon, I know you have come up from Monmouthshire.
Sir Terry Matthews: David, I am in the United Kingdom at least once a month, so it is not out of the ordinary.
Chair: It is very kind of you to come along to give evidence here today. We had a very outspoken witness on the economy last week. We really enjoy outspokenness and a bit of frank talking, so feel free to tell it as it is. Can I start by asking Jessica Morden, the local Member of Parliament, to ask the first question?

Q81 Jessica Morden: Hello and welcome. Congratulations on a very successful Ryder Cup. Can I kick off by asking what you think the economic impact will be for Newport and Wales of having the Ryder Cup in the county?
Sir Terry Matthews: There is a multi-faceted answer to that one. Most people do some sort of economic analysis. We know the number will come out between £80 million and £100 million. It depends how you bound that, but typically we think from the information we have that it will be between £80 million and £100 million. In my own case, I spent a fair amount of money putting the venue together because it had to be built from scratch. It was the first time ever for the Ryder Cup that it was a facility built from scratch for the purpose. It meant that we could pull in over 50,000 people a day between the crowds and the staff that were involved for that event. We were able to pull in over 50,000 people a day with two very large bus parks.
If you compare what we did with previous events, previous Ryder Cups could never have the logistics that we have. With the A449 on the east side and the M4 on the south side abounding the property, it meant the traffic could easily get in and out. We were able to build 140 bus parking spots, and that is continuous traffic. The previous one, which was in Kentucky, had 49 bus parking spots, so it was a tripling or more of the capacity. We were able to have hospitality on the 15th, 16th, 17th and 18th fairways, whereas in previous ones they would only have it on one or one and a half.
Doing something from scratch allowed us to have much bigger capacity. The crowds were over 50,000 people a day. Because of the weather, which was

conveniently raining on a Friday, lots of people wrote to me and said, "Sorry it was spoiled," but they do not realise that golf and business go hand in hand. The flip side of the coin is that the people who were sponsors had much more face time with their most important clients. They wrote to me and said did I do it deliberately, because it was great for business. The upshot of this is that, instead of three days, which it has been since 1926, it ended up being four days. You might not realise just how important that is, but it is a 33% increase in terms of magazine, newspaper, radio and television coverage around the planet.

Q82 Jessica Morden: How does that anticipated £80 million to £100 million break down?
Mr Gibson: All of those figures will be released next week.
Sir Terry Matthews: We will not release those. They will be released by the First Minister on the European Tour. I am giving you an approximate number.

Q83 Jessica Morden: What do you hope the long-term legacy will be for Newport and Wales?
Mr Gibson: It is the brand. I can think of no other event in Welsh history that has created such global awareness of Wales. Terry can tell you, whether he is in China or India, that people now know where Wales is. They know the Celtic Manor, they know Newport, and there is a huge brand awareness. But one of the things we have to be very careful of is that it is not perceived as a finish line. After a big event like that, people often say, "Ah, we did it," and then ease off, whereas if we consider it as a start line to rebuild the brand, it allows us to capitalise on this massive global awareness that we have created for the nation. If we just let it slip away, a lot of the effect will be wasted.

Q84 Jessica Morden: Are there any indicators particularly on golf tourism now?
Sir Terry Matthews: Not just golf. My umbrella company, which I formed in 1972, is called Wesley Clover. That was after the Wesley church in Newbridge and the four-leafed clover that I found in the garden when I was six. I created this little umbrella company called Wesley Clover. It is funny. Some people call in and say, "Is Wes in this afternoon?" They don't realise what the root is. It is mainly an electronics umbrella company. In my career, I have started up 90 electronics companies. On top of that, I have some real estate in terms of office

suites, office blocks, hotels and so on. That is on the real estate side. Also, of course, I have some golf courses.

As Simon says, it is the brand. My business takes me all over the world, whether it is throughout the UK, continental Europe or Asia. You can almost name a city and I have been there within the last five years. Wherever I go, they all know Wales, the Celtic Manor and the Ryder Cup because of the billion-plus people who watched the Ryder Cup on television. Even now I keep getting emails from people saying, "That was a terrific event. I would like to go to the Celtic Manor and play the course." I get it all the time.

Q85 Jonathan Edwards: Bore da. I was very interested in your comments about the event being a platform. What do you think specifically policy makers need to be looking at now to be able to use the Ryder Cup as a platform and build the brand up from there?

Mr Gibson: There is an obvious connection between the game of golf and business. It is a shame we couldn't publish all the attendees who came to the golf, because some of the CEOs and chairmen of some of the world's largest companies were there.

Sir Terry Matthews: These were people that we met.

Mr Gibson: We had meetings with them. They have the capacity to bring hundreds of millions of pounds worth of business to Wales and the UK if we follow up and harness those opportunities.

Sir Terry Matthews: A good example is that Simon and I spent a couple of hours with the chief executive of AT&T. That was over breakfast. It was extended to about two-and-a-half or three hours, something like that. In the person's normal environment, there would be a meeting slot of maybe half an hour or an hour and that's it. But in the context of golf you can open up and have more time. We had some great meetings and reviews with some of the top CEOs on the planet.

Mr Gibson: The hotel alone, on the Friday afternoon when we were rained in, did more than £1 million worth of bookings for corporate customers. I know that there were other large multi-million pound deals concluded in those hospitality suites during the game. A lot of goodwill is created. It is important that we continue to follow up and make sure that we build on that, and not just sit back, relax and say, "We did the job."

Q86 Jonathan Edwards: Who would be responsible for that following up? Would that be Government?

Mr Gibson: I think it is a combination of Government and then the companies.

Sir Terry Matthews: Government and private. At the end of the day there is a good brand out there. The TV coverage gave very good visibility of how pretty the Usk Valley is and so on. There was very good visibility of general coverage of Wales. A very good image was cast and now we have to take advantage of that platform. Certainly that is what I would do and that is what I am doing. Whether the balance of the nation does that remains to be seen, but a very good image was created in those billion-plus viewers, and it is quite clear from when I meet business people around the world.

Hotels and resorts go hand in hand with business. It is not very complicated. If I was to suggest to you, "Why don't you have a holiday in Iraq?", you would say, "There is no way I would go to Iraq." Why wouldn't you go to Iraq? It has fabulous history. It goes all the way back to the Sumerians. There are beautiful areas to go and visit. You wouldn't go there; you would say it is not safe. Would you make an investment there? No, because the people who work for you might get shot, clunk, clunk, clunk. It is not stable. Stability has huge value. When people visit, if they have a good visit, they stay at a hotel. They play golf. They might get a massage. God knows what their experience is, but if it is a good experience they will say, "That's a good place; I could do business there." That is in fact what happens. But if you go to a place which looks down and out, unstable and it doesn't have the rule of law, you won't go back.

Q87 Chair: I am tempted to leap in, Sir Terry, and ask if you have been to Kurdistan recently in the last five years.

Sir Terry Matthews: No. I avoid it as a matter of fact, but I have been to Pakistan. Do you want to talk about Pakistan?

Chair: I think we would like to come back to global areas later, if we may. I am just going to bring in Stuart Andrew on the graduate programme first.

Q88 Stuart Andrew: Thank you, Sir Terry. I want to talk about the graduate entrepreneurship programme and find out what your aims were when you started that in Canada, and to what extent you feel you have met those aims.

Sir Terry Matthews: This goes back a long time. I founded this little company called Wesley Clover in 1972. That was to make an investment to start a company up. I had ideas about making a particular type of electronics product. A person called Mike Cowpland joined me. The unbelievable part of that is that I formed the company with $4,000. At the time it was about £2,000. It doesn't take much of a magician to understand that you can't pay salaries with £2,000. It doesn't last long. I learned some very important lessons in that first year: first of all, the power of new graduates and people in universities. They are not married, typically; they have no children, typically; they have no mortgage, and they can work seven days a week if they are excited—and they do. I had mostly people that were out of their local universities working with me for nothing. We brought out a product because they punch way above their weight. They work seven days a week and so we came up with a product in about six or seven months. It was a product that I knew I could sell, which is another important part of the formula. I connected with potential clients first, not developed something from an idea and then tried to sell it. It is the flip way of what many investors do, inasmuch as it is connection with clients first, and then working very hard to come up with a product rapidly. Fortunately, the product sold—I never had any doubt that it would—and the company prospered.

The interesting thing is that, some 10 years later, every $1 stock option at the time in 1973 has translated to a value of $2.5 million. That made me a very wealthy person and I could afford to do almost anything. It was that 10 years, and the lessons learned were: the power of selected new graduates; the power of working with the clients up front—not taking ideas and developing a product, because if you do that it is highly speculative. This is not speculative.

The next thing was another learning that came along, which was about 10 years later. I formed another company with new graduates and developed a product, but this time with Mitel as the route to market. A new company has no credibility. God knows what it's called: Grey Suit Corporation. Who the hell is Grey Suit? "We have been in business now for three months and I am chairman and chief executive." "How long have you been going for?" "Three months." The probability of getting business with a client is zero. But if you come along and say, "I am Mitel," they have been buying from Mitel for years, the contract is already in place with the purchasing department, clunk, clunk, clunk. The client will now listen to the new proposition and probably buy it from that new group, and that sparks up the business. Once you get the first client and then the second client, away it goes. It is connection with the client up front through some credible channel—in our case let's say Mitel.

There are other strategic partners that we have today that are much, much bigger. We have $100 billion companies that are strategic partners for the companies that I start up. I start them up with new graduates. They work around the clock. Typically, after a year they end up owning 30% to 40% of the company. I have funded it. They took a low salary in return for the ownership. Out of the 90 companies that I have started up, all generally along this pattern, I have only lost six. Do you see the bags under my eyes?

Q89 Stuart Andrew: How have you aligned the scheme with universities in Wales?

Mr Gibson: Shall I answer that?

Sir Terry Matthews: You can answer it. I came from Swansea University. I have tons of friends in Cardiff.

Mr Gibson: Before I answer that, I wouldn't mind responding to some comments that I think were said in this room over the last few weeks about the quality of graduates. I don't necessarily share some people's opinion of the poor quality of the outputs. In fact, as employers, we have built very successful multi-million pound companies based on Welsh graduates. Some of them have been absolutely outstanding. In fact, if I was to turn the guns on anyone, it would not be on the young people, to be quite honest with you. It would be on some of the academics that teach them. Perhaps that is where we need to look at increasing the quality, and not having a poke at the young people themselves, because our experience has been first class.

Sir Terry Matthews: The graduates are first class.

Mr Gibson: Answering your question about the alignment of the programme in Wales, it can be a bit of a challenge because we are proposing something that is relatively new. It is completely proven as a model in Canada. We have been running the graduate

boot camp idea for about five years. So before we brought it over here it was very well tested. What we are trying to do is to make sure we follow the model that we have incorporated in western Canada, which is not only do the graduates come to our programme and a year later graduate into a company, so you get a company not a job, but the other thing we are looking for is to have it accredited so that the experience yields a master's degree in applied engineering and entrepreneurship. That has been quite challenging.

Sir Terry Matthews: It is different.

Mr Gibson: Universities here are not as fleet of foot. I can give an analogy, because it is a good one, of timing. I approached the UK Government at exactly the same time as I approached the British Columbian Government. After 12 weeks, we had the system in place and agreed, financing established and the course accredited. We are now outputting our second company from the programme in British Columbia. We are only just now, after 21 months, getting the programme up and running in the UK. That is reflective of our attitude to risk, both in universities and in Government. It is a very frustrating challenge. What we have are great graduates rotting on the vine. It is not a great time to be a graduate in the UK. You would think that we would be all guns blazing to try and create opportunities for these young people.

I am glad to say that at least we are at the finish line now. We hope to launch in the next couple of days. We will start the programme in April. We are going to locate it in Newport, in the town centre, and we are aligned with most of the major universities in Wales. We will take graduates from other parts of the world as well. What we want to do is to have the programme operating in Wales, have the companies incorporated and headquartered in Wales, but we want the best brains we can get from wherever that happens to be.

Q90 Stuart Andrew: What interest has been shown by the Welsh Assembly Government and by the Government here?

Mr Gibson: The Welsh Assembly Government have agreed to match-fund the support of both—

Sir Terry Matthews: The answer is generally very supportive. They took a look at what I do in Canada. It is not that I don't do things in the UK—don't get me wrong—but, historically, the bulk of the operations for both companies has been in the US and Canada. They look at the success rate and in general are very supportive. I can take you to a much higher level which I think you should be concerned about. If the new graduates coming out of universities are not the next generation of business people, we don't have a future. I would make that observation.

If you take a look at the salaries in India and China—and I go there very, very frequently—I can hire extremely good PhD grads on about $12,000 or $14,000 a year. It would be 10 times that in North America or here. I count out other Asian countries and don't worry about them, because between India and China there is half the world's population—2.5 billion people. So, if anyone says that eventually the salaries will come up, you are dreaming because there are 2.5 billion people and the average salary is $700 a year.

They work incredibly hard. You just have to accept and adapt a little bit. As Darwin will tell you, it is not the biggest that survive or the strongest; it is those best able to adapt. In our case, to maintain or grow our economy you have to have what I call "first mover advantage". You have to develop things before the low-cost nations are on it. In the last 10 years, you have seen Google come up from nothing and be the size of Microsoft. How can such a thing happen against the competition from China and India? It is first mover advantage.

Q91 Mrs James: We have heard a lot from previous people giving evidence about end-of-life products, and that we have become very dependent in Wales on products that really were not, as you talked about, at the beginning of the process. Do you think that is a good evaluation?

Sir Terry Matthews: I am not that sure how to answer that. Clearly things have cycles. Wales had a cycle of being the world's source of metals. There was copper in the Swansea area and iron and the ferrous metals on the eastern end. That was all created because we had anthracite, coal and lots of water, plus we had the ore. The country went through that era and then it died out, I suppose, around the second world war. In the 1950s, it started to go down and then we became a source of branch plants—low labour cost—which I hated, even when I was young, because the headquarters are somewhere else, all the decisions are made somewhere else. I hated that era. What is the next phase? I believe we have excellent graduates. We have to find ways of keeping them. They have to be in business. They have to want to be rich. There is nothing wrong with having a little touch of greed. There is nothing wrong with that.

Mrs James: Ambition.

Sir Terry Matthews: People have to have ambitions. They have to have things which are exciting and to get on selling around the product. We don't teach people how to sell in universities. The thing about a business is that it starts with selling. If you don't sell, you definitely will go out of business. As far as the commercial side and the business side is concerned, we have to bring on new graduates that end up being good business people and sell around the planet and know how to do business. That is basically what Simon and I do.

Mr Gibson: I gave a lecture in Swansea two weeks ago in the main auditorium by video, which was packed and overflowed into the second largest auditorium on the campus. I spoke to the guys for an hour and the response at the end just warmed my heart. These are really bright, motivated young people who want to do something. Trust me, there is no shortage of applications to come on our programme. The foundation itself is set up as a charity, or we are hoping it will be registered as a charity because it is engaged in education. We then commercialise the outputs of whatever comes out of the foundation, which is exactly what we have done in Canada.

One thing is worth pointing out. We have had some significant private philanthropic support of the foundation in Wales. Some of Wales's biggest names in industry are not just supporting it verbally but dipping their hands into their wallets. I will save it until the announcement, but you will be refreshed to know how much money is being put in. It is not just something that we think is a nice idea that we bring in from elsewhere. There is a groundswell of support knowing that, as Terry said, the future of Wales depends on our ability to mobilise our young people to innovate, create and exercise enterprise. As we do that, we will rebuild our economy. But if we sit back and think somehow that we are going to attract inward investment to come into Wales, I wouldn't bet the shop on that because that is going to be a long, hard process because we are up against low-cost economies that can kill us on costs.

Mrs James: That is very refreshing.

Sir Terry Matthews: You will never win on the labour cost rate. It is just ridiculous to think about that. Don't even think about it, if it is not innovation, taking advantage of what I call "first mover advantage" on new things—and you do that by connection with clients up front, not after you have developed something. Take the speculative part out. One of the things we are introducing in the programme in Wales right now is not new to me. I have done this many times and it has been honed down in the last five years a little tighter. There are some things that I could talk about, but it would take a long time to discuss in the Committee. There are many things, but take, for example, quarterly reports. You might say, "What does that mean—quarterly reports?" We bring in new graduates and I expect a quarterly report after three months. If they don't have something done within three months, why not? So every three months there are quarterly reports and then an annual report of what happens. You see, eventually along will come investors and they will ask for due diligence. "What is the background? Who has been doing what? What is the client activity? Who developed what? Are there any sales? How much did you spend?" The first page is always very simple English, not acronyms—not even acronyms like "IP networking". You might know what IP networking is, but not everybody knows what that is. In engineering, there is a tendency to be very heavy on acronyms. I forbid that, because then people can understand in plain English what is going on, what has been spent and what client activity there has been. That acts as due diligence for people who are interested.

I would like you to think about these reports, not just as something that captures the financial side, but more like a TV serial. You see the first episode, then you see one a week later, and then you see one three weeks later. Unfortunately, you miss the third and fourth ones. Damn it, what happened? Jane was about to stab somebody and they stop it for the next one. Now you get mad because you missed one. You see, these quarterly reports are a bit like that. You send it to Auntie Jane and Uncle George. They read it and Johnny is in this start-up company. When little John wants some investment, Auntie Jane says, "Yes, I know what's going on there," because it is in simple English. It is not acronyms. This is just one tiny example of honing it down to maximise success.

Another example is creating strategic relationships with very large companies that are anxious for new services and new solutions for their clients. In that regard, I think we have done an incredible job. Are we allowed to say who we are working with?

Mr Gibson: Yes. One of the other things I would point out is that, when the graduates go through the programme, obviously they reach a point of graduation. There are three things that we look for to be put in place for them to graduate. One is that we want them to have a product, an application or a service. Second, we want them to have a customer. Third, we want them to have access to a revenue stream. It sounds obvious, but I can guarantee that the vast majority of new start-ups fail because they don't have the right product, they don't have a customer and they don't have clear visibility of a revenue stream.

Sir Terry Matthews: And then nobody will invest.

Mrs James: It's a risk.

Q92 Susan Elan Jones: One of the things that fascinates me from what you said is about the ownership that the graduates have in these companies. Has that always been a pivotal part of the programme?

Sir Terry Matthews: Ownership is what drives it. In our programme, I will tell you that the students typically earn what you would call "sweat equity". In North America, you would expect people to earn, if they are really good new grads—and those are the people that we hire—$70,000 a year. They have good degrees and can get a job anywhere. Typically, they would take a job with Microsoft or one of the other large companies, but they don't; they work with me. I pay them $25,000 a year. It is what they don't earn that becomes the equivalent of "sweat equity". They get to own 30% to 40% of the company after a year. It does two things. One, it means the burn rate before you have sales is relatively low because the salaries are low. They work seven days a week anyway. They have nowhere to spend money. The fact of the matter is that they know it is about ownership. Some of the graduates' parents say, "Don't take any money, just maximise the ownership."

Mr Gibson: They sit there and within, say, a year they see their company worth $1 million. Then they do a financing round a year later and they see the company worth $10 million. These are not exaggerated. These are real case examples. If you have a company worth $10 million and you, as a group of founders, have 30% of that, thank you very much, all of a sudden I am very enthusiastic about the—

Sir Terry Matthews: And that drives them even harder.

Q93 Chair: Can you give us a brief study of a company with a product?

Sir Terry Matthews: There are many. There are about 12 on the go right now. One of them is three and a half years old. It is called Beinn Bhreagh. It is always an important thing to get a root name which has some meaning. In this particular case, Beinn Bhreagh is the name of the first home that Alexander Graham Bell built, so there is a little root to the name. The company develops notification systems. Whatever the type of business—let's suppose it is an oil company like BP—there are difficult issues every day for large companies. Retailers are the same way, but let us take an oil company. We were approached only after being in business for a year by Petrobras, the third biggest company in the world. They have emergencies every day: a pipe broken; a valve gone; an oil spill; a lorry turned over. Every day there is an issue that is significant. It might be at 3 o'clock in the morning. What this company does is build a management system that gets down to different media to get to people on an emergency or an urgent notification basis.

David, let us suppose I wanted to get to you at 3 o'clock in the morning. I would want your home number, your mobile number and probably a London number. I would want an e-mail address. I would want to know if there are any paging systems to get at you: SMS or instant messaging. These are all ways that I can get to you because there is an emergency at 3 o'clock in the morning. Not only do I use all these vehicles to get to you, but then you notify me and say, "I have the message and I am on it." It is the acknowledgement that you have actually got it and now you are on it.

This particular programme began with universities, when there was some shooting in Northern Virginia. The university made an announcement that said, "There is a gunman in the main lobby. Everybody go to the west entrance." Of course, the gunman also goes to the west entrance, so that absolutely doesn't work. We developed special IP addressed paging systems and a software system to get at every type of media that you can get at.

The upshot with this company is that the sales have grown something like the following. It took nine months to come up with the first product. The sales won't be accurate, but it will be roughly $20,000, $60,000, $120,000, $200,000, $250,000, $300,000. They are now at about $1 million a quarter. They have just taken in investment money of $4.5 million at a valuation pre-money of 10. It is three and a half years old.

I could give you other examples if you wanted, but that is a simple example where now they are beginning to sell products around the world. Verizon, which is one of the biggest service providers in the world, and AT&T, which is one of the biggest service providers in the world, both now start selling the product. They have just won business with a company called Jack in the Box. You might laugh at the name, but Jack in the Box has 3,500 restaurants. They had a case where some people died from meat which had gone off. A bad batch of beef had gone into all of the stores and it had salmonella. People actually died from it. In this particular case, like any supply channel if there is a problem, if there is a bad batch of something, once it is found there is a compliance issue. They only have two hours to clean it off the shelves. They invoked the system to get to all the managers, all the restaurant chefs, all the sous chefs, clunk, clunk, clunk, to say, "Here is a bad batch. Clean it off." They get back and say, "Got the message. We've cleaned it off." So they were in compliance. That is on the food side for such a product.

There are so many use cases on supply lines for manufacturers and so on who want "just in time". This is a company that is growing very fast.

Chair: I would be interested to know when it gets listed.

Sir Terry Matthews: Did that help?

Chair: It does help. Thank you very much.

Q94 Guto Bebb: In your view, does Wales have a good or poor track record at encouraging entrepreneurial activity?

Mr Gibson: I think the results speak for themselves.

Q95 Guto Bebb: In what way? Could you elaborate?

Mr Gibson: It hasn't been great, has it? I have been a Welsh-based entrepreneur. I formed Ubiquity in Newport. Fortunately, we had a good result. It was sold ultimately for a total value package of about £200 million to Avaya, part of AT&T. That was a great success and we could name others. It is not just a Welsh thing, so let's not beat ourselves up. It is a UK issue. Let me give you an example of a reason why. It is all right for us to say, "We think this; we think that". Let us talk about why not. There is a crisis in the access to capital. Venture capitalists are shutting down. They are not functioning any more. The reason for that is that the money supply to them has dried up. Traditionally, in this country and in North America, banks and pension funds took a certain small percentage of their assets and applied it to fund venture capital. I invite you to talk to the banks and see how many of them now apply their capital to this asset class of venture capital.

Sir Terry Matthews: It is dead.

Mr Gibson: It is dead.

Sir Terry Matthews: It is like looking for water in a desert; there isn't any.

Mr Gibson: So there we are saying we are going to rebuild the nation on an enterprise economy and we are going to encourage entrepreneurship, but there is no fuel in the tank. At a time when the Government owns some banks, whether it is carrot or stick, I would encourage the Government to put some money back into venture capital—to put some fuel in the tank to fund our plans for an enterprise economy. Without the fuel we are just going to be a talk shop. We are going to do lots of good entrepreneurship work, but not when the company needs £10,000. You can always find someone like a Finance Wales to invest those sorts of amounts of money, but you try raising money when you need £2 million, £3 million, £4 million or £5 million. It is absolutely dire, no matter how good your idea is. What tends to happen in Britain is that we build companies up, they reach a certain critical mass and they are acquired by foreign companies. The reason for that is they don't have the ability to raise the capital to keep them in the game, if that helps.

Sir Terry Matthews: Are any members of the Committee familiar with the venture capital side? Is there familiarity with this side of investments in small companies? The banks are completely out of this asset class. In Canada, the US and the UK, they are right out of it. The pension funds have also exited it because the returns have not been good. Because the returns have not been good, they say, "Okay, we will put money elsewhere."

Mr Gibson: You could build new venture funds just on the money that these damned bankers get in bonuses, to be quite honest with you.

Q96 Guto Bebb: Could I follow up on that point, because the question was in terms of the track record that Wales has? You said that the track record of Wales was not particularly bad in comparison with the rest of the UK, but then you came to the issue of the shortage of capital. Surely the problem existed before the current credit crunch. Would you comment on that?

Mr Gibson: It has always been difficult.

Guto Bebb: It has always been difficult, okay.

Mr Gibson: But, that said, back in 2000–2001, I think at the time I raised the largest venture round ever. We were a Welsh company based in Newport. We raised £27.5 million. It can be done, but I wouldn't fancy my chances doing that right now. I would be lucky to get £27.50.

Q97 Jonathan Edwards: Do you have any confidence that the so-called "Project Merlin" is going to change things in terms of finance for entrepreneurs? There is supposed to be a deal between the bankers to lend more money and they are allowed to keep their bonuses if they achieve those targets.

Mr Gibson: No.

Q98 Geraint Davies: You said there was a systemic failure in terms of venture capitalism and then mentioned that the Government has an opportunity to get in there. Historically, hasn't there been a problem in terms of picking winners and all this stuff?

Mr Gibson: Yes; I am not suggesting that the Government gets in there.

Q99 Geraint Davies: What would you propose?

Sir Terry Matthews: Geraint is saying there has always been a problem picking winners and so on. Isn't that right, Geraint?

Geraint Davies: Yes; that is right. That is one of the issues.

Sir Terry Matthews: But I don't think that is what Simon is saying.

Mr Gibson: I am not saying the Government should be the venture capitalist. I think the Government could put in incentives in terms of taxation to encourage people to get involved. It is not just banks and pension funds; it is high net worth individuals. A couple of years ago I gave a talk at Cardiff Business Club. If you are going to get a forum in Wales full of high net worth individuals, it is probably the Cardiff Business Club. From the podium I asked a question. I said to them, "How many of you have actually invested in a local Welsh company?" I'll tell you what: it wasn't a spectacular response. A couple of hands went up. If we had that same audience in Canada and we said to people who are high net worth individuals, "How many of you have put money into the local economy and invested in local companies?", loads of hands would go up. The difference is the taxation system.

Q100 Chair: Is it the corporation tax or the rules on investment—capital gains?

15 March 2011 Sir Terry Matthews OBE and Mr Simon Gibson OBE

Mr Gibson: Tax credits.

Sir Terry Matthews: Tax credits for investment in small companies. It is tax credits. It is essentially neutral to the budget. It generates more tax than the credits. If you are interested in such information, I would be happy to send it to you.

Chair: We would be.

Sir Terry Matthews: It would be wrong of me to stretch this any further than saying that it has worked very well in British Columbia. It has worked very well in New Brunswick. Ontario is currently looking at it for the budget this year, and the Federal Government is looking at it to see if it should be something that they do countrywide because it has been very effective in some provinces. I would suggest that information might be valuable in the context of this Committee and that you could encourage the Government to provide tax credits. If it can be shown in the model that it is neutral for the Treasury, then please tell me what the disadvantage is. If the advantages come because people invest as a venture capital type of thing, as an individual, and get a tax credit and the entire thing to the Treasury means it is neutral, then you encourage more people to be employed and you encourage more start-up companies. It is not very hard to understand that, if you have a company of two people, it is fairly easy to grow it to four. It is tough to take 20,000 and grow it to 40,000.

Q101 Geraint Davies: Can I come back to my particular point? I have started small businesses as well, as it happens, but it seems to me that, in terms of venture capitalists, the problem with venture capitalists for many small businesses is that they require massive returns on their investment. I think what you are now saying is that, by the route of tax credits, local people might invest in local businesses not demanding the earth from that small company.

Sir Terry Matthews: Right.

Q102 Geraint Davies: The third vehicle you have mentioned is the "sweat equity", which is obviously a very successful mechanism.

Sir Terry Matthews: Geraint, I don't wish to confuse this. On the one hand, the limited partners—pension funds and banks—don't provide money to venture capitalists. That is number one, and that is bad. That is very bad because venture capitalists look at what is called "deal flow". They look at the companies. The companies say, "Here is my business plan. Here is what I have done, clunk, clunk, clunk. I would like some financing to make it grow." That is the venture capital side. The other side is individuals that are wealthy that might be persuaded to invest in small companies, in particular if there is a tax credit, because it is a risk. At the end of the day, if somebody provides money and the bulk of it is spent on labour, the labour is taxed in any event. If the funding is used to pay for labour, in this particular case perhaps a lot of people who are graduated, clunk, clunk, clunk they will be taxed anyway. If it goes back on a tax form, what is the problem? Encourage it, because some of these companies will actually grow and employ a lot of people. It is starting the engine up.

Mr Gibson: That is the great thing about the knowledge economy too. The vast majority of the money that you need for your company is spent in human capital, in personnel. They pay taxes and national insurance, so the Treasury gets half of it back anyway.

Q103 Chair: It is something we would be very interested in having a very short—

Sir Terry Matthews: With your permission, I will send you the clearly defined British Columbia model. Other places in Canada are now saying, "This works." That information might fairly quickly help guide some changes in the way investment funding is used for companies.

Chair: We would be very grateful for that, Sir Terry.

Sir Terry Matthews: All right; I am happy to do that.

Chair: We have already asked about taxation incentives, haven't we?

Q104 Mrs James: I just wanted to tease out a little bit more about your personal experience in Wales. Obviously you have been here a long time now and you have had a huge commitment to Wales. In your experiences, has it been easy to invest in Wales? What factors did you consider the most important and is that a lesson for future investors?

Sir Terry Matthews: Siân, do you play golf?

Mrs James: No.

Sir Terry Matthews: You could. There are some great golf courses at the Celtic Manor. That is a form of investment. We do encourage young people to learn to play golf and other things. That is an important part, believe it or not, of business. I talked to that earlier. My experience in Wales started in the early 1970s with Mitel, where I started up in parallel with Canada. I started up with some people here in Mitel, first of all, to build things called tone receivers—that was the first product—and then PBXs. My experience in Wales, whether it is co-operation from the Government or whether it is the new graduates we hire—is as good or better than anywhere else. Did that answer the question?

Mrs James: Yes.

Sir Terry Matthews: I have hired many, many people in Wales and they are as good as or better than anywhere else on the planet. How we can take within Wales more start-up companies that grow is to me the biggest opportunity we have in any field. It is keeping those graduates local. It is keeping those graduates motivated. That is the most important thing we can do.

Mr Gibson: A few years ago I sat on the board of the WDA. I was asked to entertain an American in Cardiff Bay. I did so with a gentleman called Drew Nelson, who runs IQE in Cardiff. I remember he was being besieged by various inward investment packages, but he was different because he didn't have a company. He was an inward entrepreneur. I remember saying to him at the time, "All the regions will throw money at you and all of them will try and incentivise you, and in some ways almost bribe you to come to the region. The reason that you should come to Wales is the quality of the people, their work ethic, their output and their loyalty." I am glad to say I think what we said rubbed off a little bit because it was Henry

Engelhardt from Admiral. If Henry was sitting in here and we were to ask Henry what he thinks of his Welsh work force, you would be gladdened and heartened by what good things he would have to say about how good the staff are. That is the most important thing—the people.

Sir Terry Matthews: You would be pleased to hear it. Siân, you asked for my experience. The experience has been very good, whether it is the work ethic, the quality or the loyalty. It has been very good.

Q105 Mrs James: We have heard evidence from previous witnesses who have said that, in the 1970s and 1980s, a lot of the inward investment was because of the grant culture, and that they were enticed in in some ways. There is a lot of competition out there for the potential investors in Wales. How can we make sure that we are at the front and that we are the place they come to? You have talked a little bit about it, but maybe you can say a little bit more.

Sir Terry Matthews: Siân, grants are always good. You can't possibly say it is bad. When you provide cash to a company to entice them, clearly that can't be bad because you are helping to fund the operation. It would be very silly of me to suggest to you that that doesn't work. It clearly works. At the end of the day there is this other side, which is the quality of the people, the quality of the new grads and the hard work ethic, which I have found has worked very well for me.

Mr Gibson: And the innovation output of universities is very important.

Q106 Mrs James: The Techniums have been particularly successful, for example, at Swansea University.

Mr Gibson: Yes.

Q107 Chair: Have Techniums been a success?

Mr Gibson: I went before a Select Committee in the Assembly and I was asked this question. You will remember I wrote a report several years ago about the commercialisation of intellectual property in higher education. It got buried for about nine months because I think I said something negative about Technium. When I was asked what I thought of Technium, I will repeat my response that I gave there. Technium started out as a very, very good idea based on the exploitation of intellectual property and ended up a very poor idea based on property.

Q108 Karen Lumley: Can I follow on from Siân's question? Obviously, in the 1970s and 1980s we were really good at attracting inward investment, when it was 25%, and in 2009 it fell to 6%. Can you enlighten me as to why? Is it grants, or are there other reasons for that?

Mr Gibson: It is pressures of the world economy, which is shifting, and the cost base is shifting. Our cost base is very high compared to other parts of the world. A friend of mine used to work for the BBC. He resigned in the end because I think he just got fed up standing outside factory gates—he was supposed to be the business correspondent—announcing another closure. Of course, it flips over to the politician, and the politician says, "I know the factory has closed; we are moving Wales up the value chain." That is a standard kind of response, which worked years ago if we were competing with a country like Mexico, but now we are competing with somewhere like China—and you don't think they are moving up the value chain at an alarming pace? They are not a low-intellect economy. They are punching out engineers and scientists at a rate that is breathtaking. At this point I would like to prompt a question from Terry. I want Terry to talk to you about a meeting he had several years ago with an economist who was working for the Brazilian Government because I think it is absolutely key. Do you want to talk about that, Terry?

Sir Terry Matthews: Are you talking about the Indian case?

Mr Gibson: Yes.

Sir Terry Matthews: This goes back to 1978 when I was travelling from Montreal to London. I had a meeting that morning when I got into London, so I wanted to sleep. I got in the 747 and I moved back. This character was next to me. He pulled out the stuff from his briefcase and it was flopping all over me. I said, "Do you want me to put my table up? Then I can get a little sleep and you can have a little more room", because the tables on both sides could have given him a little more room. He said, "I am on my way to Delhi," and so the story began. I didn't sleep at all that night.

This guy was from Montpelier, which is the capital of the state of Vermont. I will capsule very quickly the things I learned in that discussion. Remember this is the 1970s. There is a curve—actually it is more like a straight line. On the one side is growth of GDP and on the other side is the percentage of engineers in the society. It is not complicated. It is growth of GDP against percentage of engineers, not number of engineers. It is a straight line. Sweden, Germany, the UK, the US and France is very high. India is very low in the 1970s. There are not many engineers as a percentage of the society and the GDP growth is very low, but it is a relatively straight line. It is growth of GDP against percentage of engineers.

Now, he went to India with these charts. Another chart showed that, because the growth of GDP is lower than the growth of population, standards of living keep falling because the GDP growth doesn't keep up with the growth of the population. Again, it is not very complicated to understand. He went to India and they came in with very large programmes to increase the number of engineers in the society. The upshot is that it has one of the fastest growing GDPs in the world now and the number of engineers far exceeds the number required. They do tons and tons of outsource engineering for people in the UK, Canada and the US. Outsourcing of engineering is a huge thing now. Companies that are $50 billion to $100 billion a year doing engineering, mainly software, are outsourcing because they just created so many engineers. The GDP has shot up and so the standards of living are improving.

I encourage you to think about that. How many engineers are we cranking out in our society? The first question is: how many engineers? The second thing is: how many are staying? If they take off, they didn't help create any commercialisation. Commercialisation is perhaps a subject in its own right. If you look at the amount of funding that comes from the Government into university research, the question should be asked: what parts of that research end up creating companies or being commercialised? The answer is almost none. Then the question is: are we right to keep that high cost of spending in university research instead of spending directly into companies? We should question that, because if you spend in companies, it helps them to create research and development wherever their operation is and they become more competitive worldwide.

I would argue for more direct funding into industry than funding into university research, unless the university research has a little provision that says, "Okay, I want a commercialisation plan." If there is no plan for commercialising it, no plan for an attachment to something which represents sales, boom, you don't get the funding.

Q109 Susan Elan Jones: I was very interested in what you said earlier that cash to entice is never really a bad thing. Do you think that Government has the balance wrong? Did too much of this go into what we might think of as prestige projects in terms of inward investment? Do you think it would have been better to have had more of that into regional entrepreneurialship?

Mr Gibson: Two things happened. I can't talk to the 1970s, but I can talk to the 1980s and 1990s and the early part of the new millennium. One thing you noticed was that you were definitely advantaged if you had a foreign badge on in terms of talking about support. You were also disadvantaged if you were in a knowledge economy business. The grants were always orientated towards large capital expenditure like machinery. Of course, if you are a software company or a scientific institution, you don't need tons of capital equipment; it is people. Fortunately, around the 2000 mark, they started to adjust the grants system to move it towards intellectual property and not physical, tangible machinery and assets. That was a big change in the scheme.

During the 1990s particularly, I sensed amongst the business community that they were bitter because if you had a Welsh badge on, you were sent to the back of the queue, and if you had a Japanese or American flag on, you went to the front of the queue. The multiples were hundreds more than you could get if you were an indigenous company. Fortunately, that has finished. You do sense that you are on a more level playing field when it comes to grant applications now.

Q110 Geraint Davies: I want to refer to something that people have called the "production mandate", but which in essence, as I understand it at least, is that the grants and the amount of grants should be linked to the quality of the investment and the quality of jobs that are being created. Instead of these simple jobs where they are putting something together, the grants would be higher according to the level of research, the level of responsibility and the calibre of jobs. I know

you focus quite understandably on entrepreneurial innovation and indigenous growth as opposed to inward investment, but do you think there is a role for inward investment, and do you think it should be geared in that way, qualitatively?

Sir Terry Matthews: Yes.

Mr Gibson: The score sheet was always jobs created, jobs retained, dah-de-dah-de-dah. It was a fairly blunt instrument. There was never any consideration for—

Sir Terry Matthews: Quality.

Mr Gibson: In terms of research as well, in universities you are judged on your publication history. The research assessment exercise—

Sir Terry Matthews: Wrong motivation, in my view.

Mr Gibson: As soon as you publish you can't patent; you can't protect it. It goes into the public domain and it is over. Yet why aren't we judging our academic community in terms of patents registered and intellectual property created? That should be a central part of the research assessment exercise, not just "Did I get my paper in a learned journal?"

Q111 Geraint Davies: In terms of intellectual capabilities, obviously innovation, entrepreneurial growth and inward investments are going to be geared to the level of skills delivered by our schools and universities. There has been some criticism in our hearings of the delivery and focus of both schools and universities. Is there anything that isn't being done that should be done? What is your comment on that skills offer?

Mr Gibson: Two weeks ago I sat in a meeting and I heard Queen's in Belfast present. Sometimes the best ideas are the simplest. What Queen's have decided to do is to teach entrepreneurship as a module, which is accredited—which is a really important issue. It is accredited. So it is not a waste of your time doing it and it counts towards your degree. You study entrepreneurship in every subject that is taught at Queen's. Theology: learn entrepreneurship. You might say why would a theologian want to study entrepreneurship? If he is going into the ministry, he had better be entrepreneurial to keep his flock together and financed. History: they were sending undergrads out to look at historic sites and how they could be better utilised and commercialised in terms of sustainability. I asked specifically about medicine, and the chap said that medicine was a big issue because the trainee clinicians were saying, "We have got enough on our plate; we don't need to do business and entrepreneurship." Then the Government made its announcement about the reforms of the health service. Now, every single one of these guys is queuing up to do the course.

I would hazard a substantial bet that the Northern Ireland economy is going to benefit in 10 or 20 years very significantly because it has taught entrepreneurship in higher education to every single grad that comes out of that institution. It is showing already with spin-out companies. It is why Queen's are winning so many awards around Europe. They have taken a very fundamentally simple decision— every graduate needs to be taught entrepreneurship— and they are changing the road map.

Q112 Geraint Davies: Sir Terry mentioned the distinction between research and development in companies which were commercialising ideas, and research in universities, which often weren't. Do you think there is a case to be made for investing money to bring together partnership activity between companies and universities to generate ideas as part of the delivery mechanism? I know in Swansea university, for example, they are trying to build up on Fabian Way a cluster of different companies. Rolls-Royce, Tata, Boots and all these people are getting involved. The idea is really to have the R&D, the intellectual side, networked to the real world. Rather than have a separate idea—choose this one or that one—is there a case to bring it together?

Sir Terry Matthews: We spent some time in Finland, and that is exactly what they do in Finland. They connect. There is pretty much no research that is done that is independent of some commercial operation. Correct?

Mr Gibson: Yes.

Sir Terry Matthews: It is totally connected.

Q113 Chair: Sir Terry, you talked about the need to encourage more graduates to set up their own companies through vehicles like Wesley Clover and others as well. What other strengths does Wales have? What could we be doing to develop the economy?

Sir Terry Matthews: The graduates are good. We certainly find that, and that is the raw material. Without that, you go nowhere. But then there is connection to the clients, that connection to the customers—a little bit like we were just talking about. The difference in the Wesley Clover model is that people get ownership out of that. If they work very hard, they get that ownership very quickly. The time to ownership is very short, partly because of this model that we developed.

By the way, we are quite happy to divulge more of the model that we use. I do not have some exclusive on the model. It works and if somebody else is using similar things I think that is just fine. Perhaps one of the things that is available in Wales is the fact that I travel there frequently, I would think one of the important things would be to be doing more in the way of putting on presentations to the main universities to say, "This is how you create entrepreneurs." That would encourage people. If it has been done before, why try and reinvent the wheel? Putting presentations on, whether it is in Bangor, Swansea, Cardiff, Newport or whatever, would encourage new graduates to have a go at things.

Mr Gibson: David, you asked a question about what we could do. Sometimes there is a very simple missing component in the economy, like accommodation for companies. You would think that that wouldn't be a problem in Wales. I am telling you it is. Finding accommodation for new companies once they are through the incubation phase—

Q114 Chair: What about the WISP scheme: the scheme set up by the Welsh Assembly to get high-quality office space? Has that not been successful?

Mr Gibson: We have not felt it in terms of the availability. Cardiff is obviously overheated in terms of capacity. You might say, why don't we do more in some of the outlying counties within Wales? I can tell you why: there is nowhere to put the companies that you create.

Q115 Chair: Sir Terry, you mentioned earlier on that you travel a lot around the world looking at the way different economies are developing. What trends do you see? Do you think that growth in China and India is going to carry on over the next 10 or 20 years? I am interested in this. Broadly speaking, we have a rich West and poorer developing world. In 20 or 30 years' time, do you see that there is going to be parity of wages across what is currently the first and third world, perhaps still with rich and poor, but roughly earning the same amount of money in countries across the world, if that makes sense?

Sir Terry Matthews: David, I think we have a serious problem. What you have seen in the last 10 or 15 years from India and China is just the beginning. You are going to have this higher level world economy problem. There were some major, major goofs, in my view, going back to the 1950s and 1960s with the General Agreement on Tariffs and Trade. Basically, if you review where things are at, it goes a little bit like the following. The rich nations—UK, US, Canada, France and Germany—all said, "We are the people that design and make stuff. If tariffs around the world come down, we can export more." There was a fatal flaw because it is a two-way valve. That is the bit they forgot.

There were other barriers that made difficulties for countries like China and India before. As an example, what kind of barriers? There are trade barriers. That is clear. You try to bring products through a border and there is a tariff. Those tariffs are down to almost nothing now. In the last 10 or 20 years there have been other barriers that have gone. An example is the telecommunications bill. If you called from London to Beijing 10 years ago, it would cost you £5 a minute. Now it costs you nothing. Communications costs are not a barrier.

The next thing is transportation. It was Manchester Liners that designed containers. Manchester Liners said, "Okay the issue is the logistics of not trying to get goods packaged tightly. The issue is the thing that it goes into that has to go on lorries, rail and ships. Make that a standard." That one move throughout the world meant that shipping costs are down at the point that they don't really matter any more. The shipping costs are not significant. Communication costs are not significant. The western world screwed up by saying, "We will bring tariff barriers down." Now you face the full force of the fact that labour costs in India and China are about one twentieth of the UK and we wonder why we are having trouble with blue collar workers. How can you fight that?

If you take a look at the growth, let's just take another parameter of this. Take a look at hotels. Use a narrowly defined spectrum of business. If you make systems for hotels, how many hotels were built in the UK last year? Almost none—three. How many were built in China? 2,000. 1,500 were built in India. That takes bricks, concrete, carpets, ceilings, lighting, air conditioning, beds, linen—everything. 2,000 hotels were built in China. All that the local people that make things for hotels have to do is to crank up a little more production and export it. Anybody that was in the business here is going to die because they can't meet the low costs of China; they cannot.

Q116 Chair: I suspect—in fact I am absolutely certain—you know more about economics than I do, but surely if China is exporting that much to and collecting that amount of foreign currency from Britain, say, Britain will have to export things back to China in services, patents or whatever in order to have the money to pay the Chinese. It all sort of balances out in the end, doesn't it? It has to.
Sir Terry Matthews: Does it balance out? How does it balance out? How do you take a nation of 65 million people? It doesn't even make the next decimal place on 1.3 billion. And 90% of the population are rural. They haven't actually moved into the cities yet. You will see much more automation of the farms, as happened in the UK 100 years ago, and people will keep moving to cities. Buildings will continue to go up and people will continue to work hard at low, low salaries. It is true that 2% or 3% of the population—for that, read 50 million people—will become extremely wealthy, but it is a tiny percentage of the total. We have to face the full force of the lot, and that was before I talked about India, by the way.
Chair: I had better bring in Guto Bebb for a quick follow-up.

Q117 Guto Bebb: I want to go back to the comments that Mr Gibson made in relation to Queen's University and the entrepreneurship modules. Could you elaborate on exactly what they are doing with that? I am very interested in the issue of having entrepreneurship as part and parcel of every part of academic endeavour. Could you elaborate slightly on what they are doing?
Mr Gibson: They took a fundamental decision that entrepreneurship needed to be a core component of every undergraduate's education. That alone is not an easy thing to do. You can imagine the wars that kicked off around all the various academic schools. It must have been carnage for a few months, but they stuck by that conviction. "Every student that graduates out of this institution will have an understanding of entrepreneurship."
What else seems to have happened is that all the supporting forces in the economy are now orientating themselves to support that. If you are kicking out all these young, bright people with good ideas, you want to make sure that they are supported, that they are mentored and that they have access to capital. You can see a wind of change going across the province. I think it is absolutely admirable. I would love to see that happen in Wales.
Sir Terry Matthews: Yes; we could do the same.

Q118 Guto Bebb: As a follow-up—and I speak as a member of the coalition here in Westminster—my concern is that, obviously, we are getting rid of the Regional Development Agencies in England, and one of the issues is that, as part of that, a lot of the entrepreneurship projects are being lost. The argument

that has been made is that you can't teach entrepreneurship.
Mr Gibson: Rubbish; rubbish.

Q119 Guto Bebb: I tend to agree with you on that point. Your view is that there is value in teaching this as part and parcel of somebody's educational achievements.
Mr Gibson: I deal with guys with MBAs all the time. They come in, they have been to some of the best universities in the world and they have done an MBA. They can't sell. They have studied marketing. They can take you through the four Ps of marketing with great eloquence, but they can't sell. Does marketing exist to support sales or sales exist to support marketing? It is obvious, but that is typical of a deficiency of someone who has been to a top business school, comes out and hits a crisis point because someone turns round to them and says, "Would you go and sell that for us?" They don't have a clue.
We sometimes assume that a business school is kicking out exactly what the economy needs. It is not always the case. Entrepreneurship skills don't need just to be focused out of a business school. We can have entrepreneurs who are biologists. We can have entrepreneurs who are theologians. They can come from all over the map, but we need to mobilise them and we need to show young people that there is an opportunity. It is more fun to create a job than to go and get one. We need to get that message across to young people.

Q120 Mrs James: I am very interested in this. Lots of people that I know are the best sellers who can close the deal, and closing the deal is the important thing. "Okay, sign on the line." They don't have degrees. They have come up through industry. They may have come up through call centres. What opportunities do you see within your structures for people who may not necessarily have come through the degree route?
Mr Gibson: As the companies mature, you hire outside of the graduate scale. It is interesting, because the old model was that you raised money as a team, you got a dream team together, typically more experienced people, and then eventually you hired graduates to help you out. Our model flips it on its head. We take the grads first, but the composition changes as they succeed. The company Terry told you about has many more mature executives in it now, because they have been brought in to help out. Then you hire people in sales. You hire people to help in tech support and other things. They might not be graduates, but the graduates are pulling the whole system forward and creating a critical mass underneath them.
Sir Terry Matthews: Siân, you have to have faith in the new grads that come out of universities because if they are not the next generation of business people we don't have a future. You have to get them to be business people and help them to be business people as quickly as possible.
Mr Gibson: Before you think we are delusional, I invite you to look at the top most valuable companies in the world currently. I think you will find they have

one thing in common: they were all started by graduates.

Chair: We are running a bit short of time. We have about 10 minutes left, because we have to be there on pain of death—or rather, not getting a meal, anyway. I will call Jonathan and suggest that we try and keep things fairly brisk for the next 10 minutes.

Q121 Jonathan Edwards: As a part of this inquiry, we went to Germany to see how they were working in terms of inward investment. They were investing heavily in terms of trade missions and trade offices in the emerging economies, first, to create markets for their exporters, but secondly, to attract the HQs of the new companies in these countries. Do you think it is a strategy that we should be pursuing with vigour in Wales?

Sir Terry Matthews: No; I wouldn't invest in it.

Q122 Jonathan Edwards: Why?

Sir Terry Matthews: First of all, you have to have companies that are already exporting all kinds of stuff and suitable for modification product. If you take a look at Germany, their export market for machine tools, cars and appliances and so on is very big. They already have output, and incrementally it doesn't cost much to make slight changes and ship to Brazil or whatever. It makes sense.

The first thing we need is to have a few companies that are globally capable of selling. Until you have an output that is able to be moved around the world, I do not think we are there. I just don't think we are there. It would be like another layer of cost and, like many things in life, if it is not efficiently utilised, it is a burden. Personally, if I was king, it wouldn't be the case. I would not do it. I would put my energy into innovation and new grads starting companies up. I would get the groundswell going and get some enthusiasm, not have people coming out of universities and finding they can't get a damned job. That has to be really depressing.

Q123 Karen Lumley: You talked earlier about your new venture. How helpful have you found the Welsh Assembly Government and the UK Government in that?

Mr Gibson: I have to tell you that from my experience of the last 21 months it has been fairly arduous, but I wouldn't point the finger at any politician in the Bay. Every politician that I have spoken to in the Bay thinks this is an absolutely excellent idea. That includes the Cabinet as well. One thing that I do find extremely frustrating is that we are burdened with a civil service in Cardiff that is shaped for Whitehall. It seems bizarre that, whenever you want to do something, there are 10 lawyers telling you that you are in breach of some sort of state aid intervention, market economy rule or whatever. Instead of having a discussion about how you can get things done, the discussion always starts out with, "No. Now what's the question?" I don't understand why a small, agile country like we are—or we should be in Wales—is burdened with a civil service that is monolithic in its

rule structure and based on something that was set up for this institution and for the nation. We are somewhere between a small Government and a local authority in terms of critical mass and size. Why don't we have an organisation that can move quickly?

I will give you an example just to prove my point. ProAct was a programme that was brought in very, very quickly, as you know, to support the automotive and manufacturing industries at the time the economy fell off the chart. I sat in ERAP last week—the Economic Research Advisory Panel—and was presented with the outputs of ProAct. It was an excellent programme and it did exactly what it said on the tin. They got that going in 12 weeks, which shows that you can match the British Columbia 12 weeks that we talked about earlier on.

They have been audited six times since. What does that tell you if you are the civil servant who put that together? Don't innovate; don't take a risk. There were six sets of UK auditors, Welsh auditors and European auditors. Give the guys a break. We should be celebrating and rewarding programmes like ProAct, not inflicting pain on them through six audit processes.

Q124 Karen Lumley: What was the difference between dealing with the Welsh Assembly Government and the WDA?

Mr Gibson: The WDA was not a perfect organisation, and I sat on it, so I speak from experience. There were issues in the WDA, clearly, but what the WDA was mandated to do was move quickly. A decision could go to the Board of the WDA, the Board of the WDA could make a decision, and, by the way, there was a firewall then to the Minister. If something went wrong, the Minister could say, "Not on my watch. That was their problem." The one good thing about the WDA which we need to recapture was its agility, its velocity, its ability to get things done quickly, which we have definitely lost. There was a time when you were guaranteed on a mandate that, if you put in a grant application, you would get your response and decision within 28 days. Now it is like 28 weeks, and that is not an exaggeration.

Q125 Karen Lumley: The Prime Minister talked last week about the enterprise culture that we are obviously trying to provide. What would be your one bit of advice, both of you, to the Prime Minister to get that moving quicker?

Mr Gibson: I would attack the university culture in terms of entrepreneurship and making it the norm, not the exception. I would mobilise senior business people to act as mentors. In our programme we bring loads of people in who are senior people. I typically ask them to donate one day a year to the foundation. If they are experts in law, investment banking or whatever, do you know what? The response has uniformly been always yes. People want to help; they need to be mobilised. The other thing, of course, to do is that we need to address the fuel issue. If there is no fuel in the tank, you are not going to be travelling anywhere.

Sir Terry Matthews: Whether that comes from tax credits and incentives like that or from a little bit of stick with banks and pension funds and you say, "You will do it. That is the law," it could be either way, but it needs to be done because there is no fuel in the tank.

Chair: We have about three minutes left. Does anyone have any last burning questions that they want to put briefly? If not, would Sir Terry or Simon Gibson want to make any closing comments?

Q126 Geraint Davies: It has been suggested here that Scotland are more agile and more effective in getting inward investment and entrepreneurial activity than Wales. I don't know whether this is your experience or whether there are any other lessons they bring, or any other lessons you would like to suggest to us finally that WAG, perhaps, or the UK Government could do to encourage what you are describing.

Sir Terry Matthews: I am not sure how to answer that because it is not my experience.

Q127 Geraint Davies: What—the Scotland thing?

Sir Terry Matthews: No. I understand that they have been very successful. I understand that from information I have, but on a personal level I have found the activities I have had in Wales quite good, and clearly I have an advantage there because I travel back and forth frequently.

Mr Gibson: I am not going to answer your question, but I would suggest you look at the speed of decision out of both institutions. There might be a correlation.

Q128 Susan Elan Jones: We have had some previous discussions here on the subject of brand Wales. Do you think there is any mileage in North America, whether USA or Canada, where there are links with Welsh Americans? Do you think those sorts of links make a difference?

Sir Terry Matthews: Yes, they could. I find there are a lot of people in the New York area, the LA area and Chicago of Welsh background. That could be quite valuable, I think. Certainly the Ryder Cup raised the profile enormously.

Q129 Geraint Davies: How important do you think tourism is for Wales? Is there anything more you want to say about the Welsh brand? We talked about the Ryder Cup. In terms of the Welsh brand as a place to invest, what more do you think could be done?

Sir Terry Matthews: We have to play up the fact that there are more castles per square mile in Wales than anywhere else. It has incredible history, whether it is Roman or Norman. We should play it up even more.

Mr Gibson: If you ever read my bio, I always say, "I am married with four children and I live in the beautiful county of Monmouthshire", and I am not kidding. We happen to be blessed in a land where most people would choose to go on holiday.

Sir Terry Matthews: North Wales, the Brecon Beacons: it is a very beautiful part of the world; there is no question about it. The latest generic of young people play games, and I know this is not something I particularly like, but nevertheless there are a huge number of people who play games on Xbox and other things. There are always castles involved. I get friends of mine in business who say, "Where do you recommend I go in Wales to the castles?", because castles are a focus right now of many, many games. By the way, I am not a big proponent of people spending all their life playing games. Nevertheless, in the last 10 years in particular, there have been some very powerful games involving castles.

Mr Gibson: Perhaps we should digitise every castle in Wales and sell it to the game manufacturers.

Karen Lumley: That is entrepreneurial.

Sir Terry Matthews: Raising the profile of castles is not such a bad one. Certainly the Ryder Cup helped worldwide to raise the profile.

Chair: We have a number in Monmouthshire. I was dying to end on that happy and positive note about Monmouthshire, which is the area I represent. I would like to thank both of you very much indeed for coming along and giving evidence today.

Sir Terry Matthews: Thank you very much. It has been a pleasure.

Mr Gibson: Thank you.

Monday 4 April 2011

Members present:

David T. C. Davies (Chair)

Stuart Andrew   Mrs Siân C. James
Alun Cairns   Susan Elan Jones
Geraint Davies   Mr Mark Williams

Examination of Witnesses

Witnesses: **Professor Richard Davies**, Vice-chancellor, **Professor Iwan Davies**, Pro Vice-chancellor, **Dr Grahame Guilford**, Consultant Commercialisation, Swansea Bay Science and Innovation Campus, Swansea University, and **Dr Weixi Xing**, Director of the China Centre, Swansea University, gave evidence.

Q130 Chair: Good afternoon. I am David Davies, the Chairman of the Welsh Affairs Select Committee. Although we have your names, perhaps you could briefly introduce yourselves for us.

Professor R. Davies: We will introduce ourselves one at a time. My name is Richard Davies, and I am the vice-chancellor of this tremendous university, and I am delighted to see you here.

Dr Guilford: I am Grahame Guilford, and I am a consultant working with the university on commercialisation and developing links with business. My background is 30 years in the life science industry with Amersham International plc and GE Healthcare.

Professor I. Davies: Good afternoon. My name is Iwan Davies, and I am pro vice-chancellor here with responsibility for internationalisation and also for the bay science and innovation campus. My background is that I hold the Hodge Chair in law at this great university.

Dr Xing: My name is Weixi Xing, and I am a Chinese national. I got my first Masters degree in telecommunications in China, and then I worked in the telecommunications sector for more than 10 years. After that, I came to the UK and got my MBA at Cardiff Business School and then my PhD at Cambridge University. I am now director of the China Centre at Swansea University. My main job is to manage research projects with China.

Chair: That is great. Thank you very much indeed for having us. It certainly does look like a very good university. I will hand over to the local Member of Parliament, Geraint Davies, to say a few words.

Q131 Geraint Davies: Welcome again—it is a great joy that you have encouraged the Welsh Affairs Select Committee to come here for you to showcase what you are doing. As you probably know, we are doing a study into inward investment—basically, entrepreneurship and how universities can help as an engine of growth. To start with, I was hoping that Richard Davies and others could give us an idea of how you are positioning the university as a research-intensive university, what you see to be a knowledge economy and how the development of Fabian Way fits into your plan for Swansea and Wales. I am not looking for an encyclopaedic answer to that, of course. Over to you.

Professor R. Davies: Thank you very much. That is a considerable question, and perhaps a few of us can

contribute to the answer, because to cover it we probably need to use the array of talent across the table. Swansea University was established at the behest of industry; that is what happened in the early 1920s. Heavy industry in this region recognised that it needed a university—it wanted skilled people, clever academics and it wanted science to be progressed. So, we do not recognise claims that working with industry is some new phenomenon in higher education in the UK—it might be new for some universities, but it goes back to the day that we were established as far as Swansea University is concerned; we have a long history of working closely with industry.

Over approximately the last 10 years, which takes us back to a time before I was appointed here, the governing body recognised that Swansea needed to up its game as a university. As there were more and more universities being created in Britain, we could not afford to be complacent if we were to compete in this much more lively university environment in the UK, and, of course, globally. We had to get better and we had to get bigger. I was appointed with that as a clear brief. We are hugely ambitious as a university. We do not see working with industry—creating wealth and creating high-paid jobs—as being in any way contradictory to our mission as a research-led university to develop world-class research, and to provide a very encouraging and challenging teaching environment for our students. We see those as mutually supportive activities, and that is the way in which the university has been developing and doing so extremely enthusiastically.

We have done some realigning to make it absolutely clear which academic areas of the university relate to which economic sectors of the economy, and how those different parts of the university can be supported in terms of growing and encouraging growth of hi-tech clusters in the region. We have a big strategy for that. We have also been putting in place the governance structures, the management and the leadership to make very big things happen. I am delighted that Geraint mentioned the bay science and innovation campus. That is a key part of our strategy, because we have a landlocked campus here—one of the smallest campuses in the UK. We cannot deliver on a big vision for Wales based on this small campus, so we have had to expand our thinking and, in our science and innovation campus, the whole concept leapfrogs ahead. We had fallen behind the pace in

Wales, to be honest—unlike many English universities, we do not have science parks linked to universities in Wales—but we are now leapfrogging ahead to a more modern concept than a science park. We are listening to what industry wants. On the new science and innovation campus, we are going to intermingle academic research, industrial research and development, skills training and academic courses. They will all be intermingled, with everybody contributing to everything. That, we think, will be a global exemplar. That, in summary, is the sort of thing that we are doing.

Chair: Thank you very much indeed, Professor Davies, for that introduction. We have a number of questions that we will ask over the next 40 minutes. We are very grateful to you for hosting us, and we want to get as much out of this as possible, so I ask for some quick questions and answers.

Q132 Mrs James: You have already mentioned the way that you have been working in the city of Swansea and the region, and the unique role that you are developing here. I want to find out a little bit more about how you work with other organisations. How do you engage inward investors in this area? Do you seek them out, or do firms come to you? What happens next?

Professor R. Davies: That is very much Grahame's area.

Dr Guilford: What I have been trying to do with the university is to build those links with potential investors—primarily business investors. My background in a large business is helpful there. We have been trying to develop links with large businesses to function as anchors, or a focus for the development of the critical mass that might come through building supply chains involving small and medium-sized enterprises and so on. I have tried to look at areas within the university in terms of research excellence, equipment capability, academic expertise—whatever it might be—that might be attractive to large businesses, ultimately leading to strategic links. Clearly, you have to start at a fairly small scale with some of those things, just as a normal business would do with its customers, developing an infrequent customer into a regular customer. In the same way, a university will try to develop an initial contact with a business into a strategic relationship over a period of time.

We started with some areas where the university had quite long-standing relationships—Rolls-Royce and Tata are two examples of companies that the university has worked with over a number of years. I tried to add to those existing research relationships a commercial element, whereby we could look at direct commercialisation of the research being done, in such a way that, over time, it would feed financial benefit back into the university to underpin continuing research, making the relationship more sustainable in the long term and so on. That would be one way that you would do it. Other ways might involve smaller-scale collaborations with companies that you try to build up over time into something more strategic. I think that Weixi might have some interesting examples of work that he has been doing.

Dr Xing: Huawei Technologies Co is now the No. 1 telecommunications wonder in China, with sales last year of around $27 billion. It is now second in the world. It is also a strategic partner of BT, supplying a number of telecommunications operators in the UK. I worked for the company for seven years, so I used my links to try to sell Swansea University's strengths. Some professors have links with the company. At the beginning, we secured a number of small research projects from this company. Nowadays, we have a deal for three research projects with this company. We have a framework agreement with the company that enables Swansea University to collaborate with other UK universities and industries.

Q133 Mrs James: I am aware of the link with China, and I am aware that you have links with other countries as well, so does that model apply to other countries that you work with? How would you then establish a bridgehead into a country where you have a student population, and how do you then develop that? It would be interesting to hear a little more about that.

Professor I. Davies: There are two aspects to that. The first relates to our historic role. The global footprint of Swansea University goes back to its inception, and part of my privilege is that I have been able to speak to our alumni, some of whom have had a very significant impact upon their own countries. I came back from Malaysia recently, where I met one of our alumni who was responsible for the rural electrification of the entire peninsula of Malaysia, and also for the city of Kuala Lumpur. That person graduated in the same engineering class as a UK student of ours who was responsible for the nuclear commissioning of Wylfa, for example. So, there is a story around the historic role of the university, which is very profound, and we capture these alumni in various events. Only two weeks ago, I came back from an event in India where there were alumni, in order for them to understand exactly their role in promoting Swansea and Wales as an economy. The vice-chancellor has hosted two or three events in Hong Kong and China over the last six months. The whole idea is to engage with your people so that there is a sense of presence.

The second element of your question relates to how we deal with our current alumni. In India for example, we have a bridgehead there with fairly recent graduates who work in large multinational enterprises, and we are using them as an entry into providing internships for our students. The internships issue works in two ways. First, it works in respect of UK or European students who can have a global education experience, and, of course, global employment experience is a huge asset in terms of their employability. Secondly, in terms of international students, we have to be able to demonstrate that university education here in Swansea is transferrable globally back at home. Our ability to deal with, let us say, the equivalent of the Confederation of British Industry in India is as important as dealing with the CBI here in the United Kingdom. So, it is the ability to internationalise that is key. I can give you one other illustration. In Colombia in South America, which, in terms of the UK, is an undeveloped area, we work, through the Colombian Embassy, directly with the ministry of education in Colombia, and as part of that process, this university has developed a consortium with other UK universities, including Brunel, Southampton and Leicester. The whole idea is that we are presenting UK higher education and its advantages as a mechanism for promoting development around key knowledge economy sectors. These knowledge economy sectors have an international resonance, and those are issues that inform our policy.

Q134 Mrs James: Just a quick question: are there any particular countries that you are currently targeting? You have spoken about several, but are there any other countries that you would like to be working in? Where is it happening?

Professor I. Davies: We review our strategy every year. The key things relate to the emerging economies. India and China are huge; one sixth of the population of the world lives in China, and a similar amount, if not more within the next few years will live in India. It is about a shift in emphasis. We live in a multi-polar world and the centricity of where we sit here in the UK has shifted. One of our biggest strategies relates to how we identify the emerging opportunities, because they are invisible at the moment. The ability to have early intelligence through working with our alumni, with agents, and through research partnerships, is key as part of that process. We use the British Council, which has changed its remit so that it is now very much focused on knowledge exchange partnerships; we commission work from the British Council. So, we are looking at ways in which we can deal with Cambodia, Vietnam and Laos as emerging markets for us specifically.

Q135 Chair: I would like to butt in and ask Dr Xing a question, but before I do, I should make it clear that I have some family and business interests in China. Dr Xing, do you see your role as one of marketing the university to students who might potentially come to Wales, or is it more about marketing the university as an attractive place for Chinese companies, some of which are high tech, that are looking to locate in Wales—we have heard that that is already happening in Germany—or is it both?

Dr Xing: My role is not to recruit students; we have the international office for that. The China Centre tries to help the university and local business to set up links with the Chinese Government and with Chinese institutions and industry.

Q136 Chair: So, it is about helping Welsh businesses to sell in China.

Dr Xing: Yes, and it is also about bringing more investment opportunities. Recently, we have been discussing a larger project with the Beijing Government. It wants to set up a China-Europe standards institute at our Swansea bay campus—the project is subject to discussions at the moment, but it will be worth about £ 10 million.

Chair: I am going to appeal to everyone: I know that this is an interesting area, but we only have half an hour left—although, I am hopeful that the next witnesses will bear with me.

Q137 Susan Elan Jones: I represent a constituency in north Wales, so my point will refer more generally to Wales. I would be interested in your appraisal of how the Wales Office and the UK Government sell Wales abroad. I would also be interested in knowing whether you think that there are more opportunities for links between personnel. For instance, in the 1990s, I worked on the Japanese Government's exchange and teaching programme, which the Japanese Government in the 1980s and 1990s saw as a way of making such links—I am sure that it brought some dividends. Do you think that there would be a role for the Government of this country in running a similar programme, to bring young people from China to work in this country?

Professor R. Davies: I will just jump in with a partial answer, because this is very much Iwan's area in internationalisation and external affairs. I am delighted to talk to somebody from north Wales, as somebody who lived in north Wales for many years before coming here. Wales is small, and we imagine that our influence over the developments that we are talking about currently will stretch far beyond south-west Wales. Indeed, they are already involved in north-east Wales. The work that we do with Tata is leading to the major development that was announced last week by the First Minister. We are delighted that that is capitalising on technology that was developed with Tata here in Swansea University.

There is another important point to make, because we are trying to provide context as well as detail here. Our approach is moving towards an integrated, holistic way of driving forward big, strategic agendas. One thing that has been holding us and other universities back dramatically is the bitty nature of the support and funding that we receive from many different initiatives. Each one is arguably well intentioned, but together, they result in considerable confusion and uncertainty as to how people can develop their careers and be funded into the future to drive forward these big agendas. So, we are trying to be very strategic, and it is in that context that I would like to see the sort of initiatives that you are suggesting.

Professor I. Davies: The relationships need to be put within the context of the devolution settlement. Without doubt, the relationship must be one of legislature to legislature—that is clear. The business that we operate in is devolved, but international trade is not. Core research income is devolved, but project research—around Research Councils UK and the technology standards board—is not. The nature of impact research and the requirements of commercialisation need to be fully understood as part of that process.

The vision that we have as a world-class university is not one that can simply be based upon 'Cymru fach'. If you look at some of UNESCO's global higher education reports, they are about tracking an academic revolution, and for us, effective engagement with UK Trade and Investment is absolutely critical. The global outreach of UKTI, with over 100 offices overseas, along with the networks and the facilitation of international partnerships, is something that we would look to develop. We have already worked with UKTI on the Institute of Life Science, and UKTI's engagement with the new bay science and innovation campus is critical.

If I can put it in context for you, two weeks ago President Hu of China talked about the role of universities in stimulating advanced innovation in engineering, and as part of that process he talked about funding first-class universities and their science parks. The science parks in Beijing, Guangdong province and Shanghai have research and development spin-outs from Chinese universities. We have heard from Weixi, and our key challenge has to be translating the research that we are doing collaboratively with leading Chinese universities and their science parks into commercial links here in Wales, particularly in our new campus.

Chair: I am ever so sorry to stop you, but I know that we will never get through this if we go into too much detail. I apologise for that. Could you sum it up in a sentence or two? I have to call Alun Cairns, and there is a danger that we will not get through our session.

Professor I. Davies: I will do so. Thomas Friedman wrote a book a few years ago called *The World is Flat*. He said that Bethesda, Bangalore and Beijing are just a mouse-click away, and that regions do not matter. We say that regions do matter, and that, in effect, the real challenge is the extent to which we can differentiate the offering that we have here through our research and make that globally attractive.

Q138 Alun Cairns: I want to stay with the same sort of theme, but take a slightly different angle. You talk about the importance of your relationship with UKTI, and the complexity that devolution has given to that. I remember speaking to a former Secretary of State some time ago who said that, when he was at the Welsh Office, we were punching well above our weight in terms of attracting inward investment. He said that Wales benefitted hugely from having a member of the UK Cabinet who could champion Wales. To an inward investor, that was a significant influence—that they could speak to someone at the heart of Government. I know that governance has changed completely since devolution, and that example was before the advent of devolution, but what would you like to see the UK Government do? Is that statement by the former Secretary of State for Wales still true? Also, is there an insistence in Wales on doing our own thing for the sake of doing it differently? For example, the Assembly Government has mini-embassies, as they call them, to promote trade and research and the benefits of using Wales. Could that work be done in a different way to be more effective, to help you and Swansea punch above your weight on an international stage?

Professor R. Davies: I will try to deal with those questions, because they are challenging, and they get to the heart of some of the issues that we struggle with. Certainly, as a university that has to work and compete globally, we do not recognise any borders anywhere in terms of working with students, recruiting staff and working with multinational companies. We have that international view, and I think that the whole sector is an important asset to Wales, because we have a responsibility to inform and assist Wales in delivering its policies, which may or may not differ in various ways to other constituent parts of the UK. We are enthusiastic about doing that because the sorts of policies on economic regeneration are ones that resonate with us. That leads to the point that I was making earlier, about the things that are getting in the way. I would claim that nearly all funding initiatives have got in the way in the past. There was a real problem with piecemeal funding, and some of it has always come more locally and some from a distance. You mentioned Cardiff and London, and, of course, there is Brussels. We do a lot of work with Texas, where we have American funding sources and so on. We have always had a multitude of funding sources. In terms of translating world-class research into income generation and into good, well-paid jobs, it has been exceptionally bitty.

So, I would say that the real challenge is to be strategic, and to be strategic whatever happens across several different areas of Government and locations of Government. In that regard, I would say that we are still maturing within the UK, and still maturing within Europe in terms of how we relate to Brussels. We are still maturing also in how we run relationships with the United States.

Q139 Alun Cairns: May I interrupt you there, because I want to pursue that point, particularly in relation to the role of the Secretary of State for Wales and how it has changed with the advent of devolution? To go back to what that former Secretary of State said, which is that it was a huge incentive for inward investors to know that they had a direct voice in the UK Cabinet, is that still the case, or has devolution changed it so that investors want a direct voice in the Welsh Cabinet instead?

Professor R. Davies: I would say that to transform the economy of Wales you need direct voices in every Cabinet, and that would include Brussels. I believe, however, that the situation has changed since the days you referred to. I think that inward investment is now a much more sophisticated operation. We cannot compete now with the relatively low-paid jobs that were a key part of inward investment in the past.

Q140 Alun Cairns: I accept that point. I would like to change the subject slightly. It is claimed that inward investors in Wales undertake very little research in Wales and in development and engineering, which means that universities often work with firms outside Wales. Do you have any examples to the contrary, or are there examples of what you would like to achieve if Government policy was different and allowed you to work better with firms, locally or internationally?

Professor R. Davies: I think that the situation is quite clear. There is a relative paucity of industrial research and development in Wales. Less than 2% of the commercial industrial research and development in the UK is in Wales, rather than the 5% it should be according to our population. So, the figures are stark and clear. That is primarily because we have so few large companies. Also, over 95% of research and development in companies takes place within large companies. So, you cannot compensate for the lack of large companies in Wales by doing more work with small and medium-sized enterprises; it is just not possible.

Q141 Alun Cairns: Are you saying that, if the Assembly and UK Governments want to grow the research and development base, parallel policies supporting purely indigenous business means that they are mutually exclusive?

Professor R. Davies: No. I think that what we have to do—this is a key part of our policy—is to bring multinational companies to Wales. We have to get them to establish research and development bases in Wales and build from that. With those research and development bases in Wales, and with the sort of negotiations that Grahame was talking about and the deals that we have already signed with Rolls-Royce and Tata, we can then begin to build supply-chain links with those companies. That takes us to the other problem with not having large companies, which is one of who small companies sell to. Your economy is seriously disadvantaged if you do not have large companies. We have to try to bring them in, and we can help with that. The example within Wales is Tata, where we have a very long tradition of very high-quality research. That is expanding now, with great enthusiasm coming from India.

Chair: We look forward to our visit to Tata tomorrow.

Q142 Mr Williams: I would like to thank you for your brief. For a long time, people have talked about the generality of using higher education as the focus for economic development, and it is good to see in your briefing, and from what you have said so far, that things are galvanising and beginning to happen in a very positive way. I have a quick question about the development of high-tech clusters. First, to the layman, what constitutes a cluster? Secondly, what led you to concentrate on the three specifics of engineering and computer science technologies, life sciences and medicines? What is the evidence of clustering in the Welsh economy to date? How successful are you beginning to be in those developments?

Professor R. Davies: The first question is very much for Grahame, but the second question goes back to developing policy within the university. We looked at where our links are with companies, and at the strength of those links. That led us to the three cluster areas. They are very important clusters, because depending on how you do the calculation, somewhere between two thirds and 75% of industrial research and development is covered by those three sectors, so it is very significant. Also, we were informed by consultants who undertook a major study for the City and County of Swansea some years ago called the Swansea 2020 vision. They were very enthusiastic about a cluster approach and felt that that was where universities should focus their energies and efforts.

On where we are, it is still very early days—it will be another four years before we occupy the science and innovation campus, but we have the Institute of Life Science as a small example. I am sure that Grahame can say a little more about cluster formation.

Dr Guilford: I would characterise clusters, as we envisage them—certainly for the purposes of the work that I am doing with the university—as the creation of critical mass that is capable of attracting further development and investment. The characteristics that you would see in those clusters include a strong research base, major industry partners, small and medium-sized enterprises, supply chains and spin-outs developing around that. The example of Rolls-Royce is quite interesting in this regard. As the vice-chancellor was saying, the university works with Tata, which is clearly a major company based in Wales, and the university does some research and development with Tata and it commercialises that in Wales. You might look at Rolls-Royce and say that Rolls-Royce is not in Wales, but, in many senses, from an economic perspective it is, and has been for a significant time, because it has been a major research partner with the university, and that has brought large amounts of research money in. The creation of critical mass in universities will be very important in the future, because research councils will increasingly focus their funding on larger quantums in fewer places. That funding will go to institutions that have built up the critical mass capability that I talked about earlier, which Swansea has done very successfully in terms of its work with Rolls-Royce, and which led directly two years ago to the Engineering and Physical Research Council and TSB awarding a 10-year, £50 million contract to three universities, of which Swansea was one, and Birmingham and Cambridge being the others. We have bolted onto that a commercial venture that takes the output of our research with Rolls-Royce and offers commercial testing services. That will be based on the bay campus and will employ people locally. That is an example of how a cluster can form. We are already receiving interest from other organisations that are keen to be part of that cluster. You can then begin to see something forming regionally that is perceived nationally, and, ultimately, internationally, as a cluster that is worth clustering around. That would be how I would characterise the clusters.

Q143 Mr Williams: You touched on the Brussels connection in one of your answers to Mr Cairns' questions. Your evidence noted that you benefited from European convergence funding. How have you used that funding to date, and will you be bidding for more?

Professor R. Davies: We have bid for convergence funding in the past. Two of us on this panel have to declare an interest, because we are on the programme monitoring committee for convergence funding in Wales, namely Grahame and myself. We have evolved our policies for dealing with the convergence funding opportunities alongside the approach I was explaining to you of being far more strategic, rather than piecemeal. All the projects that we now go for for convergence funding are part of a long-term development, and convergence funding is used to grow capacity in the university that will be maintained and sustained into the future. So, we are creating a bigger engine.

One thing that really worried us in our original analyses six years ago, which underpinned this whole strategy, was that the successful universities—and there are many examples in the UK and around the world—in driving economic development are large and have absolutely top-quality research. We could demonstrate the top-quality research in our engineering and science, but we were rather small compared with the successful ones. We had to grow and, therefore, growing has been a critical part of our strategy. That is one of the really difficult things in Wales. Having a large number of relatively small institutions has been a big disadvantage to Wales.

Q144 Mr Williams: I am glad that you said that. That emphasises the need for partnerships between existing institutions, does it not?

Professor R. Davies: Well, it is not clear to me. There is a conventional wisdom that one overcomes the problem of having small institutions by collaborating with others. Industry has a very simple view that, when investing in a relationship, it wants evidence that it has complete buy-in from the management and the governing body of the institution it is working with and that the policy will not change a week later and there will not be some falling out between two universities so that everything collapses. We have to be able to demonstrate governance robustness to industry before it will invest.

Q145 Chair: This question is to either Professor Davies. Do you think that there are too many people going to university and doing courses that are not necessarily going to lead straight into a job? Just to give an example, do you think there are too many people doing cultural studies courses and not enough doing mathematics and science-based degrees?

Professor R. Davies: I cannot answer that question in totality. I work, and always have worked, when I have not been in industry, in research-led universities, and I do not see people in research-led universities who I think are wasting any of their time at all.

Chair: I am sure, and that is my point.

Professor R. Davies: I know that you did not ask that. [*Laughter.*]

Q146 Chair: I am sure that you do not, and I am trying to be helpful to you here. Do you think then, as a principle, that anyone should be able to study anything they want to for three or four years, or do you think that there should be some effort by the Government, which is still funding these courses, to try to tailor the number and type of courses to the number and type of jobs that might follow afterwards?

Professor R. Davies: There has to be a certain amount of manpower planning, but you cannot force young people to do things that they do not want to do. So, it is a balance.

Chair: That is a good answer. [*Laughter.*]

Professor R. Davies: What I do believe, and the evidence is there and we could provide detailed information to the committee later, if you wish, is that there is an imbalance in Wales. For historic reasons,

we do not have as much science and engineering as you would expect. We have less than in England per head of population and dramatically less than Scotland. That is a disadvantage to us.

Chair: We would definitely appreciate that additional information. We have some other questions, but we have run out of time. I will, however, perhaps call a few Members to ask a few quick questions.

Q147 Stuart Andrew: I would like to come on to the issue of the Government funding of research. Sir Terry Matthews, in his evidence to this committee, said that the question that we should be asking is what parts of that research end up creating companies. How do you respond to that criticism? He was arguing that money should perhaps be given to companies to develop research rather than to universities. How would you respond to that, and what do you think you do better?

Professor R. Davies: Well, there is a great deal of evidence from around the world that strong, research-led universities do work that industry does not and cannot readily do, and which it does not want to do itself. Our evidence from Rolls-Royce and other companies is that they want to source that work from universities because of the talented people we attract. I know exactly where Terry is coming from, and it is arguable that there are gaps on the commercialisation side. We are not funded to commercialise research. We are a charity and we are funded for research and teaching, not to make profits. There have been major inefficiencies in the UK higher education system in translating research into products and wealth creation. So, to that extent, Terry and I see completely eye to eye. And he is a graduate of this university.

Q148 Geraint Davies: Briefly, on science versus art, is there a role for some integrating of the language offer—I am talking about modern languages—into the international global perspective of business networking? What do you feel about what has happened with regard to the technium business innovation centres in Wales, a number of which have closed? How do you distinguish yourself from that initiative and what do you think is right and wrong? Do you think that what you are doing in the bay could be replicated in the other universities in Wales? Finally, do you feel that pushing them all together, as the Welsh Assembly Government seems to want to do, to give critical mass, may not be quite the right strategy, as you have intimated?

Professor R. Davies: Oh, dear. There has been a lot of misinformation in the press about our intentions in languages. We want to extend and grow the teaching of modern foreign languages here in Swansea, but we are trying to modernise our offer with more emphasis on the use of language, whether it be in the media, business or what have you, and slightly less on traditional literature studies. So, the tension here is precisely about the issues that you raise, not about reducing our offering.

With regard to the technium, it is misunderstood. The technium was not set up as a traditional incubator; it is a modern rental facility and it is quite expensive for companies. Each one had a very narrow sector focus, but it was not always fully researched in terms of the demand for those facilities, and certainly not demand at the rental cost of those facilities. What we believe strongly in Wales, as part of our holistic approach here, is that we need genuine incubators. There are company incubators throughout England and most of the leading universities have high-tech incubator facilities. For some reason, we have never developed that in Wales. Incubators are not just the physical facility, but the set of support that small proto-companies need.

As to whether we can replicate the bay science and innovation campus elsewhere, we have to demonstrate how successful we are. We believe we will be; not only are we ambitious, but we have a degree of confidence now that this will work because we know how well discussions with companies are going. The difficulty of replicating it is that you only have two universities in Wales with the scale of science and engineering to be able to do something of this scale, namely Cardiff and Swansea. Can you get through the problems by amalgamation? Some of us would say that you should have far fewer universities in Wales.

Q149 Alun Cairns: Professor Davies, incubators is a term that many politicians like to use, but if you study the evidence you will see that it is pretty weak as regards what incubators actually achieve. Why did you say in your evidence that you were a fan of incubators? It is a nice term and gives this image that we are doing something, but, in reality, does the evidence internationally not show that they are pretty poor?

Professor R. Davies: No, that is not the evidence. If you go to Manchester, you will find incubators there, and several have made a significant contribution to the economy. This is small in comparison with the growth of large companies. That is where big growth comes, but some of those small companies will become the big companies of tomorrow.

Chair: Alun Cairns. I sense an argument, and I like that. [*Laughter.*]

Q150 Alun Cairns: There have been several studies in the *Harvard Business Review* for example that have completely lambasted what incubators actually achieve. I remember one of the economic development committee meetings in the Assembly completely destroying the argument for incubators, and the conclusion was that they were just something nice for politicians and people like us to talk about and to show that we were trying to do something. However, in reality, the economic value they add is pretty minimal, and the techniums are not far from that either, are they not?

Professor R. Davies: Techniums are nowhere near incubators. I was involved in incubation in the north-west of England before I came here. Staff here have been looking at incubator facilities in places varying from Finland to the United States. We disagree, because I think that they are part of the holistic approach to developing high-tech clusters. Not only do you need the large companies and help grow the SMEs, but you need to spin out high-tech companies that can join that cluster and be part of the growth strategy.

Q151 Mrs James: My last question on this concerns Terry Matthews's comments that we have to be ahead of the curve. We cannot have these end-of-life products coming to Wales, being based here for several years and then leaving. What do you have to offer a small business that has limited amounts of money but brilliant ideas?

Professor R. Davies: There are a number of answers to that. The biggest value added for a university is to collaborate with large companies. There is no question about that, because they pay better wages, they are better for our graduates, they take a larger number of graduates, and they pay for research and development—they do over 95% of that. That is the big thing. We need to support smaller companies as part of our total offering and responsibility to the region, and that comes back to supply chains. Perhaps Grahame would like to add something to that.

Dr Guilford: One of the best things that the university can do for small companies is to help to create clusters and supply chains. Traditionally, the role of universities was seen as being to provide direct support to small companies, and that can be very difficult for both sides. Cardiff, for example, has had its innovation network for a number of years, and there have been some successes, but it is hard work to have that one-to-one relationship. If you can create the centres of gravity or the clusters, you get something that smaller companies can sell their products to and collaborate with and so on. That is really what we see the bay campus doing. There will be, probably not a huge number, but perhaps four or five, and eventually six, significant clusters based around companies such as Rolls-Royce and Tata, and then we will try to use those clusters to grow the SME base, in terms of the provision of graduates from the university and in terms of the natural factors that would grow business through collaboration and greater expenditure on research and development.

Q152 Chair: I have a final question. What percentage, if any, of the funding for the bay science and innovation campus has come from the private sector? Have private companies been putting their hands in their pockets?

Professor I. Davies: Significantly so. BP will be investing in the campus, and we have already heard about the involvement of Rolls-Royce in collaborative research, and Tata in the same way. There is also our work with the main developer, which will be—

Q153 Chair: Will the investment go towards ongoing revenue costs for research and development, or will it meet part of the capital cost of setting it up?

Professor I. Davies: In the context of BP, it is quite simply a gift. However, as far as the ongoing revenue elements are concerned, the hope is that many of the activities will lead to commercialisation of the research. That is, coming out of the capital spend will be the creation of facilities that will engender that type of activity.

May I just say one other thing? Coming back to what Ms James mentioned, the key thing is about the porosity of an institution and what it can offer. I will leave you with this thought, which is something that

Kapil Sibal, the Minister at India's Department of Higher Education said, namely that universities should not simply be about technology transfer or higher skills for graduates; it is the concept of *magis* that is the key thing—what more can we provide? It is the ability to look beyond the simple business-as-usual approach for universities. The philosophy that we are seeking to achieve here is this concept of *magis*; the additionality that is about being open and porous to opportunity.

Chair: Professor Iwan Davies, Dr Xing, Professor Richard Davies and Dr Guilford, thank you. I am sorry that we have to leave it there, but we just do not have any more time.

Witnesses: **Peter Sishton**, Manager for Wales, e-skills UK, **Stuart Bailey**, Manager for Graduate and Apprentice Development, Cassidian Systems Ltd, and e-skills UK Wales Employer Board Member, **Aled Davies**, Skills Director for Wales, Energy and Utility Skills Limited, **Toni Eastwood**, Director of Academy and Talent, and **Neil O'Doherty**, Head of Retail HR, Operations, Morrisons, gave evidence.

Chair: I thank our next set of witnesses for coming along today. Neil and I have met before, though I did not realise it before this afternoon. We are near neighbours, but I am sure that there is no conflict of interest there.

Mrs James: That is another vote in the bag for you, Chair.

Chair: I cannot guarantee that, because I think that we met at a fancy dress party.

Neil O'Doherty: I will not say what you went as. [*Laughter.*]

Chair: We are really short of time at the moment. I will ask Siân James to start, as one of the local MPs.

Q154 Mrs James: Croeso cynnes i Abertawe, a diolch yn fawr am ddod—a warm welcome to Swansea, and thank you for coming. As Geraint's neighbour, what happens here at the university is very important for me, for local companies, for my constituency, for constituents and especially for small businesses. A lot of exciting things will be happening, and there will be lots of opportunities and thinking outside of the box; that is a good thing, and we should be encouraging and supporting it. I will go straight into my questions. This is a general one, to all of you—your starter for 10, as they say. Do you believe that specific skill shortages are either stopping firms coming to Wales or hindering the growth of firms that are already here?

Chair: Who wants to start with that?

Peter Sishton: I was just thinking that Stuart should start. I am Peter Sishton from e-skills UK, where I am the manager for Wales. Stuart Bailey is from Cassidian, and is a member of the e-skills employer board. I think that he would be much better placed to answer this question.

Stuart Bailey: There are areas like computer science skills, electronic engineering and communications engineering where we have specific requirements as a business. We certainly do not get sufficient candidates from the local area. We have to go to universities, and we particularly target the south-west, the midlands and the whole of Wales, but we are not getting enough candidates in those specific areas.

Q155 Mrs James: Is that because there is not a close enough link with schools? There are very good links at higher education level, but I am constantly hearing from small businesses in my constituency that they need to engage with young people earlier.

Stuart Bailey: I believe that that is the case. We work very much with science, technology, engineering and mathematics ambassadors, going into schools and trying to push all sorts of initiatives, whether it is CILT Cymru, which promotes languages and is extremely good, or working with Careers Wales in trying to influence the schools on STEM subjects in particular. We find it difficult—this is not pushing at an open door. However, like everywhere else, there are superb people out there, and if you get the right person and the right industry speaking to each other, a very good relationship can be built up. However, it is very much down to individuals in the education sector and within industry.

Mrs James: Does anyone else want to comment?

Neil O'Doherty: It does not stop us. We still come to Wales, and we are opening another two stores in Wales this year. Last year, we purchased a factory site in Deeside, which brought another 380 jobs, and has seen terrific growth. We are about to recruit another 200 people there because of the volume that we are putting through, so it is a big success story. We find the people of Wales as skilful and as talented as anyone else. What we believe in is growing and building on that skill, doing a lot of work within the business and with learning partners to grow careers for people here. The one area where I have most difficulty from a skills point of view, I suppose, is with pharmacists. That is the position that I find difficult to fill. I have jobs that I have been trying to fill in mid and north Wales for some considerable time. The issue there has been the supply of pharmacists going through the colleges. The problem goes back several years—there are more people there now, but they have not quite flowed out into the job market yet. That is a particular skills issue for me. It does not stop us coming here, of course, but we end up transporting people from different parts of the country to the pharmacies in our Welsh stores. That is what we have to do.

Q156 Chair: Would it be rude of me to ask what a pharmacist starting off at Morrisons might get? What sort of money are people missing out on?

Neil O'Doherty: It would be very rude. [*Laughter.*] I might want to ask our pharmacists before I answer. We have several pay levels. We have a number of what we call pre-reg pharmacists—they have qualified at degree level, but are doing their first year of training, and they are looking at a salary in the lower £20,000s. Once qualified and running one of our pharmacy departments, they will be into the £40,000 to £50,000 mark. It is extremely good money.

Q157 Mrs James: Do you have the same problem with STEM skills that other sectors and organisations have?

Toni Eastwood: No, not really, because most of the jobs around science, technology, engineering and mathematics are based in our head office. So, we tend to attract people quite easily to those jobs.

Aled Davies: I am Aled Davies from Energy and Utility Skills Ltd, which is the sector skills council for the power, gas, water and waste management sector, just to give some context. As far as employers in our sector are concerned, the feedback that we get is that the local labour market is a consideration when they consider investing in Wales. For example, wind turbines are feasible as we have lots of wind, and the topography of the country is appealing in some respects, but one of the things that employers consider is the local labour market. As Siân intimated, there is a skills shortage in our sector of people with qualifications in the required STEM subjects.

Q158 Mrs James: Do you think that we are producing too many graduates in Wales, or are we not concentrating enough on other areas? How could we ameliorate that?

Aled Davies: I could not comment on what we are producing, but to reiterate what Professor Davies from Swansea University said, we are not producing enough. We do not have the footfall with engineering expertise.

Q159 Alun Cairns: I have a question for Aled Davies. Your sector—energy and utility skills—is one of the sectors that the Welsh Assembly Government has identified in its economic renewal programme as one that it would like to grow in the coming years. However, some horrendously damaging evidence is coming out on education standards in schools and colleges, such as the evidence in the Programme for International Student Assessment report, which is a pretty damning indictment of what has happened over a large number of years—I do not want to get into a political argument about that. What I am trying to get at is that, in terms of inward investment, if I was an energy or utility company, I would think of Wales as a good place to be, because the Welsh Assembly Government has identified this as a growth area, so there would be Government support. On the other hand, is the lack of skills in that area and the educational standards that we are hearing about undermining the objectives of the economic renewal strategy, because you need both to invest?

Aled Davies: If we look at the provider infrastructure that we have in Wales in further education and the power sector engineering facilities, a lot of that training is done outside of Wales. However, we are working with providers in Wales to develop that capacity and expertise.

Q160 Alun Cairns: Who is 'we'? Is it you as Energy and Utility Skills Ltd, your company or other companies that you work for?

Aled Davies: It is us at Energy and Utility Skills working with employers. For example, the Welsh Assembly Government has just funded new wind turbine qualifications for us. We have gone through a procurement process with providers, where employers helped to select providers in Coleg Llandrillo Cymru and Coleg Powys. We are now working to develop their capacity and expertise to develop the required people.

Q161 Chair: My question is to the representatives of the skills councils and Morrisons. I have already picked up from you that we are not producing enough of the right types of graduates to fill all the jobs— you both made that point in slightly different ways. However, I also note from current statistics that one in five graduates does not get a job in the area in which they graduated or do not get a graduate job at all in many cases. Logically, I look at that and think that we are putting too many people through universities to follow the wrong courses. Is that a fair summary of what is happening? Do you think that we are putting too many people through but not giving them the right courses to follow a career in Morrisons, for example?

Toni Eastwood: As I said, we look for graduates; we do not necessarily look at a particular background or qualification. So, you can sometimes come into the organisation with a generic degree and work all over our business. In other areas, we would be looking for a specific skill.

Q162 Chair: Twenty three years ago, I applied for a management trainee scheme with a supermarket—
Neil O'Doherty: Was it Morrisons? [*Laughter.*]
Chair: I think that it was Marks and Spencer, actually, so I had to become an MP because I did not succeed. [*Laughter.*] The point is that it was only looking for A-levels in those days, but I am sure that it looks for degrees these days, because everybody has a degree. However, 25 years ago—
Neil O'Doherty: We have a mix. We look at different entry levels: we have people who join us with no qualifications who do fantastically well, have great careers and get to the top; we have people who come in with degrees; and we have various graduate programmes in our different divisions. There is definitely a need for us to take those people. We also have a particular interest at the moment in looking at people who leave school at the age of 18 and who choose, for whatever reason, not to go on to higher education.

Q163 Chair: Can they enter at the highest level, if they are good?
Neil O'Doherty: They will come in and go through some form of programme, as does everyone. That programme will vary in length from an average of 12 months, and they will then go into our process of developing the managers and leaders of the future. How they get on from there will depend not on their degree, but on what they deliver for the business.

Q164 Chair: However, you do not rule them out just because they do not have a degree. You are quite happy to say that someone with good A-levels and who has the potential will—

Neil O'Doherty: People will come through different channels. Some people who come in with a degree will do very well, and some people who come in without an O-level—in my old language—to their name will equally do very well. We believe in opportunity for everybody; we certainly do not believe in constricting opportunity based purely on qualifications. We would rather build people up and give them qualifications that are related to retailing and to their success in terms of what they deliver for us. We send people to do Master of Business Administration courses at the highest level. That is part of what we do, but we believe that anyone can show their abilities through their work in our business, which is to sell food.

Q165 Geraint Davies: I was just wondering about the chicken and egg problem. Aled Davies is involved with the energy sector, which the Welsh Assembly Government has identified as an obvious growth sector, particularly green energy. If you are a graduate, or you are trying to decide what to study, you need to see an existing jobs infrastructure into which you could feed, if you want to continue living here as opposed to going to England or abroad. Do you feel that there is an opportunity in Wales to build more of an infrastructure in order to keep people here and to keep them focused on these scientific subject areas? Where is the problem? Is it an issue of supply and demand?

Aled Davies: Interestingly, if you look at the number of people entering electronic and electrical engineering courses in universities over the last 10 years, it is down 40% across the UK. One of the challenges that we have is one of sector attractiveness. People have a perception of these traditional infrastructures and industries, and they may not be as appealing as they could be.

Geraint Davies: Everyone wants to be a banker these days.

Chair: Not now. [*Laughter.*]

Aled Davies: They often see our historically nationalised industries that have been denationalised, with infrastructures in place, not as fast-moving industries and do not have the sexy image of some other sectors.

Q166 Geraint Davies: When we, as a committee, were in Germany, we were told, 'We manufacture things in Germany; you do not do that anymore in Britain—you just have a load of banks'. They were talking about whether to invest, and the perception was that we were not gearing ourselves up for that. Your job is partly about trying to gear us up for that, and you are meeting resistance in terms of people's perceptions of those paths.

Aled Davies: What we need is a better-value proposition and sector attractiveness. A National Skills Academy for power was established last year, and it is trying to change that perception. For example, it is working with pupils in junior schools at the age of eight or nine, asking them 'What would happen if

there was no power? You would not be able to use your PS3.', or whatever.

Q167 Geraint Davies: Is there any success in that, Peter?

Peter Sishton: The issue for our sector, which is technology and business, is that applications for the computer science A-level have fallen 63% over the last 14 years, for example, and we have a huge gender imbalance within the sector. Our research shows that, by year 6—the end of primary school—girls have made up their minds that IT is not a career for them. That is an invidious problem: if year 6 kids are deciding that technology is not for them, where do they go? They go down a different pathway. A sector requiring 3,000 jobs a year, growing at 1.2% a year, is really important for Wales. Growing that future talent is critical, and, rather like you were saying, it is a case of career attractiveness and pipeline talent. We must have a number of interventions to ensure that we can get the message across that technology is growing and will provide the high-value jobs.

Q168 Mr Williams: To follow on from that, I spent 12 years in a classroom and I very much agree with that point and I am aware of the extent to which information technology has been debased by having a very general cross-curricular approach in primary schools. People have not seen the essential linkages that need to be drawn later on. You talked about the problem and I think that you know where the problem lies. Can you quantify the scale of the IT shortage problem and the ramifications of that? In your brief you say that, in the longer term, skills and recruitment issues often lead to delays in developing new products and services, to difficulties in introducing technological change and to the loss of business orders to competitors. That is hefty stuff and shows the real interface of the problem and reality. How big a problem is it? I find it very depressing to read that the most commonly advertised jobs in Wales require the specific technical skills needed to use SQL.Net, SQL server, ASP, JavaScript, Java, PHP, HTTP and Visual Basic. I must admit that I do not have a clue what any of that means, and that is worrying.

Peter Sishton: Those are essential skills that employers are crying out for right now in Wales. That is coming from IT recruitment consultants; it is coming from small to medium-sized enterprises within the sector that are turning down work because they cannot recruit the skilled staff into the business.

Q169 Chair: Then why have we got so many people going off and doing, dare I say it, media studies at university when we are crying out for people who have—

Peter Sishton: Again, there is not an easy solution. It is about getting the message out, frankly; it is a mantra that has to go out loud and clear to schools, teachers and careers advisers. It is about getting that sound labour market intelligence out into the marketplace.

Q170 Mr Williams: You mentioned in your note the need for ongoing professional development for teachers because the fact is that the IT component of

many teaching courses is minimal. As part of postgraduate courses it amounts to two or three afternoons a week in a year-long course. Teachers have not been equipped, and many of the unions—and I am a member of a union still—would testify to that. They have not been given the professional knowledge that they need to deliver the curriculum.
Peter Sishton: There are two issues. One is the continuing professional development of teachers, and the elephant in the room is that employers—there are 15 of them—like Cassidian and Fujitsu, and the employer board for Wales are saying very frankly that they want to engage with local schools and offer CPD to teachers, but, in reality, the schools do not release the teachers because there is no funding to backfill the places, or, at least, that is the argument that you get. So, it is very hard when you have the likes of Stuart hammering on doors, as you were saying this morning, and having it shut; that is a very real reality.

Q171 Mrs James: It is the same for us as employers as well. I thought that a person who came for a job with a European driving licence could drive in Europe and it had to be explained to me that it was a computer qualification. We have no idea what it means.
Peter Sishton: That is an IT user qualification.

Q172 Alun Cairns: The Government clearly has had a responsibility in the past, and will have in the future, in terms of championing certain areas for strategic purposes, for good governance and for economic development in general, but there is a balance between Governments picking winners and saying, 'This is a sector we need to grow' and encouraging people to go in there. However, does more of it come down to what the industry can do itself in terms of championing an area? Let us take the energy sector as an example, because we have been quite explicit in that. Is it not up to energy companies to say, 'Look, come and work for us; we have high levels of salary and good conditions of work', because the demand is low? As you get a shift in that direction, there will be a gap elsewhere, which then creates a bit of dynamism to attract people. I am not saying that you are blaming Government, but is it unfair for some commentators to blame Government for not having planned, when there is a danger in Government planning because it ends up trying to pick sectors that it should be growing?
Aled Davies: I would not say that we are blaming Government. However, we are fortunate to have some very large employers, particularly UK-wide organisations, that do a lot of work with schools and a lot of work to promote their attractiveness—it is just such a big elephant to eat. However, we are trying to push a new value proposition through the national skills academy, but it is a huge task for us to change that perception. It is not only about inward investment: the age profile of our sector means that, within five years, 20% of the people will have retired, and by 2024, between 80% and 90% of the people currently employed in the sector will have retired.

Q173 Alun Cairns: Do universities communicate that kind of information? If I were an A-level student

thinking about what subject to study, I would think, 'Wow; this is a pretty good area to get into', because of what you just said and because of the salaries that would be available. I might do that instead of media studies, to pick up the Chairman's reference.
Aled Davies: We do provide all that stuff to Careers Wales, and we have a sector skills assessment, but I could not comment on the rest.

Q174 Geraint Davies: Stuart Bailey, you mentioned the elephant in the room, and then eating the elephant was referred to, but I am interested in this banging on schools' doors to get them to take up the skills that you are offering. Could you just elaborate on that?
Stuart Bailey: Sure. It comes down very much to an individual relationship with one particular teacher. In any school, it could be the deputy head, it could be the head of the sixth form, or it could be the careers adviser—anybody in the school could be the right person. Often, the way into a school, to start interfacing with them, is through an individual introduction rather than in writing to schools—we wrote to five schools in Newport when we introduced apprenticeships, and we did not get a single response. We were trying to tell them that we were introducing apprenticeships in the area, but people were not interested at that stage. We now find that it is down to individuals, but, if an individual leaves for some reason, you might invite someone else, but that person might be disaffected and not see the benefit in what we can offer schools. We have a fantastic high-tech industry and a fantastic customer facility that we can demonstrate—it is technology five or 10 years in the future, and I can guarantee that every child who has visited has gone away totally enthused about the IT-telecoms sector's work with Governments to secure critical national infrastructure and stuff like that.

Q175 Geraint Davies: Do you think that the Government—WAG in this case—should be more proactive in bringing both sides together rather than it being a voluntary exercise; that is, to leave the elephant outside the room? People have talked a lot about apprenticeships and the need for industrial growth. You seem to be saying that you have these apprenticeships to offer and the schools are not allowing you to make that bond. Is that right?
Stuart Bailey: I am not saying that they are not allowing anything; I am saying that we are getting limited take-up. Some schools are excellent, while other schools appear to be disinterested. I do think that it is schools so much as the individuals within the schools.

Q176 Geraint Davies: So what should happen? Should the Government intervene? Is that what you are saying?
Stuart Bailey: I think that Careers Wales has the responsibility at the moment. However, it would be good to see some means of pulling industry and education together, by which you get key people from industry talking to key people from schools to start developing this relationship. At the moment, it is done on an ad hoc and individual basis.

Q177 Susan Elan Jones: I will ask specific questions to the representatives from Morrisons. In terms of the economic effects of retail, beyond employment, which has a clearly important effect, what would you say are the main economic effects of the retail sector, and how would you rebut the criticism that some people might make that those effects were limited beyond employment?

Neil O'Doherty: We would argue that we make a big contribution to the economy of Wales and the rest of the UK. In Wales, we currently employ something like 6,400 people. I know that you refer to more than jobs, but it is important to note the point, and that number will be over 7,000 by the end of this year—it is an area that grows. Our payroll in Wales is at the thick end of £100 million, and that money goes into the Welsh economy, so it has a multiplier effect in the economy. That is purely within our own operations. We also contribute significantly in terms of the number of services that we use to run our stores and our factory, including local contractors. If you owned a JCB anywhere near one of our stores in December, you probably did quite well out of us from clearing our car parks. So, there are all sorts, ad hoc or otherwise.

We also get into technology. The systems that we use to run an operation such as ours, like those of any major retailer, are enormous. We have a project at the moment to replace or upgrade our computer architecture. It is one of the biggest IT projects in Europe at the moment, and it is a fantastically important business.[1] So, that generates stuff.

We have impacts in terms of links with schools. Every time I go into a shop, I have a school in there having a look around, with kids visiting and seeing what retail is about. So I think that we play a major role in terms of the economy.

Q178 Susan Elan Jones: Would you say that it is a major role in terms of small and medium-sized enterprises in the areas where you have stores?

Neil O'Doherty: Yes. We are based in Yorkshire, so the impact around our heartland, if you like—and what a fine place to be based—is much more substantial, with professional services and all sorts of things. However, because we are nationwide, there is an impact in all areas across the UK.

Chair: Mr Davies wants to play devil's advocate with you and ask you a tough question.

Neil O'Doherty: Thank you for the heads-up. [*Laughter.*]

Q179 Geraint Davies: This is the Chair's fault, of course. We have an array of people here—skills providers and people in energy—but, in terms of Morrisons, which provides a lot of apprenticeships, given that the headquarters is in Yorkshire, are most of the jobs that you are providing in Wales stretching jobs that require qualifications?

Chair: The phrase I heard bandied about was 'stacking shelves'.

Toni Eastwood: One of the issues in trying to attract people to the retail industry is the fact that people say

that about the skills required. There are some amazing careers at Morrisons in all sorts of areas, so it is not just about stacking shelves. There is a wide range, from field to fork.

Q180 Geraint Davies: I appreciate that you have buyers and so on, and it is all very interesting, but, in terms of the jobs you are delivering in Wales, they tend to be more mundane, do they not, because your headquarters is not here? What sort of things are you talking about, other than pharmacy, of course, where you cannot get the people?

Toni Eastwood: We have the manufacturing side of the business in Wales, and we have transport and distribution in Wales, as well as the shops.

Q181 Geraint Davies: Do you manufacture in Wales, then?

Toni Eastwood: Yes.

Neil O'Doherty: We have a food manufacturing plant in Deeside, which we recently acquired. It is an issue for Morrisons, as well as for every other retailer, how people perceive some of the work available. I should say that some of our jobs are about filling shelves and replenishing, but most of our jobs are about serving customers, even when you are filling a shelf. That interaction and buzz, and the selling, which is the big thing that we do, means that it is quite an interesting and exciting job. I could point to numerous people around our shops, in Wales as much as anywhere else, who have university degrees in all sorts of subjects and who have ended up in a retail environment because they love it, find it exciting and find that what we provide, perhaps better than most industries—and perhaps we do not tell enough people about this—is the ability to progress rapidly. You can do well if you are good, if you take the opportunities and are prepared to develop yourself. We are growing all the time, opening new stores and creating opportunities for promotion. I think that we mention in our paper that we have promoted some 3,500 people within the business in the last 12 months. That is a massive amount of progress and opportunity for people, and that is what retail is all about. It is about dealing with people, selling and providing customer service, but it is also about career opportunities, which is an important aspect. We would like everyone to recognise that, whether at Welsh Government or UK Government level, around the country.

Q182 Chair: With your apprenticeships, you are training people to gain qualifications in baking and in your delicatessens and in butchery. Presumably, people could walk out after doing an apprenticeship with you and get a job on the high street.

Neil O'Doherty: Yes, and some do. With craft skills such as baking and butchery, we are fortunate to some degree that some of our competitors have got out of butchery and that their meat is all prepacked in factories and not butchered in-store. However, we still do that, and we are forever dealing with situations where a competitor down the road will offer a few extra pence per hour, which means that the baker will go, for example. We can get into a bit of a spiral in that regard. So, we have to compete on rates for those

[1] *Note by witness*: This IT project will in turn generate additional investment.

skills, and they are difficult, but we feel that we have cracked that one through a good apprenticeship scheme. We grow our own people.

Q183 Chair: Is it one of the biggest in the UK?
Neil O'Doherty: I think so. We put some figures in the paper, but I have updated figures that show that we currently have 54,000 people signed up on QCF level 2 and 27,000 people going for apprenticeships. The numbers are massive, but it is really important that we recognise and value what our people do. Our business is very different from the businesses of some of my colleagues on the panel here, but it is still important that we recognise what people do and build their skills. We want their skills to improve, and the better we are, the better our customers' lives.
Chair: Susan Elan Jones has the next question.
Susan Elan Jones: No, I think that probably answers my question.

Q184 Geraint Davies: Could I ask a question on the balance? The Westminster Government needs export-driven growth to reduce the deficit rather than just making cuts, but, on the retail side, to a certain extent, there is no export market for you, is there? The area that we should be focusing on, surely, is electronically driven, skills-based stuff. Would you agree, Peter?
Peter Sishton: Absolutely. All our research shows that, if Wales, for example, can embrace technology, and the small and medium-sized enterprises and the managers and leaders in Wales can take it and apply it in the workplace then £1.2 billion in gross value added would be available to Wales over the next five years. We know that there is a big problem there. We also know that the large companies on the e-skills employer board are high-value research and development companies, and if we can grow the pool of talent there it is all to be had. I turn to you, Stuart, as the employers' voice.
Stuart Bailey: I must admit that we are looking to expand within our markets, but we primarily operate in the Ministry of Defence and the defence market, and that market is shrinking—it has been cut by 7% in the last year. We also operate out of France and Germany, and there are similar situations there; I think that France is stable, but the German market has gone down by 7%, and Spain has gone down by 7.5%. As an organisation, the global family has to look to expand, and we are expanding into countries such as Brazil, Russia, India and China, as well as the middle east, on border security and things such as that. So, our area of growth is overseas.

Q185 Mr Williams: Turning specifically to the energy sector for a moment, you have touched on some of this before, but could you elaborate on the specific skills challenges that confront new investors in the energy sector in Wales? More generally, is the uncertainty over the direction and pace of energy policy having an effect on long-term skills development? How would you like the UK Government and the Welsh Assembly Government to respond to that?
Aled Davies: The answer to that is 'yes'. There are two dimensions to this. One dimension that we have

not really discussed is the impact that planning consent has on energy projects; I imagine that the situation is similar in retail, with the opening of new stores, or whatever. The feedback that we are getting is that there is a need to free up planning consent much more. Before I came here, I looked on the Renewables UK website, and there are currently 23 windfarms in planning, which would produce 1,228 MW of power—that is equivalent to supplying 689,000 homes. All that is tied up in different stages of planning consent.

Q186 Chair: How many nuclear power stations is that equivalent to? About one?
Aled Davies: I could not tell you exactly, but I suppose Wylfa would—
Geraint Davies: You need greater planning permission for a nuclear power station than a windfarm, as in Japan.
Aled Davies: It is not just the planning. The issue with planning consent, and all the things that need freeing up, is that it is hard for employers to plan their skills development because of the time taken to get people on the road to competence. When do you start training? If you do not press the button, they will not start the training and so might not be ready. What is the mix? When do you start that ball rolling? When do you start investing? You do not know when things will occur.

Q187 Mr Williams: Those of us in mid Wales who have a healthy scepticism about large windfarms are very keen nonetheless to talk about the opportunities of tidal power, turbines out at sea, biomass and geothermal—the range of renewable energy that will make up the mix. Put that into the context of what you have just said about the skills shortage, and the extent to which those skills can be generated within Wales, rather than generated outside Wales and bought in.
Aled Davies: What I said about windfarms also holds true for tidal energy. There is a tidal energy pilot scheme off Pembrokeshire currently awaiting consent. As I understand it, the Welsh Assembly Government can give consent to schemes of up to 1 MW, and the pilot scheme is 1.2 MW, so it is tied up with planning consent issues. The scheme is hoping for a way through that; it is not an issue. Tidal energy is not as mature as wind energy, but the whole planning process need to be freed up.

Q188 Mr Williams: Is there still a skills shortage in all those technologies?
Aled Davies: That is the challenge—we need to develop the people so that when the planning and everything is ready, we have the skills sets ready.
Chair: That sounds like a 'yes'—that there is a skills shortage.
Aled Davies: Yes.

Q189 Alun Cairns: I think that the planning issue is important. I previously quoted a former Secretary of State; that person said that, when he could call a local authority leader to ask whether planning consent could be delivered on a project—whatever the industry might be—relatively quickly, it was a huge impetus in terms of attracting inward investment. We will all have our own views on wind energy and other renewable energies, but, for the industry, in relation to securing inward investment, do you think that a quick 'no' is better than a long wait for a 'maybe', which is what you seem to be getting at the moment?

Aled Davies: An employer's answer, rather than mine, would be that clarity would be preferable.

Q190 Chair: That brings me back to Morrisons, thinking about the development that I hope will go ahead soon in Abergavenny. [*Laughter.*] We have heard evidence that some employers are concerned about the standards of basic reading and arithmetic among some school leavers. Some employers have said that they are lower than they should be. Is that a concern that you share?

Toni Eastwood: Yes, and it is true right across the UK. In certain job roles, there are real basic skills needs.

Neil O'Doherty: We do some work on it. Key skills form part of our apprenticeships, so we are able to help colleagues who have issues with their levels of literacy and numeracy.

Q191 Chair: Should Morrisons have to train people in key skills? Is that not what schools are for? It is good that you do, but—

Neil O'Doherty: We take the view that it is part of what we do, and that we need to do it. Away from literacy and numeracy, what often gets forgotten—and I think that we will become more and more of a service economy as time goes on—is service skills. One thing that worries us is the level of interpersonal skills of some young people when they leave school. I wonder what we could be doing to increase the level of interaction and educational activities to build that up. Do not get me wrong—we have some fantastic young people, but we also have some people who turn up for interview who are barely able to raise a smile and say 'hello'. That is a worry, because that will not work in a service environment like retail. We have all probably been in places where we have seen it—

Geraint Davies: I have—the House of Commons.

Neil O'Doherty: In terms of growth and the basic skills levels that you accept, that is kind of important, and we see too much of it. Information technology is important, but I have three kids at home and getting them off the computer is a challenge, so that may be a wider issue.

Chair: We have run out of time. Thank you.

Tuesday 7 June 2011

Members present:

David T. C. Davies (Chair)

Stuart Andrew   Susan Elan Jones
Guto Bebb   Karen Lumley
Geraint Davies   Owen Smith
Jonathan Edwards   Mr Mark Williams
Mrs Siân C. James

Examination of Witnesses

Witnesses: **Professor Stuart Cole**, Professor of Transport, University of Glamorgan, **Mr Alec Don**, Chief Executive, Milford Haven Port Authority, and **Mr Ian Jarman**, Environmental and Legislation Manager, Owens (Road Services) Ltd, gave evidence.

Q192 Chair: Good afternoon, gentlemen. Some of us know one another of old, but perhaps I might ask everyone to introduce themselves for the record. May I also point out to all Committee Members that a few people have had to give their apologies and will be leaving early? It will not in any way be an effect of the evidence we hear from you today, so please do not be offended.

Ian Jarman: I am Ian Jarman. I am the environmental and legislation manager for Owens Road Services. We are based in Llanelli with depots along the M4 corridor.

Professor Cole: I am Professor Stuart Cole, emeritus professor of transport at the Wales Transport Research Centre at the University of Glamorgan. It is interesting to be on this rather than that side of the table.

Alec Don: I am Alec Don, chief executive of Milford Haven Port Authority.

Chair: It is very nice to meet you. I was rather remiss in not introducing myself as David Davies, Chair of the Committee, and somebody who had previously had an interest in haulage.

Q193 Geraint Davies: Professor Cole, you will probably notice I have a Swansea City tie on, just to ensure that, on record, we remember the Premiership, which will be very important for bringing more traffic flows and inward investment to Wales. First, how important do you think investment in transport systems is for inward investment in Wales, in particular rail, and with particular reference to the electrification to Cardiff? Secondly, do you think the case for Swansea has been made and what difference would it make to inward investment?

Professor Cole: Thank you very much, Mr Davies. I think we have to consider two things here. One is that, as you quite rightly pointed out, Swansea is now a tourist attraction from the sports point of view and therefore we have to provide for those kinds of traffic numbers, which will be going to Swansea on a regular basis, hopefully for many years. We also have an important tourist industry in Wales anyway. I am not talking just about south Wales but north Wales. The competitive position that we have to be in is one which means that we are competing not only for tourist but for industrial investment, which is one of the primary elements in this inquiry.

Taking the position of Wales on the periphery of the European Union, we are a country in competition with countries far nearer to the primary markets of the EU—the so-called "golden banana" from Milan through Germany to the Netherlands and the southeast of England—where the wage rate is much lower. We are in that kind of competition and, therefore, our transport system has to be that much more efficient in order to compete with those countries.

Going on to your question about rail, certainly this has been one of the key elements in transport, particularly in south Wales. It is fair to say that electrification came to Cardiff with a considerable amount of struggle. This Committee has already heard evidence in an earlier inquiry about the original plan to go only to Bristol with electrification. That plan was then developed, and proof was provided that Cardiff would also justify an investment. It was not as good a rate of return as Bristol, but it was nevertheless good enough to get that decision made in a positive way.

The next stage is the Swansea to Cardiff section. I am sure that discussions are going on between the Welsh Government and the Department for Transport, probably on two things. One is the rate of return. It may be that the information that was placed in the Library of the House some months ago does not give a clear picture of what rate of return could be achieved. Certainly, Swansea now has to make a considerable effort both on the numbers side in terms of rate of return and also on the perception of Swansea as being on the edge if it does not have a rail connection.

Q194 Geraint Davies: The rate of return or the cost-benefit analysis will be done on the basis specifically of the benefits in terms of traffic flows. Obviously, there are these issues about the Premier League and future possibilities. It is chicken and egg. On the cost side, do you think there is a prospect of some convergence funding that could be applied which would reduce the cost and possibly tilt the balance in our favour?

Professor Cole: As far as I can see, it is certainly the case that the Department for Transport did not look at convergence funding as a source of funding, and therefore that would bring down the total cost. It would perhaps be useful to pursue the position. The Department for Transport now appear to be saying that they will take only those costs that apply directly to them, so if some convergence funding comes in they will deduct that from the investment amount and work out the resulting rate of return on the amount of money they have to pay net of anything like convergence funding. The Treasury do not see it in the same light; they see convergence funding as something that just comes in to fund the total amount, and I think that issue has to be resolved with the Treasury.

Q195 Geraint Davies: But convergence funding would be available only for that bit, because it is certainly not available for the English bit.

Professor Cole: But the Paddington to Cardiff bit has effectively been decided by the Department for Transport as an investment programme that they will pursue. The section from Cardiff to Bridgend in the main does not attract convergence funding but Bridgend to Swansea does.

Q196 Mrs James: We have heard a lot recently about the perception of Swansea. In a recent meeting I attended on this matter, the issue of curvy rail was introduced. I was told that the railway was too curvy in south Wales to take electric trains. I am a little sceptical about this. Perhaps you would like to comment on it.

Professor Cole: The railway is a curvy railway. Essentially, when the Great Western Railway was built to Swansea—we are going back a long way—the designs were done by Brunel. The railway originally went through Gloucestershire, Monmouthshire and then into the rest of Wales. When the railway got into south Wales, there were issues of geology or perhaps geography. The hills came down almost to the sea and Brunel had to build his railway around that. At the time local land owners very often objected, and perhaps he did not have as much influence over the land owners in Wales as he did in England. There are some very straight sections of the Great Western Main Line on the way to south Wales. Some of them were built by Brunel and some built later, but there are very good, straight sections where speeds of 140 mph are easily achievable. That is not so in south Wales with the present structure.

Q197 Mrs James: I find it difficult to believe that, given new technology and new answers to issues, we cannot address this without putting in a new straight line.

Professor Cole: The only trains that can use a track which curves significantly are trains like the Pendolinos, and even they have limits. These are trains which, if you like, tilt. For the passengers, they seem to be upright and they do not feel as though they are going sideways, but those are expensive trains and they are certainly not among the Department for Transport's options at the moment.

Q198 Chair: That is odd, is it not? We all know the topography of Wales, but I thought that corridor in the south was not particularly topographically challenging; I thought it was basically pretty flat.

Professor Cole: It is flat but not particularly straight for a continuous period. There are certain straight bits but nothing as long as you have in England.

Chair: I admit that I had never thought about it before.

Professor Cole: Once you have a curve which reduces the speed of the train, it will not run at 140 mph but more like 90 mph.

Chair: I bow to your superior knowledge. I have never thought about it in my life.

Alec Don: I am not sighted of the technology or anything like that, but, just thinking about the issue you raise, the wire over the rail has to run in straight lines between two points and you cannot make it follow a curve. I can imagine that if the track is too bendy there is an engineering difficulty in suspending a wire over a curved track that has too big a curve on it. I do not know whether that is helpful in answering the question.

Q199 Chair: Just before I bring in Jonathan Edwards, getting away from curves for a moment, what will the respective impacts be on both you two gentlemen in your different industries? Presumably, it will be quite good for you, Mr Don, but perhaps not quite so good for Mr Jarman.

Ian Jarman: Speaking for myself, electrification will not be for freight movement but passenger movement. That is where I see electrification in south Wales. Freight movement will still be on the old-fashioned diesel line going from Port Talbot or Llanwern steelworks. I cannot see it going on to electrification.

Alec Don: As far as freight movement is concerned, the gauge of the railway is very important to us. The wagons likely to be emanating from Milford Haven will not necessarily be container wagons that require the biggest amount of space and height under bridges and so on. We have had a lot of discussions with Network Rail. I think there are a lot of train paths. You get a conflict between passenger and freight services. Passenger trains want to go at 100 mph or so and freight trains want to average about 40 mph or 50 mph. I do not know whether faster passenger trains would increase or reduce the overall freight capacity on the railway. Beyond freight, Milford Haven is an important economic area. It is important for the people working in that area to be able to get quickly to the places where they have to meet customers and so on. It is unquestionably important that the links connecting the remoter parts to Cardiff and onwards should be as fast and efficient as possible.

Q200 Jonathan Edwards: As to potential inward investors, what kind of message do you think will be conveyed in terms of the wider south-west Wales economy if electrification stops at Cardiff?

Professor Cole: I think this is a key element. The Department for Transport can look at the numbers and come up with whatever rate of return and cost-benefit ratio they can assert. Electrification is possible. Notwithstanding what Mr Don has just said, the lengths of overhead wiring are quite short so getting around bends is not difficult, certainly not for the bends on the South Wales Main Line. It is the speeds that trains can achieve. In terms of additional speed, there is probably not an awful lot of difference between bi-modal and electric, although the figures that the Department for Transport put before the House through the Library do not show exactly what that difference is. Perhaps that is a question they ought to be answering. As to perception, if you are an inward investor sitting in Spain, Italy or France and you are deciding where to invest, you look at the road network and you may have a bit of a concern about the Brynglas Tunnels, but you look at the rail network and see that electrification finishes at Cardiff. Then you begin to wonder why the Department for Transport—the British Government—have not invested west of Cardiff. Perhaps it is not worth your investing west of Cardiff. You might think that is not the way in which businesses work, but very often it is. It is a matter of, "What else is there? What facilities are there for us?"

Chair: With the utmost respect, perhaps we could try to keep the answers a bit briefer; otherwise, we will not get through much.

Q201 Mr Williams: Following on what Mr Don said in his professional role, I am quite clear about the case that Swansea is making and you make very valid points about why electrification should be extended to Swansea. You talk about perception, but what practical representations do you think are happening, and should happen, from areas in south-west and west Wales more generally to advance the case? I am aware of constituents in the south of Ceredigion who would instinctively travel to Swansea, Llanelli or Carmarthen when they are going to travel in an easterly direction. How far is the catchment area that is affected by this?

Professor Cole: If you take electrification or the improvement of the services to Swansea, Swansea's catchment area for trains, including Port Talbot because of Parkway station, extends way beyond Carmarthen, certainly as far as the dual carriageway system is concerned. As to whether more work has or should have been done, I think the simple answer, sadly, is yes. A lot of work was done by Cardiff, Bristol, Wiltshire and Swindon in a group called the Great Western Partnership. There was representation on that body by the South West Wales Economic Forum, but clearly it was very much geared towards Bristol and Cardiff. As I understand it, SWWITCH—the South West Wales Integrated Transport Consortium—are now working on the next stage, which is to push for the electrification plan to be extended all the way to Swansea.

Q202 Mr Williams: It is very easy to make generalisations about the south-west of Wales and the west of Wales. I am convinced of that, but we need to build a concrete case about how this will benefit those of us further west.

Professor Cole: We do, and I think you will find that that is in progress at the moment.

Q203 Mrs James: Given we have now been told that at a later date they will be able to extend from Cardiff to Swansea, are you sceptical about the costs at a later stage of meeting certain requirements? Is it not best

to electrify all the way now and have the cost ratio lowered, or do we take our chances and wait until some later date and it might never happen?

Professor Cole: Unless electrification is carried out continuously as one programme on that line beyond Cardiff—the same thing applies to the valley services, services in the Vale and commuter services—the costs will go up by at least 30%. If you are asking what my forecast might be—

Chair: I think that is a yes.

Professor Cole: —the answer is, no, it will not be extended.

Q204 Owen Smith: As a point of clarification, a moment ago you seemed to imply scepticism about the cost-benefit analysis placed in the Library, which says quite clearly that there would be no additional gains in reduced journey time if you had fully electric trains all the way through to Swansea. Is that because you do not understand the argument about the line speed between Cardiff and Swansea or you do not understand why the bi-modal train, when in diesel mode, will run as fast as the electric mode?

Professor Cole: The simple answer is that that analysis is not comparable. The first set of analyses to Cardiff is about electrifying to Cardiff. The Cardiff to Swansea analysis is about the incremental effect. It does not indicate what the difference would be between the intercity 125 and electrification to Swansea, and what that rate of return would be, and that is the figure that is really needed.

Q205 Owen Smith: To put a very simple question, do you think that analysis was the one on which the decision was predicated, or do you think that was a post hoc justification cobbled together for the purposes of putting it in the Library?

Professor Cole: I suppose I should say that you ought to ask the civil servants in the Department for Transport. Certainly, the analyses in the two columns in that document are not comparable.

Chair: Thank you for that tactful response.

Q206 Karen Lumley: To move to transport links in general, you argue on the one hand the notion that good transport links leading to investment are not fully proven but, on the other hand, that such links are a prerequisite for inward investment. Can you explain that to me?

Professor Cole: Most companies will look at a number of elements when deciding where to invest. In the surveys which Lloyds Bank have carried out over the years transport has always been in the top four. It has never been top. Labour costs are invariably an important element, as are utilities and land cost factors, but transport has always been one of the significant decision-making criteria. I think it is a prerequisite. You cannot guarantee that a good railway network will bring investment. If there was a motorway all the way to Haverfordwest and Pembroke Dock, which I am sure Mr Don would like to see, there would be no guarantee that investors would go all that way. But without a good motorway network, which we have as far as St Clears in south Wales and as far as Holyhead in north Wales, getting that

7 June 2011   Professor Stuart Cole, Mr Alec Don and Mr Ian Jarman

investor interested will be difficult. Therefore, it is a prerequisite, but sometimes it works the other way. Like most roads, it is two-way. It can be a good attractor for an inward investor. As we have seen on a number of occasions, when, for example, the M4/A48/A40 corridor was complete, the response of the owners of the Whitland Creamery and Carmarthen Dairy was to close them. With new methods of production and the chilling of raw milk before it goes to be processed, processing is now done in Gloucestershire because that is a good distribution point for south Wales, the south Midlands and the south-east. That is the downside of providing a really good means of moving goods for companies.

Q207 Karen Lumley: If your analysis is correct, do you think that undermines the case for investing in transport infrastructure?

Professor Cole: As I said, transport is a prerequisite for most companies. If you do not invest in good transport links, we are on the periphery and are competing with low-cost economies like Poland and Lithuania that have far lower costs. We have seen companies leave Wales and go to those countries. Without that prerequisite we are at a disadvantage. The downside risk is that some companies already in Wales will go somewhere else because they can shift their goods just as quickly.

Alec Don: Clearly, there is transport infrastructure and transport infrastructure. Road and rail are clearly very important for certain commodities, particularly containerised or ro-ro-type traffic serving on the ferries. I would like to take a slightly broader view of transport, which is obviously about pipelines and, indeed, electricity cables. I am not sure whether real enhancement of the road and railway network will create a cluster of general industrial activity around Milford Haven, but I know that enhancement of the gas and fuel products, pipelines and electricity cables plays exactly into the equations in which the major companies which potentially will invest in that area— the Exxons, Valeros and British Gases of this world— are very interested. It would definitely make a significant difference. Dragon LNG has the scope to build additional tanks and bring in more gas and do more with it. The message that the creation of additional capacity on the pipeline might take seven years to deliver has basically made them put all their plans on hold.

Q208 Owen Smith: A general question, if I may. In respect even of that broader definition of transport, if you like, is there any obvious evidence of companies choosing not to invest in Wales because of transport infrastructural deficits?

Ian Jarman: As to infrastructure, you have the Severn bridge coming across into Wales. Tesco is moving out of Wales from Magor. One of the factors for Tesco must be the cost of the Severn bridge tolls, so the infrastructure has to be correct for the economy of Wales rather than just bringing goods out of and into Wales. It has to be the whole picture: tourism; transport; network links; and it has to be cheap. That is the big thing. We spend £200,000 a year just bringing lorries from England back into Wales. Is that

justified? Why do we not base ourselves in England? We have opened a depot in Droitwich where we now see a lot more work.

Chair: That is quite worrying. Would you like to come back on that, Mr Smith?

Q209 Owen Smith: I would quite like to hear what Stuart and Alec have to say in response to the same question.

Professor Cole: I recall that the report of the Federation of Small Businesses only looked at why people came to us and why they did not like the Severn bridge tolls. The Welsh Government have commissioned another study into the impact of the tolls and queues at the bridge on inward investment. Presumably, in that report the consultants, who I think are Arup, will try to find companies that did not come to Wales. It is not inordinately difficult to do that because local authorities will have had approaches from companies over, say, the last five years. The WDA, as was, and the new Department within the Government will have had those inquiries. It may be that those companies might be asked why in the end they did not come to Wales but went somewhere else. I understand that report is to come out quite soon.

Q210 Mr Williams: You are talking generally about Wales. Quite rightly, so far, the discussion has focused specifically on the M4 corridor and also rail links. Can you break that down geographically? We do not have any fast roads and I do not have a stretch of dual carriageway in my constituency. It takes two hours to access motorways. We do not have anything approaching a direct link yet to London. Would you accept that that has impeded areas like Ceredigion and parts of the west of Wales, in particular, right along the west Wales coast, and certainly the north-west of the west coast, in terms of our economic development? We have heard about creameries in Carmarthenshire. I place on record that Rachel's Dairy in Aberystwyth, which is now an international player, is still based in Ceredigion despite all the impediments of freight and haulage charges.

Professor Cole: In terms of the overall picture, you are absolutely right. As to Aberystwyth and the roads that lead to it—the M54, A5, A483 and, to the south, the A44—none of those is a particularly good road. The companies that have grown in that area have tended to have some local connection. Rachel's Dairy is one; Laura Ashley is another. Laura Ashley went to Caersws because Laura Ashley liked Caersws. It was not a logical investment decision. When the Dutch company took it over, a number of those factories closed. I think that supports the argument that if you do not have really good transport infrastructure, particularly if you have just-in-time road haulage operations, which after all are 90% of total movements, companies will not go there, or, maybe when they are taken over by somebody else, an international corporation, they are going to move out.

Alec Don: Mr Smith has gone. In terms of companies that have not come forward, we have had discussions with power generators interested in biomass and those have disappeared back into the mist. West Wales is a fantastic potential location for tourism and particularly for what I term the marine leisure sector. We are there in competition with the likes of the Solent and Cornwall, and the ease with which people from Birmingham or the Greater London area can access Pembrokeshire will be a key determining factor in whether they put their boats there or somewhere else. In the wider context, you set the investment programme in roads and rail against what is happening in other countries. How visionary is the UK and Wales in terms of bridging that gap between what the private sector will happily finance, because there is a guaranteed return, and what will stimulate and drive investment? It is important for Wales to recognise that and step up to the plate wherever possible.

It is worth mentioning what has happened that is good. In Milford Haven, we have had £2 billion of inward investment over the past five years entirely financed by the private sector. Effectively, they put in their own motorway, which is the gas pipeline connecting Milford Haven to the grid. That sort of thing can happen around a port which offers all the dynamics that fit into a global distribution chain appropriately, which clearly Milford Haven does, but it is also important to lead that wherever possible.

Q211 Mr Williams: My frustration, as you will appreciate, is that in my county we do not have the benefit of the potential spin-offs from port developments and we lack that key infrastructure. You can also throw in infrastructure such as broadband or the lack thereof. We are not talking about that this afternoon. That presents companies with a huge challenge. Pembrokeshire is a very good example to cite in terms of the progress it has made and particularly the opportunities for tourism. We have not really built on the links between, say, the Midlands and Aberystwyth or Borth in my constituency in the last 100 years. There has been a rather inadequate infrastructure.

Alec Don: Yes, but I strongly believe that increasing the commutability to where the employment naturally wants to sit is important to Ceredigion. Milford Haven has the potential to be a strong centre for economic activity for all the reasons we have explained, and if it is easier for people living up towards Aberystwyth to commute down to it they are as much beneficiaries as the people in Pembrokeshire. That is where I would seek to put the emphasis.

Ian Jarman: Again, you must have the transport links to get the people from Aberystwyth to Milford Haven.

Mr Williams: Absolutely.

Q212 Geraint Davies: In your view, what should Swansea be doing to develop its port? In addition, I understand that, with European funding, there may be transnational transport funding available for this last electrification link between Cardiff and Swansea in the light of the port link on the ferry from Swansea to Cork. Mr Don, from an expert's point of view, what more do you think can be done for Wales in terms of the port of Swansea? What should they be doing?

Alec Don: I think ports generally, generically, have huge scope to be a driver of economic activity. There is no question about that. I would almost ask the

question: which came first—London or the port? You can put it in those sorts of terms. Port-centric development is very important. Swansea has its characteristics and its hinterland. For an inward investor, as often as not, the biggest constraint is how quickly he can get his project off the ground. Can you put a planning regime around that port and around Milford Haven that allows an inward investor to say, "I want to invest £1 billion. I can do it in six months in Milford Haven or Swansea. If I want to go and do it in Le Havre, I know it will take three years"? He will come to Swansea and Milford Haven. I emphasise the importance of how the ease of getting something done is ranked in the decision-making halls in the international investment companies that we talk about.

Q213 Geraint Davies: How is it ranked in Wales? Obviously, there is the Welsh Assembly Government and there is planning law, which is non-devolved. How does it rank?

Alec Don: There are two answers to that question. Clearly, in the case of Milford Haven in particular—forgive me; obviously I am from Milford Haven and I know it slightly better—we have had a good record of driving inward investment. The key factor that attracted Dragon and South Hook, in addition to the depth of water, was the availability of sites. They look at the fact that there is a jetty on the site and know they can get from A to B in planning terms in two rather than five, six or seven years, or whatever it is. We know that the potential time it will take to get a second gas pipeline—it is mooted as seven years—is definitely deterring further investment by British Gas and Dragon. It has a very critical impact on them. We have a record of success; potentially there will be more of it provided the framework supports it. The other half of the equation is about the generic reputation of living day to day, trying to operate a complex plant in an environment that is highly regulated. Can they get things done, or does the management at the facility at Milford Haven constantly have to report to the board in America that an important bit of dredging has been delayed because of some regulatory impact, or whatever is going on? On the latter point, the fact that you have a Welsh Assembly Government's set of rules, UK rules and local rules means that it is not necessarily such a good, encouraging story, but let's recognise that Milford Haven particularly has been successful at attracting major amounts of inward investment. That is great, and let's try to build on that.

Q214 Guto Bebb: I am afraid I am going to drag you up to north Wales. Referring to your comments, Professor Cole, in relation to the fact that investment in transport infrastructure, particularly roads, can be a double-edged sword, to what extent do you believe that the A55 has provided a corridor of opportunity to north Wales? Has it simply facilitated people's ability to commute from north Wales to the north-west of England? Indeed, it could be argued that the local development plans being adopted across north Wales are an indication of the fact that the Welsh Assembly Government see north Wales as a commuter area for the north-west of England.

Professor Cole: Certainly, the ease of travel to Chester and Liverpool, or the Merseyside conurbation, has made north Wales an attractive proposition for commuters for years. In the time I lived in Chester people were commuting certainly from Denbighshire and Flintshire. The A55 makes it easy to travel just that little bit further, and of course that may have other social effects. The A55 construction certainly had impacts on local communities in that, when the old roads were there, people stopped at cafes or restaurants; they stopped for petrol. That does not happen as much any more and a number of those smaller settlements have suffered as a result. So there is that negative element. In terms of the corridor of opportunity, I think you are referring to what Peter Walker said some years ago. It was intended to be an attractor for inward investment. It did not do that in the same way. It has certainly encouraged the tourist industry in north-west Wales; it has not brought manufacturing industry, maybe because the population size was not there or companies did not think of north Wales as being a manufacturing area. But certainly it has enhanced the tourist industry and spread that further along, because people can now travel in the same amount of time a much longer distance along a very good piece of roadway.

Q215 Guto Bebb: I accept the comments about tourism, undoubtedly. The second question I want to ask is about the railway line in north Wales. We have talked a lot and incessantly, it could be argued, over the past few months about the electrification from Cardiff to Swansea. I am all in favour of people arguing their case. My understanding—I suspect that this question is for Professor Cole—is that the north Wales railway line is not particularly bendy or curvy. Having had discussions with various railway companies, it would appear that the main drawback for a faster service in north Wales is related to signalling on the line, which, in comparison with the cost of electrification, is a very low-cost solution. Indeed, I have been informed quite reliably that the people who are tendering for the North West railway franchise would be happy to provide hourly services from north Wales to Euston if the signalling on the north Wales line could be improved. Is that hyperbole on behalf of the companies or the reality?

Professor Cole: There is a lot of truth in what they say. There are two issues related to the North Wales Main Line. One is that certain sections of it are still subject to 75 mph. Companies do not like going there for up to 90 mph or 100 mph and then having to slow down; they like to keep a fairly constant speed. It is better in terms of train maintenance and fuel. That means a lot of the passenger trains are capable of doing far more than that. The 175s are travelling at 75 mph along that track. Part of that is to do with signalling. There is some track improvement to be made, but signalling is a major issue. On the calculations that I carried out recently, the North Wales Main Line electrification, which has been on the cards since 1977—I worked on it then—is £300 million. It is not an enormous sum of money. To get the journey time from Bangor to Cardiff down to just over three hours from its present four hours and 20

minutes, the total cost of the Marches Line and the North Wales Main Line—the South Wales Main Line is now being improved anyway—was about £120 million, when I made those calculations about two years ago. We are not talking about enormous sums of money to get good journey speeds on that line.

Q216 Guto Bebb: Obviously, the journey time to Cardiff is important if you are a bureaucrat or politician, but in terms of economic development is it the case that the journey time to London Euston is the one that counts?

Professor Cole: The journey time to London Euston is certainly the important one. Let's not get away from the fact that London is a major financial centre; it is a major investment source worldwide, not just for Wales or the UK. Therefore, an important element is a good journey time to London. Electrification will improve that journey time as well as the quality of the North Wales Main Line. Similarly, a lot of the movements are not to do with just Cardiff to Bangor, or north Wales to Cardiff; there are sectional movements along that line which, again, will improve a whole range of journeys.

Q217 Mrs James: It is a well-known fact that over 1 million people live along the South Wales Main Line. Economies of scale there have given it the edge, have they not?

Professor Cole: When it comes to the cost-benefit ratio calculation by the Department, numbers of passengers are an important element, as are numbers of trains. Of course, that is what makes the analysis between Cardiff and Swansea more of a challenge than the analysis to Cardiff.

Q218 Chair: Mr Don, to move slightly away from trains and towards ships again, given Milford Haven's distance from EU and UK markets and the competitiveness of ports like Felixstowe, how do you compete? What are your main challenges?

Alec Don: It is true. You can ask the question why the LNG terminals got built in Pembrokeshire rather than, for the sake of argument, Rotterdam with a simple pipeline under the sea. We are operating in an international competitive marketplace as a port, but that encompasses many different markets. We are not in the same container industry-driven market as somewhere like Felixstowe. If you look at Milford Haven in terms of a logistics map, it is very close to the Atlantic trade route in terms of deep sea shipping; it is about the transmission of cargoes from a wide variety of sources, such as Africa, the Middle East and the North Sea, and retransmission of processed product to other UK ports, European ports and the eastern seaboard of the United States. It is worth thinking slightly outside of the immediate Welsh boundary and in terms of that global logistics map. That is why Milford Haven is in a good location, which is driven by, it has to be said, these important pipeline links into the UK heartlands. Our business is energy. We have a fabulous natural deep-water harbour, and all those factors will combine to make it a good place for further investment by those sectors.

I suspect that we will not be another Felixstowe or Southampton.

Q219 Chair: One issue that has been raised by other ports—it may not affect you directly—is backdated business rates on businesses within the curtilage of a port. My understanding is that, in England, the Government decided that they could not possibly backdate rates because it would be unfair to businesses that had not built in those costs, but the Welsh Assembly Government have decided to do so. A number of businesses based within the curtilage of a port authority are now faced with a whole load of charges that they never faced before. Broadly speaking, is that correct? What opinion, if any, do you have of this?

Alec Don: For me, I think the most important factor is that businesses in Wales have the opportunity to be treated in the same way as businesses in England. If the rebate has been made in England, it should probably be made in Wales.

Q220 Chair: Are you aware of this happening in Milford Haven?

Alec Don: Some businesses are affected. I think that in the grand scheme of things probably for us and our client or tenant businesses, the impact has not been particularly significant, but it is a shame that the Welsh Government received money from UK central Government to deal with the issue and decided to use it for other purposes.

Q221 Chair: The UK Government gave the Welsh Assembly money and said, "This is your money to prevent you from having to put a charge on Welsh businesses."

Alec Don: Not for ever and a day but to deal with the backdated element that they would be faced with.

Q222 Chair: They said, "Here is money which is given to you specifically so that Welsh businesses will not lose out in comparison with English businesses", and the Welsh Assembly Government spent it on other things.

Alec Don: Yes; that was exactly what happened. That is a fact. I guess that, much like the discussion about the extension of the railway to Swansea, there is a value calculation about what, for the interests of Wales, is the best way to use that money. I think it was in that context that there was some evaluation of it, but essentially the facts that you relate are correct.

Chair: Would anyone else like to come in with any questions about shipping and ports, given that some of those who were going to ask those questions have had to go elsewhere?

Q223 Mrs James: We have had evidence previously from Associated British Ports that ports are more than simple transfer points for goods, ships and things on to the road; that they are multi-modal hubs. There is a good connection with rail and roads. You may have realised I am a little interested in rail.

Alec Don: Yes.

Mrs James: These are backed with very good statistics. We need to develop storage and sites around

it. Can you give us a better picture of what that would actually mean? What would we need to do in Wales for that?

Alec Don: My personal view is that, in policy terms, it is worth defining ports areas as areas where you can get things done quickly and investment is directed. One of the reasons I say that is that transport networks are about commutability and the efficient movement of goods. Manufacturers never want to be located off route for what is the main source of supply and main market for their goods. If you have them off route, you are building in £1 or £2 a tonne deviation costs. That will steadily undermine an entire industry. They want to be close to these points of interchange, be it ports, motorway junctions or airports. This is the essence of what I say. I think ABP also say very well in their submission that it is worth seriously backing a port-centric approach, an airport-centric approach and perhaps even a motorway junction-centric approach— but I am a port guy, so a port-centric approach—to the question about ease of planning and definition of sites. As well as transport links, good sites are very important.

Q224 Mrs James: One of the things that I come across—I tell you because we have a port site in Swansea and it is near me—is a dichotomy with development for leisure and tourism. How do we maintain those areas of industrial activity, yet all see a better standard of living, better housing, etcetera?

Alec Don: To a certain extent, the market will have its way whatever you decide. In policy terms it will go where the market wants to go. I would, broadly speaking, encourage the decision makers to say, "If that is what you want, that is what we will support", because ultimately how fast you can make things happen is a key determinant of how much investment you get. That's it. I come from Liverpool. Perhaps it is worth talking for a second about something that is completely outside Wales. Technology changes. The central part of Liverpool was where the port was. It dealt with ships whose depth was about five or six metres. Ships get bigger and bigger and you build more and more deep docks that go out towards the sea, and the shallower ones fall off being economically useful as ports and get turned into flats, offices, shops and so on. That's fine; the world changes. I think it is very important to back that process and see the new money going in wherever it wants to go.

Q225 Guto Bebb: On the issue of ports as a natural hub for economic development, obviously in north-west Wales we have the transport links heading towards Holyhead, which is a gateway to Ireland, but the transport links are predominantly passenger transport rather than commercial. Do you think that the concept of an enterprise zone located on something like Holyhead port has merits? Is that enterprise zone-type approach one that Milford Haven has considered in any way?

Alec Don: Yes, I think it does have merit. Whoever has that site will have to work up a plan that attracts someone to that site for the merits it offers. It might be depth of water; it might be proximity to a particular trade route. If it does not tick any of those boxes, he really is proverbially pushing water up hill, but from a policy point of view you have to support him in the effort. It is a key site. There is talk about the installation of an undersea electricity connection essentially from Anglesey right the way round to Milford Haven to connect to the Pembroke spur. That would be a fantastic thing to do. It would create a ring main and you would immediately have a much higher utilisation of the electricity grid capacity. You could put biomass power stations anywhere on that ring main and it would feed into Cardiff, Swansea and the rest of the UK in a way that had lower logistics costs and used bigger ships and the existing berth infrastructure more intensively. I do not know whether that is the story that the market will eventually buy, but by all means it is absolutely right to back it, focus on that site and say, "What can we do with it?"

Q226 Jonathan Edwards: Building on that slightly, ports policy is essentially a reserved matter for the UK Government, yet access to the ports is a devolved matter. In your view, do the UK and Welsh Governments work well together to assist inward investment?
Alec Don: My answer to that is yes, broadly speaking. They all have a common policy objective of stimulating growth. We are in an economic environment at the moment where we want to stimulate growth and investment, and that is very important. Our instructions—we are not a devolved matter—from the Department for Transport is to get on with growing the business on a commercial basis, and they will back whatever we have to do in that respect. The Welsh Assembly Government have exactly the same objective. Milford Haven, as a port, at certain times delivers up to 30% of the UK's instantaneous gas demand. All the assets there collectively are a phenomenally important installation. I do not see a particular conflict in any of that. At the micro level, we would be concerned about whether a unit like the MCU, which is our consents unit for certain licences to do with the disposal of dredged material, might charge higher fees than the English equivalent, which clearly would disadvantage Wales. There are little concerns like that about the interaction between the UK and Welsh Assembly Government, but in terms of the big picture I do not see a particular problem.

Q227 Jonathan Edwards: Any there any specific joint forums?
Alec Don: I think the short answer is that I spend quite a lot of time talking to both of them but not conveniently in one place. A lot of effort goes into building up things like the Wales marine spatial plan and the Wales regional plan working from a UK top-down approach. They spend a lot of time trying to integrate those things. Those sorts of documents are really useful as long as the attitude of the political leaders who manage and control the impact of the bureaucracies, if I may call them that, on the operation and development of the ports is as conducive as it possibly can be. Fundamentally, if we have a customer, a financier and a site all lined up and we

have to wait for five years for a consent, or we have to get 10 different types of consent in terms of licences and so on, you just cannot hold the equation together. It is like the man from Del Monte. The Government is the man who says yes. If we have got all those things together, broadly speaking it makes good sense, and you can get a single decision as quickly as you possibly can, investment will happen and it has happened.

Q228 Jonathan Edwards: As part of this inquiry we went to Germany and had a meeting with UKTI. In their promotional material they do not include infrastructure as a reason for investing in Wales because they deem it to be so poor. Does that surprise you?
Alec Don: I am looking at it through a particular lens quite a lot of the time in so far as I am very focused on the energy sector, and the infrastructure for us is pipelines, electricity grids and our deep water. We also have a ferry service and the opportunity to try to stimulate a ferry service that connects Pembroke Dock with Spain. Those kinds of incremental improvements would be great. Once you have a node of interchange of commodities on ro-ro services you might see some value-added services coming into the area, such as warehousing and RDC-type activities, and it might develop from there. But we are working on projects that may very well lead to making a greater demand on the railway. When we are talking seriously to the market that might want to use those services, they will be asking questions. How many paths are there? How fast will the trains go? What will it cost me? Can I get a train to turn around between Milford Haven and Crewe once a day, or will it be one-and-a-half times a day? If it is one-and-a-half times a day, it is just not going to stack up. You see the approach. As soon as you get into those sorts of discussions, the level of infrastructure available in Wales will be very critical.

Q229 Chair: Mr Jarman, what would you say? Do you think the level of transport infrastructure, which we are thinking of here primarily, is something that we should be boasting about or keeping quiet about?
Ian Jarman: We have two trans-European networks which link Ireland, Wales, England and Europe: the A55, which is predominantly dual carriageway with the exception of the Menai bridge area, and the M4, which is basically dual carriageway to St Clears. St Clears is not the best road; it is not the worst road. But you will not get people to invest around Milford Haven because the reliability of the road network isn't there. If there is an accident, there will be long detours to move your goods and people and get your staff to work. I mentioned in my submission the closure of the M4 twice. That hit us extremely hard and cost £20,000 on both days that the M4 closed. For a family business in south Wales that is big money.

Q230 Mr Williams: That leads on to my questions. Do I detect, therefore, a slight note of irritation that the debate to date, perhaps even this afternoon, has focused largely on rail, understandably? I don't deflect from my prejudice on Swansea. It is quite right that they should raise it; I agree with them on that matter.

But a big debate needs to be had about investment in road. I suppose that the question I am leading to is: do you believe it would be more cost-effective to enhance investment in roads rather than rail?

Ian Jarman: My opinion and my answer would obviously be that Wales is a just-in-time manufacturing base. You cannot do just-in-time delivery on a railway network; it just does not work. Just-in-time has to be by road, having regional distribution centres and shipping the goods out by HGVs. There is a severe lack of investment spurring off the trans-European networks up in the north and in the south. There is not enough road going north.

Q231 Mr Williams: We will come on to the middle in a minute because there is a particular interest there. Do you know of inward investors who have been dissuaded from investing in the country or have voiced concerns because of those difficulties?

Ian Jarman: I was asked a question when the First Minister for Transport, or whatever his title was, announced that the M4 relief road would not go ahead. It was just after Amazon had come to Swansea. One of the questions I was asked by the CBI was whether I thought Amazon would have located in Swansea on the basis that they would not have that relief road. All they want is a reliable road network to ship their goods to the Midlands and towards London from their Swansea distribution centre. I would say that investment in road infrastructure has to be taken into consideration for locating any inward investment.

Q232 Mr Williams: Professor Cole, what do you think about that?

Professor Cole: Ninety per cent of freight goes by road. Many people might think it is wrong but that is the reality. Therefore, if we are going to be competitive on the edge of the European Union we have to have a really good road network. As we have seen, Amazon have come to Swansea; Macmillans have just moved from Basingstoke to Skewen. They already had a small distribution centre at Skewen; now their main distribution centre worldwide is there. Clearly, they think that the M4 motorway is adequate for their distribution. To some extent, we are investing in the right way. I am sure that Mr Williams would like to see more investment on the A44, maybe an extension of the M54 westward, but the reality is that governments have to look at where the most likely impact will be and therefore concentrate on those areas.

Q233 Mr Williams: I was going to come on to prioritising. In the context of shrinking infrastructure budgets there is inevitably a need to prioritise areas of particular investment opportunities. But you would accept, though, that those of us in mid-Wales have particular challenges and difficulties on which we touched earlier. I am quite aware of them; I get the business people coming to my surgeries and talking about them. What is your perception of the problems we face not just in the road infrastructure but, to digress a bit, on the railways? The fact is that we do not have a direct service from London to Aberystwyth. If you look at a map, that is one of the

few peripheral areas that do not have that. I hope that Arriva Trains will make some progress on that in due course, but these are big problems for us, are they not?

Professor Cole: They are. To take the road network first, clearly in terms of prioritisation any government will go for those investments which will give them the biggest rate of return, and that is what they have done. The Welsh Government is the responsible authority for roads in Wales. To go back to Mr Edwards' earlier question, where they can get co-operation with the Department for Transport, some years ago we saw issues to do with the construction of the A55 and the ongoing problem with the A483, which comes into England as an unimportant road but in Wales is a trunk road. Of course, that has an impact on mid Wales. As an economist, I am sorry to say that prioritisation is almost bound to be based on the cost-benefit ratio. What returns will we get in terms of employment? What numbers of vehicles will travel on those roads? Consequently, the big investment will be where it is from. There are discussions about the A465. Clearly, that is an important road. Again, it has more of an impact on south Wales than it does on mid Wales, although one could say that there are roads in mid Wales that could go on to that road. It is dualled for part of the way. There is an expensive job to be done at Clydach Gorge, and that would make it a good road into the Midlands. It would not give best impact certainly on the western part of the canolbarth or mid Wales. It would have a greater impact on the Brecon area more than the western section, but almost inevitably we will have an investment prioritisation in roads across north and south Wales.

In terms of rail, the Aberystwyth to Shrewsbury line now has capacity for an hourly rather than a two-hourly service. With the demise of the Wrexham and Shropshire private railway company, they are now part of the same group as Arriva. The Deutsche Bahn company that owns Arriva might well decide that this is perhaps a good opportunity to introduce a commercial service giving access to the network from Aberystwyth to London. That was what Arriva had planned to do some years ago.

Q234 Mr Williams: In one of your earlier answers you talked about the importance of perception. That is linked to what Mr Don said about Pembrokeshire and the ease with which people could get about. Mention was made of Crewe and all the rest of it. That perception is important. That is what we are lacking at the moment. I do not doubt that very few business people will want to do a daily trip from London to Aberystwyth, but it is a strategically important area; it is a university town; it is a tourist centre of growing importance, and we need to enhance that.

Professor Cole: One thing about which we have to be clear is that the Aberystwyth to London service is not doing only that job. The Holyhead to London service has a lot of intermediate changes of passengers. For example, Chester and Shrewsbury are important centres. It is not just thinking about how many people travel from Aberystwyth to London but how much business can be generated along those different and important sections of that route, which of course goes through parts of England and therefore will stop at certain stations. You are absolutely right about the perception. The perception is that Aberystwyth is difficult to get to by train. If you are talking about it from a railway perspective, it is difficult to get to. It is a two-hourly service, and it makes little sense for anybody to use the train other than for casual, leisure or maybe student journeys because no car is available. To get people to shift from car to train and for Aberystwyth to be, if you like, in people's perception a connected town by rail, then an hourly service at least is essential and those trains need to be of good quality of the type, perhaps, that Wrexham and Shropshire were operating.

Q235 Chair: I am going to come up with a bit of controversy here just for the fun of it. I have often heard it said that Aberystwyth, Monmouth and all sorts of very nice but small places that are hard to get to ought to have absolutely first-class rail links or whatever, but is not the reality that some people like these places precisely because they are out of the way and a bit hard to get to? If they were within a two-hour commute of London, they would become the new Readings or Swindons, would they not, and we would be paying rather a lot of money for something to happen which many would not want? I am playing devil's advocate.

Alec Don: People are brought up in areas and they want to live there. Sometimes they just cannot because there aren't the jobs there. What is really important, perhaps a little more so than how we can create a rail service that is on the very margins of profitability for an operator, is the creation of good IT infrastructure. What is it that people in somewhere like Aberystwyth have, because it will not really be on a central route for manufacturing or logistics of goods in terms of RDCs or warehousing? It will never quite fit that sort of profile, but does it have the skills base? That is a very important part of the infrastructure of a place like Aberystwyth and the ability of those people to communicate and work in this ever-more IT-connected remote working world with the rest of the planet. The traditional themes of road, rail and so on are important sector by sector and activity by activity in different ways. In Milford Haven, what we are interested in is not rail services that can carry containers but pipelines and electricity grid connections. That is one of the things that will drive our business. I am sure that Aberystwyth has to be interested in really good IT connections and selling on its skills base. You get different answers in different places, but I think the overriding theme in each area is to concentrate on what it is good at, not try to disperse activity away from where it is already successful.

Q236 Geraint Davies: When my father was a boy in Aberystwyth, two or three trains a day carried tourists from the Midlands. Obviously, now people go to Spain and all the rest of it, but at that time an enormous hub of people were feeding that economy. Given the points Mr Don has made about technology and that Aberystwyth is a nice place to live, if there was that speed of connection, more and more people who perhaps went to the university there would stay

there and set up their IT businesses in the knowledge that if they wanted to go to London they could, but at the moment they cannot. More people are looking for environmentally sustainable holidays rather than getting skin cancer with climate change and all the rest of it, and perhaps people from America want to go round castles or whatever it is. Unless we have that infrastructure to support modern international tourism with people living longer and all the rest of it, Aberystwyth will have a big problem, but if we provide infrastructure, we might also provide the demand that justifies it.

Alec Don: You have to put it together with sites. You could build a really good service to Aberystwyth, but what is at the end of it in terms of hotels, other activities and, in our case, marinas? There has to be a bit of a plan around that to get from point A to point B over a two or three-year programme. The other very important thing is to have local ownership of the businesses in areas like that. The people who want to stay in Aberystwyth are, I presume, those who own businesses there.

Q237 Mr Williams: You have responded to references to Aberystwyth. The simple fact is that we have the highest proportion of small businesses per head anywhere in the United Kingdom; we have a university town with a high skills base; we have huge tourist opportunities; and, above all, if you put them all together, it is about an economic imperative now. The fear is that those opportunities cannot be realised to their full potential without those links. On many occasions I have come across examples of American tourists who want to come to the west of Wales but are put off, quite frankly, by having to mill around the dreaded Birmingham New Street station for some time waiting for a train connection and then having a shambolic service to get them to the west of Wales. That is not the way we are going to promote it. I think that requires immediate action. I am sorry; there was a question. Mr Jarman and Professor Cole enlightened us on many of these things before. You have reiterated some of the very important messages, but particularly some of the experiences in terms of road freight and the difficulties that you and other companies have had in mid Wales.

Ian Jarman: We operate a pallet network service from Llanelli as far as Aberystwyth.

Mr Williams: You do not have to restrict it just to Aberystwyth; we have heard a lot about Aberystwyth this afternoon.

Ian Jarman: That is our boundary. We cannot send an articulated lorry to anywhere other than Pembroke Dock and Milford Haven because it just will not get through the narrow, windy roads. The road infrastructure is not in place there for HGVs, not that you would want them trampling up the coast from Newquay to Aberystwyth, but the road network is not there for you. You need a good route, whether it is an upgrade of the A44 or something coming up from St Clears. I do not have the answer to that, but we cannot operate HGVs deeply into west Wales because the road infrastructure is just not there.

7 June 2011   Professor Stuart Cole, Mr Alec Don and Mr Ian Jarman

Q238 Guto Bebb: Obviously, we appreciate that 90% of commercial traffic will be on roads rather than rail, but to what extent are Welsh haulage companies looking at integrating with rail transport?

Ian Jarman: The only real option at the moment is the rail freight terminal at Wentloog. We do not go into Wentloog purely and simply because the money is not there for operations. It is a very cut-throat market and they work on extremely low margins, even lower than those on which we are already working, so it is not a market we have even tried to tap into.

Q239 Guto Bebb: My second point relates to the constituency that I serve. I have a quarry next to the A55, but predominantly that uses the rail infrastructure to transport its product which is basically low value hardcore. Is there a level at which the price per tonne of a product becomes uncompetitive to transport by road?

Ian Jarman: In response to that, there are hauliers out there who would undercut and do it below cost price at the moment purely and simply out of desperation.

Guto Bebb: The point I am trying to make is the fact that that quarry is next to the A55 but it needs to access the rail network.

Ian Jarman: Are they using the railway to ship their goods?

Guto Bebb: Yes.

Ian Jarman: Where do they ship their goods?

Guto Bebb: To the Manchester area. What I am getting at is that there is a possibility of developing quite significantly the market for slate waste from Blaenau Ffestiniog, for example. That is being stopped by the fact that the road network is so poor that you cannot get heavy goods vehicles up to that part of the world. Is that the type of context where the railway which is already in place is an option that should be looked at, because road transport would require a huge investment right through the heart of Snowdonia, whereas the railway lines are already there? The point I am getting at is that perhaps it is not always the case that the road transport network is the way to go.

Ian Jarman: It is an option. I am from the road haulage industry, so I would always say that the road haulage industry is the best method of transporting your goods because it gets from A to B and you do not have to have large quantities of it. You can send it out in a convoy of one lorry or 50 lorries if you want to.

Q240 Guto Bebb: But the specific point that I am getting at is the low value of the item in question. I come back to the question: if the value of the product is comparatively low, is there a cut-off point where road transport is not competitive, apart from in the midst of an economic recession such as we currently have?

Ian Jarman: It all comes down to the volumes you are shipping.

Q241 Chair: As a former hauler with an HGV, perhaps I may ask some quick questions. We are running a bit short of time. Would you like to see weight limits increased? Is it now 44 tonnes?

Ian Jarman: It is now 44 tonnes. We have the DfT consultation on longer semi-trailers with no increase in weight. We will max out on weight before we cube out on volume for the majority of the product we carry for our diverse customers. We do carry for Georgia-Pacific tissues and toilet rolls where longer semi-trailers would work. Again, the road infrastructure is not really built for 54 or 58 tonnes.

Q242 Chair: It would be all right on a motorway, would it not? It would work on a motorway.

Ian Jarman: But those roads off the motorway from your distribution centres would have to be upgraded, so it is a cost.

Q243 Chair: Is it a problem for you that foreign drivers are breaking tacho rules and the rest of it and then do not even bother to pay fines, and as a respectable company you find it hard to compete with that?

Ian Jarman: Through the trade associations we have lobbied hard for VOSA to have better stop and on-the-spot fines. It is getting better. It is not perfect at the moment. There are a lot of unscrupulous foreign counterparts out there who do illegal operations through cabotage. They carry excessive weight; they drive beyond their hours; they do not take the required breaks set out in the European regulations.

Q244 Chair: I do not know whether it is still the case, but years ago it was difficult to pick up back loads from abroad if they were not coming back to the country of origin. Therefore, you could not pick up in Italy and drop off in Germany. Is that changing now because we are all in the European Union? It may not be something that affects your company.

Ian Jarman: Not as a company. We do very few European movements now. We used to have a department that was a European department, but we probably do one European transaction a month. What we have seen of late are vehicles being impounded by VOSA or stopped. VOSA stop the foreign drivers. All they are doing is winding down their windows by two inches and passing the credit cards straight out of the window. They know it will be a £200 fine. They park up for nine hours and they are on their way.

Q245 Chair: Lastly, do you have concerns about the standards of rest facilities for HGV drivers?

Ian Jarman: Yes. There is a lack of UK Government and Welsh Assembly Government thinking on rest facilities. Every driver after four and a half hours must take a 45-minute break; after nine hours the driver must park up for a daily or nightly rest of nine or 11 hours. Load security is a major factor where you park. We are very fortunate in that we offer other UK hauliers parking facilities and they offer them to us, but facilities around the UK are not good enough and are very expensive.

Chair: I think this will be the final question, hopefully, on trains again.

Q246 Mrs James: It is about freight as well. Mr Jarman has already picked that up. Basically, will electrification work for freight? We have heard conflicting information on it that most providers in Wales are very reliant—and quite happily reliant—on diesel.

Professor Cole: I think the issue is for some of the very big operators. I am sure that Ian is not going to agree with this. We have a large company called Tata Steel which is manufacturing in Trostre, Port Talbot and Llanwern. The issue goes back to Mr Bebb's question. Where does rail work for freight, for example? It works where you have a siding at either end, direct deliveries and you do not have to transfer to road because that incurs a cost. With electrification, the benefit to Tata as a user of the railway at the moment is that they do not have to change from diesel to electric. It would not be at Cardiff but it would be somewhere on the Cardiff to Newport main line. They would have to attach an electric locomotive. If they could run straight on to the electric main line not at Llanelli but Port Talbot and Llanwern, that would be an advantage to them, in that they would not have that extra cost.

Mrs James: They have supported the electrification to Swansea; they have been very supportive.

Professor Cole: Yes.

Chair: Gentlemen, thank you very much indeed for coming along.

Tuesday 14 June 2011

Members present:

David T. C. Davies (Chair)

Stuart Andrew   Susan Elan Jones
Guto Bebb   Karen Lumley
Geraint Davies   Jessica Morden
Jonathan Edwards   Owen Smith
Mrs Siân C. James   Mr Mark Williams

Examination of Witness

Witness: **Sir Roger Jones OBE**, gave evidence.

Q247 Chair: Sir Roger, diolch yn fawr am dod heddiw.
Sir Roger Jones: Diolch i chi, am y gwahoddiad.

Q248 Chair: I am afraid there are no translation facilities here.
Sir Roger Jones: That's all right.

Q249 Chair: We all know who you are, Sir Roger. I am not sure whether there is any point in asking you to introduce yourself, but perhaps I should, just for the sake of form.
Sir Roger Jones: You have got me worried now.

Q250 Chair: We will take it that you are Sir Roger Jones. I am David Davies. Basically, we are conducting an inquiry into economic development in Wales. We are very interested in how you saw the role of the WDA in your time there. To kick off, in particular what changing patterns of investment did you see? What was the difference in the types of companies and industries that came into Wales in the years when you were with the WDA?
Sir Roger Jones: Prior to the time I started I was involved with the training and enterprise councils and sorting out the LG mess. We had put all our eggs in a single basket; there were very little funds left over to encourage other investments, and, as we all know, tragically, it did not work out.

Q251 Chair: Was the problem that we were just going round the world saying, "Have some money and come to Wales", and people were taking the money, coming and then disappearing at the first opportunity, or is that too simplistic?
Sir Roger Jones: That is probably too simplistic. Proper companies do not establish a business just because there are grants there. They are much more interested in skills and markets. If a television assembly or electronics plant in Wales gave them market entry, I believe that was the major reason they were there, not because of the grants.

Q252 Chair: In your paper you have been critical.
Sir Roger Jones: I have rather, haven't I?

Q253 Chair: You have not pulled your punches, which is great and we like that. To play devil's advocate, is there not an argument that we were bound to lose out on those kinds of manufacturing industries because of the growth of China and the Far East? Was it not inevitable that it would be harder for us to compete in manufacturing?
Sir Roger Jones: With hindsight, all of us have 20/20 vision, have we not? We really were not to know. I am going back now to 2001 and 2002. Yes, there were signs of the Far East markets changing substantially, but they had not done so at that point. Upon reflection, we could have done better. There were different things we could have done, but it was a big beast and the big beast was captured and brought to Newport. You can't really knock it. I think we should have looked more carefully at the political risk because, if we saw the places in the UK where LG had other plants, then any cutback they were going to be making could have been in south Wales or elsewhere. I do not think that risk was properly evaluated.

Q254 Mrs James: In the 1980s and 1990s we had huge success in Wales in attracting inward investment, but was there too much emphasis on creating low-skilled jobs and not enough on the long-term need to invest in skilled labour?
Sir Roger Jones: The point is that if you do not have a highly skilled work force you will not get the jobs. You have to bring in the industries that can use the level of skills you have currently. We can complain and say that these were low-skilled jobs, but by and large we had a low-skilled work force. We start off by improving the skills of the work force so it is ready for investment.

Q255 Mrs James: You talked about the LG factory. In a previous Welsh Affairs Committee inquiry we visited where LG had gone. We visited Poland where the factory went and it is now empty and being used as storage space because they have moved on to China. I was quite interested in what you said earlier about the need to know what the market is and to be at the entry level of the market. Will we ever be in that position, because things are moving so quickly?
Sir Roger Jones: Unless we are tracking the markets very carefully, that is where it starts off. You then see what industries are required in order to enter those markets. But it all starts off with the markets. If you do it the other way round, it is a recipe for failure.

Q256 Mrs James: I want to ask you a question about the Massey report. It identifies a deteriorating performance in Wales in attracting inward investment in the period post-2000. Why do you think Wales lost its competitive advantage in attracting inward investment?

Sir Roger Jones: There was not a lot of inward investment around. Things dried up fairly quickly. I think the Welsh Assembly Government were minded that the sun would stay in the sky for ever, that all these things would happen and all the glory would descend upon them when it happened. They did not look at the downside risk and the skills required in order to stay afloat and win in a more difficult market.

Q257 Mrs James: Is trying to attract inward investment, including foreign investment, still a valid policy?

Sir Roger Jones: We do not have the capital base ourselves. I do not see any other solution. We cannot go to government and ask for handouts. We are at 75% of UK per capita in Wales at the moment. What are we going to do? We have got to get more investment in, upskill the work force, earn more money, just playing up GDP.

Q258 Mrs James: We need a successful investment policy then.

Sir Roger Jones: We need a successful investment policy.

Q259 Mrs James: How would we judge that?

Sir Roger Jones: If I had the skills, I would be living in the south of France or somewhere now. I wouldn't be living in Brecon.

Q260 Mrs James: Come, come, come! Brecon can compete any day.

Sir Roger Jones: It is a matter of risks. You have to understand the market, go there and evaluate what industries and companies we can go for. What is the purpose? What advantage do we give to a company for investing in Wales? If we are not doing all of those things, we will never succeed.

Q261 Mrs James: What you are talking about is the requirement to be fleet of foot, is it not?

Sir Roger Jones: Yes.

Q262 Mrs James: We have got to be really reactive and be able to change quickly.

Sir Roger Jones: Absolutely.

Q263 Mrs James: How do we grow that culture?

Sir Roger Jones: To start with, you do not get anyone who is fleet of foot—sorry, sorry, sorry—in the civil service. You are asking the wrong people to become fleet of foot if you are asking the civil service to do so.

Mrs James: I think there are some questions about that later.

Q264 Jonathan Edwards: If you were formulating an FDI policy now, would it be based primarily on grants, or would you be looking at a favourable tax environment?

Sir Roger Jones: I have never been a major advocate of grants. The only advantage of grants for indigenous companies or companies coming in is that, if you get a letter from the Government saying, "We're going to give you this much grant", you can take it straight to the bank and say, "Lend me money at favourable rates against this letter." That is a huge advantage of having a grant. The actual quantum of the money that you draw down is not that important. Access to markets is the most important thing. Companies do not need grants; they need business. That is how I would try and do it. I would use government influence to try to help people to enter markets that otherwise might be difficult for them.

Q265 Karen Lumley: What do you think the strengths and perhaps the weaknesses of the WDA were?

Sir Roger Jones: It was an organisation ready for change. There were some serious flaws in the WDA, and I readily admit that. The management style was wrong. Its weakness was that it encouraged interference from civil servants and Ministers, saying, "Are we doing all right? What are we doing today? Are you happy with this?", instead of having a board that said, "This is what we intend to do. We will come back and tell you in six months whether or not it has been successful." Micro-management by people who do not know very much is a very dangerous practice.

Q266 Karen Lumley: In what way did it insulate politicians and civil servants from the risk?

Sir Roger Jones: There is someone there to say, "It was my fault; I got it wrong. The Minister said this to me. He was quite right and I was wrong."

Q267 Karen Lumley: How did you sell Wales as a location for inward investment?

Sir Roger Jones: The environment and quality of life for employees was a big selling point. Unfortunately, it was very difficult to sell our skills base because it was not that good. Certain people, like tool-makers, were in very short supply in Wales from 2000 onwards. It was very difficult. Key skills were missing. So we could not sell those but we tried to sell what we could. We sold training. We said, "If you come here and do not find the right skills, we will give you money. You tell us what training you want and we will implement that on your behalf", so that is worth while.

Q268 Chair: At this point perhaps I may say how much I appreciate the very frank and short answers that you are giving to us. Perhaps you will give another one on the quality of the people who are coming out of universities at the moment and the courses that some are undertaking. If 50% of those who go to university are undertaking courses that may, some argue, not be that pertinent to industry, is that good or bad? Is this the right way to go?

Sir Roger Jones: As pro-chancellor of Swansea university my answer will be somewhat clouded. I cannot simply say and write off that 50% is too much, but what is important is where our universities are in the league tables. Swansea university is No. 4 in the UK in engineering after Leeds, Sheffield and Imperial College. We have some very good things happening but you build on your strengths. You find out what you do well and then tell the world about it.

Q269 Guto Bebb: I want to go back to the question asked by Karen Lumley about the strengths and weaknesses of the WDA. You specifically said that it was an organisation ready for change. To clarify that, do you believe that in terms of the WDA in general, or are you talking specifically about the part of the WDA which tried to attract inward investment? This inquiry is looking specifically at inward investment. Do you believe that that department was having problems, or was it a general problem?

Sir Roger Jones: I was looking at the general picture. The structure was one where you had the Welsh Assembly Government handling trade and the WDA handling inward investment. As I said earlier, what people want are markets. That is the main driver. I do not think that separating the two in the way the Welsh Assembly Government did was an effective strategy at all because we did not know where the markets were.

Q270 Mrs James: You mentioned the lack of tool-makers. Can you see a direct link with the demise of heavy industry? People like my husband, who was apprentice-trained and qualified, came out of the heavy industries; they worked in the big factories.

Sir Roger Jones: I had a factory in Tredegar. I think it is probably the most successful indigenous company. I sold it to the management it was so good. I had taken it as far as I could take it, so I gave it to them. But you are quite right. We have wonderful skills available if you are prepared to find them and work with them. It is difficult clay to work. My goodness, once you have got the right stuff, it is magic; it is a very good work force, so we can do it. Those skills came largely from the coal industry. These were the engineers, electricians and so on who were used to much more robust machines but they could turn their hands to smaller stuff. The makings were there. What did we do? We declared many of them redundant and came out of the work force altogether. That is a dumb thing to do.

Q271 Mrs James: My husband is 59. He came out of the collieries and went into a factory and stayed there.

Sir Roger Jones: Do you understand what I am saying?

Mrs James: Yes. They are very much needed.

Q272 Chair: Does anybody want to come in on this point?

Sir Roger Jones: I am sorry.

Chair: Not at all. We are fascinated by this.

Q273 Geraint Davies: In your view, grants are not very important and it is about skills and markets, but, given your experience of Swansea, do you agree that one of the key successes there is to establish a research and development cluster that is networked into industry and works with it to develop globally relevant products, like Tata out of Swansea, Rolls-Royce and Boots? It is not about selling tellies down the road in England; it is a matter of having that cluster of activity and building on the engineering and equity you mentioned. You can then provide a platform for future jobs based in Wales rather than being an outpost of a big multinational.

Sir Roger Jones: I like to think I had a small influence in taking the university in that direction, but it is for others to decide that.

Geraint Davies: So, yes.

Q274 Owen Smith: That is a very interesting take on the skills deficit, and I think all of us can agree that is evident. Is that not a much longer-run problem? Is it not true that perhaps the relative success of Wales in respect of heavy industry masked a more profound long-run deficit in education and skills? Is that not what we were dealing with in the era of relative success that you talked about? Is it not very difficult to imagine how any agency, whether it be the Welsh Assembly Government, WDA, or its successor bodies, can address that quickly? Will it not take a long time to turn round?

Sir Roger Jones: The longer answer to your question is yes; the shorter answer is no.

Owen Smith: Now I am confused.

Chair: By one letter in fact.

Sir Roger Jones: It works both ways. We were doing things right, if you bring in employers to decide on obtaining the skills and the level of skills required. Lots of jobs are becoming deskilled. I can bore for Wales on this subject. I will not try to give you a diagram, but, if you look at a bell-shaped curve, the skills requirement is biphasic. There is a huge peak there, it levels off for management skills, and then you have the technical skills. These guys run the process; these guys manage the process; and these guys design and set up the process. I am sorry; I should have had something to show you. Getting the right level of skills is the trick to industrial development. You are quite right. If you give people insufficient work to use their skills, they become very dissatisfied and it does not work out. On the other side, if you give them work that is too difficult for their skills, that, again, is disenabling. It is a matter of pitching the right level of skills for the job. The people who can best tell you what level of skills is required are of course employers because they buy competencies. You do not buy qualifications but competencies—people who can do the job—and we call it employment.

Q275 Jessica Morden: Earlier you were very honest about the flaws you saw in the WDA. When Dr Ball from Swansea university gave evidence to this inquiry, he commented that he did not feel it was arm's length from government, which you mentioned; he did not feel it had the appropriate policies; he thought it was poorly managed and led; and it did not have clear objectives. Do you think that is a fair assessment based on what you said earlier?

Sir Roger Jones: Yes. As I say in my paper, about half the employees of the WDA were inward-focused, making sure that the information was available for the civil service and their political masters, which left you 50%, at best, to go and interface with the private sector, which is where the jobs were.

Q276 Jessica Morden: When you were chair of the WDA what did you do to try to address those weaknesses? What was your aim?

Sir Roger Jones: It was very difficult. I pleaded to be left alone. "Let us get on with the job."

Karen Lumley: No chance.

Sir Roger Jones: Therefore, what I am advocating is that, if you have an arm's length agency, make it arm's length so that all the instructions and everything else come in to the board, which then discuss them and accept them, leaving the operation to carry on in the way it should.

Q277 Mr Williams: How successful was the WDA in working with UKTI? What was the relationship in the promotion of Wales?

Sir Roger Jones: It was rather strange. I was the representative on UK overseas trade for Wales; I was there even before I was chairman of the WDA. UKTI is a strange organisation. In a way, it gets taken over by the export manager in the company. The company making widgets has an export manager and he is the one who goes on to UKTI. He goes on the trade missions and various other things. The guys you really want in UKTI are those who are designing the widgets and understand what other widget makers are doing. By and large, I think it is represented by the wrong people. I find it very boring.

Q278 Mr Williams: In your submission you say that you felt the decision to have a spread of offices in all continents was flawed. When this Committee went to Germany, we heard that the German Chamber of Industry and Commerce had 120 offices in 80 countries, and the Länder often had their own representation throughout the world. To what extent should Wales have a spread of offices across the world, and how should those offices be utilised?

Sir Roger Jones: The need to have offices overseas is now probably less. You have Skype and various other things. If you have a centre looking out into the world that has good language skills and people there, you can cover the ground from the UK, followed up by two, three or four trips a year. You then have much better control over those people than if you have them in Los Angeles and they send you a postcard once a month. It is difficult to manage them.

Q279 Mr Williams: It is more a case of getting the right people out there.

Sir Roger Jones: Yes.

Q280 Mr Williams: Like the Chairman said, it was very refreshing to read your very robust submission about the origins of International Business Wales and the end of WDA. At the time a joint ministerial statement was made which talked about the hope for a new, sharply focused commercial organisation which was the best of its kind not only in the UK but in Europe, but your written evidence is very concerning and robust. Would you like to say more about the impact of the abolition of the WDA?

Sir Roger Jones: I remember him saying that. They were not my words but the Minister's.

Q281 Mr Williams: I suspected as much. Can you say more about the impact of the abolition of the WDA?

Sir Roger Jones: This is a very important point. If you get only one thing from the discussion this morning, it is that the private sector is interested in one thing only: outcomes. The public sector is obsessed with process. In my life, personally I do not give a bugger for the process. I am concerned only with the outcomes I can get. I get paid only when the stuff gets on the truck and leaves the factory. You must have process to get to that, but it is not the be-all and end-all; getting the outcomes is the important thing.

Q282 Mr Williams: What was the debate like at the time? You gave warnings about the three years to realise the mistake; three years to decide what to do; and another three years to implement change, with dire implications for parts of the Welsh economy.

Sir Roger Jones: I was not afraid to say it.

Q283 Mr Williams: What was the debate like at the time? What was the political reaction?

Sir Roger Jones: I was ridiculed. "We've got to do this. These wonderful civil servants have got to be able to understand how to get industry going. Yes, they understand everything. After all, they all have MBA degrees, so they will hit the ground running, won't they?"

Q284 Chair: Everyone wants to come back again, Sir Roger, including me. If I understand it, are you saying that, rather than have lots of offices round the world, we would be better off simply having a group of people who can fly off on trade missions, follow up very quickly with meetings within 48 hours anywhere in the world with anyone who shows an interest in Wales, and this would be considerably cheaper than locating offices all over the place and having staff to man them permanently when there may not be much to do from month to month?

Sir Roger Jones: I believe so. The management of those staff is the difficult thing. They are far, far away.

Q285 Chair: If we did that, presumably we would have to be honest with the public and say it will mean that a lot of people fly off in planes and do not get any business, but it is still a lot cheaper than having them going off in a plane once a year, not seeing them for a year, having to pay their wages and create an office for them.

Sir Roger Jones: Yes.

Q286 Guto Bebb: I was very supportive of the WDA and I think that the loss of the WDA has been problematic in the Welsh context. You said that the end results were more important than the process, but is it not true that when, for a period of time, the WDA was very concerned about the end result and not so concerned about the process it got itself into hot water? Because we are dealing with public money, the process will always be important in the context of a body that is fully funded by the taxpayer.

Sir Roger Jones: That is the dilemma. What you have to have are individuals within a board who accept total responsibility. If they get it wrong, they are the ones who face the sanction. Fire them.

Q287 Jonathan Edwards: On the job of selling Wales and the discussion about UKTI, should it be for UKTI to sell the Welsh economy abroad, or should it be a matter for the Welsh Government?

Sir Roger Jones: I think it is for the people of Wales to ensure that the representation they get in the large cities of the world is the right kind of stuff. We have missed out on a really big opportunity. If you look at the Joneses and Williamses in North America, we do not do anything to try to pull in these people. Why do we not have a Jones day at some time?

Q288 Chair: Or a Davies day.

Sir Roger Jones: Yes; a Davies day would be better. There is no ambition; there is nothing there at all. One morning in Chicago the announcer on ZF Radio said, "This is March 1; it is St David's Day. St David is the patron saint of Wales, dolphins and other marine animals." There rests the case for the defence, m'lud.

Q289 Owen Smith: You seem to be saying that one of the problems is that the Government, whether it is the Welsh Government or another government, do not really have insight into what industry needs and what the trends are in order to direct investment. How do government do that better?

Sir Roger Jones: By talking to a man or woman who knows and being prepared to listen. We have the expertise; there is enough experience. There are some very successful businessmen and women in Wales. Why do politicians think they know better than anybody else? I am sorry; that is a rhetorical question.

Q290 Owen Smith: That is very clear. Once these know-nothing politicians or their envoys have listened, what should they do, because I cannot see that you are saying anything beyond, "Get out the way"?

Sir Roger Jones: A good start.

Q291 Owen Smith: Clearly, that is what you are suggesting, but is that always necessarily the case? If markets are key, government can in part make markets or help to make markets, or certainly inspire them, and there are other things government can do. What should we be doing? What should the strategic vision be?

Sir Roger Jones: The strategic vision should be for government to sign up to agreements on markets, market sizes, products that are required and costs, and then you can get the product into that market with the Government. To give an example, I had a company called Zymed in St Asaph. It made a fantastic device that monitored the drips in a bag in hospital. It did not need pumps; you just hung up the bag and it would count the drips. Every single trust in the UK bought that equipment, with one exception. Guess which one that was: Wales. We could not sell one in Wales. They said, "No, no, no. We haven't approved it." We can work with government. You are quite right. Working with the big spending departments is a great opportunity.

Q292 Susan Elan Jones: Probably our next inquiry will be into the validity of international Jones day. It is a rather good idea. Do you have any concerns about the restructuring that is currently taking place in the Department for Business, Enterprise, Technology and Science and the abolition of International Business Wales, with the proviso that some members of this Committee recently visited Germany and spoke to staff at UKTI who said that, because of that organisation, there had been little or no communication with International Business Wales? How do you think this will affect the ability of Wales, if indeed at all, to attract inward investors?

Sir Roger Jones: I am out of touch; I have had no contact whatsoever with that Department for the last four or five years. I do not know what is happening there. What I asked for and the Welsh Assembly Government promised was a heritage document. I asked to get all the facts about the history and performance of the WDA. Yes, you scrap it, but let's get all the numbers down in a single document so that we can have something to compare it with. Guess what? Nothing happened. They absolutely refused. I did follow it up but they refused to provide us with a heritage document. As I said, they do not like outcomes; they stay with the process.

Q293 Susan Elan Jones: I am thinking of a subtle way of putting this. Do you think that, with the abolition of the RDAs in England, there is any way that Wales could benefit from that?

Sir Roger Jones: I think so. If we get our act together and can get a proper, effective arm's length operation, we can take on anywhere in the UK.

Q294 Geraint Davies: When we were in Düsseldorf and Berlin talking to UK Trade and Industry, their function, in part, was basically to get prospective inward investment from Germany. They would have a list of factories that wanted to come to Britain, and then RDAs would draw down those and bid for them in terms of skills, location and all the rest of it. Because the RDAs had been abolished, all of these bids were available that Wales could have taken advantage of, but we were told that they were restructuring and essentially that opportunity was not being taken. I was wondering how in your view an arm's length body should be structured to take advantage of the infrastructure of UK Trade and Industry and to organise Welsh industry to take best advantage of the Olympics, for example, where we did very badly in bidding for the £6.2 billion. I think we got £0.5 million of business. How should we have an arm's length, or quasi-arm's length, structure that can take advantage of big trading or procurement or inward investment opportunities? How would it look? Presumably, it would not just be WDA2, would it?

Sir Roger Jones: Do you know what the value of that brand was? We spent at least £50 million in establishing the WDA brand, and these people just said, "No, no. We want a little white dragon now; we don't want that one. Throw it away." I would argue that really belongs to the people of Wales, not some folk in the Assembly building. My personal view is that it is a complete mess. Your question was: how do we establish this?

Q295 Geraint Davies: Do we work with UK Trade and Industry and what does the arm's length body that is accessible look like?

Sir Roger Jones: If they do not pay us, then we just go home. All of this world is competitive. Let's go and play. I do not think we should divvy it up so the north-east has that one and the south-west that one. Let's get in there, because the decision will be taken by the German investor.

Q296 Geraint Davies: But what would the arm's length successor to the WDA look like as an organisation?

Sir Roger Jones: I would encourage them to get in there and become competitive.

Q297 Stuart Andrew: Six key sectors have been identified by the Welsh Government for investment. Are they the right ones?

Sir Roger Jones: The short answer to that is that I do not know. I suspect not. Certainly, life sciences have to be in there. As to high-value tourism, we were doing very badly with that. I think we can do much, much more with high-value tourism.

Q298 Chair: Do you agree with things like gamekeeping courses? Is there a lack of this?

Sir Roger Jones: That is why I am partly deaf; I have been doing too much shooting in my life.

Q299 Chair: In all seriousness, we run courses for surf studies on the basis that lots of surfing goes on in Wales, but there are no gamekeeping courses—

Sir Roger Jones: Not one.

Q300 Chair:—because it is politically incorrect, but am I right in thinking that some Americans will pay thousands of pounds for a weekend in Wales?

Sir Roger Jones: I did a calculation. The political correctness that we have in Cardiff Bay is palpable. The value of shooting to the Welsh economy was about £80 million throughout the season. That was about the same size as the lamb export business. That

could be doubled ever so easily if only there was a bit of focus. We could have done it. We still choose not to do it; we do not train. It is the Department for Education that chooses what skills people are to be taught. It is the guy who employs them who needs the gamekeepers, so we go to Scotland for them, don't we?

Chair: Thank you very much. I see lots of pens scribbling furiously in the back.

Q301 Owen Smith: As a keen and committed fisherman, I completely agree with you.

Sir Roger Jones: There you go.

Q302 Owen Smith: Would you add, I take it, that training gillies and capitalising on our fantastic rivers and fishing is another area where we fail to come up to the mark as yet?

Sir Roger Jones: Absolutely, yes. The river Towy is excellent; it provides the best sea trout in the world, and yet we have never trained a gillie, as far as I know.

Q303 Guto Bebb: I also agree with you entirely when you say that tourism should be one of the six key sectors. It is inexplicable that tourism is not seen as a priority area for economic development in Wales, but that is an aside. The evidence we have collected so far in this inquiry has identified the fact that there has been a lack of co-operation between UKTI, the Welsh Assembly and even the Welsh Office. You stated that you had not been involved in the past four years, but, if you were given a magic wand, how would you try to develop a working relationship between the Welsh Assembly and UKTI to try to ensure that the image of Wales was made available to investors in all parts of the world?

Sir Roger Jones: It is an awful thing to say, but when this subject has been broached with me by well-meaning individuals I have made the comment that not enough time has passed yet and there is not enough pain yet to go back and re-engage. They will make the same mistake again unless they understand the pain it has caused them. I am sorry. That may be small-minded but I feel that way. For me, re-engaging is probably not an option.

Q304 Guto Bebb: Even if you are not going to re-engage but you were in a position to influence, how would you see the Welsh Assembly working with the UK Government to try to ensure that Wales had a fair crack of the whip when it came to attracting inward investment? Granted that in my view the decisions made have been problematic, how can we try to improve the situation?

Sir Roger Jones: By establishing a new organisation that requires a strong board with some really good people, explaining what is required and letting them get on and do it.

Q305 Guto Bebb: And take responsibility for it.

Sir Roger Jones: And take responsibility, yes— every penny.

Q306 Chair: Sir Roger, we are about a minute away from our allocated time. I feel that we ought to end on that high note. I thank you particularly for the way you have given evidence, which is far more entertaining, frank and direct than many, and also for the written evidence. As far as I am concerned, those who are submitting written evidence may follow your example, because that kind of evidence gets read, even if some people would disagree with it. Diolch yn fawr iawn.

Sir Roger Jones: You are all very kind. Diolch yn fawr iawn i chi.

Witness: **Mr Glenn Massey,** gave evidence.

Q307 Chair: Good morning, Mr Massey. Thank you very much indeed for coming along today and for the report you sent us. Perhaps you would elucidate why you believe Wales lost its competitive edge after the WDA went and whether or not that had anything to do with it.

Glenn Massey: Before coming specifically to the WDA in Wales, I think it is true to say that in about 2000 the UK—in those days it was the DTI—took the view that manufacturing was not particularly important, that we were almost a post-industrial society and that there were far more interesting sectors on which to focus. As a result, the UK as a whole, not just Wales, lost its way in terms of inward investment. I think that is the starting point for this. If you look at the statistics, in relative terms Wales has gone backwards rather than forwards over the last 10 years or so. I suspect there are quite a number of reasons for that. If you go back to the 1970s, 1980s and up to the late 1990s, Wales had a very competitive package in terms of being attractive to inward investment.

If you think back to the types of investment that were around at that time, it was mainly consumer electronics. There were a few exceptions to that. They tended to be large scale, not particularly capital intensive, with a few exceptions, but very job-oriented. Wales had a very compelling package at that time. We had a lot of unemployment, relatively low wages compared with Western Europe, an open-house policy towards inward investment, a grant regime that was pretty attractive, going back to the early 1980s when regional selective assistance came in. At that time in the development areas it was based on five times someone's annual salary. It was a pretty attractive package.

What happened? Lots of inwards investment came in. There was not much competition around at the time. The RDAs did not exist at that time. Wales and Scotland basically had a free run at all those inward investment projects and were very successful. Obviously, things changed during the 1980s and 1990s. England got its act together and became much more competitive. By the time we got to the late 1990s and into the early 2000s eastern Europe was now part of the EU. They had by and large highly educated work forces, with big grant regimes and much lower taxes than the UK. Suddenly, the UK fell off a cliff for those large types of inward investment projects. That is not to say the UK was not successful for FDI; it was. It still remained No.1 in Europe, and that was likely to continue. However, there was a shift away from the regions. Scotland, Wales and parts of northern England were very successful in the 1990s. From 2000 onwards, most of the FDI, with a few exceptions, is now in London and the south-east of England. The centre of gravity has changed.

Q308 Chair: That is probably because most of the FDI in terms of money now goes into financial services which tend to cluster around London. Is that right?

Glenn Massey: Technology and life sciences. It is not just financial.

Q309 Mrs James: You have given a very good overview of what happened and your report, etcetera. You have covered a lot of the questions I wanted to ask you. I want to tease out a little further what you have just said. You talked about going backwards, not forwards. Obviously, we have all got our eye on the prize. Everybody is chasing the same investments and jobs. What do you think is the offer in Wales that can put us back in the position where we are competing?

Glenn Massey: When I did this study back in 2009, it became pretty clear that the business proposition Wales was selling overseas was regional selective assistance grants, which had been around since 1982. Sadly, that was fine when you had the type of projects around that I mentioned earlier in the 1970s, 1980s and up to the mid-1990s, where that was a very attractive proposition, but inward investment is not like that now. Those types of consumer electronics and automotive-type projects and many jobs tend to gravitate towards eastern Europe or China and the Far East. We have to recognise that we are no longer in that game. The problem Wales had was that the toolset it developed to attract that type of investment did not change to reflect the new world economy. The FDI that is coming into the UK now is not really looking for regional selective assistance; that is inappropriate. As a consequence of that, we should have developed a suite of other instruments—whether it be skills, a property proposition or R and D through universities, a whole raft of things—to make things attractive to inward investment companies. We have not done so. I think there is a recognition in Wales that something needs to be done, and I still think it is in the process of trying to figure out what it is. Sadly, that has been going on for a long time.

Q310 Mrs James: When I speak to the public, this is the question that I get asked day after day, and I am sure many of my colleagues do. When are we going to go back to attracting big industry? When are we going to go back to manufacturing? We have heard lots of experts speak here in this inquiry.

Glenn Massey: We are never going to go back and be attractive to low-value manufacturing. That has gone, unless we become a low-wage economy again, and I do not think any of us want that. What we have to do in terms of manufacturing is attract high added-value projects, and there are still lots of them around. Roger Jones touched upon the problems we have in terms of a skilled economy. We have a few very high quality companies in Wales which have very well-trained work forces that are world class. Sadly, you can count them on one hand. A major investment needs to be made to upskill the work force. It is not necessarily at the bottom end; it is at the top end where management are concerned. Management skills in Wales by and large are not great. One of the jobs I had with PricewaterhouseCoopers, or PwC as it is now known, is that, for my sins, I was on the listening end of lots of presentations from development agencies around the world. I used to spend my life listening to them, so I know what to look for in a presentation. I think that over the last 10 years Wales has not had a compelling presentation.

Q311 Chair: Do you think that the merger of the international division of the WDA and Wales Trade International was good or bad?
Glenn Massey: I do not honestly know because I have never dealt with the trade side of it. It would be unfair of me to comment on that.

Q312 Chair: Your report undertook a benchmarking exercise of International Business Wales. What were the key findings of that particular study? What do you think? Were they doing a good job or a bad job?
Glenn Massey: You have to look at this in context. You cannot look at IBW in isolation; that is unfair on the management and staff. You have to look at the department as a whole. What seems to have happened over the last few years—it was even true of the WDA—is that it was a big organisation and people operated in silos. You had a budget for which you were responsible but you did not look left or right. If you were the grants team, you had a budget; if you were IBW, you had a budget; if you had a property budget, you were over here. Very rarely was this ever integrated into a coherent package.

Q313 Chair: You heard the comments made by Sir Roger and echoed by some here, including myself. Do you think there is a case for saying that IBW should not have offices all over the place?
Glenn Massey: Roger probably went too far, so I do not agree with him on that. One thing I have found out doing business in the world is that you have to be in front of the decision makers; you cannot do that over the telephone or by Skype. You have to be there. You can argue about whether that means people actually flying out to do the business or having an office out there. I think you have to have some representation overseas. About half of FDI coming into the UK comes from the US. To me, it would seem unusual if Wales did not have some representation in this major market.

Q314 Karen Lumley: How would you judge a successful investment policy?
Glenn Massey: Something that Roger touched upon several times was outcomes. Roger is quite right that it has been a process-driven activity. It is changing. If you look at the success of the overseas offices over the last 10 years or so, it has involved lots of people, resource and cost. Bear in mind that Wales was costing twice as much as any other region in the UK

with the exception of Scotland to deliver very little. So the costs were there, the budget must have been there to pay for all this, but the outcomes were not.

Q315 Karen Lumley: If we are delivering very little, how do we get to the stage where we are delivering good stuff for Wales?
Glenn Massey: Expensively delivering very little.

Q316 Karen Lumley: A reduction from 25% to almost 6% or 7% in the last few years is not good news, is it?
Glenn Massey: Some would argue, given the population base of Wales, that is a reasonable performance. Personally, I do not think it is but some would argue that. Given the fact that Wales has the biggest budget other than Scotland and it has more staff than anyone else, it should be getting at least 10%.

Q317 Geraint Davies: To what extent do you think the strategy for inward investment should build on existing clusters rather than go outside them? I am thinking specifically of a conversation we had with GE Aviation who said they would be happy to host a joint meeting with Boeing to get them into Wales. In your paper you mention that Boeing has a joint venture in Yorkshire. Given we are a small country, rather than going out and doing everything, do you think we should say, "Where are our strengths?", build on those and use the universities as part of that mix?
Glenn Massey: Yes. We have a few world-class companies in Wales and we should leverage those as much as we possibly can. I do not think we have world-class universities in Wales, but we have some reasonable ones. One of the disappointments for me over the years has been the fact that the Welsh universities have not spun out lots of exciting new projects, or not enough. They have spun out one or two but not many. Why that is so needs to be looked at. There is lots of research going on in Wales. There is a lot of very high quality research going into Wales. Again, unless that moves into some kind of business, personally I would challenge why we are doing it, but I have a very business-oriented viewpoint on these things.

Q318 Geraint Davies: How do you translate a good idea into a commercial product? What are the best examples of that, and where are we going wrong in doing that?
Glenn Massey: We should look at MIT, which is an obvious example of how lecturers are basically entrepreneurs; they mix the two. Unfortunately, not enough people are doing that in Wales. As to the way Welsh universities are funded, you should get more money if you can spin out companies and ideas rather than pure research; in other words, there has to be an outcome.

Q319 Owen Smith: To continue that theme and return to the question I asked Roger about the extent to which government can act to try to create markets, one area in which universities in Wales are very good is research in respect of hydrogen, in particular hydrogen fuel cells for motor vehicles. The universities of Glamorgan and Swansea are working hard on that. It struck me that the difference between the UK, not just Wales, and Europe and places like Japan is that governments there are investing, for example, in creating a network of hydrogen fuelling centres to allow hydrogen fuel cell cars to become a reality. They are spending billions of pounds to do that. Japan and Germany are doing it. Are those the kinds of big, bold things government across the UK should be thinking about? Is it feasible that Wales could take a lead in trying to come up with something like that?

Glenn Massey: Not for billions of pounds, but Wales can take the lead in creating the right environment. I do not think government creates jobs, but it can create an environment in which business can flourish and pump prime various initiatives; it can help businesses feel secure and also want to grow in Wales. I think that is the role of government, but those initiatives at the moment are lacking and they need to be worked on.

Q320 Owen Smith: You implied earlier that over the last 10 years Wales had got worse at attracting FDI versus the south-east of England. You also said you thought that was not all related to financial services or other services. What is the mix? How much of that FDI that the south-east has attracted is services or financial services-related and how much is advanced manufacturing?

Glenn Massey: When I drive along the M4 I see Microsoft all over the place. They must have half a dozen very large facilities around Heathrow and Reading. I can understand that, when they dipped their toe into the UK market, they wanted to be near Heathrow and be able to jump on an aircraft and go to and fro. But they have been here for more than 20 years now and they still have a huge amount of investment in that area. I do not see why Wales cannot compete for that kind of business. It needs to have a proposition that Microsoft want to buy, like a skilled work force or some relationship with universities that they do not currently get from Reading or London. What we have to do is to go and talk to these companies at a very senior level—this is the real knack—and say to Mr Microsoft, "What do we need to do in Wales to get one of your big R and D or software facilities down there? Tell us." I am not certain that anyone has ever had that discussion with them. We guess. We try to sell them quality of life; we say there is a factory over here and a site there and we have fantastic universities. I can tell you that I have heard that a thousand times from every region of Europe, so why are you different?

Q321 Jessica Morden: You have touched on what you think the Welsh Government are not doing. If you do not think it is enough, is there an argument for setting up a body similar to the WDA?

Glenn Massey: I have never been a big fan of structures, by which I mean that it is really about management and people. Management and people can work within any structure if they are good. I am not hung up on reinventing the WDA. What I am hung up

on is having a delivery team that can actually deliver something, and I am not bothered where it is.

Q322 Jessica Morden: Do you think that Wales is taking full advantage of the abolition of the RDAs, or could it do more?

Glenn Massey: For the last 18 months it has been inward looking, for obvious reasons. We have had the economic renewal programme and the abolition of IBW. A lot of staff, not all, have become very disillusioned and morale is quite low. If you are working in that kind of environment, motivation is hard.

Q323 Jessica Morden: Is that a no then?

Glenn Massey: I think it is a no. Take it as a no.

Q324 Chair: Is there an argument for saying that all these things—IBW, WDA and UKTI—are a waste of time and any company wanting to come to Wales or any region of England, to Europe or anywhere at all will look at utilities, tax rates and employment costs, and if somebody will give them a little extra that is fine but it will just be the icing on the cake? All we are doing is throwing money away which we could be spending on improving the utilities, the transport infrastructure and broadband or reducing taxes and that would have more effect.

Glenn Massey: The truth of the matter is that probably 90% of FDI would come to the UK regardless of anyone's involvement. Why? Because there is a market opportunity that a company wants to exploit and so they will come. The other 10% are genuinely footloose and are looking at Ireland, France, Germany and the UK. Those are the ones on which we should focus. The other 90% will come anyway. When I read all these FDI statistics that UKTI put out every year, I take them with a pinch of salt because most of them would have come anyway. The first port of call for most companies coming from America is not UKTI. They phone up their lawyer or accountant and ask for some advice about how to structure the business or what they should do. The first port of call is not UKTI, the regional development agency and the Welsh Government. People tend to forget that.

Q325 Chair: It sounds like you half agree with my deliberately slightly outrageous statement.

Glenn Massey: No. I am half agreeing with you that the 90% will come and, therefore, government or any development agency have no role to play in those whatsoever; for the other 10% they do.

Q326 Geraint Davies: As to those who are concerned about the decision to scrap the WDA, the reasoning behind it is that a recognised brand was lost. In terms of your previous answer, you do not think that is an issue at all.

Glenn Massey: It is for those 10% of companies that are looking and are genuinely mobile. There is no doubt that the WDA had a brand name around the world. Roger Jones is quite correct that they spent a lot of money on that, and it was a shame that it was lost. Despite all that investment, Wales, frankly and sadly, is not a well-known brand in many parts of the world even now, and it certainly was not when the WDA was there as well, so it is not quite right.

Q327 Geraint Davies: I want to ask a couple of related questions. First, are the six key sectors for investment that have been identified by the Welsh Assembly the correct ones? We have already heard that people think high-value tourism might be included. I have mentioned aerospace. Given the size of Wales, do you think that maybe the marketing strategy should be much more targeted on particular sectors in particular countries for inward investment to match what we have got, and to have insight that most big companies will decide to go to Britain as opposed to Wales and look at our competitive offer versus other regions that are at that point taking prospective inward investment decisions?
Glenn Massey: What I can tell you from my experience of how this tends to work is that I am sitting with a company looking at half a dozen countries in Europe, so we are one of the 10% that is genuinely mobile. We will look through a whole raft of things that you would naturally consider: taxation; ease of doing business; regulation; salary costs; and skill levels. At the end of the day, you will come down to a few regions. As to where you go, it is almost decided by the flick of a coin. If you are sitting in California, you have probably never been to Wales; you have never been to Saxony. How do you make that call? It is very difficult. It often comes down to soft things that never get on a list. Long ago in the annals of history—it was 12 years ago so I can tell you the story—MBNA was going to come to Wales. It was all set up. At the final minute the managing director of the company came over with his wife and she did not like Cardiff, so they went to Chester. There was no business reason for that whatsoever; it was what I would call a soft issue and that made the choice.

Q328 Owen Smith: I think there is a lot of truth in what you say. Before I came into this place, I was UK director on the board of the world's biggest biotech company. The difficulties of getting those companies to make big decisions about relocation are legion and I will not go into them. Is not one of the quick wins we could have in Wales massive improvement of infrastructure and connectivity down the M4 corridor and the rail infrastructure? Fortunately, we now have some investment in rail. Is not the other quick win far better marketing of the lifestyle benefits of coming to Wales—the beauty of the country and the lifestyle opportunities it provides? Looking at northern California, the success of that part of the world in attracting companies out of other parts of America was predicated very much on lifestyle opportunities. Should we not be thinking about that in the short term?
Glenn Massey: The infrastructure problems in Wales are not a short-term fix, are they? We are talking about a 20-year investment programme. I used to travel to London two or three times a week. I came up again this morning, and it is still difficult. Trains are slower than they were 25 years ago. They are more comfortable and more expensive. I do not think there

is a quick fix on infrastructure, but it certainly needs to be put in place and I would put road, rail and air infrastructure way above broadband.

Q329 Susan Elan Jones: I want to tease out some sort of answer about overseas offices. A number of times people have been in front of us answering questions on this subject and we seem to get totally divergent answers. Is it true that overseas offices may be absolutely key in certain cultures where it is about building those long-term links but in other cultures it might not matter at all? Do you think that could be?
Glenn Massey: Bear in mind that often these projects can take five years to happen. Therefore, you have to build up a relationship over a period of time with them. Whether it is cheaper to have someone who is local and pops in once a week, has a cup of coffee and discusses where they are in terms of the project, that can be one way; or it could be, as tends to happen with most companies, that they do not involve the public sector until they are very close to making the decision. They have done all the work in terms of where the market opportunity is, whether they will buy a company, whether it will be a greenfield site, how they will structure it in terms of taxation, etcetera. Once they have done all that, they will engage. I would say that, if you could have a delivery team made up mainly of people experienced in business rather than the public sector, who can fly out at a moment's notice and try to win the project, that is probably as good as having somebody in an overseas office who is not quite as effective.

Q330 Susan Elan Jones: But how do you marry that idea with the fact that you say that brand Wales often is not heard of in certain places?
Glenn Massey: All I am saying is that, after 20 years of trying, it still has not worked and we have had lots of overseas offices with lots of people in them.

Q331 Chair: I must be careful how I suggest this. It is the kind of question that can easily get me into trouble. There was a row about the Duke of York in his role as ambassador. The argument was that, on the one hand, he should not have the job; there was no application. On the other hand, it was said he could always get in to see the top people and, whether or not we like it, the top people are always willing to see a member of the royal family. In some cultures, the top people are more willing to see a British Member of Parliament than somebody who works in an office for an overseas development agency. Is there not likely to be a problem in some countries and some cultures that the people who work in the offices for IBW will not have access to the top decision makers? In some cultures there is an issue about face and seniority, and people who possibly would be willing to see somebody possibly like Sir Roger Jones, the head of an agency from the UK, a British MP, a Cabinet member, or a member of the royal family, might not be quite so willing to see the guy who sits in that office for three months of the year sending back a postcard, as Sir Roger said. Do you see what I am getting at? Have I put that in a way that will not offend everyone?

Glenn Massey: It is correct. It is true of every culture. Every culture is the same. They want to see the decision makers or the people who can influence a decision. If the person they see has no influence and has not got much to say by way of a proposition, why do they want to waste time? The average meeting for an inward investment agency talking to a company like Intel is 20 minutes. You have got 20 minutes to make a proposition for Wales, and that is it. Bear in mind that they have another 150 to see after you.

Q332 Owen Smith: This has been a personal view of mine for years. Could we do better at desk-based analysis of which companies and sectors are likely to want to invest next in the UK? Take, for example, a Japanese pharma firm that does not have a location anywhere in Europe. They will always want a location in Europe at some point. Why do we not target them better?

Glenn Massey: It is a bit like investing your money with a fund manager, is it not? You are relying on the fund manager's research to get it right. Sometimes they do and sometimes they don't. Looking at my personal position, they do not always get it right; certainly, they get it wrong more often than they get it right. Obviously, there is a case for that, but it is a question of whether you know the industry sufficiently well to draw out the conclusions you want. Often I find that talking to senior executives in companies is a much easier route than that.

Q333 Geraint Davies: One thing that seems to come out of this is that you need the right person at the right time to make the decisions. You have intimated that some of the decisions are about knowing the prospective buyer for inward investment and perhaps forming a relationship, whether that is short term or long term, or, as the Chair said, it may be the case that certain doors are opened by certain people at the right moment, whether they be MPs or whatever. The question that follows from what Owen said is: how do you map out some of the likely new opportunities and flexibly arrange yourself in such a way that you can present yourself preferentially to get that win? Would you agree with that?

Glenn Massey: Yes. One of the things I found out working for PwC is that people are often prepared to share information with you because it is mutually advantageous. I am dealing now with a project that involves aluminium cans. It is a pretty standard product, but I discovered from talking to the chairman of the company that, because there is a worldwide shortage of tinplate, manufacturers of tinplate have told the people who make aerosol cans with tin that in two years' time they will cut them off. Whether they like it or not, they will be forced to go to aluminium. Half the market currently with tin will change in two years to aluminium. That is a huge marketing opportunity. It is uncovering things like which you do through discussion. It is through talking to people and captains of industry. One of the problems that many development agencies have, not just Wales, is how to get access to these people to find this out. A lot of the time you can do it through

intermediaries like accountants and lawyers, who are dealing with some of these big issues.

Q334 Geraint Davies: One of our previous witnesses suggested that events like the Ryder Cup could provide those scenarios. People who move around picking up these titbits are in the right place at the right time to take action to deliver those. I want to ask a separate question about India and China. How do you think we could do better there? Do you agree with me that foreign university students, particularly from places like India and China, are not ordinary people? They are all from rich backgrounds and are probably prospective inward investors, who could at least become high-value tourists in Wales. Is there an opportunity to take advantage of people from emerging markets to make those links and bring in tourism and inward investment, or should we do something else?

Glenn Massey: I think there are big opportunities, for the reason that if you had made a lot of money in China—lots of people have made a lot of money in China—you would want to get some of it out of the country. Where do you put it? We are talking now about people with serious money. If you look round London, they are buying property and infrastructure; they are also probably starting to think about buying companies. The next stage on from that is to do greenfield developments. This will not be in consumer electronics but in high added-value-type technology projects. If you think about it downstream, we are educating a lot of overseas students in Wales, who, hopefully, go away with a great impression of Wales. They are probably from moneyed backgrounds, as you say, they will want to do something with their own careers, which may or may not be in China; they may want to go overseas and do things. I think there are big opportunities there.

Q335 Owen Smith: To go back to your point about the opportunity relating to aluminium cans, are we employing the right kind of people either to pick those things up in conversation or conduct the analysis that will allow them to see those opportunities from their desk?

Glenn Massey: No.

Q336 Owen Smith: Why not?

Glenn Massey: It is a good question. I think it comes back to money at the end of the day. If you can earn £100,000 or £150,000 a year working in London, that is what you will do. Why would you want to work as a civil servant in Cardiff?

Owen Smith: For the good of the people.

Chair: Most of us would absolutely agree with Owen.

Q337 Jonathan Edwards: I know that you are not obsessed with structures, but perhaps one of the key areas of debate between us on the Committee is about who should be responsible for promoting Wales abroad. Should it be a matter for the Welsh Government, should we go solely through UKTI, or do you see a role for both?

Glenn Massey: I see a role for both. I think Wales has missed an opportunity over the last 10 years in paddling its own canoe. UKTI has recognised that, and most of the inward investment projects that it handles which are genuinely mobile go to England.

Q338 Jonathan Edwards: From my understanding, Wales is the only nation or region that has no UKTI presence domestically. Should UKTI have a presence in Wales to work closely with the Welsh Government, or is that not necessary?
Glenn Massey: I do not think so. What I think Wales should do is second people to UKTI.

Q339 Geraint Davies: Interestingly, you mentioned that Wales makes a presentation and so does everybody else, and it is difficult to differentiate. Maybe the best idea would be to go to the managing director of Microsoft, or whoever it is, and say, "Well, what do you want?", and then restructure or offer to fit that. For example, do you think that in this particular forum possibly we should be inviting big prospective investors to our hearings to ask them what they want, helping that process and literally getting jobs into Wales?
Glenn Massey: Yes.
Geraint Davies: Let's do that, Chair.

Q340 Guto Bebb: I am intrigued by your reasons why you do not think the staff are appropriate for the work being undertaken. In view of the fact that the whole structure in Wales has been restructured, should the Welsh Assembly Government consider just privatising the whole issue and offering the contract to a private sector company in a performance-related deal?
Glenn Massey: No.

Q341 Guto Bebb: Why is that? If we agree that the quality of staff cannot be recruited to the public sector, how do we get across that?
Glenn Massey: When I was in PwC I remember that one of the development agencies spoke to us about that very thing, but there were so many conflicts of interest we had with clients that it just was not worth it.

Q342 Guto Bebb: I am not sure where the answer is taking us. You are saying that we cannot get the quality of the individual in the public sector, nor can we go out and privatise the contract.
Glenn Massey: I did not say you can't get them.
Owen Smith: You have to pay for them.

Q343 Guto Bebb: You have to pay for them.
Glenn Massey: Yes. I would have a delivery unit largely drawn from the private sector with annual contracts. If they perform you keep them; if they do not perform you kick them out.

Q344 Guto Bebb: The problem is that we will say we will not employ anybody who earns more than the Prime Minister. That might be a problem.
Glenn Massey: If you take into account the Prime Minister's stately homes at weekends, I do not think that is a problem, is it?
Chair: I think I shall move swiftly on.
Owen Smith: A creative accountant to the last.

Q345 Karen Lumley: If you were in charge of bringing companies into Wales, what would you do? What would be the one thing you would do to help us?
Glenn Massey: I would develop some propositions which were attractive to companies who might be interested in Wales, and at the moment we do not have any.

Q346 Geraint Davies: On the issue of getting the best officials in place, do you think the problem is that, basically, you have to say you can speak Welsh before you can be a top civil servant in Wales and therefore a lot of civil servants will not apply? Similarly, do you think Welsh is an obstruction to inward investment generally?
Glenn Massey: It has never been an issue with any company that I have dealt with.

Q347 Geraint Davies: What about people who are applying for jobs there?
Glenn Massey: I do not know. I do not think I am the right person to ask.

Q348 Chair: If you want to attract the best people to work for an inward investment agency, presumably you would not want to stipulate that Welsh would have to be spoken, because the people they would be dealing with, by definition, would not speak Welsh, would they?
Glenn Massey: No.
Chair: On that slight note of controversy, does anyone want to come back to it?
Susan Elan Jones: Mr Massey's answer was not remotely controversial. It would seem to have good sense in it.
Owen Smith: I am more worried about going to Germany and not speaking German.

Q349 Chair: Lunch is beckoning. Thank you very much indeed, Mr Massey. It has been a most entertaining session.
Glenn Massey: I enjoyed it.
Chair: All these people who do not turn up to the Welsh Affairs Select Committee don't know what they are missing out on. It has been good. Thank you very much.

Thursday 30 June 2011

Members present:

David T. C. Davies (Chair)

Stuart Andrew   Jonathan Edwards
Guto Bebb   Susan Elan Jones
Geraint Davies   Mr Mark Williams

Examination of Witnesses

Witnesses: **Ms Katherine Bennett OBE**, Vice President, Head of Political Affairs, and **Mr Steve Thomas**, Government Affairs Executive, Airbus, **Mr Leighton Davies**, Financial Director, GE Aviation, and **Mr Tim Wheeler**, Industrial Participation Specialist, Boeing, gave evidence.

Q350 Chair: Good afternoon, ladies and gentlemen. I thank you very much indeed for coming along and also for the courtesy that you have all extended to the Committee in different ways recently. This is not meant to be some sort of an interrogation. We are conducting an inquiry into inward investment in Wales and we are just looking to you to give us help, advice and suggestions on how we can increase inward investment, and what will keep you here and keep your companies and others like them developing and growing. If I can kick off with Airbus and GE, perhaps you could tell us what made you come to Wales in the first place and what is it about Wales that has worked particularly well for you as organisations?
Katherine Bennett: If I could kick off, we came to Wales back in 1939. There were obviously some events going on in Europe at the time so the factory was created for a particular reason with considerable investment by the Government at the time. You could say that was a good piece of government support there.

The other reason for choosing that site was its location in terms of the airfield location and good all round flying facility and support, and essentially a local workforce who were happy to come in and work and support such an immediate start-up. That was the reason why we were founded and, of course, we had some celebrations recently on the milestone of that foundation.

It is a significant investment for Airbus in Broughton. Millions of pounds worth of cost goes into the capital investment and investment in our employees and, believe you me, Airbus does not spend money lightly. This continues. In the last few years we have spent £7.5 billion worth of work on the A380 facility across both sites and that is a significant investment. Why do we stay here? Well, the workforce is very supportive. We have spent a lot of money on training so they are there, they are trained up, and it is the kind of place to which people want to send their sons and daughters. It is a continuous project. Steve could confirm there are quite a lot of fathers, daughters, sons who have worked at the factory over the years, so that is a key thing. The other thing, which Steve can perhaps touch on a little bit more, is that the local supply chain has grown very strong and, of course, the supportive environment that we have found from the Welsh Government and, of course, the English regions nearby, because we are very close to the Cheshire area.

Q351 Chair: That happily leads me to my next question. Katherine, you and Leighton at GE have both worked very closely with the Welsh Assembly Government and been supported by them in different ways recently. I am not so sure about Boeing, but we will find out in a minute. Obviously, there are other things going on at a national level that will be affecting your organisations. This is a leading question, but you obviously would, I presume, think it important that the Welsh Assembly Government and national Government are working closely together. In your experience, is that actually happening at the moment?
Leighton Davies: In terms of the Welsh Government and the national Government working together, we have not really seen much evidence of that. On whether we are interested, I would say we are more focused on our relationship with the Welsh Government.

To go back to your question of why we came to Wales, GE came to Wales back in the early 1990s when we acquired the site from British Airways, which had also moved down from London to the Welsh Valleys around 1939 to avoid some activity around that area. Since then, it is important to say that we have invested nearly £200 million in the site with a lot of support and advice and guidance from the Welsh Assembly Government and previously the Welsh Office. Our salary bill every year is £70 million, which goes into the Welsh economy. There are 1,100 people working there. There are 1,000 highly skilled jobs on site. I think that has been built up over time with the good relationship that we have built with the Welsh Government. It is important to us that we have that avenue to interact with the Welsh Government effectively. From a national perspective, Mark Elborne, who is the President and CEO of GE UK, is engaging with Westminster on a national scale as well, so importance is placed on that, yes.
Tim Wheeler: Perhaps looking at the questions through the prism of an international business into the UK, I should explain that the UK market, the aerospace market, is one of the biggest international parts of the supply chain to Boeing, so there is lots of supply base in the UK. The interaction you are specifically asking about with the Welsh Government has been proactive. The Welsh Government has made sure it has understood what Boeing is doing and what its activities are in the UK, which are primarily supporting the aircraft platforms that the Government

has bought: C17, Apache helicopters and Chinooks. Inevitably, where Boeing is gaining a footprint in the UK, the locations tend to be where those aircraft are operated and, therefore, where they need to be supported. Those locations mean that Boeing Defence UK Limited now, as a UK business, this morning actually was 686 people and there are about another 300 Boeing staff in the UK.

On the interaction with the Government, I was just looking at the job titles of some of the people who have come along and explained what was happening and, very importantly, listened to what Boeing was up to and explored opportunities. We have a chief executive for the Americas, of International Business Wales, a senior vice president who talks to us frequently—he spoke to me last week—an aerospace sector leader and a strategy and development manager for UAVs, talking about our proposed developments. In terms of an engagement there has been a structure in place that has kept Boeing very up to date with opportunities in Wales.

We have also attempted to represent where we could Welsh companies' business interests in the US if those interests were not directly in Boeing or its supply chain. Probably one of the most recent events was something called "Washington 80", where 80 Welsh companies came to the States and visited various prospective US customers. The interaction, I would say, has been high and compared with any of the regional development efforts, has been pretty high.

Chair: I should have said at the start, by the way, that because of trains, we are rather short of time at the moment, so I am going to try and rattle through things a little bit more quickly than normal, if that is all right. I hope everyone will bear with me there.

Q352 Susan Elan Jones: If I could just ask this question to Mr Wheeler, please, from Boeing, I wonder what factors you took into account when looking where to base the company in the UK. For instance, did you consider establishing a subsidiary in Wales?

Tim Wheeler: Thank you for that question. The factors I guess can best be described by answering where the company is. The company is head-officed in Central London because its primary customer is the Government, so it is there. There is the Boeing Commercial Airplanes office in Heathrow that looks after UK and a lot of Europe from Heathrow and that is the central hub. When we look at the other operations, it is reflective of the point I was making about where those operations are. As with, indeed, GE taking on a BA business, our sites have generally been government facilities, government aircraft maintenance, so our single largest site is in Gosport where helicopters are maintained. We have just taken on a contract with 13 UK centres, an MoD contract, and TUPE transferred 230 staff into Boeing. Inevitably, their work and where they live and operate to some extent determines matters, so those are factors. Not surprisingly, you would find our operations in Brize Norton and Lakenheath and those sorts of location. The factors are whether it is really a new or established entity that you are taking on. Then for a new entity it would be the staff and

infrastructure, communication links, transport links, but bear in mind pretty much anything that we would take from the UK will be exported to the US for further assembly on aircraft.

Wales is featuring in a couple of significant developments at the moment. We are looking at a combination of some of our operations and Wales is certainly one of the locations we are considering for that. It will then come down to affordability, economic factors, because they are government contracts and you have to get best value. Those are the sort of factors and the sort of reasons that have drawn us to certain locations in the UK.

Q353 Susan Elan Jones: One of the things that very much featured in our informal discussions as we were going round Airbus this morning was the idea, the great benefit, of being a large fish in a smaller pond in Wales and the added incentives that would come from that. I wonder what you feel that the UK Government can do to make the UK, but also Wales in particular, a more attractive place in which to invest.

Tim Wheeler: I think when we look at the things Boeing takes from the UK as an international customer, I am pretty accurate in saying as an international customer Boeing is probably the biggest customer of the UK aerospace industry. What we take from it is high degrees of innovation in systems and sub-systems. The new electric wing on the 787 Dreamliner, the de-icing system for that, is made in the UK. It is this innovation. I think it is really important to keep a flow of that innovation and those ideas, the things that we seem very, very good at doing in the UK, because from an export point of view it will always be something that is then scooped up and put into an integration factory in the States. That would be the encouragement. We are not a low cost economy in most of Europe, certainly not in the UK, so you do not come here for the low cost economy. There is a great relationship, 70 years in Boeing's case. It supplied Harvards into the UK. All those things are important, but what is really important is the great ideas, the design and the realisation of it that Boeing then takes from the UK.

Chair: I think Jonathan and Geraint might have very, very quick, brief questions.

Q354 Jonathan Edwards: Thank you, Chair, for indulging me. Just quickly, there is a big debate going on in the UK about empowering the different national Governments through corporation tax powers to levy different rates. What sort of effect do you think that would have in terms of—

Chair: Good or bad, from everyone. That would be an interesting question.

Katherine Bennett: Perhaps I could just say it is interesting to hear comments from my colleague at Boeing. We are very proud not only to be a customer of the UK aerospace industry but to be resident in terms of our business here. Corporation tax levels are an interesting factor. Airbus is obviously a global company so corporation tax is not something necessarily that is a big focus for us in deciding where to locate a facility. Other things—and you will come to this a bit later, I am sure, with your other questions—are important, for example, the economic climate, as to where a company would invest or invest more. I think we all want to talk more about investing more in this country. I understand there has been a lot of debate in Wales about enterprise zones and there are other attractive things like that that could be done. Whether stamp duty income goes to the local authority or the Welsh Government is another factor. Really, probably I would like to say this is something for the politicians to worry about—businesses like ours obviously are happy to be consulted but we would say maybe a better answer would be a good package of business support measures rather than just focusing on one tax versus another.

Q355 Chair: Any further thoughts on whether it is good or bad?
Leighton Davies: I concur with the views just provided by Katherine, really. I think corporation tax, while important, is not viewed as the be-all and end-all. I think there are more important aspects such as encouraging academia to invest in engineering, maybe encouraging industry to invest in apprenticeship schemes. We take on 25 apprentices every year and for those 25 jobs there are 500 applications. We go down to the local college; there are 26 in the class, 25 of which have come from GE. I think that that is a reflection on the amount of investment that goes into apprenticeship schemes in Wales or particularly Mid Glamorgan. So, while it is important, I do not think it is going to really make a big impact in terms of where they decide to invest.

Q356 Geraint Davies: Obviously Airbus and GE are now well established in the Welsh economy in ways I think we all understand. Mr Wheeler, can you foresee a situation where Boeing might join that very significant cluster in Wales? Under what circumstances you imagine that happening on a scale approaching what we enjoy from GE and Airbus, or don't you think that is a possibility?
Tim Wheeler: The Airbus operation here is a manufacturing operation and GE is an aftermarket operation. We would be more synergistic, I think, with the aftermarket operation. That is why our operations are in the UK. I do not see any immediate move to put a European manufacturing base together. Evidence of that is that we have just put in place a new factory for one of the new aircraft in the US. But I would go to the programmes that are relevant for the UK and the employment that Boeing is generating in the UK, and there would be no reason whatsoever why that should not be based in Wales.

Q357 Guto Bebb: My first question really is to Airbus and GE Aviation about the training within your workforce. Quite clearly, from the visit this morning and from the evidence that we have already received, you invest heavily in training and you have a highly skilled workforce. That has been done, from what we saw this morning, in partnership with local higher and further education institutions. Could you expand upon that partnership that you have built?
Steve Thomas: Yes, we are very proud of our apprenticeship programme in particular. We have over

400 apprentices currently undergoing some form of training, whether that be craft or higher engineering apprenticeships. It is done in conjunction with our local further education college, Deeside College. I myself am the Vice Chair of the Governors of Deeside College and so we have strong links embedded in that relationship and also Glyndŵr University, the proprietors of this facility we are in. We were also fortunate this morning to go round our Composites Training and Development Centre, which is run in conjunction with Deeside College and Glyndŵr University. That for us was a real step forward in embracing further education, higher education and a mainstream employer. That combination enables our employees to embark on an apprenticeship or continue potentially a craft apprenticeship to a higher apprenticeship, foundation degree, master's degree and even chartership. The complete spectrum is available should the employees and the business need to complement each other.
Also Wales has an added advantage from the Welsh Government in the all-age apprenticeship scheme that is on offer whereby our employees who are not previously designated as apprentices can actually up-skill themselves by embarking on an apprenticeship scheme. That for us is a tremendous opportunity that is not available elsewhere in the UK.
Overall, we invest very significantly in our training programmes across the spectrum. Airbus spent last year, for example, £3.6 million on training and development of our 10,000 employees throughout the UK and the key to that clearly is the investment that we also spent at Broughton specifically.

Q358 Guto Bebb: Just on the work that went into that, was it difficult to build those partnerships? That is the first question. Secondly, do you think that the partnerships that you have developed could be replicated by other sectors of the Welsh economy?
Steve Thomas: Was it difficult? It was challenging at times, I have to say, particularly with the higher education side because it was our first foray into that arena. We have a longstanding relationship with further education. Our involvement with Glyndŵr University was a new venture for us, but can it be replicated? Certainly. We have learnt lessons and Glyndŵr University has clearly learnt lessons. It is definitely something that we are looking to build upon as we move forward, and as we want to expand our training facilities to embrace all the new technologies that we are looking to introduce to support our A350 programme.

Q359 Guto Bebb: Just a question to Mr Wheeler: does Boeing have any concerns about the skills level in the UK as a whole?
Tim Wheeler: No, I think there is a broader skills issue, but it is not just the UK that it affects measurably. At the moment, the average age of an engineer in Boeing is 47 and in the next five years 25% of the engineers could come up for retirement. Now, being newer in the UK our issue is not quite as pronounced. The average age is 36; they are babies, it is great. But that skills gap I think comes from a time when a lot of engineers were not trained. I am a time

served apprentice who went on through higher education and a significant proportion of my counterparts at school left and pursued that route. There is a pent-up need to be able to replace some engineers, we recognise that. We contribute significantly to research and development because that is what we take from the UK through key university partnerships. I was looking, and found that there are 86 universities or entities, businesses or universities, or collaborative partnerships that we have worked with in the last three years, so a significant footprint. But our interest in those often is research, development, delivery, products and services perhaps more than the training of skills. As I say, certainly in the response concerning factors we would look at, you do have to have the right skills and they have to be in the right places.

Q360 Guto Bebb: A final point just to clarify, the figures you gave in terms of engineering and the age of engineers, was that a UK figure or is it just a Boeing figure?
Tim Wheeler: No, that is a Boeing figure.

Q361 Guto Bebb: That is a Boeing figure particularly?
Tim Wheeler: To qualify it a bit, there are 157,000 people across all disciplines in Boeing, and of the engineering community that average age is 47. I am told, and I believe, there is an ADS figure, which I do not have locked in my head, that actually the age is higher. It is north of 50, as I recall, about 51, 52, the average age of aerospace engineers in the UK.

Q362 Stuart Andrew: Can I ask all of you if you think that there are specific skill gaps in Wales and, if there are, how would you try to overcome them?
Leighton Davies: Well, if I can just talk about the recent recruitment that we have gone through, we announced at the Senedd earlier this year that we were going to take on 100 people, and 1,000 applications were received. We saw that there was not a surplus of the skills that we were looking for in qualified aircraft engineers. I think if there is an area that the Welsh Government could encourage industry to train people up on, it is around aircraft engineers because there certainly was not a surplus of the workforce available there.
Steve Thomas: I think from an Airbus perspective and just to build upon my previous response, certainly in terms of the money factor in engineering skills, we are investing heavily to overcome any potential skill shortages. That goes back to our initial links with the schools. For example, we have a full-time schools liaison officer; his prime role in life is to go out, share the message of what we are about in Airbus to primary schools and secondary schools—not just to extol the virtues of Airbus in the UK but of engineering in general. He emphasises that this is not a dark, dour organisation that most people could spend the rest of their lives in. It is quite the converse; it is quite an exciting opportunity, a career opportunity, for these people. We invest heavily in our people. We invest heavily in our links with schools and universities and FE colleges to overcome those skill gaps.

Q363 Stuart Andrew: When we went to Tata Steel they said exactly the same thing, that the reputation before among young people in the area was they did not want to work there, but the engagement changed perceptions. Are you saying that if more companies did that, the future for Wales could look an awful lot brighter?
Steve Thomas: I think there is a really exciting prospect of that and it was really brought home to me earlier this year when we held an open day in the West Factory where the wings for the A380 are assembled. We had an extensive advertising campaign and we invited along all potential recruits, whether they were interested in apprenticeships, direct entry graduates or internships—the whole spectrum—for an evening just to view what is on offer in Airbus in the UK. Four thousand people attended that event and from that we were able to select some real quality people to actually pursue their careers. It is a fantastic take-up and I am sure if that was replicated elsewhere, Wales as a whole would benefit.
Tim Wheeler: If I could just come in on Steve's point there, I think businesses are beholden to paint that picture and start engagement at that very young school age. Boeing runs something called "Build a Plane" where we take a kit for a three-axis microlight, give it to a school, they get to make it, then they have to sell it, then the money recycles into the scheme. Now, that is one business with 1,000 employees in the UK trying to engage and excite children about engineering at that early age. For the next stage, the university relationship with the Advanced Manufacturing Research Centre has a truck that comes out and opens out. It is a very attractive pantechnicon and shows a number of engineering experiences. Thousands upon thousands of youngsters have gone through that and seen the Mantra truck. Those are the practical things that organisations like ours can and do do, but somehow it needs more effort behind it and more businesses involved.

Q364 Geraint Davies: Many of our witnesses in the past have said there are low levels of business expenditure on research and development in Wales and I know, Steve, you mentioned I think that there was £367 million of research and development in Airbus in 2010 alone. How does the panel think that firms can be encouraged to invest in research and development?
Katherine Bennett: Well, I think it goes back to what I was saying earlier about the general supportive business climate provided by authorities or governments. The climate now for bidding for technology support across the UK is obviously to encourage partnerships, so university links and supplier links are absolutely key. You cannot get anywhere unless you are working. It would be dumb anyway not to because both Boeing and ourselves are extensively using the supply chain very, very early on in research and technology. We do engineering at Broughton as well as manufacturing, so a certain element of research and technology investment goes into Broughton. We obviously like to link in with universities across the UK, but we are strengthening our links a lot with local universities, too. Yes, we are

one of the top 10 investors in R&D in this country and let us maintain that. You are asking me—I guess why the Committee is looking at this subject—what more governments can do, and really perhaps going back to the skills debate, rebalancing the economy. Don't talk about the sector bankers and the service sector and the media companies. I am not an engineer, I did a history degree, but I find it fascinating to work in a company that produces things that can help develop the future and help develop young people in the future. We are seeing the Government, both the Welsh Government and, of course, the Government in Westminster, changing their dialogue with us. I have really noticed that in the last few months. Engineering is a big focus and I think that would also then create a climate where more research and technology is done because more ideas are developed as people see a supportive climate.

Q365 Geraint Davies: Is there a case for companies like your own, and we found this with Tata as well, perhaps to be more vocal about how exciting the R&D you are doing is and how it generates real change and a new future to excite the imagination of the public and prospective employees and whatever, children or anybody?

Katherine Bennett: You have asked me a perfect question. Just last week Airbus started a debate all about flying in the future—so what kind of cabins you could be flying in in the future in terms of different technology, whether new kinds of materials could be used that perhaps had not been thought of before for aircraft. Some of that technology is beginning and is happening in the UK. Composite technology for Boeing and ourselves obviously is absolutely key.

Q366 Chair: I feel I ought to bring Boeing in at this point just so that the score is even.

Katherine Bennett: Ten thousand employees versus 1,000.

Chair: Quite a task to umpire this.

Tim Wheeler: The excitement that you can generate and the interest is probably well articulated in that research and technology aim by the first of the TICs, the Technology and Innovation Centres. The policy was announced by David Cameron from the Boeing Advanced Manufacturing Research Centre at Sheffield University. What I think businesses can bring is their requirements, and I think they can say, "We need research a bit nearer 52 weeks a year. We need more office hours. We need things to be spun round very quickly". In the case of Boeing, we recognise the gap from great research and technology at the lower technological readiness levels to the ability to go into production. Do we make enough noise about it? Well, we try to.

Q367 Jonathan Edwards: Can I move to supply chains? Both Boeing and Airbus have given us some substantial evidence on this already in written form. Could Airbus expand perhaps about the clusters in northeast Wales based on your supply chain?

Steve Thomas: Yes, certainly. First, it is appropriate to say that we are a global company with a global supply chain, but nonetheless we really view any

opportunities that arise as important. In some businesses it may be entirely appropriate for close proximity to our business. Indeed, we had the opportunity to see that this morning in terms of a local business park that is situated adjacent to our site where already three businesses have moved on to the site and are dedicated to the supply of components to our final assembly lines based at Broughton. Indeed, if you look at the local supply chain on or about our site, and many of our subcontractors are actually physically located on the 700-acre site based at Broughton, over 2,000 employees are directly employed in our supply chain wholly and exclusively dedicated to supporting our business. That is 2,000 employees over and above the 6,100 employees of Airbus' own employment base. It is vital for some industries but it is within the context of an overall global supply chain.

Q368 Jonathan Edwards: In terms of Boeing, your evidence was based on a UK outlook. Do you have any Welsh specifics?

Tim Wheeler: Yes, there are. I think in terms of a business that is going to export, unless there are synergies in businesses exporting together, the cluster probably is not quite so important as the benefits one gets from being in the supply chain close to your primary customer. I think sharing knowledge and information if there is a cluster of businesses and possibly, as we look at this area of SMEs, developing more business with larger organisations, the ability for them to work together and potentially come up with a more complete product or a higher tiering of product can be beneficial to clusters and the information that they exchange among themselves. However, from the prism of an exporter from the UK, I guess, it is less significant than being closer to the factory.

Q369 Mr Williams: I think the time is increasingly against us. You have already talked about the importance you attach to the links with the Assembly Government. First Airbus, in your written submission you made it known your extensive links with UKTI through trade missions, and you have had a great deal of success in the last week. What are your views, though, on the effectiveness of the Assembly Government's activities overseas and the extent to which they are effectively embedded in UK marketing? I could summarise the question: how successful is the Assembly Government in promoting Wales abroad? What are your experiences of that?

Katherine Bennett: Well, there are two questions there, really. First, obviously Airbus orders of Airbus aircraft is a global sales issue. Thank you for mentioning it—yes, we had 730 orders at the Paris Air Show last week, which is a considerably nice thing for our employees up in Broughton to reflect on. Yes, I work very closely with the UKTI operation. I am a member of their Advanced Engineering Board. I am forever beating the drum here. I am forever nagging. I am probably a bit of a pain, because I want British Ministers to do more on this. Because in my role I can see what the French, German, Spanish Ministers do—the other three Airbus home countries in Europe.

Q370 Chair: In a nutshell, what are we not doing or what are British Ministers not doing?

Katherine Bennett: To be honest, the previous President of France used to describe himself as the biggest Airbus salesman, and I would like Lord Green and David Cameron to also become an Airbus salesman and promote our company abroad. Certainly, President Obama does that for Boeing. I would like my country to do that as well. UKTI have recently reformed the way they work, doing a lot of work with PA Consulting, and they have really focused on what needs to be done to help big companies like us with sales.

Q371 Mr Williams: Just carrying on very quickly from that, I think intimating from what you have just said, is it the case still that the UK Government can open doors and create opportunities that perhaps as yet—some of us are optimistic devolutionists—Wales Ministers cannot at this stage?

Katherine Bennett: I think that—and we were talking about this earlier—the First Minister of Wales has a very powerful position in terms of influencing the UK Government and then globally to maybe do a bit more. Maybe he should be banging on at Westminster a bit more to say, "Hey, come on, let's support aerospace".

Chair: Our door is always open to him, I can assure you of that.

Katherine Bennett: I think that is a useful thing and I am trying not to support party politics here—we do not want to get caught up in that. But from the position I see it now, based in Airbus' head office in Toulouse, I want Wales and I want the UK to fight harder and louder.

Leighton Davies: A question was asked earlier about R&D and what could we do to encourage more R&D. In GE in Wales we do not undertake that much R&D because most of it is done at the headquarters in Cincinnati. GE also has global research centres—there is one in Munich and I think there is one out in India as well. What can the Welsh Government do to attract more of that type of investment? I think they could engage with large companies' headquarters. We are headquartered in Cincinnati. I do not think anybody from the Welsh Government has ever spoken to anybody in Cincinnati and I think maybe that would be a really powerful way of getting engaged with these companies and just advertising what Wales has to offer. We are constantly trying to do it in terms of attracting investment to our plant in Nantgarw and we are competing with GE sites around the world in so doing. We are helped by the Welsh Government when we have attracted investment, but I think if the Welsh Government could engage directly with these headquarters, it would be a really powerful message.

Q372 Mr Williams: In answer to my question, how successful is brand Wales abroad? What about the responsibility of the Assembly Government to promote it? That is not a partisan point. Has it not been effective to date in your view?

Leighton Davies: I think they could always do more and I think I would welcome that.

Tim Wheeler: I think generally from a UK point of view the UK is a great economy but there is a big world out there. Some of the parts should be greater than the sum of the whole. I think all of the reach that the United Kingdom has into global industries would give a lot more touch points if that were then brought back and viewed in a particular way. To a business in North America, it might or might not be important what part of the UK we are talking about, but start talking about the UK first of all. I echo the Airbus point on that. We have to sing the praises of the UK. Discrimination then between the different parts of it is the next level of conversation.

Chair: We have about two minutes left. Guto, you have a very, very quick question.

Q373 Guto Bebb: Just a quick clarification. Mr Davies, you said that nobody from Wales has been to Cincinnati. Have you had anybody from the UK Government or anybody representing the UK Government?

Leighton Davies: Not that I am aware of.

Guto Bebb: Not that you are aware of. Thank you very much.

Q374 Geraint Davies: In the written submissions there is concern expressed about the lack of an aerospace representative on sector panels. I think this is in the Welsh Assembly Government's industrial sectors and did not seem to mention aerospace. Do you think they should?

Chair: Perhaps we can have a couple of quick-fire answers to that one.

Steve Thomas: I think from an Airbus perspective it is early days. From Airbus in the UK we have been designated anchor status. We have held initial discussions with the sector chair—very productive discussions they are, too. We are mindful of the fact there is no separate designation in terms of the aerospace sector and we are part of the advanced materials sector. We are hoping that will not dilute the focus that we previously enjoyed. I have to say there are no immediate signs of any such dilution but it is something that we are mindful of.

Q375 Chair: We should build on our strengths, basically?

Steve Thomas: Absolutely.

Tim Wheeler: I agree totally with Steve on that point.

Q376 Chair: Excellent. Thank you very much indeed. I am sorry it had to be very quick, but I am afraid we have another panel and we have discovered that we might need a little more time to get various people to trains. I do not have to rush off, though, so if anyone is here afterwards I shall be more than happy to stay behind for a few minutes.

Tim Wheeler: Thank you very much for having us.

Witnesses: **Professor Michael Scott**, Vice-Chancellor and Chief Executive, **Mr Tony Hawkins**, Managing Director, Glyndŵr Innovations and **Mr Andrew Parry**, Executive Adviser to the Vice-Chancellor and Head of Corporate Communications, Glyndŵr University, **Ms Karen Padmore**, Business Development Manager and **Mr James Goodman**, Programme Development Manager, Bangor University, gave evidence.

Q377 Chair: Thank you very much indeed for allowing us to be here and coming to give evidence. If you do not mind, we are going to get straight into it because I am told we only have about 25 minutes. We will all try and be as quick as we can with the questions and the answers. Could I just start off by asking you, perhaps anyone who wants to speak, what links you have with inward investors in Wales, how you find inward investors, what you do to build up a relationship with them, if there is a quick answer to that?
Professor Michael Scott: Well, it is a huge question and a huge answer, really.
Chair: I was worried you might say that.
Professor Michael Scott: We are working all over the globe to try and bring investment back into Wales. I will just say straight away that I have been in Vietnam quite recently. We have gained a £5 million contract over five years to train technicians for the Vietnamese Television Corporation, but as I speak I still have a team out in Vietnam. Tony has just come back from Vietnam because we are talking with the Vietnamese Government and with the Vietnamese Media Corporation about extending that kind of work. It is all inward investment because we bring all that back. We bring back the expertise that we gain there to our new Creative Industry Centre in Wrexham, which we share now with the BBC. Of course, part of that was to link the BBC with the Vietnamese Television Corporation. Yes, that gives an example.
Karen Padmore: I would just add that we have had the Technium programme and obviously OpTIC, which came from that, and also CAST. Part of the work that we were doing there was actually about inward investment and using it as a catalyst to attract inward investment companies. We obviously have a natural link with anybody who is in the buildings and we currently have 20 tenants there.

Q378 Guto Bebb: A question to Bangor University. There is a question mark about whether there will be a second nuclear power station at Wylfa, but some of us are still hopeful. The question is what type of links would Bangor University try and develop in order to facilitate that development?
James Goodman: We are making extensive links with the Anglesey Energy Island project. In fact, in a previous role I was involved in looking at the different energy options for Anglesey, not just nuclear but, of course, wind, tidal, biomass and so on and so forth. There is quite a deep engagement. I think it is important also to state, in regard to engagement with the nuclear industry, that it is very easy to pigeonhole it and think that this is just about nuclear, but the opportunities around, for example, a company like Horizon coming into the area, which would bring something like 5,000 to 6,000 jobs over I believe a six-year period and a project the size of around the Olympics but with a legacy of 60 to 100 years, are

quite phenomenal. They include socioeconomic type studies, infrastructure studies, economics, grid type issues around distribution of energy and so on—there are many opportunities. Where we are looking at the moment is around the gap. As I am sure you know, there is decommissioning at the present Wylfa, and also staff are coming from Trawsfynydd. It was interesting that your previous correspondent mentioned the ageing workforce. One of the things that we are looking to do is provide an alternative means of delivery of accredited skills; for example, work-based learning type programmes that will actually help nuclearise people who are not in the industry so they can respond to the need and then we can keep some of the skills local.
Karen Padmore: There is a group that meets—it is a whole forum that is signed up to a constitution, which will meet tomorrow morning, and I sit on that forum as well as a couple of other members so that we are engaging with all the partners who have an interest in energy more generally than on Anglesey. I would just like to add that the other stuff about the work-based learning is that we are talking about skills that will be needed in 2020 or whenever and these kids are still in school, so there is a whole programme around STEM Dudes, this idea of us promoting STEM to schoolchildren—those initiatives are under way.

Q379 Guto Bebb: Certainly the partnership approach, which has been played out in the Nantgarw project, was apparent when we went to Düsseldorf, where we saw all the names of the partners at the presentation. To what extent do you think that the fact that the catalyst for change might be the nuclear sector is creating problems for you in gaining support from various levels of government?
Karen Padmore: I would say that there is an awful lot of local support for wind, so I see that in that sense it is not a problem. It is actually seen as an opportunity. Maybe I do not understand the question, but I do not see it as a political problem.

Q380 Guto Bebb: For example, my understanding is that the Energy Centre in Llangefni has been described as "energy" skills rather than "nuclear" skills because certain individuals in certain government agencies in this country have a problem with the word "nuclear".
Karen Padmore: I guess that there are elements of that, but if you look at Anglesey as an entity, you have tidal, wind and so on. It actually makes sense to look at it as a holistic issue, so I think that is very much the way of encompassing it. While it might actually have some political connotations, I think in practice it is probably a really good, sensible approach.
Chair: No doubt you will have been heartened by the *Daily Mail* this morning, which I am sure you have all read, and Chris Huhne telling us that we all need nuclear power stations, which I thought was a

misprint, but I read it three times and it really was there.

Q381 Jonathan Edwards: I will move on to my questions. We are interested in how the universities work with companies on their research and development. Can you provide any examples of how your universities have transferred successfully knowledge to some companies in the surrounding area?

Tony Hawkins: Following on from the previous panel and the aerospace focus, it was interesting listening especially to Steve Thomas in the Airbus team, with whom we work closely. As you know, Deeside, ourselves and the Assembly have created a composite centre at Hawarden, which was a challenge, is now up and running and is great, with a mixture of skills training and research. Now, what we are bringing in addition to what we set up originally in that building is research from overseas. We have some very strong links in Russia with Bauman State Technical University. We had a conference recently on site that involved Airbus and some of the key supply chain. It was evident from that that there are a number of technologies that sit around the world and, if we pull together, they will make a big difference to the aerospace industry.

What we are doing at present is trying to move on from the first composite centre into a second generation centre, so that we work much closer— going back to what Steve was saying—with kids from a very, very early age. Engineering is seen as a career that is dirty, unpleasant and there are skill structures. What we want to do is create a pathway all the way from year seven right through to degree and masters, et cetera. At the moment we are working with the Assembly's new Advanced Materials research team and with Flintshire County Council and with our Funding Council to create a new centre that will be innovation, knowledge transfer, skills, research, that will go all the way back through, from junior school, right through senior school through degrees.

Q382 Jonathan Edwards: Is there any evidence of companies locating now to be near to Glyndŵr?

Tony Hawkins: Not directly as a result of what we are doing, but I think Flintshire County Council— Steve was saying this—were trying to create a hub or a cluster of businesses around advanced manufacturing. Flintshire has 33% manufacturing. It is the highest density of manufacturing companies anywhere in the UK. Hawarden is the ideal venue for that around the Airbus site, so the more we do to help manufacturing in a broad sense, not just the Advanced Manufacturing Composites move, the better it is for the region and the economy and the skills.

Professor Michael Scott: There is evidence of spin-out, of course, with something like this building, so that two companies went out of this building just over the last month, actually on to this park here. So, there is that. We have not brought Toyota in but we are working with Toyota, obviously, and with Sharp, for example. You mentioned the TICs earlier. Sharp actually rang us up and asked whether we would be

partners in a bid for a technology innovation centre because of the work that we are doing in this building on solar panels.

Q383 Geraint Davies: Innovation now in Airbus is around carbon wings and carbon planes and this sort of thing. The suggestion was made this morning that the power potential in Anglesey could be harnessed to have locally produced carbon material that would be lightweight both for aeroplanes and in the future for cars. How do you think we should take that forward?

Professor Michael Scott: I think there is an issue there in terms of us being behind in the game in the sense that, as far as Airbus is concerned, my understanding is that the majority of the research based on their carbon materials comes out of Germany. Airbus required us to give them solutions to the assembly of composite materials and also the repair of composite materials because you cannot repair a wing in the same way as in the past. If you got a wing in the past that was hit by a flock of birds, which takes a bite-sized chunk out of the wing, you just riveted another piece of metal on. But you cannot rivet with a composite material. Our concentration at the moment has been in the context of what is being asked by the industry—research into the repair of the composite. If there is a case that what is coming out of Anglesey is more revolutionary than their present supply chain, obviously then there has to be talk with the local universities, with the industry, and then pressure to try and ensure that Airbus changes its view as a global manufacturer about where the composite materials come from.

Susan Elan Jones: The development of Glyndŵr University over the last 10 or 15 years has been one of the massive successful stories of northeast Wales and I do not think you can ever say too much about that, to be honest.

Professor Michael Scott: Thank you very much.

Q384 Susan Elan Jones: If I could just ask a quick question of Glyndŵr and one of Bangor. Now, for Glyndŵr, your submission highlights the role of the universities in supporting high technology clusters such as OpTICs, advanced engineering and renewable. Could you expand on this a little bit?

Tony Hawkins: Well, the Vice-Chancellor took the decision to take on OpTIC a couple of years ago and it was obviously built around a successful OpTICs business around Pilkingtons originally. That has become a successful business now and we have developed a successful chain of companies coming through that are fledgling and then growing outside. We obviously have the huge research project here for the ESO telescope, which you may or may not have seen while you have been here. This is a very successful model that will continue to grow. I know there are aspirations to grow this centre to be more vibrant and to have a bigger role as a science park, if you like. I think this is very successful. I think the work we have done at Hawarden has been great so far, in the early stages. The composite centre is up and running. The next stage will be to continue to develop that, knowing how important manufacturing is in this part of the region.

Q385 Susan Elan Jones: A very, very quick question for Bangor. What special challenges does the university face in developing links with international firms by virtue of the location of Bangor, which clearly is not anyone's fault?

James Goodman: Well, of course, it is pretty obvious that there are not that many large-sized companies, and we mentioned earlier the engagement with the Energy Island. We have used pre-existing links to, if you like, strengthen links with, say, Horizon and open up those discussions. Our friends at Wylfa have been very helpful in helping us do that. Many of our engagements come through partnerships and we partner up with our Glyndŵr colleagues here in a number of initiatives—for example, the Low Carbon Research Institute, which gives us through some of our academics an input into companies like Tata on things like organic photovoltaics, which I guess you are familiar with. A lot of it comes through partnerships and some through overseas visits. Of course, we have just come back from a mission to China to increase our links there. Clearly, the Chinese market in terms of students is a key one for us, but we also use our alumni.

Karen Padmore: I think that a connection into London City Airport would be great. That sort of thing would actually help enormously if we can shorten the time on that international connection. I think that is one of the points we would make in terms of collaborating with overseas organisations; how they actually get to us and have that access. It is a challenge, but we have I think now nearly 2,000 overseas students so I guess that hopefully we are creating a market and a demand that will justify better transport links. Obviously, from Wales we all recognise that we want to be more successful in Framework 7 projects, so again if we can actually increase that activity, I think some of these transport links will perhaps become more economically viable.

Q386 Mr Williams: You have answered my question about the importance of renewed international activity. This is one for Glyndŵr. In your written submission, I was a bit concerned to read, in terms of the potential for more work for the national centre, it should be able to support such research activities, "It is concerned, therefore, at increased pressure applied on the university by the Funding Council to move away from research and concentrate solely on teaching". You have obviously identified a potential problem there and a potential role there for the Assembly in bridging this gap.

Professor Michael Scott: Well, it was not specifically the Assembly but it was just a disappointment with the Funding Council. For every pound that we receive from the Funding Council in terms of research, Glyndŵr University actually earns £11.50. The closest university to us in that, though it is in a different proportion, of course, is Cardiff. For every pound that Cardiff gained from the Funding Council, it actually made £3. We are making £11.50 and they are making

£3. Perhaps that was seen to be to our disadvantage because they have now removed the pound.

To be fair to the Funding Council, it is saying that we really need not just to cluster our research together but focus it into one particular area. We believe that we have done that in advanced manufacturing. This advanced material manufacturing, this building, is all about materials, but so is the composite centre. Perhaps from our point of view, we should have said that it is the composite centre and this together in one research institute in order to get the money.

Having said that, I think that there is a problem related to applied research and pure research. All our research is applied research. All our research comes from the market. We go into companies and we do not say, "This is the research that we do. Here it is". We actually go into companies and say, "What do you want us to do or what is your problem? What is your difficulty?" If we cannot find an answer to it within our university, we will go to another university to do it. It is all applied. That is not to criticise our colleagues in any traditional university. Traditional universities do what they do and they do it very well. I think that we do something slightly different in the applied nature, although some of the traditionals are doing applied work, of course, as well, but we concentrate on that. I do not think that within the culture of the UK generally that has been recognised to the extent that it should be. The decisions about research funding are still on research assessment exercises, peer review in terms of research papers and all the rest of it. Very important, no doubt about it, but actually for the economy what is really important is that you actually get the research into the industry and get the solutions that get the product made, that get the product sold. That is what we are talking about.

Q387 Mr Williams: Presumably that is a debate you are still constantly having with the Funding Council?

Professor Michael Scott: Yes, they come in force to see us next Thursday and I look forward to it.

Mr Williams: Good luck.

Professor Michael Scott: Can I quote you on that, Mark?

Q388 Stuart Andrew: Do the Welsh Government and the local authorities actively make use of the location of universities in promoting the various potential places for inward investment?

Karen Padmore: I have an observation on that because I spoke to the Vice Chancellor, and he sadly cannot be here today in person, but he has just come from Ireland and he was saying that in his view Ireland tend to make more use of their universities and their research in the toolbox when they are promoting Ireland overseas. He thought that there may be the scope to do that better in the UK. He cites an example I think that he was personally involved in, which was with Intel. That was very much driven by the universities getting Intel into Ireland.

James Goodman: Can I add to that as well? Having come from a local authority background, of course, you probably should ask them the same question. But very often when we have had engagement it is quite a revelatory experience for the local authority to see what a university can do and has on its doorstep. For example, when CAST on Parc Menai opened up on the outskirts of Bangor and we had really the top level equipment for visualisation there, it was quite a revelation for the local authority to see that we had one of the top pieces of kit, certainly in the UK if not in the world, on the doorstep. I think perhaps more could be made of that. Saying that, we are regularly cited as an important element of the local economy; in fact, I would argue that we are a very, very important element of our local economy.

Q389 Chair: Is there any way of measuring the success of trade missions?
Karen Padmore: Industry presumably has a better answer to that just in terms of sales and the international—
Professor Michael Scott: I have to say that missions, not necessarily trade missions, but the fact that David Willetts went out to Russia and visited universities in Russia actually helped us when we followed on a bit later and started talking first to the British Ambassador, because the British Ambassador then knew that there was a—well, she would have known there was a policy, but was then enthusiastic for the policy to go forward and so helped us. Secondly, at the Bauman State Technical University in Moscow they knew that they had had the Minister there and that we were following on and that this was a policy that was being followed from Westminster. Therefore, we got a good reception. Actually, within three days of us getting back, talking particularly about OpTIC technologies out there, we had a phone call from them to say they had already been to the Russian Government and there was money available to enable some joint research. I think those kind of missions are good, but they cannot be in isolation. They have to be followed up.

Q390 Chair: The British Embassies abroad fulfil a different function from the Welsh Government, do they? Are they working well together, do you think?
Professor Michael Scott: I think the British Embassies, when we have been abroad, are actually representing the whole of the United Kingdom. Obviously, they are well aware of the Welsh Assembly Government, the Welsh Government's agendas, as they are of the United Kingdom's as a whole. We have not found any tensions there at all between the two. In fact, I cannot thank the British Embassy enough in Moscow for the work they have done for us.
Karen Padmore: If I could just add that Bangor has an internationalisation policy now and obviously, with this new Vice Chancellor, this is very much driven. They have just opened an office in Beijing to assist students and they are actually getting more and more presence in the international market. I think it is a real priority, and then we will be able to see where the trade benefits come on the back of that so there is more of a symbiotic relationship.

Q391 Geraint Davies: Following through on that, whose responsibility is it to, as it were, sell Welsh universities abroad and get inward investment and partnerships? Is it universities taking the initiative or the Welsh Government or the Wales Office in the UK Government? How do you think that should fit together?
Karen Padmore: I think that we have to bear in mind that the UK is more than Wales and that we are selling a UK product out there through the British Council and other things when it comes to education. We need to be selling at different levels, and I think that universities are not going to sit and wait to see if the Government can do something for them. I think that you actually all have to work at the different levels. I think the most important part is that there is some coherence to it and that there is some consistency so that we know what is going on in each of the different areas and that we are presenting a common face. I think that is the real challenge. I think that the Vice-Chancellor was invited recently to—was this the Vietnam one that David Cameron was heading up? I think that there is that level of engagement.

Q392 Geraint Davies: The Beijing visit, was that successful in promoting inward investment or students?
Karen Padmore: Over 50% of our overseas students are from China and we are looking to increase that, so I think that it has been very successful.
Professor Michael Scott: When the Vietnamese Government was over in North Wales, the First Minister met them. The very fact that he met them and talked about the university and the backing that the Welsh Government was giving to the projects that we had with them was very, very important. Consequently, when we went over there, we had Ministers and a message from the Prime Minister in Vietnam and so on and so forth. But also the equivalent to a select committee in the House of Commons was in touch with us to ask how they could support the work that we are doing in Vietnam. I believe that there is a mission that is going down from that Select Committee to Vietnam, and part of the evidence is to do with us, to do with the development of our projects out there. I think it is trying to line up the two Governments irrespective of their political—
Chair: We completely agree with that, Professor Scott. I am so sorry to cut this short, but I know that there is a train that all the other Members, or many of them, have to catch. I thank the university for having us here and all of you for coming along and giving us that evidence, which was most helpful. Thank you very much.
Professor Michael Scott: Thank you for asking us. Certainly, if anybody is not going straight away and wants to see the telescope—
Chair: I am not going straight away so I will volunteer.

Thursday 15 September 2011

Members present:

David T. C. Davies (Chair)

Guto Bebb   Jessica Morden
Geraint Davies   Mr Robin Walker
Mrs Siân C. James

Examination of Witnesses

Witnesses: **Professor Mark Drakeford AM**, Welsh Labour Party, **Nick Ramsay AM**, Shadow Minister for Business, Enterprise and Technology, and **Eluned Parrott AM**, Welsh Liberal Democrat Shadow Minister for Enterprise, Transport, Europe and Business, gave evidence.

Chair: We are all on camera now, so perhaps we should bear that in mind. *Diolch yn fawr iawn am ddod yma heddiw.* It is a pleasure to see Nick Ramsay, Eluned Parrott and Professor Mark Drakeford. I congratulate Eluned and Mark on their recent election and Nick on being re-elected in Monmouth. This is meant to be a fairly friendly occasion. We are just looking into inward investment in Wales, which is something in which we all have a shared interest. We have some specific questions, but please feel free to throw in whatever you want or any observations you think are relevant to the inquiry. I will start with Siân.

Q393 Mrs James: *Bore da.* During this inquiry, we have heard a number of theories about why Wales is no longer seen as a place to invest. My question to all three of you is whether you have any opinions on, or ideas about, why Wales is losing that competitive advantage and becoming less successful at attracting inward investment.

Eluned Parrott: If I may begin, one reason why Wales was so successful in the 1990s, which is obviously seen as a critical time, was that we had a particular market position that was attractive. We were able to market ourselves on the basis that we were a relatively low-cost but also relatively high-quality location—which meant good value for money—and an entry point to the European market, which was a critical factor for inward investors, particularly from the far east. The problem is that we live in a completely different world now. We cannot recreate the conditions that made that a competitive advantage. We are no longer the lowest cost location in the European Union, since the entry of several eastern bloc countries to the EU. In no way are we able to compete on that, and nor do I think we should try to compete on cost with the far east. I do not think that a developed economy such as that of Wales ought to be trying to compete on the basis of how cheap the labour is. That would be a real mistake.

Places such as India and China have removed many of the practical barriers to investment that previously prevented big investors seriously considering basing themselves there. There is improved infrastructure as well as improved political stability—particularly in the case of China—and that makes those much more viable locations for long-term investment. The trouble that Wales has had is that we have not responded to that. We have not developed an alternative market position that is as viable, distinctive and attractive to

potential investors as the position we had previously. We have not responded to that changing world.

Professor Drakeford: I agree with a great deal of what Eluned has just said. I think that you have heard that from a series of witnesses in your earlier meetings. Glenn Massey particularly drew out the fact that you can only understand Wales's position if you understand the changing wider picture of foreign direct investment—

Q394 Mrs James: The global economy.

Professor Drakeford: Absolutely, the global economic conditions; the changing nature of the Department for Business, Innovation and Skills's view of inward investment, particularly its lack of interest in manufacturing; the fact that the centre of gravity of FDI across the United Kingdom has altered so that most FDI goes to London and the south-east in contrast to the pattern of 20 years or so ago. As he said to you, 90% or so of FDI would come regardless of anything that was done, because it was investment that was looking for market share and so on. The question for us in Wales is how we make ourselves attractive in relation to the 10% of investment that is genuinely mobile.

It seems to me that it is as Eluned said: we cannot return to marketing Wales as a place that is cheap to come to and where you will get a grant. We must find a way of persuading the companies that could go anywhere on the globe why they should come to Wales in particular. That means mobilising our competitive advantages in economic terms but also in social, cultural and other terms in a way that says to companies, 'If you come to Wales, you are not simply coming to some anonymous posting that could be anywhere in the world. You are coming to somewhere that has a sense of identity, that offers you a combination of possibilities in social as well as economic terms, so coming to Wales will allow you, your company, your career and your family to thrive'. We must concentrate more on mobilising, bringing together and making coherent that overall sense of marketing offer that we can make.

Q395 Mrs James: To follow that up, Professor Drakeford, you did not mention training, skills and education. We hear constantly that we must be a clever small country and target our workforce towards being mobile and up to the level of skills required.

Professor Drakeford: That is quite a complicated question and a bit more complicated than the headline kind of way in which it is discussed would sometimes suggest. If you look at the evidence of organisations such as the Resolution Foundation, you will find that—I think that Sir Roger Jones said something about this to you as well—the nature of the skills that are required has altered over the last 10 to 15 years. If you look at the shape of skills within developed economies, you will see that many jobs requiring the bottom end of skills continue to be created: a lot of face-to-face work in restaurants, catering and care, and stuff that you cannot do without someone else doing it with you. Other jobs are being pulled up the skills ladder so that they are at the top, graduate end, but there has been a hollowing out of the middle. Many of the skills that were previously associated with white-collar jobs and the higher end of blue-collar jobs, to use those terms, have disappeared and been pulled in those bipolar directions.

Firms often say that, in a workforce, they look for the potential to acquire the skills that they will need. That is very much what Airbus said to you. It did not say that it came here because people had the skills already; it came here because it has a workforce that is dedicated, loyal, hard-working and keen to associate itself with the success of the company, and the company, alongside the Government, further education, higher education and so on, is able to mobilise the skills package that it needs. It has a workforce that is capable of learning and relearning new skills as the skills package that it needs develops. That is definitely something that we are able to offer in Wales and it is a message that inward investing companies continually repeat. It is not just about having the skills already, important though that is— and there is more that we can do to ensure that that is the case—but the willingness and the potential to go on acquiring skills in a rapidly changing economy are what really matter.

Nick Ramsay: First, I would like to thank the Committee for inviting us here today. I think that I speak for us all when I say that we welcome the opportunity to look at ways in which we can progress matters with regard to inward investment in Wales. Some very good comments have been made, particularly those relating to the types of skills and jobs that we would like to see developing in Wales in the future.

There is no doubt that, if you look at the economy at any particular point in time—such as the 1990s or, to go back further, the 1950s, or even further back, the nineteenth century—the economic conditions at each point are different and the global economic situation at each point is different. Any Government, whether in Westminster or Cardiff, has to deal with the economic reality in which it finds itself. At the moment, things are clearly difficult. That said, we have to ask whether we will simply accept that we are constantly battling against the forces that be and against the problems that arise when other countries, such as those in eastern Europe, or China, enter the game. I do not think that we should.

A key statistic, which I think was included in our submissions, is that the figure for inward investment in Wales stands at around 4% or 5% of the overall UK inward investment figure. It stood at 15% in the mid-1990s and was more than that further back into the past. Therefore, there has been a decline. I hear a lot from my colleagues in the Assembly and from the Welsh Government about the need to address this, but I do not always hear solutions. Mark Drakeford made a point about anonymity; I agree that we need to market Wales in a different way and that we need to ensure that Wales punches its weight on the global stage. However, to be frank, there have been key mistakes in terms of the loss of the Welsh Development Agency. I do not think that International Business Wales ever completely filled that gap. We are still waiting for a successor to that and we do not know whether it will be as successful as the WDA. Therefore, there are all sorts of ways in which we can market Wales better, both now and in the future. I am not convinced that we are there yet, but we would all value the opportunity to contribute to that debate.

Chair: That was a very good opening. I appreciate the opening comments and it was right that you were able to set out the direction in which you feel we should go. However, I will say gently that we have quite a lot of questions, so from now on, we will have to be a little more brief.

Q396 Mrs James: Building on what Mr Ramsay has just said, do you think that stimulating the Welsh economy, all of the work that we have talked about, and all of the important things that we have to do in the future, should be solely the preserve of the Assembly, or do you see a role for the Government in Westminster?

Eluned Parrott: Parts of the economic strategy for Wales lie in the hands of the devolved Welsh Government, while some powers and things that have a strong and direct influence on the Welsh economy are in the hands of the Westminster Government. It is therefore critical that we are able to collaborate, co-operate and work together. That is why I am so disappointed that Edwina Hart has not joined us here today to put forward the perspective of the Welsh Government and to share in the mutual respect agenda. That is genuinely a source of disappointment to me.

In terms of the way in which we collaborate and co-operate, this meeting in Cardiff is a symbol of what is possible when we have a shared agenda and a shared commitment to tackling some of the problems that we have. I am sure that I speak for colleagues here and elsewhere when I say how grateful we are—

Q397 Mrs James: We have done it several times in the past.

Eluned Parrott: I recognise that.

Chair: It perhaps also demonstrates what is not possible on occasion.

Professor Drakeford: The response to the question has to be that the effort to bring investment into Wales is not something that the Welsh Government can do by itself; it relies on the conditions that are created at a European level as much as the UK level. If we are interested in a manufacturing-led growth strategy and an export strategy, what happens in the eurozone and in European countries—which are all retrenching, are not spending money, and are not buying goods—matters as much to the Welsh economy and investment here as anything that the Welsh Government can do. Eluned is right to say that it takes a combined effort.

Nick Ramsay: I will give the Chair a short answer as I know that he will appreciate that.

It has to be about partnership. We talk to local authorities about collaboration and partnership, and there is no doubt that some of the answers lie here with regard to small-scale matters, fiscal stimulus and what the spokespeople on economic matters here can do. However, Westminster has the macro-economic levers; the Assembly Government has no fiscal power in that sense. So, we should work together. The three parties' representatives in front of you today are singing from a similar hymn sheet in many ways, despite the differences. That is the way ahead: to work in partnership.

Q398 Geraint Davies: I want to ask about how convergence funding—and, indeed, any other funding streams—can be used to make infrastructure in Wales better for inward investors. Do you think that you should have a dialogue with prospective inward investors on how that should be done, rather than simply deciding without consultation? Do you think that convergence funding could be considered for the electrification of the railway line from Cardiff to Swansea? I represent Swansea, and we are very disappointed in that respect. The idea would be for us to use our allowance and to have it match funded by Westminster. We would not use any Welsh Government money, but use that convergence funding allowance to bridge the gap and to enable the electrification, thereby sending a signal to inward investors that we are in the network.

Chair: I beg the contributors to try to be brief, because we have quite a few questions.

Professor Drakeford: I chair the programme management committee for current convergence funding, and I will chair the programme board that will draw together the thinking on whether there will be a third round of convergence funding for Wales. That will include heavy representation from investors who are already in Wales, and others from the business world. My view—others can respond to it and be part of the debate—is that, if there is to be a third round of convergence funding, infrastructure investment must be higher up the list of things that we use that funding for than was the case in the first two rounds.

Eluned Parrott: It is important for us to look at all the potential options and that we are creative in how we approach funding in times as difficult as these. Convergence funding is one possible route for some kinds of infrastructure projects. The introduction of things such as tax increment financing schemes in Wales might also be an interesting option to explore. We need to keep our options open and keep an open mind on what could be achieved from different sources.

Nick Ramsay: Convergence funding should be invested in a way that will stimulate the economy; it

should not be just a sticking plaster or given almost as a sop, if someone says 'You are not doing very well'. The fact that we are talking about convergence funding suggests that something has gone awry. There was a time when we were hoping that Wales would not even need convergence funding at this point. So, that is sad. However, if we are going to qualify, it should be used for investment.

My final point is on institutions such as the European Investment Bank. Wales has not always benefited from them; it has not always sought support from institutions such as the investment bank in the way in which other countries such as Spain have done. So, there is not just convergence funding; there are other avenues that we can look at.

Q399 Mr Walker: Siân touched on the area of skills earlier, and it is a key determinant in attracting international investment to Wales. We have received written submissions, particularly from the energy industry, expressing concerns about science skills. Do you feel that there are areas in which firms are being put off from coming to Wales at the moment by a skills shortage or gap?

Eluned Parrott: The perception of Wales as having a low-skill economy is unfortunate, because our capacity to build skills here, the amount of university places and the opportunities that there are for people of all ages to develop their skills are a real source of potential competitive advantage. This is one area that I would like to see identified as a key selling point when we are working overseas. We are in a vicious circle at the moment whereby we have low skills and fail to attract skills-led jobs, so we lose skilled people, who go back over the border to England when they have graduated with their science-based qualifications. We need to create the conditions to develop a virtuous circle. There are some practical things that we could do. For example, we could help our universities to compete for more research funding and invest in their innovation programmes. We could look at creating a graduate science programme for Wales in order to provide those postgraduate opportunities for talented young people to stay here and to become part of the innovation structure. We can also learn from some existing successes in Wales. Some of our leading universities are leading the way on things such as innovation networks and so forth. So, there are lots of practical things that we can do.

I am also looking forward to lobbying the Welsh Government to include things such as training grants for small and medium-sized enterprises in its jobs fund, so that it can work to build the skills capacity that we have to develop the very job-specific skills that we need.

Nick Ramsay: I agree with most of the points that Eluned made. There is also a broader question about the perception and the reality: is the science base there or is there more of a perception that it is not? The things that have been mentioned would be excellent. When we eventually see it, the economic renewal programme will try to refocus—you might be asking questions about this later—on the six new areas, and science clearly plays a part in that. However, our job and your job will be to look closely at whether that actually happens. There are concerns at the moment within the university sector, as Eluned mentioned, that it will not deliver in the way that we would hope.

Professor Drakeford: The energy sector has been the largest new investor in Wales in the last 12 months, so it is vitally important to the future of the Welsh economy. If you look at Wales's geography, here we are perched on the western edge of the European Union, furthest away in terms of supply chains and so on. In some ways, that geography has been a problem for our economic development, but you could argue that, in looking ahead, particularly in relation to renewables, our geography is our biggest asset, in terms of wind, wave and other forms of renewable energies.

I tend to agree with Nick about the difference between reality and perception, and that perception can sometimes take a while to catch up with reality. If you look at what is going on in higher education, you heard evidence from Richard Davies about the new bay campus at Swansea University, which is hugely exciting for science and science education in Wales. It puts us right at the edge of what the interface will be between universities, commercialisation and business needs in the future. So, in some ways, maybe we just need to bang the drum a bit louder about what we are doing and about the real determination that there is out there in parts of the higher education sector in Wales to put ourselves where we need to be.

Q400 Mr Walker: One of the big opportunities that Eluned mentioned is European funding. When we were over in Brussels, we heard a lot of evidence about the importance of European funding and the opportunities that exist. However, there was a feeling, particularly among the Welsh Members of the European Parliament of all parties, that Wales might be punching below its weight in that area at the moment. Do you feel that the focus on Objective 1 capital funding is detracting from the focus on chasing research funds?

Nick Ramsay: From my discussions with colleagues, it seems as though we are punching below our weight. It is not always clear why that is the case. I have mentioned the European Investment Bank. I remember asking Andrew Davies, the previous Minister with responsibility for economic development, who is no longer an Assembly Member, about the EIB. At that point the funding coming to Wales was very limited, particularly from the Government avenues that we could be making the most of. At that time, a high-speed railway line in Spain benefited massively from such funding. Looking at the types of infrastructure capital investments that you want to make here, there is no doubt that that sort of money would be very useful in a Welsh context. As for why it is not happening, and why we are not making the inroads that we should, as Eluned said, it is a shame that the Minister is not here for you to ask her that question. However, we continue to raise those questions in the Chamber, and we will hopefully get some answers.

Professor Drakeford: It is not right to say that because we do one thing, we do not do the other. Convergence funding consists of a substantial slice of money that is specifically for research and development purposes. We need to capitalise on Wales's very strong reputation in Brussels as far as the running of convergence funding is concerned; we are very well thought of for the way in which those programmes have been set up and delivered, their financial integrity and so on. We need to use the platform that that has given us to make sure that we take advantage of whatever other European funding opportunities there are—it is not one or the other; it is both.

Chair: I will bring Guto in, and then Eluned can answer.

Q401 Guto Bebb: I specifically want to push on the issue of convergence being a distraction for the higher education sector, because one of the MEPs whom we met went as far as to say that, if Wales qualifies again for convergence funding—which would be an indication of failure in my view, because it would mean that we had not progressed in any way, shape or form—there would be a question as to whether the Welsh higher education sector should be allowed to go for convergence funding. In the view of this MEP, it was a distraction from opportunities to develop cross-border initiatives with other institutions in the UK and in Europe. There was almost an insular approach to funding.

Eluned Parrott: In terms of European funding for higher education, there are a number of other issues that put off Welsh universities from applying. Mark and I have both come from the higher education sector into the National Assembly for Wales, so this is something that we have experienced in our work—the kind of problems that Welsh universities will encounter if they go for that funding. First, it requires high-profile partnerships across EU borders, and frankly, it takes time, money and a strong reputation to deliver those kinds of partnerships. Secondly, you really need a huge investment of time to put together a bid. The European funding procedures, particularly in terms of research, are extremely time-intensive—more so than with the UK research councils. The scale of the projects that are funded is often off-putting to smaller institutions, and many of our universities are smaller than the national average. To take the European Organization for Nuclear Research in Switzerland as an example, no Welsh university is planning anything on that scale. Of course, there is perhaps a perception that support is not available to the universities. We could be looking at some kind of seedcorn funding programme for the universities so that they can really tackle this and start attracting that kind of investment, because it is an opportunity that we are not making the most of at the moment.

Chair: I will take a further, brief supplementary question from Geraint.

Q402 Geraint Davies: We were told in Brussels that, because £13 billion a year was being spent on skills and innovation grants, it was as easy to apply for a £200 million grant as a £2 million grant. Given that we have clusters such as the Institute of Life Science in Swansea, would there be an opportunity to attract extra, Beckham-type players in the academic world?

It would pay to get these people in to secure these massive investments from Europe. Would that strategy be considered?

Eluned Parrott: We already have some of those players. Cardiff University has two Nobel prize winners.

Q403 Geraint Davies: So why are we not applying for the big bucks? That is the issue. Are we just going for a few million?

Eluned Parrott: There is a perception that it is a big, difficult undertaking, and we need to break down that perception, as well as the practicalities.

Professor Drakeford: There are huge opportunities for universities that put a lot of eggs in a single basket, but if that does not come off, they might have lost all sorts of other, smaller opportunities that could have been gathered with some of that effort. So, this is not simple for the universities.

Nick Ramsay: I am just wondering which mountain we will hollow out for a CERN project if we attempt to create black holes in Wales—probably not. [*Laughter.*] I agree with the comments made. This is a complex area. At the moment, a lot of the small institutions that I speak to are concerned about whether they will even exist in a few years' time. So, when we are talking about the long-term planning necessary for making these bids, we should be giving some of the educational institutions in Wales the sort of stability that they need for that.

Chair: We could easily be here all day discussing this, but unfortunately, we cannot, because we have someone else coming in at 11.15 a.m. I therefore appeal for brevity.

Q404 Jessica Morden: I will be brief, then, Chair, and just ask for views on the impact of the UK Government's planned enterprise zones, particularly as some will end up on the borders of Wales—for example, the Bristol enterprise zone will potentially impact upon an area like Newport.

Professor Drakeford: The Welsh Government has said that, given that enterprise zones are tools that will be available, it will deploy them. There are anxieties about the border, and about what enterprise zones will do, given their history of simply sucking activity from one place to another rather than leading to new activity. That is part of the reason why the Welsh Government has taken its time in ensuring that enterprise zones in Wales will do the job that we want, rather than simply grasping an opportunity quickly and finding that we are replicating difficulties rather than creating opportunities.

Jessica Morden: What is the consequential again? Could you elaborate a bit more on your plans?

Professor Drakeford: The consequential is not huge. I do not have a figure in my head, but I would say that it is just under £5 million. It will not transform the Welsh economy by itself, and while it is a matter for the Welsh Government—and I am not a member of the Welsh Government, so I am just reflecting the thinking that we hear from it—it will want to deploy that money in a way that leads to genuine additionality, which is what these zones are meant to provide, rather than running the risk of them just

taking goods and services and activity from elsewhere.

Q405 Mrs James: I will make just a quick comment on that. Not many people seem to be aware of the fact that the first and biggest enterprise zone in the country is based in my constituency—it was known as the Swansea enterprise zone and has different parts bolted on to it now. What traders in the city centre are telling me is that it is sucking in all the shopping business and that the big mistake was, in the first place, planning. I will make a plea here: the planning issues must be really tight, or you could damage other fledgling industries.

Chair: Perhaps Eluned could respond to that.

Eluned Parrott: Although you are not representing the Welsh Government, I am absolutely delighted to hear someone who is close to it asking for a clear lead that the enterprise zones will be here in Wales, because I am sure, Jessica, that you must be extremely concerned about your own constituency and the kind of impact that a big enterprise zone in Bristol and another enterprise zone in Hereford will have in leeching potential investment out of your local area. That is very important.

We also need to look at other things because, if we are matching the enterprise zones position for position, there are a couple of other barriers and stumbling blocks that prevent people coming to this side of the Severn estuary—this is where we come on to Severn bridge tolls. We have seen investors move out. For example, Tesco is moving its distribution centre out of Chepstow literally across the water to avoid the £0.25 million worth of tolls it was paying each year.

Nick Ramsay: Someone once said that a week is a long time in politics. It is good to hear this movement from the Welsh Government's perspective.

I have listened to some of the comments that Edwina Hart has made about enterprise zones over the last few months and there is no doubt that they are not a panacea—they will not solve everything. However, there is no doubt at all that if you are going to have an enterprise zone just across the border in Bristol, Liverpool or the north, to compete on an even playing field, Wales needs to be investing in, if not exactly an English model enterprise zone, something similar to that. I am very pleased to hear today that the Welsh Government is looking at what options are available to do that.

Q406 Guto Bebb: Moving on from the issue of enterprise zones, I accept the argument about the displacement that could happen, but obviously, I would be very concerned as a Member with a constituency on the A55 in north Wales that an enterprise zone in the north-west would be problematic. However, hand in hand with the issue of displacement is the issue of powers to vary corporation tax rates, so I wonder what the view of the panel is in relation to Wales having the ability to vary corporation tax rates as a means of attracting inward investment.

Chair: Eluned is first and then Nick—we will do it in a fair and impartial fashion.

Eluned Parrott: Thank you. As I stated in my submission, this is something I am concerned about, because Northern Ireland has a specific challenge on its border, in that the Republic has a much lower rate of corporation tax. However, if we are not very careful in how we plan the devolution of these kinds of powers, we will enter into some kind of price war over corporation tax, and that would be very damaging. We need to work together to ensure that that is not the case. If responsibility for corporation tax is devolved to Northern Ireland, I am sure that the devolved administrations will all ask for it.

Nick Ramsay: You could spend many hours on this, but I can see the Chair beckoning me to move on—I know that look only too well. [*Laughter.*] At the risk of pre-empting the commission that will look at all these areas—and I sat on the Assembly's Finance Committee when Gerry Holtham did his review into funding in Wales—you can see some of the benefits of Wales having a lower corporation tax rate, but I am certainly not convinced. As Eluned Parrott said, you would risk a kind of competition with England that I am not sure would be entirely beneficial. It might be, but I am not convinced at the moment. I am looking to see what the commission says. When I was on the Finance Committee, I found that many of the people who defended a reduction in corporation taxes in Wales or our having the ability to vary it separately looked at corporation tax because it was an easier thing to do than deal with other taxes. We need to look at the taxation issue as a whole. I do not think that we should look at corporation tax as a panacea that will suddenly solve all Wales's woes.

Q407 Chair: Does the power to vary corporation tax mean the power to reduce it or the power to reduce or increase it? Everyone is talking about variation, which could mean going in either direction.

Professor Drakeford: In theory, variation could mean putting corporation tax up as well as down. However, the whole economic debate is about lowering it, because it is said to give you a competitive advantage. The risk, as Eluned has said, is that it leads to a race to the bottom. From a Welsh Labour perspective, we are sceptical about corporation tax, but if it were to be given to other devolved administrations, we would have to—or would want to—have the same opportunity in Wales. To be completely clear about it, the Azores judgment means that a quantum of resource available to Wales will not go up as a result of corporation tax. It can go down, because, if you do not make more money as a result of it, you will lose that extra, but if you gain money, you simply lose it out of your grant funding from the Treasury. You cannot gain, in a quantum sense, from corporation tax variation.

Nick Ramsay: That is an important point. If we have power over corporation tax, then we lose the amount of money coming from the UK to start with. That money can be evenly spread across the whole Welsh economy and Wales as an area, and although you may well benefit in pockets such as Cardiff where you are attracting business, other areas may lose out. So, as I said before, corporation tax is not quite the great bonus, but it is something that should be considered.

Q408 Chair: Presumably, you could fiddle with the local government funding formula to even that out. Anyway, as you said, we could spend hours on that one.

I will start by asking Nick a question about the six sectors that have been identified as priorities for the Welsh Government. Where does tourism stand in that? It was not in the original six.

Nick Ramsay: It does not.

Q409 Chair: Feel free to tell me what you think of that. [*Laughter.*]

Nick Ramsay: Are you giving me complete freedom?

Chair: Within the space of about 60 seconds, yes.

Nick Ramsay: I think that it is unwise. We all appreciate that, to a point, with economies of scale, less money will be coming to Wales because of the necessary cuts over the next few years. So, we have to be specific in where we target the funding. The Government's idea to focus it on ICT and on areas that it thinks will have durability and will put Wales on more of a high-skill threshold is a good one.

I do not have the figures to hand, but I think that 4% of Wales's GVA, which is falling overall as a proportion of the UK, comes from tourism. I think that the amount was £1.5 billion or so in 2010—I am quoting from memory here. The sums are nonetheless huge. So, for tourist industries not to be able to go to the Welsh Government to be considered as part of the strategy seems to me to be barking. I am sure there will be other opinions from the panellists.

Q410 Chair: I want to throw in another thought. Moving from tourism to the environment and energy, which is going to be a priority, if we encourage the generation of electricity from renewables, which, by their nature, are more expensive and therefore require subsidies in one form or another, is there a danger that we will encourage manufacturing industries, which require large amounts of electricity, to move elsewhere and therefore negate the green jobs that we create? Feel free to respond to the point about tourism as well.

Eluned Parrott: I share Nick's concern about tourism being missing. I also think that agriculture and food production are obvious omissions from the six sectors that are being targeted. At the moment, the Minister for business is planning to review those, so we will see what kind of direction she is going to take. I have queries over a couple of the sectors, to do with how unique they are to Wales, ICT being one of them. Yes, we have a core of knowledge, but is it unique? Is it better than other places? Are we going to convince Silicon Valley that we have the silicon Valleys? I am not convinced.

In terms of the sector approach as a whole, energy generation is going to be important. We have some very good research expertise in this area, as Mark will be aware. For example, the Seren project is looking at ways of creating sustainable energy, though not necessarily windfarm-based. We look forward to those kinds of technological developments, because they create opportunities for us. Generally speaking, the UK has relative energy stability at present, but we need to ensure that we are looking to the future. It would be a mistake to say that all renewables are obsessively subsidised when it is even more so for something like nuclear power.

Professor Drakeford: The Minister has said that she is willing to look at the sectors, and that is an invitation to people who believe that tourism, for example, should be included. I read the evidence that Nick has provided, and it makes a powerful case on that front. The message is that if people have cases to make, now is the time to make them. There will always be an argument about the margin of the list and whether the sixth-placed sector is the right one.

On energy, I suppose that it depends on where you think oil prices are going to be. If we are in an era of peak oil, or an era in which, once the global economy starts to recover, the oil price will go up again, you will come to a point—we were at this point during a previous peak—where renewables become competitive on price. Eluned said it: companies are looking for stability and continuity of supply, as well as looking at price. If we are entering a hugely volatile period as far as oil pricing is concerned, being able to offer a steady, guaranteed alternative is a competitive advantage for Wales.

Q411 Mrs James: I accept the point about the price of oil. However, oil is a fossil fuel, and we are going to run out of it eventually. You speak to any nine-year-old child—my granddaughter, for example—and they can tell you about saving the planet and so on. Here we are in Wales, sitting on our greatest natural resource, namely our coast. We have the second highest tidal range in the world—second to the Bay of Fundy—and we are not seriously looking at wave and tidal power. How do we move forward on this to achieve a mix of energy sources? That mix has to be there to take us into the next stage and beyond.

Chair: It will no doubt be difficult to get a quick answer to that, but we will try.

Professor Drakeford: It is disappointing that the UK Government did not agree to go forward to the next stage of the Severn tidal opportunities, however they would be configured. We have to find other ways to put some packages together to allow that to happen.

Eluned Parrott: It is exciting that Wales has some real expertise in alternative energy generation, and I look forward to the kinds of solutions that those projects will bring for us.

Nick Ramsay: The stone age did not end because we ran out of stones, and the end of the oil age will probably be similar. You hit the nail on the head when you said that we need to have an energy mix—I think that everybody accepts that. It is good that the current UK Government is pressing ahead with nuclear energy. Certainly in the medium term, that will give us a stability of supply.

No decision was taken on the Severn barrage by the previous Government. There were huge issues, mainly to do with where the funding would come from. If you look at the enormous investment required by a Severn barrage, I do not think that it would be easy at present to persuade the private sector to get involved without a huge commitment from the UK Government. I think that what the UK Government is doing on energy supply at the moment is a lot better than what has been done for a long time, not only in the last ten years, but further back, too.

Mrs James: There are miles of coastline besides the Severn area.

Q412 Guto Bebb: I am glad to hear the comments about the tourism sector being allowed back into the fold, as it were. The announcement that the six sectors did not include tourism knocked the industry, because it was perceived as a low-skills sector. That is certainly not the case in my constituency, where there have been huge investments in improving tourism infrastructure. In terms of the review that we have undertaken in Brussels, Berlin and even Dusseldorf, if I remember rightly, the loss of the Welsh Development Agency as a public face for Wales abroad was noted by almost everybody we spoke to. The strategy of the Welsh Government in marketing Wales abroad appears to be in disarray. How should Wales be marketed abroad? How should the Welsh Government be responding to the challenges? Clearly, at this point in time, we seem to be missing from the top table when there are opportunities abroad.

Professor Drakeford: I am not going to re-fight the WDA battles for you. I have read the transcripts of those being thrashed out in front of you by many other previous witnesses. I think that we have to use the economic renewal approach and the sector skills approach to doing it. When attempting to raise Wales's profile abroad—which I entirely agree is fundamental to how we attract inward investment—we need to do it in that more focused way, going out to attract companies into Wales based on the extra investment and organisation that we are going to put around the sectors we think are the future of the economy.

Chair: Siân has a very brief supplementary question to put to Eluned.

Q413 Mrs James: Is there a case for re-establishing the WDA? Is it too late?

Eluned Parrott: I would not wish to see the WDA re-established as a quango. Democratic accountability is very important for this sort of work. However, the WDA brand is still highly recognised. International Business Wales did not step into its shoes with any great degree of success, and a team of people who have been lost in the ether of Welsh Government bureaucracy in sector teams is not the best or most marketable approach. The WDA is a brand. Companies spend billions of pounds on brand awareness. We already have it. It is a massive asset. Whatever the successor should be, being cheeky, I would say that we should use the initials 'WDA' even if we are using different words.

Q414 Guto Bebb: I have a final point on this. I am not trying to pick issues with the Assembly Government over the past 12 years, but we have heard evidence that there has been constant reorganisation of the way in which Wales sells itself abroad. Today, for example, we have heard evidence that the reorganisation of the higher and further education sector in Wales is resulting in it looking inward rather than looking for opportunities. Is it possible for the

Assembly Government to provide some stability in this important area to allow us to develop for the benefit of Wales rather than reorganising all the time?

Nick Ramsay: This process of putting things into silos is an ongoing problem for Wales and the Assembly Government, and we all fall into it occasionally in contributing to debates here. It is important that Wales continues to look outward. I think that it was a mistake to abolish the WDA. It did a great deal of good work. Wherever you went in the world, when you got off the plane, somewhere nearby there was WDA branding. As has been said before, IBW certainly did not step into its place. There is no doubt that civil servants are too risk-averse to be able to deliver the sort of brand success that the WDA delivered. You cannot go backwards. You probably cannot recreate it—I think that the name may be being used elsewhere now, so it may be impossible for the Government to go back—but, moving ahead, I think that we would all agree that the people involved in marketing Wales abroad need to be at arm's length from the Welsh Government. If that is not the case, you are never going to get the sort of agility needed for Wales as a brand—although I do not like to use the word 'brand'—particularly in new markets.

Q415 Mr Walker: The written evidence that we received from Professor Garel Rhys was that there was a feeling in some places that Wales is just not really interested in this area any more. I think that what we have heard from the panel is that there is certainly an interest in sorting it out. What are the most straightforward steps that can be taken to deal with that, show interest and move away from what I think he described as a perception of chaos and indecisiveness in this area?

Professor Drakeford: I certainly would not accept that as a description of the way things are. It is problematic to achieve stability, which I think is a very sensible goal, in such a rapidly changing context. This Committee heard, one after the other, from Sir Roger Jones and Glenn Massey, both of whom are leading figures in this field. Roger Jones told you that you do not need people permanently based in other countries representing Wales and Glenn Massey immediately disagreed and told you that you do. Both of them were relying on a series of different ways in which you can do business, including Skype and so on. It is easy to say that we should have a single model and stick to it, but, when the operating context is changing so quickly, some ability to be adaptable and to change to meet that is important. We now have a plan and the Minister has indicated a willingness to fine-tune it at the edges, but pursuing it is the way that we—

Q416 Jessica Morden: What are your views on the role and location of the Welsh Government's overseas offices? For instance, we visited the Brussels office, but its remit is policy gathering. Is there an argument for widening its remit to engage in inward investment?

Eluned Parrott: It is very much worth considering that, because we have a base and people there. So, as well as gathering information, why not use them as a

proactive tool to get the word out about Wales? We are not getting that word out effectively at the moment. So, that is a real opportunity and we could get an efficient result from it.

Nick Ramsay: The idea behind the overseas offices was probably a good one at the start, but I am not sure that they have achieved their aim. I have also been to the Brussels office. Whichever future model we adopt—I agree that there is a need for stability, namely whatever the Welsh Government does, we need to have something in place and stick to it—rather than having an office there that says 'We are here', we somehow need to get Wales's name out there to other organisations. I do not think that the offices have worked. I do not even know why the one in Brussels is in that location. It is a high-rate location and I do not think that it returns the dividends that an office in another location could do. However, rather than just having an office as a physical base, it is about getting the brand of Wales out there. We can all talk about how we do that, but, however that happens, we must then stick to it.

Q417 Jessica Morden: Nick, you referred to a London hub. Can you expand a bit on that idea?

Chair: But not too much. [*Laughter.*]

Nick Ramsay: We should not operate in silos. The south-east of England is the one part of the UK that is currently producing more money than it spends in the area—

Q418 Jessica Morden: What is the London hub practically?

Nick Ramsay: The London hub is the centre of the UK economy as a whole. You have the City of London. There would clearly be benefits for Wales from tapping into that, rather than just turning inward. That was the point, which I probably did not make in a successful way. However, that does not mean that we should not have hubs elsewhere, but, as I said at the start—I will finish on this, Chair—it is about partnership and all of us working together for the good of Wales.

Q419 Geraint Davies: As you will all know, UK Trade and Investment markets Britain for inward investment trade, but, because the current Government has got rid of regional development agencies, there is now a queue of inward investors and there is an opportunity for Wales to take advantage of that. When we went to UKTI in Brussels, Dusseldorf and Berlin, there was no obvious relationship with Wales. The focus of the Wales Office in Brussels tended to be on grants, legislation and profile and not inward investment. I wonder whether anyone thinks that the priorities of the overseas offices and the focus on working with UKTI should be improved to attract more inward investment to Wales.

Eluned Parrott: As I have said, these overseas bases are an opportunity that we need to assess critically on a regular basis and refocus their activities to ensure that we are getting the greatest return possible on the investment that we are making. On collaboration and co-operation with UK Trade and Investment, it is crucial that we have not only operational-level interaction, so that the people who are on the ground doing this kind of work are liaising effectively, but also strategic interaction between Government Ministers in Wales and the Westminster Government to ensure that everyone, at every level, is singing from the same hymn sheet.

Chair: Guto, would you like to ask your supplementary to Nick?

Q420 Geraint Davies: I do not know whether Mark knows if there is a move to take advantage of UK Trade and Investment in terms of inward investment.

Professor Drakeford: Our key message is that Wales is open for business and welcomes companies that wish to do business here. Any sensible Government would want to do anything that it can to broadcast that message loud and clear.

Q421 Chair: Would anyone like to add to that? If not, perhaps I may be a bit cheeky and ask the last question in a brief way, because we have another guest waiting. We were going to ask each of you what three recommendations you would make to improve inward investment in Wales, but I will ask each of you to just give one; we will end up with three, that way. Does anyone wish to come in first on that, and make a brief suggestion?

Professor Drakeford: My key suggestion would be to not lose sight of the fact that we have many

competitive advantages in Wales, but we have to assemble them better into a package that gets that message across.

Eluned Parrott: My suggestion is in the shopping list in my written submission. The critical point regarding infrastructural development is the one on devolving borrowing powers to the Welsh Government. Please can we consider doing that in order to give it the tools that it needs to do its job.

Nick Ramsay: A number of good things have happened. For example, the decision on the electrification of the Great Western main line—

Q422 Mrs James: To Swansea, please.

Nick Ramsay: That is for another hour of discussion, probably. I will be cheeky and give two points, if I may, because there are two scales here. In the immediate term, we need to do something practical such as providing enterprise zones in some form, which will be key in making sure that we get people across the border. Secondly, we have been talking about the WDA, and we need to market Wales on the international stage in a way that is somehow at arm's length from the risk averseness of the civil service. That is key.

Chair: *Diolch yn fawr am ddod heddiw*—thank you for coming today.

Witness: **Mr David Stevens**, Chief Operating Officer, Admiral Group plc, gave evidence.

Q423 Chair: Good morning, Mr Stevens, and thank you for coming here today. I would like to begin by asking you once again—although it is very clear from your submission—why you came to Wales. It was an excellent story, and I wonder whether you could summarise it for us. There is a lesson for us all in there.

David Stevens: Yes. Five of us wrote a business plan in London in the early 1990s for a new car insurance operation, and recognised that car insurance, which is a people-intensive, low-margin business, needs to be in a cost-efficient location. So, we were never going to set up the business in London. Once we secured financial backing, we went through a process of approaching cities to ask them why we should come to their city. We had two stipulations: they had to be clearly competitive in terms of the availability of space and people, and the costs of those, and they had to be within two hours of London, because our backers stipulated that they wanted easy access to us. That has a lot to do with personal lifestyle issues—many of these things are always about personal lifestyle issues. We drew a map of places that were two hours away from London, looked at those that would be attractive in the context of labour and offices, and wrote to people in Folkestone, Dover, Corby, Leeds, Cardiff and so on. Cardiff did a phenomenal job from the word go—it was South Glamorgan council at the time. It was the only council to send people to see us; a number did not respond,

and some only wrote. They came to see us in a fairly dingy little office up some stairs on Borough High Street, yet they persevered with the idea that this could be an interesting company in the long term, and invited us to Cardiff. We spent a weekend in Cardiff; we came here about five or six times, and ultimately chose Cardiff.

Q424 Chair: There was even a piece in your presentation about Royal Ascot.

David Stevens: A problem for an inward investor such as us with regard to Cardiff was that there was no established labour pool that had the specialist skills relevant to our industry. So, we had to take some specialist people with us. One individual, who was key in the perception of the investors, was unwilling to move from Brighton, where he was living. We contacted Paul Gorin from South Glamorgan council and said, 'We are really sorry. We would love to come to Cardiff; the rest of the team is on board, but there is one individual whom we cannot move. We therefore feel that we cannot take up your invitation to Royal Ascot.' He said, 'That is very sad, but do please come. It is all booked; it would go to waste anyway. There are no hard feelings.' He told us to bring the individual along, and he spent the afternoon persuading that individual of the benefits to him, and of the delights, of Cardiff, and did so successfully. As a result, we came to Cardiff.

There are two reasons why we are here. There are the hygiene factors such as the proximity to London and cost efficiency, and then the factors that clinched it were a £1 million grant and the salesmanship of Paul Gorin.

Q425 Chair: What has happened to Paul Gorin? He sounds like an excellent individual.

David Stevens: He runs an employment agency, Smart Solutions. One thing that I said in my submission was that it is very important in the context of inward investment that you have people interacting with potential inward investors who are entrepreneurial, motivated, clever, not bureaucratic, not risk-averse, and not slow. So, it is not just a question of how many people, how many offices, and where the offices are located; it is the mentality, motivation and quality of the individuals.

Chair: He sounds like just the sort of person who could be running whatever is set up to replace International Business Wales, but there we are. He obviously has another job, which is sad for us. Siân is next.

Q426 Mrs James: Thank you for being so patient. First, I would like to say that I have a wonderful welcome from the team in Swansea whenever I have to go to SA1. The team is an important part of my constituency and is doing you proud. Thank you very much for that. Is the Welsh Government's six-sector strategy the right approach to stimulating inward investment?

David Stevens: The identification of priority sectors is logical in a time of constrained budgets, but, in and of itself, it does not really make a huge difference to whether you attract inward investment. They have to be run very well by the right people, and they have to be targeting the right companies. I listened to the three predecessor witnesses, and the discussion was fascinating, but the thrust of it was about how to market Wales on the global stage and I wonder whether that is the right target market. Have we not learned from the 1990s that big multinationals with mobile investments bring you mobile investments and are not necessarily the long-term future for the Welsh economy? Certainly, nowadays, if you are going head to head for a big multinational investment against Slovakia, Portugal, Singapore or Vietnam, you could win some, possibly, but—and this is not just a Welsh thing, but a UK thing—you would probably have to pay hand over fist and lay gold at their feet. Is that really the right thing?

Admiral came to Wales at the beginning of the 1990s with a £1 million grant at almost the same time that LG got £250 million. Which was the right strategy? To my view, the strategy should be to find 25 Admirals. Find 25 start-ups—which would probably be UK-based, incidentally—and compete to put those UK-oriented operations in Wales. The reason why that is a valid strategy is because small companies, start-ups, tend to be geographically mobile; they have not laid down such huge roots that they cannot move. They also tend to be cheap to move. A small amount of grant makes a big difference to a start-up, and it could even be a loan as well as a grant in some

contexts. Also, when they come, they bring the whole kit and caboodle—not just the satellite jobs, but the heart and the brains of the company.

Q427 Mrs James: There is a lot of criticism of the call service sector. I have quite a lot of call service centres in my constituency, and I think that they are doing a great job. However, they are seen as providing jobs that are not good jobs, somehow. We have had evidence previously that these are face-to-face jobs, providing services. What is your opinion of the detractors of call centres?

David Stevens: I would make two points on that. First, I would differentiate between a satellite call centre—which only has the face-to-face, front-line people, with the complicated stuff happening elsewhere—and a place such as Admiral. Admiral has 4,500 people in south Wales, including 250 IT people, 70 or 80 specialist marketing people, some amazing specialities on car insurance pricing, and 40 or 50 people who handle massively complicated bodily injury cases—essentially, they are complex legal cases. So, to look at a company such as Admiral and think of it as just a call centre is to misunderstand the added value that it brings. The added value of that quality of people is massive for the local community, because the Admiral office is also the decision-making place and so we use local suppliers. A satellite operation would probably use a printer somewhere else, but our printer is on the northern edge of Cardiff. It—A. McLay and Company Limited—has grown with us and has some of the most sophisticated printing technology in the UK and has been able to use that investment and equipment partly for our contract to attract other contracts, so it feeds into the economy.

We set up Confused.com and a couple of companies have spun off from that, such as Go Compare and another one which is about to launch in Llantrisant, so that south Wales is now the centre of the UK price comparison market. Had we just been a satellite call centre operation, that sort of value to the local economy would not have been delivered. Then I will flip around and say that call centres are actually fine and that a lot of the employment growth is around face-to-face services that can only be delivered in the language of the consumer and take up time. A lot of the jobs therefore will be in the call centre area; what is important in the call centre area is that you make those jobs as engaging as possible and make them a stepping stone to better jobs. If you look at our claims department of 1,500 people, almost everyone in that department started taking the first notification of claim—the simplest job—and then they moved up to handling thefts, complex accidents and liabilities and legal cases. So, there can, in certain companies, be a way through. It also has a real value in society and what we try to do at Admiral is to make the experience of dealing with Admiral as pleasant as possible, both for the employee and for the customer. We have been in the top 20 companies to work for in the *Sunday Times* survey ever since it came out, and yet these are jobs that are sometimes disparagingly called 'call centre' jobs and are not as highly paid as some of the competitors in that survey. You can run a call centre in a way that delivers value to the employees and a real positive experience to the customer.

Q428 Mrs James: Do you feel that motivation when you enter the building and that commitment—
David Stevens: Yes. It is very strong in Swansea.

Q429 Mrs James: You have talked about the call centre sector, but do you think that there are other types of companies that we can successfully attract to Wales? Do you have any ideas, or is there anything that you have seen?
David Stevens: It is very difficult for the public sector to spot which companies to attract. At the end of the day, when we crossed the desk of whoever it was in south Wales 20 years ago and they said, 'Hmm, car insurance—£1 million, okay, fine, but, hey, I have this semi-conductor thing which is really exciting', well that is rubbish. Everyone goes after the sexy sectors. If you had had a bunch of bright people who had wanted to do internet gambling, and if you had known what internet gambling was going to be like 10 years ago—okay, some people recognise that as a service sector—that might have been something that could have come here. Then you might have someone who wants to do something very prosaic and day-to-day, but who has a plausible business plan and people who are willing to invest in it, who says, 'I will come to Wales if you give me a reason to come to Wales, because I have a personal stake in the success of this'. The reason why we valued £1 million at that point was because we did not know it was going to be successful. We thought that we might make a mess of it first off and £1 million might be enough to give us a second bite, and, therefore, it really mattered to us. If you were to offer £1 million to Xerox, which might want to build an assembly plant, or to Amazon, which might want to do a distribution centre, although that is not a good example, it is neither here or there; if you offer it to a start-up, it could mean that they are willing to move. One of the things about Cardiff, and I say this a lot, is that it is about the personal. One reason why we are here that I did not mention is because the management team is very happy to live here. That is a really important variable that sometimes gets left out. One of the five used to come here on camping holidays. We have heard about tourism, and it is the shop window of Wales. He used to do camping holidays in Wales and had very happy memories of Wales. We came and visited five times and we loved it, so that is a factor as well.

Q430 Chair: I will just make a quick intervention. In an era when we are less able to pay out a large amount in grant funding for businesses to come to Wales, are there things that we could be doing to sell Wales? For example, you have just mentioned the area, the schools and the fact that it is a nice place to live. Is that what we need to be doing, or are there other things that we can do apart from offering money to get companies to come here?
David Stevens: The principal responsibility of a Government, in the economic context, is to make the country as easy and pleasant a place in which to do business as possible. Ultimately, the success of Wales

is more about its existing businesses than it is about inward investors. So, what you do with regard to the infrastructure, education and the pleasantness of the place is really important. In terms of the economic renewal document, the fact that it led by talking about infrastructure and the environment in the wider sense is valid—that is: make it better.
You then get the issue of how you sell the country to people outside, because there is a bit of a deficit, in the sense that people's perception of south Wales is not necessarily as positive as south Wales deserves. That probably goes back to the quality of the people selling the place. It does not necessarily go back to spending money on inserts in in-flight magazines on transatlantic jumbo jets. It is not about buying spots on television. You do not have the money to move people's perception of a country. You need to do it face to face with individuals.
Chair: I see that everyone wants to make an intervention. Siân can go first.

Q431 Mrs James: You mentioned infrastructure, and you know that we are keen to get electrification of the railway line to Swansea. Can I honestly say that Admiral supports that?
David Stevens: We are very supportive of investment in railways in south Wales. Beyond electrification of the line to Swansea, we would love to see the Valleys lines turned into an asset rather than, arguably, a problem.

Q432 Jessica Morden: When we were in Brussels in particular, collecting evidence about how other UK regions attract inward investment, we found that one thing that they do that is quite effective is to have successful businesses in their regions talk to those other 25 Admiral-type companies. How are you engaged with the Welsh Government, and does it ask you to do similar things on its behalf?
David Stevens: We have featured in documentation, and we have talked to people on occasion. It would be dishonest of me not to say that, actually, we have quite busy day jobs, and so there is a limit to how much we would be available for that. Sorry.

Q433 Guto Bebb: What can I say? We appreciate the fact that you are here, despite your being very busy.
I was delighted to hear you comment on career progression and skills development within the company. Could you elaborate on any problems that your organisation has experienced in sourcing higher-level skills in south Wales?
David Stevens: There are some challenges. Given the lack of a very developed private sector and, particularly in our context, a very developed insurance sector in Wales, we have either to grow our own or to bring people in who have to move house. As soon as you are in the universe of bringing people in who have to relocate, it is much trickier. That is partly because they are taking a bigger personal risk. If you ask an insurance professional to move from Guildford to St Albans, the chances are, if their new job in St Albans does not work out, they would not necessarily have to move the family again, as there is quite a strong possibility that they would be able to commute from

St Albans. If you come to Wales and your job with Admiral does not work out, you know that you will have to move again, and that is a drawback.

You also have the perception issue. When we run advertisements and talk to head hunters, we hear from them that Wales is a barrier. Sometimes, you will not even get them to come here, which is a key to persuading them that it is not a barrier.

Q434 Guto Bebb: Can you elaborate? Why is it a barrier? Are any reasons given?

David Stevens: It is not a universal view. Some of our best recruits are people who know Wales well and are anxious to return or come here. There is a perception, funnily enough, that it is further away than it really is, which is bizarre. There is also a perception that it is grimmer than it really is. There is a still a legacy— I loved the FA Cup, which was brilliant for Wales, and some of the things that have happened to change Cardiff's image and to give people a look at the place, but some people are stuck with an image of it from another time, one of greyness and soot.

Q435 Jessica Morden: With hindsight, do you have any regrets about having your headquarters in Cardiff?

David Stevens: Wales has been brilliant for us. Earlier, someone—I think that it was the Professor— mentioned the flexibility, loyalty and quality of the labour force. Siân referred to the Swansea office; there is a real buzz there, which is partly cultural, I think. We have also benefitted from being a big fish in a small pond. Admiral is important in the Welsh context. Were we in Guildford or the west there, we would be much less important. So, that has been nice. It creates a real fellow feeling around the company that our staff are essentially Welsh-based and we sponsor the Welsh team and all that sort of stuff. That creates a real togetherness, which has helped us. That all sounds fuzzy and not necessarily very valuable, but it is incredibly valuable. The car insurance market has gone through rapid change, and our business has therefore had to change; it has gone from a phone business to an internet business. Our staff's attitude is, 'Fine, we have to change'; there is no resistance to change. It is a collective endeavour, essentially. You are in the lift and someone says, 'I can't understand why we do x' to one of the senior managers. That freedom of communication is really important. So it has been very good for us. Having to have everything home-grown and not having other insurance people around has proven very valuable to us now, because there is no-one to pinch our good people—and we have a lot of them.

Q436 Geraint Davies: You seemed to be suggesting that a barrier to the relocation or start-up of key companies in Wales is the perception of how nice a place south Wales is. Obviously, we have lovely countryside and, certainly around Swansea and the Gower, a lovely coastline, and good schools and so on. Do you think therefore that there should be a refocusing on those sorts of assets, that Wales is a great place to live and be outside the smog of London? When I spoke to the general manager at Amazon, he said that he was happy to be an ambassador, as it

were, for Swansea. It is great to see you today saying all these good things about being based in Wales. Would you be prepared to help in the marketing strategy in terms of getting people to invest in Wales?

David Stevens: Up to a point. I would say that to communicate the attractiveness of Wales, the key is to get the key individuals here. It is not necessarily about having glossy pages in a magazine or television advertisements, and it is not necessarily about a big budget. It is about finding the people who make the decisions and are potentially interested in being mobile and getting them here.

Q437 Geraint Davies: So events such as the Ryder Cup, for instance, would be important networking opportunities.

David Stevens: Yes. It is also important to time it right—we came here six times and it did not rain once before we decided to move here. So that was clever. We said, 'We love these Victorian arcades' but had not worked out why they were there.

Q438 Geraint Davies: I know that Siân has already mentioned this, but you mentioned in your evidence the importance of being able to get to your destination within two hours on the train. Obviously, Swansea is a bit further. To reiterate the point, I presume you would very much support electrification of the railway to Swansea from Cardiff, if only to give the perception that we are on the network.

David Stevens: I support it. I have to say it is not about Cardiff to Swansea, but Swansea to London. It is also, incidentally, about Swansea and Cardiff to Heathrow, because there is a possibility of a Heathrow hub out of Reading, which I think would be really valuable. One thing that we find challenging now that we are an international company operating in four countries is interacting with our international operations while being based in Cardiff. That is a challenge. Some of the infrastructure improvements that would mean you have a better chance of getting the people and the money from London are also relevant to companies that go to an extra stage that then have to work on a wider stage and to addressing the question of whether Cardiff is the right place to be based if you are trying to run a multinational company.

Q439 Geraint Davies: The airport is there.

David Stevens: I am talking about ease of travel to Heathrow, because there is a real challenge around making Cardiff airport successful where it is. To my mind, it is such a tragedy for south Wales and Bristol that we did not put something near the Severn bridge—I know that it will never happen—that could almost be a third London airport, sucking in people from Birmingham and Bristol. Bristol airport is in a stupid place, as is Cardiff airport. It is the classic big investment that the UK Government collectively will not make.

Q440 Mr Walker: Thank you very much for this evidence. It is clear from what you have been saying that Admiral is a great Welsh success story, and that the way in which it was attracted as a small entrepreneurial business was key. You made it very clear that that was all about individuals. You mentioned not having a bureaucratic approach—not printing leaflets, and so on. We do not want to look back at history, but do you think that it would be better in future for Wales to have an arm's-length body promoting Welsh business, rather than doing it from within government bureaucracy?

David Stevens: I think that I am out of my area of competence. Paul Gorin was in the economic development department of South Glamorgan council; he was not in the WDA, which became involved later. I do not know what it is that lets some parts of government operate with a freedom and effectiveness that other parts struggle to operate with because of bureaucratic constraints. You are probably in a better position to judge that than I am.

Q441 Mr Walker: It was absolutely key that local government was the key element, rather than central government. As an organisation, do you have regular dealings with the Welsh Government?

David Stevens: Yes, we do, and it is a nice thing about Wales that it operates on a scale where it is quite plausible to have that access. Ultimately, it could be a selling point for Wales, if it was able to translate that into speed of action and into a perception that the Welsh Government is creative, fast-moving and very business-friendly.

Q442 Mr Walker: How important is it for the Welsh Government to focus on these smaller businesses? You made a very persuasive case that bringing in smaller businesses and growing them can sometimes be much more successful than bringing in big overseas investment. What would you like to see change in order to deliver that?

David Stevens: I should first of all qualify what I am saying by saying that I am a car insurance executive who does car insurance well and who has one experience of inward investment into Wales, and that that is the prism which I see through. The option of going for start-ups would imply that you are looking to interact with venture capitalists, business angels and a different network of individuals that will probably be based in the rest of UK, and probably primarily in the south-east. That is how you will be marketing Wales—you are saying, 'You're an investor and you are backing something that is interesting and still mobile; we'll come in and provide you with some money as long as it locates in Wales'. So, it is a different target market and it is a different sales approach.

Q443 Guto Bebb: You commented that five of the six executives were persuaded of the merits and the competitive advantage of south Wales when you decided to come here, and that the sixth was persuaded at Ascot. Do you think that Cardiff and south Wales still have those competitive advantages that you noticed when you decided to invest in the area?

David Stevens: Very much so; they have the advantages. In the briefing note, one of the potential questions for me was about what the barriers were to inward investment. I will switch it round and say that lots of places qualify as attractive places for inward investment. I cannot see really big barriers to inward investment in Wales, but you have to go one step forward and ask, 'How do I differentiate myself from all those others; how do I say that I am better and different?' All the hygiene factors are in place, but you need to ask whether the salesmanship and the grant/loan option are there, which were the two things that pushed it over the edge for us.

Q444 Chair: You made a very powerful point about how one excellent individual can make the difference, but what can the Government do to give that individual something to sell? Are there any particular policies that we could recommend to the Assembly or to national government that would help?

David Stevens: I am sure that Paul would say that he had a team working for him, and it also makes sense to point out that he introduced us to a lot of individuals when we were on our trips to Cardiff who were universally positive and helpful. So, although Paul was key, it was a piece of teamwork.

In terms of policies, it is probably about who you target, where you spend your money and the type of people you employ in the process.

Q445 Geraint Davies: The west midlands had what was basically a soft-landing package for inward investors. Investors were told, 'Come to the west midlands and we will give you free accountancy and legal advice to set up a company, and we will give you free office space for six months, so that you de-risk your trial'. In your case, you had a £1 million buffer in case things went wrong, which would allow you to have another go. Do you think that the Welsh Government might look at such an option? That is, putting together a package of a certain value that would allow people to come, try it out, suck it and see and see what it is like without having too much of a downside in the first instance. If it works, they could then go forward.

David Stevens: Providing services in kind, which is what you are talking about, is a valid approach. The chances are that, if you spend £1 million on services in kind, you do not deliver £1 million to those you are spending them on. If you give them the cash, they can spend it more cleverly than you can. However, it may be helpful and it may be a valid way forward. I do not understand the constraints preventing regions from offering money. If it addresses some of the constraints regarding what they are allowed to do, then that is certainly a valid approach.

Chair: You have gently pointed out that you have a very busy time doing what you do. It is drawing near to 12 p.m.. Do any Members have any quick-fire questions that they would like to ask before we finish? No-one is catching my eye, in which case we will finish a few minutes early. I thank you very much indeed for coming down and for sparing the time to talk to us today.

Tuesday 8 November 2011

Members present:

David T. C. Davies (Chair)

Stuart Andrew	Jessica Morden
Guto Bebb	Mr Robin Walker
Geraint Davies	Mr Mark Williams
Jonathan Edwards	

_____

Examination of Witnesses

Witnesses: **Mr Nick Baird**, Chief Executive, **Mr Martin Phelan**, Director, Investment Projects and FDI Transition, and **Ms Kirstyn Boyle**, Head of Strategy and Business Partnerships, UK Trade and Investment, gave evidence.

Chair: Good morning. We are not being televised today so you can make any slips that you want and it will never be held against you. I am going to let other members kick off and I might interject, but this is not some sort of Rupert Murdoch-style grilling. We are just trying to inform ourselves more than anything else; so feel free to tell us anything you think is relevant. The only thing is that we have about an hour so I may have to speed up the questions. I usually do at some point in the proceedings, but we will see what happens.

Q446 Jessica Morden: Thank you very much for coming. Can I start off by asking you to explain UKTI's role within Government?
Nick Baird: UKTI is effectively the Government's investment promotion and export promotion department. It has two parents: BIS and the Foreign Office. In terms of inward investment, we have agreed targets which are essentially to bring 750 new inward investment projects to the UK each year. We do that both through the teams we have in our embassies and missions overseas, and our new private sector partners, PA Consulting, in this country. On the export promotion side, we also have agreed targets in terms of the volume of services and the number of interventions we provide through our services in support of British companies. I can describe those services more fully, if you would like. Those are delivered by teams in the regions, who operate through a private sector contract and, again, our trade teams in the missions overseas.

Q447 Jessica Morden: In terms of being overseen by the Foreign Office and BIS, how does that work in practice and what are the advantages and disadvantages?
Nick Baird: It is a very good system. With BIS, you are integrating trade and investment fully into the growth strategy, which is led by BIS. I work extremely closely with my colleagues there. I sit on the BIS board on all the more domestic aspects of the growth strategy. My own background is Foreign Office, and I worked before this job on the Government's campaign to commercialise it. We work very closely with the broader Foreign Office agenda on prosperity, which includes issues such as market access, building up big relationships with all the emerging powers, and our work on the European

Union to extend the single market and so on. It is a very good system. I sit on the boards of both organisations. I work very closely with the Foreign Secretary, the Business Secretary and my own Minister, Stephen Green, who sits in both organisations as well.

Q448 Jessica Morden: Can you explain practically how you go about attracting inward investment and your experiences when you talk to CEOs of how they feel, particularly about Wales? What are the protocols?
Nick Baird: Our system has some new aspects to it, which I should bring out. Essentially, it begins with the setting of targets, which I have described, and then it moves to a lead generation phase, where our teams overseas will be proactively scanning the horizon in our key inward investment potential countries, looking for companies that are already global or going global which have skills and sector competencies to match our own economy, and then making contact with those companies, pushing for investment into our country. That is for new companies. We also work very closely with our existing inward investors to encourage them to expand further. Underpinning all that, we engage in generic and sector-specific events which showcase the excellence of the British economy, both generally and sector-specific. That is the lead generation aspect.
When we get some interest under the new system, the project goes into what we call a pipeline, managed for us by PA Consulting. That pipeline then triggers a process whereby different parts of the country can bid to host the particular investment. Then, a process starts of working with the client on where the best place for them to locate would be. Then, PA Consulting, working with our own staff, will take an inward investor through the whole process towards landing a project, whether it is to do with taxation issues, grant, planning, skills and so on. Then there is a process of aftercare as well.
In terms of the second part of your question on Wales, we are extremely proactive right across the world through all our embassies, working very closely with the Welsh Government in showcasing the particular advantages of Wales around the skills that arise from the very strong clusters, the aerospace cluster in particular, but advanced manufacturing also. There are also life sciences, sustainable energy, media, legal

professional services—all those strengths—plus the proximity of Wales to big centres, in particular London. I was very impressed to hear that, apparently, one can get from Cardiff to London in one hour 36 minutes now on the train. There is, also, the relative low cost and quality of life. We are very heavily engaged right across the world in showcasing those advantages.

The figures for last year on inward investment were not great. All of us acknowledge that, but, quite interestingly, the figures for exports are very good. In Wales, in the last financial year, exports went up by 30%. The year to date increase in exports retains that. That is higher than any other part of the UK except London. It arises very largely from the FDI into Wales, which is very heavily engineering, aerospace and other advanced manufacturing-based. There are certainly some good statistics out there as well as the tricky ones on inward investment.

Q449 Chair: How much are PA Consulting paid each year?
Nick Baird: Martin, do you know the exact figure?
Martin Phelan: Yes, I do. Depending on how they perform, because it is very much a results-based contract, were they to achieve all the target outcomes, of which there are several layers, the total management fee for delivery would come to just shy of £1 million. That is out of a contract of just over £13 million.

Q450 Chair: What made you choose a private company to interface with the private sector?
Nick Baird: Our own view is that, bringing in the expertise and the private sector links of a company, and a process of strong incentivisation as well, will increase the quality of our performance. We have also done this through our trade teams—our export support teams—across the country. We have tracked very considerable improvements in performance by doing that through a private sector approach.
Chair: If you have a written breakdown of the figures that you could send us, that would be helpful.[1]

Q451 Mr Walker: Wales's proportion of FDI has fallen over the years. We have been hearing in this inquiry some of the reasons for that. In your opinion, is there anything that has happened over the last decade or so which has made Wales a less competitive place for foreign direct investment?
Nick Baird: It is a challenging picture; that is undoubtedly true. I know you have looked very closely at the figures in the '80s and '90s. They were really impressive figures for inward investment—in fact well out of proportion with the size of Wales as a proportion of the economy as a whole. Over the last decade, it has been in the high single figures most of the time, although it has dropped to lower single figures in the last year or so, which is for much of that time more in proportion with the size of Wales's economy as part of the overall economy of the UK.
There are a number of factors. I would not claim to be a huge expert on this, but what strikes me in terms of general, global trends which may well have

affected Wales is, first, the type of investment that increasingly we have seen into this country. The balance of investment has moved away from engineering and manufacturing over that period toward services, although there is a lot of very good manufacturing investment coming in. It is an issue of scale and balance. That is one element of it. The second element—and this is again very noticeable globally—is the increasing concentration of investment around big urban centres. You see that in the UK as a whole, and the concentration of investment around London is very strong.
There is no doubt a range of other factors, too. The other thing that is, to me, very impressive is the way that Wales is adjusting to that. Although it is terrific that it is fantastically strong in aerospace, advanced manufacturing and so on, there are new sectors emerging. There is media around Cardiff, and financial and professional services such as Legal & General, Admiral and so on. If we push forward that diversity, that would be very beneficial to Wales.

Q452 Mr Walker: Other regions are affected by the same global trends. Are there any particular reasons for them standing out in terms of their performance?
Nick Baird: The big pluses tend to be recognisable clusters. You have seen recognisable clusters, for example, in Manchester, which have taken it forward. Martin was there yesterday and may want to say a few words about that. High-tech clusters help particularly as well. We see the huge success, for example, of clusters around Cambridge university and the success that we are able to make in Tech City in the east end of London, again, because it is high-tech. We have also seen a lot of success around the old, automotive industries in Birmingham and Liverpool. That is because of traditional skill bases which have adapted, adjusted and upskilled to the new requirements. The big Tata investments in Liverpool and Birmingham have been fantastically valuable. I do not know if you want to say anything about it, Martin.
Martin Phelan: Just a little. We have seen some real growth in the big cities. London, particularly, has grown. It is not necessarily so much about a climb in one area as growth outstripping some areas, London being the most noticeable in terms of how it has managed to grip the issue of foreign investment. That is part of the trend of FDI globally. Manchester, where I was yesterday, as Nick said, has very successfully managed to market its brand as a city of certain things—creativity, for example, but, at the same time, industrial capability. The way they have projected themselves is quite interesting. They have built one of the more effective city structures for inward investment around MIDAS, which gathers the partnerships together and operates as one single, coherent unit.

Q453 Jonathan Edwards: When we were in Germany, Germany Trade & Invest seemed to have a mission statement to rebalance their economy geographically, partly as a result of the reunification process. They have been extremely successful. Is it in your mission statement—because, presumably, the UK has greater wealth polarisation at a regional

---
[1] See Ev 219

level—to target investment into its poorest areas, or is it more a free-for-all approach?

Nick Baird: The Prime Minister and the Business Secretary made it very clear that they are looking for rebalancing in a number of ways. They are looking, of course, for rebalancing from an economy which is fuelled by debt and based on domestic consumption; they are looking for a rebalancing from services to manufacturing; and they are looking for a rebalancing from London to other regions. In terms of the way that we as an organisation operate, we will not particularly prioritise any regions, but we will take in all the investment that we can possibly get from countries and companies around the world, and we will work very closely with the different parts of the United Kingdom to showcase their particular advantages and attract investment in those directions.

Q454 Chair: Do you find that employers are complaining about educational standards in Wales or in other parts of the UK? A comment that has been made to me in the course of this inquiry is that people in an area of high unemployment are applying without even basic social skills, a basic level of mathematics or spoken English. Is that an issue that has been raised with you before?

Nick Baird: Yes. I have had raised with me issues around the importance attached to engineering in this country through our education system and the need to encourage greater enthusiasm. There is a lot of support from inward investors around the Apprenticeships Programme, for example. It is more an inward investor here and an inward investor there rather than a consistent picture from inward investors talking to me about lack of the basic skills required to operate in a business environment.

Q455 Chair: Is that UK-wide or specific to Wales?

Nick Baird: I have been doing this for only two months so it is not a very long period. I have certainly not heard anything specific to Wales in that sense. I have talked to a lot of inward investors active in Wales, particularly GE, which I talked to at some length. It very much enjoys and benefits from its experience in Wales.

Chair: I will probably have to speed it up a little bit now, if I may.

Q456 Mr Williams: I have a question on some of the figures in your submission. You stated that between 2003 and 2010 an average of 173 jobs was created for every project in Wales compared with a UK average of 105. What is the explanation for that?

Nick Baird: I think it is true that job-intensive projects, in particular, have gone to Wales for the simple reason that costs and labour costs are cheaper there. The kinds of projects that have traditionally gone into Wales have been more job-intensive than elsewhere in the UK, particularly London. It remains true that that is the case, because, although Wales got only 2.6% of the projects last year UK-wide, the figure for jobs was 5.8%.

Q457 Mr Williams: You mentioned earlier and in your submission the four areas where you feel Wales

still has a strong, competitive advantage. I am glad you mentioned skills. That is obviously critical. You also mention proximity to UK hubs in Europe, competitive property prices and the quality of life. As you promote Wales, which of those four is the most important?

Nick Baird: It is probably quite difficult to identify one as more important than the other. The package is very important. To me, it is a very persuasive picture on skills. When you look at the aerospace clusters and the really good experience that Airbus, GE and BA have, the advanced manufacturing beyond that with terrific experiences through Ford, Sony, etc, and the way that we are moving to new sectors, which is really impressive and needs to be pushed forward, all that is absolutely critical. It is that, allied with the fact that it is a cheaper place to do business and a beautiful, beautiful country. These are, all together, what give it the edge. It is the collectivity of those points.

Q458 Mr Williams: How much of an edge does Wales have over eastern Europe when one looks at some of the benefits of investing there, not least lower labour costs? In short, are those benefits strong enough in themselves to promote Wales positively?

Nick Baird: That also links in to the UK-wide picture for attracting inward investment. A number of things on a UK-wide basis that the Government have taken forward are relevant to the balance between the attractiveness of the UK, including Wales and eastern Europe: corporation tax rates, the work that is going on with regard to regulation, the skills that exist already and the way that they are being supported. Across the UK, it remains, as we know, the No. 1 destination for FDI in Europe. Although it is a challenging time for FDI, the reductions we are getting are pretty small. If you look at the reductions elsewhere in Europe, including eastern Europe, they are more significant than we are getting.

The other very important areas for the next period in which Wales shares are the big infrastructure developments going forward and some of the Welsh aspects of those, such as the big offshore wind farms and all the infrastructure around those, and nuclear generation at Wylfa. These are really big projects, not just in themselves but in terms of the supply chains and the associated infrastructure with them. I am going on to a really big infrastructure investment conference with the Chinese straight after this, and we will absolutely be stressing the opportunities for them as well in the Welsh aspects of this big infrastructure development programme.

Q459 Mr Williams: In terms of infrastructure, I do not represent a part of Wales in the south or the north, but I could relate to at least three of the four positive ways in which you could sell Wales in my constituency. One in which we could not compete is through the absence of an adequate broadband infrastructure. The starting point for a lot of the companies you are talking to is that there is a robust, fast broadband cable, is it not?

Nick Baird: Yes. It is absolutely critical. I do not know whether this happens in Wales—forgive me—

but with the enterprise zones in England fast broadband is a priority. The Government are moving forward as fast as they can with the 4G auction as well.

Q460 Mr Williams: In an area like mine, there is excellent research work being undertaken in one of my universities in Aberystwyth. If our capacity to build meaningful hubs is impeded by that, I would imagine that would be a great negative.
Nick Baird: It is true of my conversations with inward investors that fast broadband is very important.

Q461 Guto Bebb: Can I follow up on the issue of proximity to hubs? You mentioned in your initial statement that Cardiff, after electrification, will be within one hour and 40 minutes of London. How important is proximity to London for people making decisions to invest in Wales?
Nick Baird: It is extremely important. It is really important for the Welsh Government to build on strong contacts with London HQs over the next period. We have clear evidence that a good way into expanding inward investment in other parts of the UK is to have very good relationships with the London HQs as they try to develop and expand their engagement in the UK. They are going to look for other parts of the UK in which to put some of their expanded capacity. In those circumstances, it is absolutely critical to be able to get to them fast. That is one aspect of this.
For all companies, it is very rare that you will get an inward investing company which does not need, by definition, to be travelling globally a great deal of the time. They need to get to Heathrow very quickly, or other airports which have extensive, international connectivity.

Q462 Guto Bebb: You also mentioned in your evidence that you co-operate with the Welsh Assembly in trying to attract inward investors into Wales. Can you expand on your relationship with the Welsh Assembly and the partnership work you are undertaking?
Nick Baird: Yes, indeed. We work extremely closely with our Welsh colleagues. We are now working quite closely with the new arrangements in the Department for Enterprise. I will go and see my colleague for my first proper meeting with him on 24 November.[2] Martin and his team work extremely closely with their colleagues. There is a new major projects team under an official called Jason Thomas, which has been set up in the last two to three weeks, and we want to work extremely closely with them.
It is important to stress that the process I have described is quite new. The key focuses of our joint working over the next period need to be making sure that the Welsh Government and its officials understand the new process and can fully access it. It is basically the idea that, when a company bites and a project goes into our pipeline, the Welsh Government are straight in there and have all the information to present their offer for that particular project if it is relevant.

Secondly, I want to work very closely on showcasing with the Welsh Government. We have a very good narrative, but we need a renewed, compelling narrative that every key inward investment country overseas has our ambassador at their trade teams so that they can get across the four or five key points.
The other thing I want to do with my opposite number in Wales is make sure that everything my organisation and I know about best practice in inward investment is being carried out effectively in Wales. I am thinking of practical things like having really good business champions to speak on behalf of Wales. Are we getting Tom Enders and GE out enough everywhere, championing Wales as a business destination? Do the universities of Wales work closely with their alumni overseas in getting them to champion Wales in their particular countries? Are we sufficiently active in working with the embassies in London to get consulates in and so on and so forth?
To underpin all this, we have put in place two particular things: first, one of our own inward investment relationship managers, Gareth John, who has experience with the Welsh Development Agency from the past, to manage our relationship with Wales to make sure all these things are being pushed forward. We have also signed a memorandum of understanding with the Welsh Government to underpin all this.

Q463 Guto Bebb: I welcome everything you have just said, but you used the word "new" several times. Is that an indication that the relationship has not been what it should over the past few years?
Nick Baird: I have only been around for the last two months. The relationship has been perfectly good. Martin, perhaps, will have a longer perspective on it. I am a new chief executive. We have a new approach, and I want to put energy and drive into this and really understand myself what the issues are in Wales. I am uncomfortable with the figures we had in terms of the number of projects for last year. We must not have that again. I am determined to work closely with my opposite number to make sure that does not happen.

Q464 Chair: Who is your opposite number?
Nick Baird: James Price is the relevant director general of the Business, Enterprise, Technology and Science Department.
Chair: We probably are going to have to start speeding this along a bit.

Q465 Guto Bebb: Significant changes are being undertaken in terms of the relationship with the Welsh Government. How can you ensure that there is no duplication of effort in this age of austerity to make sure that all resources are being used in a constructive manner? Are you confident that can be done?
Nick Baird: Yes. The answer to that is by really close working. We need to be absolutely aware at all points of what the Welsh Government are doing, their particular priorities, where their resources can be best focused, what we can do and make this complementary. We need to do that in terms of the Welsh Government's offices overseas. Where the Welsh Government have offices, we will be in

---

[2] See Ev 220

support; where they do not, we will be acting very intensively for Wales. Here, in this country, it is through a real understanding of what the Welsh Government are doing to make sure that our action is supportive and complementary. The way you do that is by being aware of what they are focusing on and how our skills can be applied.

Although we are not here to talk about export and trade issues today, I have looked at the figures and they are not good enough in terms of Welsh company use of our export support services. I want to make sure that Welsh companies are coming on trade missions a lot, using the reports that our embassies provide and properly accessing our funding to support companies in exhibitions overseas. Wales is performing well on exports but we can also help them do better.

Q466 Guto Bebb: I have a very short final question and a yes or no answer will do. In the eyes of potential investors, is the fact that Wales has a devolved Administration a positive or a negative?

Nick Baird: I think the answer to that is that, particularly with new investors, it is always a question. They do not start with a perception that it is therefore bound to be more difficult but with a perception that they need to understand how the two organisations and Governments work together, and I think that is really important.

Q467 Geraint Davies: I am very encouraged by everything you have said, but, during our visits to Brussels and Berlin, the impression was given in the UKTI offices that there is typically little or no contact with the Welsh Government and not very much involvement. While I support what you have been saying in terms of ambassadors, alumni and the marketing strategy, this has not happened to date. Would you like to comment on that?

Nick Baird: My main comment would be that it will not happen on my watch. I will be really determined to prioritise Wales and give it proper priority in the overall picture. It is critical for all of us, right across the United Kingdom, that we push on the inward investment side. I am absolutely determined. The way one does this most effectively is by having a really clear, simple message that everybody across our organisation understands on the benefits of Wales. You have a longer history of this, Martin. What is your sense of the overseas awareness of the Welsh offer?

Martin Phelan: To be absolutely honest, it is probably variable, but that is probably true of the rest of the UK as well. Over the years, the relationship has been okay. I think it has been as good as the relationships with any other parts. The sorts of things that Nick has talked about we have not done in the past. There is a lot more opportunity now to help through the extra resources we have with the new arrangements and the physical closeness of the relationship which we can now achieve through Gareth and one or two others operating in an employed way in England, which we have not had before.

Q468 Geraint Davies: Wales's GVA is something like 74% of the UK average. At a time of austerity and public sector cuts, the dependence of Wales on public services is particularly important now we are getting new investment in trade. At a time when the RDAs have been abolished, I would have thought there would be a greater opportunity for Wales to draw down these potential opportunities. That does not seem to be happening. Kirstyn, you are involved in partnerships and strategy. Is there a new opportunity to talk to the Welsh Government about their priorities in their offices? What they said in their offices in Brussels was that their three priorities were grants, policy development in Europe and profile. They did not mention inward investment or trade at all. UKTI said they were happy to do something. In fact the officials said very little. What do you think about that? I thought I would bring you in because you have not said anything.

Kirstyn Boyle: We are co-located with the Welsh investment people in New York and in the UAE, and we get 80% more FDI from the States than we would ever get from Brussels. In that sense, they are right. They are prioritising key markets. Wales used to have an office in Germany and, with the reorganisation, that person was moved out. That is what you alluded to earlier: that it is all being re-formed now and picked up. There is always a danger with putting investment officers in Brussels that you can get sucked into the politics of the euro rather than talking to businesses. Businesses are clearly in Germany, France, America, China and India. They are probably the key markets that the UK, as a whole, should look at, and Wales possibly as well.

Q469 Geraint Davies: Mr Baird, you are a fresh pair of hands and eyes, driving this forward. There have been a number of changes in the Welsh Government since the reorganisation of their economic development. We have a new Minister, Edwina Hart. Have you made contact? Is there an opportunity there for a new, happy marriage, moving forward?

Nick Baird: I am determined to work with her as closely as possible. I very much hope I will be able to see the Minister on 24 November.[3] That would be my ambition. I have been in contact with my official opposite number. I speak a lot also to the Welsh Secretary. I have talked to the Welsh Secretary twice about these issues since I started.

Q470 Geraint Davies: The levers now are devolved so it is important, is it not, to work hand in hand?

Nick Baird: Absolutely.

Q471 Geraint Davies: Mr Phelan made a point about Manchester and city brand development. Representing Swansea, I am particularly interested in Swansea. Are there opportunities for Swansea and Cardiff? Are you working on that sort of thing or is that off the radar?

Nick Baird: Yes, we absolutely are. There are real opportunities around that. That is part of the compelling narrative that we need to develop. One of the things I have not talked about as much as I should have done is the really strong research base backing that we have in the manufacturing, engineering and aerospace industries in Swansea university and its

---

[3] See Ev 220

associated cluster of high-tech companies. I am really interested in visiting there.

Q472 Geraint Davies: We celebrate the centenary of Dylan Thomas in Wales, particularly in Swansea, in 2014. We are interested in building tourism opportunities and brand values in Swansea with the Dylan Thomas brand, which is international. Is that something with which you would be interested in helping us?

Nick Baird: Absolutely. We have this new Great campaign, which has been very much led by Number 10, which is this big, new campaign of showcasing British excellence in industry, which is of interest to us, but also Britain as a tourist destination. I sit on the Great board and I will absolutely ensure that we have enough Welsh involvement and Welsh branding as part of that. Taking advantage of these big anniversaries and events like the Dylan Thomas centenary is really important. The other thing I want to do is bring many more big, UK-wide events to Wales. For example, if we have a big China investment event like the one we are doing today, why not do it in Cardiff? We are, for example, planning the next Britain/China JETCO meeting in Cardiff. That will be Vince Cable and his opposite number in December.

Q473 Geraint Davies: That is very encouraging. Would you be prepared, for instance, to come down personally to Swansea to meet the vice-chancellor, some representatives from Amazon and other main investors to talk about showcasing and encouraging inward investment?

Nick Baird: I would be delighted to do that.

Geraint Davies: Excellent. I will be on the phone.

Q474 Stuart Andrew: We heard from Sir Roger Jones, the former Chair of the Welsh Development Agency. He said that the abolition of the WDA would sentence Wales to nearly 10 years in the wilderness in terms of industrial development. Do you agree with that statement? Do you think that the brand of Wales suffered with the abolition of the WDA?

Nick Baird: I really do not know the answer to that question, I have to say. From where I am sitting, I will work with whatever organisation is there, and I will work as strongly as I possibly can with them. I am very encouraged. It is a really good move that my opposite number, James, has set up this new major projects unit. We are very keen to be heavily engaged in that. I really do think it makes sense to put a lot of resource into this over the next period. We all know the issues around constrained domestic demand at the moment. We all know that exports and inward investment are what we have to do to get ourselves back to sustainable growth as a country, as a whole. It is really worth investing in this area.

Q475 Stuart Andrew: What do you think the skill mix should be of the people involved in such an organisation? Should it be just civil servants or do we need to broaden the scope of expertise?

Nick Baird: We should definitely broaden it, in my judgment. The vital skill sets are strong marketing capability, real knowledge of the sectors in which the country is strong and real capacity to build relationships with key investors going forward. That is another area that we are trying to take forward in UKTI, which is much better client account management of our relationships with inward investors. At the top level, the Government have introduced new ministerial level client account relationships with some of the biggest inward investors, including some who are very active in Wales, and exporters. We are going to expand that. There will be ministerial level accounts, but then we will have accounts for companies managed at a lower level, right the way through our organisation. I am very keen to talk to my opposite numbers in Wales about really good client account management of inward investors as part of this.

Q476 Stuart Andrew: Can I go back to the overseas offices again? The Massey report mentioned that they wondered why more staff were being recruited in India, for example, where the returns have not been that successful, whereas those in America have been. Do you think UKTI is better equipped than the Welsh Government to promote Wales abroad? Are the Welsh Government right in spending money on resources like that?

Nick Baird: I certainly think it makes sense to do so. The existence of an office in a particular country, even if the embassy as a whole can do a perfectly good job in presenting Wales, has power symbolically, in terms of saying, "We really want your investment in Wales." There are difficult judgments about where you put these offices. The United States is so obviously the biggest investor that it is important to pay attention to that market. I am very struck by the speed with which Chinese and Indian investors are growing. There is huge capacity there. UK-wide, India is now our third biggest investor. As you know, Tata is the biggest manufacturing employer in the UK bar none now.

There is that balance between the present, in terms of size of investment, but also the opportunities for the future, which may not be a particularly distant future either.

Q477 Stuart Andrew: Finally, on the operations in the United States, the Massey report says that the decision to centralise all the operation in New York goes contrary to best practice. What is your view of that?

Nick Baird: It would be very difficult for the Wales Office, I suspect, to spread its resource much into other cities, but we have that network. Because we are co-located in New York, that will strengthen the ability of the Welsh Government Office to access the broader network. I was in the United States a few weeks ago talking to all our teams and they are fantastically active. It is a best of class performance out there, not just waiting for companies to come with their offers but going out, engaging with companies and seeking to attract them to the UK.

Q478 Jonathan Edwards: Where is Gareth John based?

Nick Baird: He is effectively peripatetic. A lot of our investment promotional advisers work from home. I think he lives in Wales; so effectively he is Welsh-based.

Q479 Jonathan Edwards: In an earlier answer, you said you wanted to improve Welsh presence on trade missions. For example, with regard to the recent trade mission to India, how many Welsh businesses went on that trip?

Nick Baird: I would have to write to you on that.[4] The figures I have been given are that 40 Welsh companies came on our trade missions overall last year, which is not enough. I cannot tell you what proportion that is, although I am sure we could give you that, but it is not enough. As part of this big, new approach that the Prime Minister will be launching on Thursday to get 100,000 new SMEs exporting between now and 2015, we intend to use intermediary organisations to work in partnership on that: chambers, trade associations, banks, lawyers, accountants and so on, those with big SME networks. On the back of that, we are going to hold big SME conferences across the UK, including, if the Welsh Government agree, in Wales, and then have SME mega-missions into some of the big growth markets, including India. We will make absolutely sure we take a good number of Welsh SMEs with us to present the real opportunities there and be honest about the challenges.

In the context of India, Tata are very interesting because they have a particular ability to help companies, partly those in their supply chain but others as well, including in Wales. They have already offered to take a number of SMEs into training centres in India to help them engage better with the Indian market.

Q480 Jonathan Edwards: We were talking earlier about the UK Government's strategic aim of geographically rebalancing the economy. How are you going to play a part in that if you do not have any targets? Is there a danger, if we have this free-for-all, that the nations, the regions and the state are competing against each other?

Nick Baird: It is a very good point and something I ought to discuss with my colleagues in BIS. If we have that broader approach clearly set out by the Prime Minister and the Business Secretary, my organisation should in some way latch on to that. I cannot give you an answer now but you are absolutely right. I ought to be talking to BIS about how we make that a reality. We will engage really closely with the Welsh Government to make sure that we have the best possible case for putting to companies overseas, but we need to think more about what we as an organisation can do to help the Government's overall objective to rebalance in the way that we have said. We will come back to you on that.[5]

Q481 Chair: What would be the impact of differential tax regimes across the UK? Is that likely to confuse or encourage potential inward investors?

4 See Ev 221
5 See Ev 221

Nick Baird: That is a very good question. It is probably not easy to provide a single answer. I suspect bigger inward investors will employ expert financial advisers, who will give them judgments as to what that, therefore, means in terms of where they should place all or part of their productions. For smaller ones, it is probably confusing, I would imagine.

Martin Phelan: I agree. The answer to your question is probably both. Generally, we see a call from investors to try to simplify as much as possible rather than complicate the tax environment and to try to avoid continuous change, which then affects predictability issues, which are a big factor for investment decisions.

Nick Baird: I emphasise Martin's point about certainty. I have had that message very strongly from inward investors. If they are going to make a medium-term commitment, they like to know that there is going to be certainty about taxation, regulatory planning and other issues. They do not like uncertainty.

Q482 Chair: I can understand that. You have been there for two months, Mr Baird, so this might be more relevant for Mr Phelan, but have any inward investors ever mentioned the issue of the Welsh language to you in either a positive or negative sense?

Nick Baird: Certainly not to me over my two months.

Martin Phelan: Not to me in my years. That may or may not be an issue, but it certainly has not come to my attention.

Q483 Chair: Do you have any quick view on the potential for enterprise zones to stimulate growth in a given area?

Nick Baird: It is a really good way of getting a focus and prioritisation around particular areas.

Q484 Chair: We will want to see a few in Wales then.

Nick Baird: Of course, this is very much for the Welsh Government to take forward. My understanding is that they are taking forward enterprise zones. In the ones I have seen and visited in England, there is huge enthusiasm in the relevant areas to use them as a basis for growth.

Q485 Geraint Davies: Coming back to this issue of competing regions, when we were in Brussels, I received a copy of the West Midlands presentation, "Why should you invest in the West Midlands?" From your point of view, all the different regions and nations of Britain will be interested in inward investment. I do not quite understand how we can get you to promote Wales as a place to invest when you have Yorkshire or whoever it is knocking on your door. How do you discriminate and differentiate?

Nick Baird: It will depend largely on the specific benefits of a specific part of the country. There will be sector specialisations. If we are engaging with a particular company from a particular sector, in the aerospace sector it is absolutely obvious that we would be pushing Wales. If it is a sector in which Wales is not particularly strong but Newcastle or the north-east is strong, for example, we would push them. But we do not want to just be doing it ourselves. When we get a project into the pipeline, Wales, the different English regions and others are competing for that project if it is an area they want. A big American company project goes into the pipeline. The details of that are available to everybody. If Wales thinks it is right for Wales, they need to be actively selling, and using us to sell, the reasons for investing in Wales. No doubt English regions may bid as well. I think you know this process quite well, Martin, so maybe you want to add something.

Martin Phelan: Historically, with the devolved Administrations, although not with the RDAs in the past, we have shared our pipeline through a system called DocStore, which has enabled the Welsh Government, or the Invest in Wales Bureau beforehand, to respond to us within the context of that pipeline.

Q486 Geraint Davies: Have they responded?
Martin Phelan: They have. They have not always responded to all of them, but they will look at them and make a decision about their competitiveness within a particular project and respond to those that they see as ones in which they could compete. We work with them and others to build the overall UK proposition, which may be one of a number of options in which Wales could be a part. We are improving the system as part of the benefit of the PA relationship which will make it easier to use, to work within and search. It has some quite neat searches around sectors and other functions which will make it a little easier.

Q487 Geraint Davies: Can I finally ask a couple of very quick fire questions? First, £1 million to PA Consulting does not seem much money in terms of the value of the work they are doing. Could you

comment on that? That is my instinct, anyway. Secondly, do you feel the Severn Bridge toll impeded inward investment in South Wales as a tax on trade? Finally, I was going to ask about how we use foreign students as ambassadors for tourism and inward investment. I am sorry about all those but we are running out of time.

Nick Baird: It is probably best for us to set out for you in writing exactly how that contract works and is financed, and the incentivised elements of it.[6] The Severn Bridge I have not heard about particularly. Students are really important in all sorts of senses. It is important that universities work closely with other economic authorities to be quite systematic about using their alumni networks to showcase the benefits of Wales in this case. I have seen it done quite effectively by universities. It has been done well in Manchester, for example. It is really effective.

Q488 Chair: My last challenge is for you to give us three bullet points as to how we could improve inward investment into Wales.
Nick Baird: First, get a really simple, compelling narrative about the specific and distinctive benefits of Wales. Secondly, I would encourage engagement with the big London HQs. That is vital. Thirdly, I would encourage engagement with embassies in London and try to get more consulates in Cardiff, particularly with the big, emerging economies. I do not know where it has got to, but I am engaged, because of my particular background, with my Turkish opposite number about the possibility of a Turkish consulate in Wales. There is quite a lot of enthusiasm. I don't know where that has got to.
Chair: Excellent. Thank you very much indeed.

---

[6]   See Ev 219

Monday 5 December 2011

Members present:

David T. C. Davies (Chair)

Guto Bebb	Karen Lumley
Geraint Davies	Jessica Morden
Jonathan Edwards	Mr Robin Walker
Nia Griffith	Mr Mark Williams

Examination of Witnesses

Witnesses: **Rt Hon Dr Vince Cable MP**, Secretary of State for Business, Innovation and Skills, and **Lord Green of Hurstpierpoint**, Minister for Trade and Investment, Department for Business, Innovation and Skills, **Rt Hon Mrs Cheryl Gillan MP**, Secretary of State for Wales, gave evidence.

Q489 Chair: A very good afternoon. Thank you very much, indeed, to all three Ministers for coming along here this afternoon. This is obviously an inquiry we are doing into inward investment in Wales. It might help us if you could just briefly tell us what you think the respective role is that each of you has within your ministerial portfolios in promoting inward investment in Wales. Perhaps we could start on the left with Dr Cable.

Vince Cable: Thank you, Mr Chair. To answer your question directly, we have a mixture of generic policies and very specific relations with big inward investors. In terms of generic policies, of course there is the UKTI—Lord Green will talk in more detail about that—and specific support measures are the Technology Strategy Board and credit measures which affect companies across the UK but are clearly of particular interest to you.

The other aspect of it is what I and my colleagues in the Department do in trying to build up a relationship with major potential or actual inward investors. I have been in Wales and to the overseas headquarters of, for example, Ford, Toyota and Tata, and tried to develop personal relationships with the people at the head of those companies. In several cases—as with Tata and, more recently, Toyota—the relationship the British Government have with these companies has borne fruit, and Wales benefits indirectly from that.

Mrs Gillan: Good afternoon, Chairman. The Wales Office has a slightly different role. As you know, we are a fairly small department and a lot of the areas of trade and investment are delegated and devolved to the Welsh Government, but the Wales Office has a great role to play in bringing people together. Certainly, when I came into the Department, one of the first ports of call for me was not only with Sir Leon Brittan to talk about trade, but also with my colleagues to the right and to the left of me in making sure that they went down to Wales, both north and south, and visited as many people as possible, and I continue to do that.

We have another role, which is equally as important, and that is Wales's voice around the Cabinet table. You will appreciate from some of the evidence you have taken during the course of this inquiry that elements such as ensuring that Wales goes forward on the infrastructure front and so on is exceedingly important. Also, we now have our own excellent contacts developing with diplomats and with other countries, and with organisations. Therefore, it is very much a co-ordinating and linking role—an important role—that you see for the Wales Office.

Lord Green: I am responsible for UK trade and investment performance overall and, specifically, I have oversight at ministerial level of both the UKTI and also of what we now call UK Export Finance—the former ECGD—and for the Foreign Office's commercial diplomacy function. I see all of those three as kind of interlocking; they are not three completely separate areas of activity.

The strategy is, I think, fairly clear. Indeed, you heard some of this from Nick Baird the other day. We need to target our services particularly on SMEs. On the export side, we need to focus particularly on high-value opportunities overseas, which is partly about making sure we support the big companies already engaged in those, but crucially is about encouraging and finding ways for SMEs to become more active in those opportunities, too. We need to focus on inward investment, which is the subject of today's hearings, and—Vince has already mentioned it—on strategic relationships at a very high level with the major inward investors as well as exporters.

Q490 Chair: Lord Green, you might have a point of view on this. You will be aware that the percentage of inward investment coming into Wales has been falling over the last decade or so. Do you think that that is partly due to global economic trends—for example, the rise of China, and the fact that we are now having to compete for manufacturing business with China and the south-east Asian nations, or is it entirely due to policies pursued by the Welsh Assembly Government and the Government in Westminster? Is there more that we can be doing back at home to reverse that?

Lord Green: It is a complex situation. Yes, of course, you start from the global situation in which competition for inward investment is becoming more and more intense with every year that goes by. If I may have a minute or two on this, I think it is worth making sure we start by looking at this from their end of the telescope, not from our end. I was in China last week, as it so happens, in Beijing and Shanghai. I met businesses from both cities, as well as the Governor of Anhui Province and various other quite important interlocutors there. It is very clear that when they look at outward investment—and they are busy encouraging Chinese companies to go global—they look first at Europe. The first question they ask themselves is, "Should we be investing in Europe?" Assuming the answer to that is "yes" or "maybe", they then say, "Where in Europe?"

In one case, for example, I had a conversation on Thursday with a company that is looking at investing both in setting up a European headquarters and also some manufacturing operations within the European Union, or within Europe, because the three countries they are looking at are the UK, Switzerland and Germany. They start from that perspective. If they end up majoring on the UK, as I hope they will in this particular case, they then ask themselves, "Where do I go within the UK?", and the answer will be different from the perspective of the head office and from the operating unit, for obvious reasons, and the answer will possibly be different again if they are thinking about R and D. In that particular case, R and D is not a big deal.

The only point in saying all that is that if we are going to have success in this very competitive world, we have to start from that end of the telescope. What does it take to attract inward investment in the circumstances when there are dozens—if not hundreds, certainly dozens—of other countries competing for that same flow of outward investment?

Q491 Chair: Is the focus therefore on expanding existing Chinese companies by setting up a branch effectively within the UK, Germany or Switzerland, or is it on buying existing companies within those nations, which may do a similar thing to the Chinese company, and basically take them over?

Lord Green: I think you will see examples of both those things, plus greenfield investment, which the company I have just described would be involved in, plus also R and D partnerships. So I think there are different ways in which both the Chinese and, of course, other countries think about investment. In that context, at the UK level we need to be ensuring that we have a competitive offer, obviously in terms of tax, the story about regulatory environment, the skills base, costs and infrastructure. These are all the kinds of criteria that they weigh up. I have found that companies do this quite systematically. It is almost as if they are building up a grid: here are the criteria, here are the countries and we are scoring each country, and we come out with a decision in the bottom right-hand corner.

Q492 Chair: Lastly from me to the Secretary of State. Is Wales's performance in terms of getting inward investment something that is replicated across other regions of the United Kingdom, or is Wales doing particularly badly compared with other regions at the moment, and compared with how it was 15 years ago?

Vince Cable: It seems to be doing relatively badly, but you can look at the trend in different ways. It reached a peak in terms of attractiveness for inward investment round about 1990–91, when much of the rest of the UK was in some trouble at the peak of that boom before it bust. It has since declined and has plateaued for the last five years or so. I think the

answer is that it has done relatively badly in recent years.

Mrs Gillan: It is not always straightforward. The figures released in July showed a fall of 29% in new jobs created by inward investment projects into Wales, and that Wales contributed only some 4%, that is 38 projects, to the number of FDI projects brought into the UK in 2010–11. That emphasises the need for both the Welsh and the UK Governments to work closer together to look at what we can do to make sure that the offer from Wales is so much more attractive, because I believe that there is a great future, and we can achieve that by working together.

Q493 Mr Williams: I want to turn the clock back a little and reflect on the fact that in the past, Wales's offer to inward investors was based on grants and low costs in terms of land and labour. How relevant are those inducements now to inward investors? Over and above what Lord Green said about the importance of research and development, what are the new inducements? If we are looking through that telescope, what is the whole package that people are looking for and how relevant are those historical inducements?

Vince Cable: All those factors are relevant. Indeed, one of the big, new departures in policy has been the creation of enterprise zones. Wales is proceeding with five of its own, and they are trying to differentiate locations through taxation, capital allowances, business rates, in this case, and flexibility in planning policy. Those are the issues that come to mind.

As Lord Green said, most companies have a matrix of things they are looking for and there is a limit to the extent to which any Government can lavish grants and tax reliefs. It is probably fair to say that the boom of inward investment in Wales 20 years ago was accompanied by fairly substantial grant assistance. It was expensive, and many of those companies drifted away, because it was temporary support.

Mrs Gillan: We have to make sure that we have the right situation for companies to consider Wales as a destination. You heard some of the criteria from Lord Green, but inward investing companies will be looking for skills and capacity, and infrastructure—broadband has been particularly important. The indications are that we have had such good inward investment in the past that we can build on that footprint and move forward. For example, I know that Tata Steel has been looking at helping some of the SMEs in its supply chain to look at what opportunities they can have in India. There is a lot to be done on building on the existing footprint of those companies that came in.

The Welsh Government have a good policy of looking after the anchor companies, which, again, lends itself to looking at a good, attractive policy for inward investors. There is always more that can be done, but I am certainly optimistic about the signs.

Lord Green: Looking forward, the role of the universities is becoming more and more important—not just in Wales, but everywhere. Their role as centres of R and D that are closely connected with the business environment is becoming increasingly prominent in investors' decisions, particularly in advanced manufacturing, in life sciences, in ICT—even in the creative industries. If one is looking forward as opposed to looking backwards, it is very important to work to ensure that those links are as close and constructive as possible. I think Wales will have a good story to tell.

Q494 Mr Williams: I am glad to say that I have two universities in my constituency—that's the plug—and building those partnerships is critical.

There has been a debate in Wales about the relevant balance between larger inward investment projects and support for SMEs. Secretary of State, we have heard about the drive for exports from SMEs, what is your view on the balance between the two? Again, from an anecdotal, constituency point of view, I have the largest proportion of small businesses per head of population anywhere in the UK. There are a lot of small businesses that need and want support. What will you be doing for them in the context of the big debate?

Vince Cable: Well, I would certainly argue that in order to build up sustainable forms of economic growth SMEs are absolutely critical, but not SMEs in general. A lot of analysis has been done—the CBI has done a lot of this work—that suggests there is a particular group of the Ms rather than the Ss. They are called gazelles and are the 10,000 companies that are SMEs with a real ambition to expand. They are British based. That is the group of companies that are probably the most crucial to growth. Obviously, inward investment is an important part of the mix, but no economy can be dependent on that; it has to be domestically based. I was looking at the figures within Wales and I noted that Ceredigion had a relatively low share of inward investment relative to its own domestic small companies. One can understand that.

Mrs Gillan: May I make a point on that because it is quite important? The UKTI has a programme of market visit support that provides assistance to new-to-export or new-to-market SMEs visiting overseas markets. Previously, the Welsh Government made use of the UKTI's funding, which was up to about £50,000 per annum, but, over the past two years, they have not taken up that offer. It is only a small amount, but it is important in the greater scheme of things. As it had been taken up previously, having missed doing so for two years, I hope that the Welsh Government and SMEs will be looking to take advantage of that.

Chair: Obviously, there are two Secretary of States here and so we are confusing things a little bit. I better gently move things on.

Q495 Jessica Morden: You referred to building on the footprint of companies such as Tata Steel. I would like to ask you and the Business Secretary what you are doing to protect the investment we have already got. In my constituency last week, Tata Steel mothballed the hot strip mill, with the loss of 115 jobs. A month previously, 70 jobs had gone in a construction products part of the business. The company obviously cites low demand for steel, high energy prices and things like the future carbon floor price. You have obviously tried to adjust some of those things in the autumn statement—although

crucial details remain unclear for the company—but I am keen to know what kind of immediate help you can offer to companies to protect the investment we have.

Mrs Gillan: May I just start with an overview in particular relating to Tata Steel? Last week's situation has happened before and it is a mothballing, thank goodness. We are hoping to look to the future and to that opening again at some stage. My colleague came down and visited Tata Steel alongside me at a very early stage. Of course, the big issue was to look at the carbon intensive industries particularly, but also at how we can take forward the investment. We have worked together very successfully and my colleague will have a lot more to say on the detail of that.

Vince Cable: Various things. First of all, Lord Green and I have developed a personal relationship with the top people in Tata. It is the biggest overseas company investing in British manufacturing, not just in Wales. It is therefore a very important relationship. I think Tata is positive about the UK. In terms of Port Talbot, which is the biggest installation, it has made a big commitment. The fourth blast furnace replacement was a very big commitment by the company and all our conversations with it suggest that it regards its investment in Wales, particularly in Port Talbot, as massively important to its group. It has put a lot of capital in already and is committed to doing more.

There are two issues now. One is the energy intensive industry problem. When the Secretary of State for Wales and I visited some months ago, that point was made very strongly. Actually, that visit, as much as any other factor, triggered the detailed negotiations with the industry about the kind of support it needs to offset higher costs. The package we produced in the autumn statement is very substantial, at least as regards the costs of the EU ETS and the carbon price floor. There are issues still remaining in terms of the electricity market review and what that means for energy intensive industries, but we have gone a long way to meet the concerns expressed.

As far as Llanwern is concerned, I discussed—as the Secretary of State for Wales did last week—with Dr Köhler why that particular mothballing had occurred. He was quite clear that they have been hit very badly in terms of market demand and what is happening in Europe. They have taken a measure that replicates what they did in the middle of the recession in 2008–09, namely using flexibility agreed with the labour force—mothballing rather than closure. In general, this is an exemplary employer that is very considerate towards the labour force and tries to handle these situations as sensitively as possible.

Q496 Jessica Morden: My point was that a lot of these things are not going to kick in until 2013, such as the carbon floor price and the help that you are offering in the autumn statement. I have one more question from a local perspective. The Army specialist vehicle programme will be very valuable to companies such as General Dynamics, in terms of both highly skilled jobs and future exports. Are the Government committed to delivering that programme?

Mrs Gillan: I have spoken to both General Dynamics and the Ministry of Defence. We have been committed to delivering that programme, and we continue to consider that that is a very valuable part of the Defence portfolio. We have a large Defence footprint in Wales, and I will be having some more discussions with the Ministry of Defence on Scout shortly.

Q497 Nia Griffith: Lord Green mentioned earlier how companies use a chart to tick off which countries score on which features. In the joint submission from the UKTI and the Wales Office to the Committee you mention four areas where Wales may have a competitive advantage: skills, being close to the rest of the UK hubs in Europe, property prices and quality of life. To what extent do you think those criteria attract inward investment? Do they rate highly in what the companies choose? Does the UKTI encourage investment in Wales and discussion of the reasons why companies may or may not come in?

Lord Green: The criteria that you have just mentioned are helpful, but they are not sufficient on their own. Wales sits within the overall UK tax structure, and tax is clearly an important factor for many investors—not all, but many. Infrastructure is a broader issue than just Welsh infrastructure, and the state of Heathrow airport is one thing that occasionally comes up in conversations. Those things are helpful.

To what extent does the UKTI help? If I can look forwards rather than backwards—I am still relatively new in this role, although after 11 months that is perhaps wearing a bit thin—there seems to me to be goodwill on the part of both the UKTI and the Welsh Government towards making a constructive and forward-looking approach to marketing Wales. We are in a competitive environment, and there is no country that has a completely distinctive set of attributes that will win investment without further ado; you have to market the proposition. Marketing Wales as part of the UK is clearly a job of the UKTI overseas, as well as the way in which it processes inward applications. You heard from Nick the other day about the way in which the hub for investment possibilities is managed centrally and made available to the Welsh Government, as to other devolved Administrations and regions.

The branding is important. In some senses, I hate to use that terminology because it risks sounding crass, but it does matter. Brand Britain is something that means something internationally. Wales has a brand that there is potential to invest in. By invest I mean not primarily put money behind, but build on. Wales clearly has an identity. Lying behind it are the kind of things you have just mentioned: the quality of life, the attractive environment and the university base in particular areas, so the brand is not something that sits up in the atmosphere unconnected with real facts. It is important to market the concept of Wales, however, and that is part of the UKTI's responsibility.

There are some interesting things to build on, looking forwards. I am not sure that, looking backwards, we have necessarily made the most of these things. For instance, Wales attracts some 6% of all the overseas students that study in this country, so against a population base of 5% of the total it is doing better

than the UK average. There are 24,000 overseas students at any one time, and they are the basis for an alumni network that can be worked. At its best, I have seen that done very effectively. Anecdotes are only so valuable, but I know of a very senior official in the Shanghai administration who did her English language training in Cardiff, and indeed speaks English with a slight Welsh accent, and that is the kind of contact that is well worth nurturing in the short, medium and longer term. That is one example, and the Welsh diaspora is another one.

The Scots do a brilliant job with global Scots working their own diaspora. I think that Wales could work its diaspora. I was in Korea two weeks ago. The Chairman of the British Chamber of Commerce there is a Welshman—very proud of the fact, too. It is an example—again, by anecdote—of how you can enhance the brand, and I think that that is well worth doing in this highly competitive international environment.

Q498 Geraint Davies: Taking that forward, this question is again for Lord Green. In passing, may I give thanks to Nick Baird, who was in Swansea with his team recently with Swansea University? Swansea University is very focused on Tata and industrial R & D. We have another university—the Met—which is the largest producer of SMEs of any university in Wales. Presumably, the UKTI can link into something like Swansea Met and help those SMEs grow and so on, but I really want to ask about branding.

Beneath the Wales brand, you might have something like the Swansea brand, which is known now to 500 million people thanks to its premier league status. A particular event we have coming up is the Dylan Thomas centenary in 2014. That in itself is a brand, and obviously Dylan Thomas was born in Swansea. How creatively could the UKTI help to build all the opportunities around that Dylan Thomas event, not just for Swansea, but for Wales and the UK, in the way that the Ryder cup a few years ago did, bringing millions of pounds to Wales? What are your thoughts on that?

Lord Green: First, on the general point about sub-brands, if that is the right phrase, I think there is absolutely nothing wrong with the UK saying to itself that it has a UK brand—or brand Britain—and a Welsh brand, in the context that we are discussing this afternoon, and individual brands within that: Cardiff, Swansea and no doubt others. Again, I can think of other examples around the country—Liverpool—and Shanghai is fresh in my mind because I have just been there.

Geraint Davies: Let's go back to Swansea.

Lord Green: Let's stick with Swansea.

There is evidence, without naming them again, that you can raise your profile very strongly. Forgive me: the population of Liverpool is around about 300,000—I may have the number slightly wrong—and its visibility in Shanghai, which is a city of 14 million, is really quite high, because it has worked the brand. Therefore, I agree that there is plenty of scope for promoting individual city images. In the context of Dylan Thomas, I am tempted to show off by quoting the only lines of *Under Milk Wood* I can, but I will not.

Geraint Davies: Go on.

Lord Green: "It is Spring, moonless night in the small town, starless and bible-black".

I think that it is an interesting idea. Dylan Thomas would be well known in America. I am not sure how well known he would be in Asia—I just don't know. It is an interesting thought.

Q499 Geraint Davies: I know that President Jimmy Carter is a great fan and is supporting Dylan Thomas's house. The issue is whether networks can be built two years in advance, so that tour operators in America put together packages to go to South Wales, including Laugharne and Swansea and so on. Could the UKTI help? Rather than waiting for the event to happen and not taking full advantage, can there be help in supporting infrastructure development, including private sector investment, and international linkage to make something bigger than just an event in Swansea—a Wales and a UK event?

Lord Green: I imagine that that is something the Welsh Government ought to lead on, but I think that the UKTI should be there to help. If this is a significant inward investment opportunity built around a particular cultural event—the Olympics is a major opportunity of that kind—I think that the UKTI should certainly be ready to help the Welsh Government, who would clearly want to take the lead on this kind of proposal, in marketing the proposition overseas and doing whatever it is reasonable to do.

Q500 Geraint Davies: Obviously, when the torch comes through Swansea, I am hoping that they will have a Dylan Thomas T-shirt on. I hope the press got that.

If I can move on to infrastructure, obviously connectivity is very important. I want to raise two issues: first, the extension of the electrification to Swansea, which we are very keen on; and, secondly, the Severn bridge toll and so on. Obviously, we want to do everything we can to be able to get goods to market quickly, and to get inward investment. I do not know whether any supportive or positive words are going to be said about the bid towards electrification to Swansea and reducing the costs of transportation. After all, the Humber bridge tolls went down, and tolls are up on the Severn bridge.

Mrs Gillan: First, may I just congratulate you on what you have been doing on marketing Swansea? Reports have reached me.

Geraint Davies: I will send you a T-shirt.

Mrs Gillan: I hope you will. On that, we will see what we can do to assist. I am sure that our embassies abroad and others will be interested, because Dylan Thomas is, after all, an international figure, and well known. As America is such an important market for Wales, it will be a good opportunity, because it has such a high recognition factor.

Briefly, on the electrification to Swansea, as you know, we have kept that option open, and I am looking at electrification of the valleys lines; in fact, I put in another business case on that recently—last week. I am still optimistic and keep pushing for that.

The door has still been kept open; it has not been closed on the electrification to Swansea. I think that that is really key.

Vince Cable: On your infrastructure question, broadband is obviously particular to that, and this has been rolled out. There was more in the autumn statement. Cardiff is one of 10 cities that will have a very dense, superfast broadband connectivity.

Q501 Geraint Davies: That is welcome but the concern in Swansea, as the second city, is that with the railway, the broadband, the electrification and so on, everything stops at Cardiff. That is the fear, but obviously we want to reach out beyond that.

Mrs Gillan: On the Severn toll bridge, there have been discussions on improving the road infrastructure in south Wales. What we said in the autumn financial statement is that if the Welsh Government come forward with sufficient, or some elements of, capital towards those improvements, we will look at what we can do from the UK Government end, including looking at what happens to the Severn tolls after 2017.

Chair: Geraint never goes gentle into that good night, but there are many people on this side, including Jessica, wanting to come in.

Q502 Mr Williams: On the broadband point, my colleague has said that the barrier ends somewhere near Swansea, and I am glad that you mentioned broadband, Secretary of State. I mention it in the context of mid and west Wales. If we are going to develop those small businesses, it was very alarming to hear from Nick Baird, when he gave evidence to the Committee, that a prerequisite to anything in terms of growth is adequate broadband provision, when in many areas, we do not have broadband provision at all.

Mrs Gillan: We have done a study of what is needed for the rural areas, within the Wales Office. The Parliamentary Under-Secretary of State carried it out on our behalf, and this figured highly. We have £57 million going into Wales in terms of broadband, but the city region money for broadband was money over and above that, so we are hoping that this will be rolled out.

Q503 Guto Bebb: In the submission you provided, you mentioned skills as being a competitive advantage that Wales has. I take it that that is a comparative figure, but who is the comparison being made against?

Vince Cable: I have not made the comparison, so I cannot answer your question directly, but in terms of the underlying premise, it clearly is crucial. This is an area where devolved powers kick in. We have very aggressive progress of apprenticeships, but that is in England. I cannot make comparisons with exactly what the Welsh Government are doing, but it is obviously crucial.

Mrs Gillan: Obviously, skills are very important. We have some tremendous skills in Wales, not least in north Wales, as you know, with the manufacturing hub up there, and materials. We have a first-class apprenticeships scheme based on Deeside college as a hub, which we are very keen on. It therefore makes that area very attractive, as far as that type of activity is concerned.

Q504 Jonathan Edwards: You both mentioned the autumn statement and the capital investment programme that was announced. That was £30 billion; £25 billion coming from pension funds and £5 billion from the Treasury. The only element that is Barnettised is the Treasury, which means we are only getting £216 million, so what will you do to make sure that we get the £1.25 billion that we should be getting from the pension element?

Vince Cable: Well, as you say, the Barnett consequentials for capital I think are £216 million, but the large sums of money that are talked about relate to private investment and big infrastructure projects. What has happened is that the Government have reached a memorandum of understanding with the big pension funds and insurers, where we know there is currently a lot of money locked up and looking for a secure home with a decent rate of return. How that money is spent will depend on whether good infrastructure projects are available. You presumably have in Wales a kind of inventory of your top priority infrastructure projects, and if they are good projects and if they produce a return, they will attract some of that money.

Q505 Jessica Morden: A question for the Secretary of State for Wales: you mentioned earlier that your role was to bring people together. In terms of inward investment, who have you brought together and what has that resulted in?

Mrs Gillan: Starting off right from the beginning, I was bringing my colleagues into Wales and introducing them, but I was working with the previous Government and the previous Minister for Business on looking at what we could do jointly in terms of highlighting the offer we have in Wales. However, for example, just simple things I have been doing have included working with the Bangladesh chamber of commerce, and, indeed, I encouraged and inspired the first visit of a whole group of Welsh companies to Bangladesh. I have been looking at how we can work with the UKTI from the Wales Office, and we worked together on the DSO conference, which was very successful and which was held in south Wales. I am also obviously seeking to work with the new Minister for Business, and I hope that we will have a fruitful relationship moving forward to see where we can jointly assist. Those are just a couple of examples.

Q506 Jessica Morden: So far, what have been the achievements of the Business Advisory Group that you have set up?

Mrs Gillan: The Business Advisory Group was set up right at the beginning so that we can understand better the business climate in Wales and get feedback from a variety of businesses in and across sectors. It has been able to inform the Prime Minister's business group, and the outcome from his business group, about what is happening in Wales. In fact, it has been addressed by both my colleagues sitting either side of me, and we are going to be looking at FDI specifically next year, because one thing that is important is to

allow the new Welsh Government to settle down and to see against what background business in Wales is working.

Q507 Jessica Morden: How many inward investors have you met recently in your time as Secretary of State?

Mrs Gillan: We have a huge number of inward investors. I can provide a list for you[1]—from Airbus to Tata and from General Dynamics to Sony and Sharp—so it is a large number that I have met.

Vince Cable: In terms of the different models of engaging with investors—other than at the high level that Ministers do in London—there are essentially two approaches. One is the state agency, as we had with the English RDAs, which still exist in Scotland and Northern Ireland. Alternatively, there is a business-led approach, as we now have with the English LEPs. Wales does not have either, but this structure that the Secretary of State has established does provide business leadership in a slightly different way.

Q508 Mr Walker: The Welsh Secretary mentioned earlier the importance of the different Governments working together, and I am interested in how closely the Wales Office and the UKTI work with the Welsh Government at the moment. How does that work day to day?

Lord Green: I think it works quite well now. I am not sure that that was always true looking backwards. You have heard from Nick Baird, and he was down in south Wales recently. I am due there early in the new year and that will be my third visit since taking on the task. As I think you heard from Nick, they have appointed a relationship manager in Gareth John, who lives in Wales and who—you can tell from his name—has a resonance with the Welsh image. There is to be a major event in Wales for SME exporting, which follows on from the national event that we recently held in London, and we are rolling that out around the country. I am hoping that Edwina Hart will chair that, and if invited I will be delighted to go and be a keynote speaker, as I will be doing for the English regions and for Scotland—

Q509 Chair: Did you say that she is going to chair it?

Lord Green: I am hoping. We are still in discussion about pinning down a date for the event, but it will happen some time in the reasonably early new year. I am working on that assumption. That, I think, is an important opportunity to engage not the SMEs themselves so much as their supporters. In Wales, as in everywhere else in this country, our task is to get more SMEs looking at the international markets for all the reasons we understand. That involves clearly the Governments doing things right in terms of support so it is the responsibility of the Welsh Government and of the UKTI, making sure that those work well together. But it is also, critically, a matter of engaging banks, lawyers, accountants, chambers of commerce and trade associations in the project as well. That is what that conference is about. As I say,

[1] See Ev 222

we are rolling that out around the United Kingdom. I am hoping that Edwina will host that.

Q510 Mr Walker: You mentioned Nick Baird's evidence. Disappointingly, we have had written evidence from the UKTI which mentioned that the meeting he'd proposed with the Welsh Business Minister did not go ahead on 24 November. I was wondering whether the three of you have met with the Welsh Business Minister and, if so, how regularly.
Lord Green: I have not.
Vince Cable: I have not.
Mrs Gillan: I have met with the Welsh Business Minister. I have had one meeting and I was hoping for quarterly meetings, but I think we have arranged now to have meetings every six months if the Welsh Minister considers that there is something we need to talk about. However, it is really important because there is concurrent responsibility between the UK Government and the Welsh Government on trade and investment in terms of the UKTI and the Welsh Government. It is definitely my view that we can strengthen joint working and strengthen the possibilities of putting the best possible case forward for Wales.
Certainly, I have met with Gareth John, who is a former senior member of the WDA and lives in Wales, but I acknowledge that there is scope and certainly a willingness from this side to do more. As Lord Green knows, I was keen to see whether there was any possibility of enhancing the UKTI's presence in Wales, particularly because I know through the Business Advisory Group and through many other contacts in the business community that they have often been uncertain where to call on and whom to talk to for advice both on exporting and on attracting inward investment. I hope that we will be able to improve that co-ordination over time. But let me stress, the Welsh Government is only new in office. It has now got a lot of money coming to it. We have secured a good deal for the Welsh Government at UK Government level and it now has the powers, and I am hoping very much that we will now make more progress.

Q511 Mr Walker: Just for the record: Dr Cable, I saw you shake your head. I don't think you have had a chance to meet the Welsh Business Minister.
Vince Cable: No.

Q512 Mr Walker: And Lord Green likewise?
Lord Green: No. I have not.

Q513 Chair: Have you offered to meet with her?
Vince Cable: Not specifically. I have had correspondence, inevitably, on UK-level matters that relate to Wales.

Q514 Chair: For the record, there would be no problems on this side?
Vince Cable: Absolutely not.

Q515 Chair: If a meeting does not take place, it is not through any lack of enthusiasm?
Vince Cable: There is no lack of enthusiasm.

Lord Green: We would like to meet. We look forward to that.

Q516 Jonathan Edwards: When we visited Germany and met the German Trade and Investment, they were specifically tasked with helping geographically to rebalance the economy, primarily because of reunification. Despite reunification, they are a more equal state geographically than the British state. Therefore, in evidence the UKTI said that they were willing to look at that but it would take a political decision to say that you had to target investment to the poorest parts of the state. The UK Government have a strategic objective geographically to rebalance the state, so are you going to look at that or are you still going to maintain this free-for-all approach to inward investment?
Vince Cable: I wouldn't describe it as a free-for-all approach. We are trying to attract as much inward investment as possible, particularly when it contributes to rebalancing the economy, and that is both sectoral and geographic. I am not sure that setting targets is the best way of doing it, but certainly if big inward investors—particularly those from emerging markets where much of the growth is now in inward investment—were to want to come to Wales and express an interest, we would certainly want to encourage that. As you say, rebalancing is a big strategic objective.

Q517 Jonathan Edwards: If you are not going to set targets, how will you rebalance the economy geographically?
Vince Cable: As Lord Green said at the very beginning, we have to look at this problem through the other end of the telescope—the way that inward investors look at us. We cannot go out to China, India or, for that matter, the United States and say, "Come forward all those people who want to invest in the north-east of England or Wales, and the rest of you step back." That is not the way it happens. There is a series of processes, and we are trying to attract people interested in investing in Europe and in the UK. We do our best to encourage them, and if there is a Welsh dimension to it, and if it is a strategically important industry, advanced manufacturing for example, obviously we work very hard to attract them.

Q518 Jonathan Edwards: Several witnesses have told us that in recent years Scotland has been outperforming Wales in attracting inward investment. Why do you think Scotland is doing far better than Wales at the moment?
Vince Cable: I am not sure that is necessarily true. Again, as Lord Green said earlier, there are areas where Wales has world-beating companies, lots of them based on inward investment—aerospace, motor vehicles and life sciences among them. There are the creative industries around Cardiff, a lot of which are inward-investment driven. I would not be negative. Scotland has one particular advantage in that it has had a very big offshore oil and gas industry. As I saw a few weeks ago, there is a very well developed supply chain around Aberdeen, much of it inward

investors who are attracted by that particular piece of geography.

Q519 Karen Lumley: I apologise for being late. I had a question in the Chamber.

Do the Secretary of State for Wales and Lord Green feel that the UKTI or the Welsh Government are better placed to promote Wales to overseas investors? Do you think they are duplicating their work?

Mrs Gillan: I cannot say whether they are duplicating their work, because I do not know extensively what the plans of the new Welsh Business Minister are as yet. I think there is joint responsibility, as I said earlier. The UKTI is charged with all parts of the United Kingdom, and Wales is part of that United Kingdom. We need to make sure that Welsh strengths and capabilities are covered in our national offer by the UKTI. In the way the UKTI shares with the Welsh Government its portfolio of existing investors and the way it makes sure that the pipeline is transmitted to members of the Welsh Government, there are some statistics about the number of individuals in the Welsh Government who have access to the UKTI data sets, which have not been taken up to the fullest extent recently. I think that could be improved on but it is a question of joint working, which, from my perspective and from what I have observed, makes the offer from Wales stronger.

Lord Green: I do not think there is a need to fear duplication, but there clearly is a risk of it if you do not organise it properly. Wales actually has an advantage over some regions of England, but it does have a separate—I used the word earlier, probably before you came, and in some senses I am almost reluctant to use it—brand, image, let's say. Wales has an image, and building on that through Welsh Government representation overseas is helpful.

That goes back to the previous question. One of the ways in which you work your best to ensure that Wales gets its fair share/more than its fair share of inward investment is to promote the image. I think the activities overseas clearly need to be co-ordinated. There are six Welsh Government offices overseas, two of which are co-located. My own view, for what it is worth, is that, in general, co-location is a good thing because you can then trade on each other's strengths. Putting two offices in two different parts of a city is not the best way to organise the effort. Wales needs to, as it were, piggyback on the activities of the UKTI, but it has an opportunity in so doing to reach further than it ever could on its own and probably to do better than if it were just the UKTI. So I do not feel that duplication is a risk, but it does need to be managed.

Mrs Gillan: May I make one further point? The UKTI invited the Welsh Government to contribute responses to 68 investment leads last year. Since May 2011, 24 UKTI projects have either been transferred to Wales or have expressed an interest directly in Wales. It is obvious to me that the complementary activity pays off in terms of prospects for Wales.

Q520 Karen Lumley: Have UKTI offices overseas experienced budget cuts?

Lord Green: There were some budget cuts in the spending review, but actually the Chancellor's autumn statement has given us extra resources, which will be used for different sorts of things. Some will be used for those medium-sized companies that the Secretary of State for Business, Innovation and Skills referred to a few minutes ago, and some will be used for investment and overseas support.

Q521 Chair: Lord Green, when you were running HSBC, were you aware of the Wales overseas offices, for example in China? You must have been in China a lot, and you would have been aware of the UKTI.

Lord Green: If I am honest, I am not sure that I would have been, and I am not sure how aware I was of the UKTI, which maybe goes to a wider question of how good a job either Government, jointly and severally, do in ensuring the services of Government in its general sense—

Q522 Chair: What about the WDA?

Lord Green: The WDA clearly did have a strong brand. One of the most obvious points is that this whole effort has twice undergone a substantial reorganisation in the past few years. I think it is coming out of that now. It is obvious that you need a stable environment within which to do the best possible job.

Q523 Geraint Davies: Self-evidently, Wales has only got 3 million out of 60 million people in the UK, so it cannot do it on its own. It is unclear that we are getting the same message from Lord Green and Cheryl Gillan. There was something in the press today from Cheryl Gillan saying: "You've got the power, now do something", implying that Wales should just get on and do its own thing.

Wouldn't you agree that it is critically important that there is a partnership approach, that we get our fair share of the UKTI, and that any tax that emerges from wealth creation from that goes back to Westminster anyway? Obviously the money to Wales has got to be given through the budget formula. Have I got this right? I think I might have misunderstood the quotes in this article. What the Secretary of State is presumably saying is that we should work together in partnership for a stronger Wales, not just get on with it, you have the power.

Mrs Gillan: Mr Davies, I am not responsible for writing the headlines for *Western Mail*. If you delve slightly deeper into the article and some of the direct quotes you will see that I am very encouraging and willing always to work in harness together with the Welsh Government. They are quite rightly, in devolution terms, responsible for certain areas. For example, in this area I know that the Business Department in the Welsh Government is rebuilding, and I think there are some concrete joint working opportunities that we can take forward, particularly on the UKTI front. I think my colleagues will attest to the fact that right from day one I have been keen to ensure that that joint working is fully realised.

Q524 Geraint Davies: Can I ask Lord Green, in a nutshell what should be the USP focal point in marketing terms for Wales?

Lord Green: I am not sure about the "U" bit of that. I don't think there is one single headline. Clearly, the universities—we have talked about that before. There is an existing base of major investing names in Wales. That is both reassuring to other inward investors, as well as a set of relationships to work on in their own right. The proximity to London is a helpful part of the case for Wales.

Q525 Geraint Davies: Presumably also, quality of life and Dylan Thomas, of course.
Lord Green: Quality of life and Dylan Thomas.
Vince Cable: May I reinforce the point about joint working, with an example that partly answers Jonathan Edwards' question? One of the success stories for inward investment in the past few weeks has actually been a big Michelin investment in Dundee. That happened primarily because the UKTI first established contacts early in negotiations at an exhibition in Paris. That was passed on and Scottish Enterprise became involved in the detail of the negotiation and the funding. Such is the politics of this that both sides have claimed credit. Actually, the truth is that without both sides—the UK level and the devolved Government level—that would not have happened as smoothly as it did.

Q526 Guto Bebb: Dr Cable, in 2010 the Welsh Government announced that it would focus resources on a sector-based, strategic approach to business support. Originally, six sectors were chosen for support, but that was expanded by a further three in September 2011. Are the nine sectors chosen by the Welsh Government the right sectors for Wales?
Vince Cable: Certainly at a UK level we do not try to specify sectors in quite such a detailed way. There is the old jargon about picking winners. Certainly, while I have been head of the Department, we have not gone down that road. What we do have is a commitment, more broadly, to rebalancing the economy. That means a greater emphasis on manufacturing, particularly advanced manufacturing, creative industries and business professional services. We have not tried to break that down to a lower level of sectoral specificity and we do not intend to do so. To the extent to which someone has to make strategic judgments, we leave that to bodies such as the Technology Strategy Board. Those bodies make choices on our behalf, rather than doing them politically.
Lord Green: It is perhaps worth adding that the six sectors that BETS had identified are pretty coterminous with a number of the sectors that the UKTI has arranged itself around, which I think is a case of great minds thinking alike. The new three are very new. The UKTI will have to think about how it responds in its way of doing things to those three new sectors in order to support them properly.

Q527 Guto Bebb: I think you have already responded to my second question, which was to ask whether, when the UKTI goes out trying to market Britain, it targets specific sectors.
Lord Green: It depends. The UK economy is very broad-based. What you certainly don't do—in a sense

I am repeating what the Secretary of State just said— is identify a small number of so-called winners. Yet it is obvious that in some major emerging market opportunities, where there are high-value opportunities where huge infrastructure projects are being developed in places such as China, India and Saudi Arabia, there are particular sectors that are relevant to that if you are trying to engage more businesses. For a lot of these infrastructure sectors, you are obviously looking at engineering services, contracting, project design and those kinds of activities. The sector gets defined by the opportunity there. I do not think, however, that we should go out with a general proposition that that UK is only interested in three or four or five sectors, because, actually, we are quite a broad-based economy.

Q528 Guto Bebb: Dr Cable, we have heard a lot during this piece of work about how successful the WDA was in the late '80s and early '90s, but there was also criticism from other parts of the United Kingdom. At that point, I remember well people saying that Wales was buying projects at the expense of the rest of the United Kingdom. My question is: do you think it is possible for different regions within the UK to compete for work overseas, or would that be counter-productive?
Vince Cable: I think that I would be worried on two levels. The first is revenue, if you get into a revenue bidding war—that relates to the wider argument about corporation tax in the UK—and the second is duplication of effort. One of the reasons why we made the decision to move away from RDAs in England was because a lot of effort was going into duplicate promotional work overseas, which was not terribly sensible. That is an important qualification and why it is important not to waste a lot of energy and money in competition of that kind. As Lord Green has been saying, Wales has an identity, it has a brand and it has distinctive positive things to offer. Obviously you have to try to sell that.

Q529 Karen Lumley: Secretary of State for Wales, you have talked a lot about working with the Welsh Government, which is good. Do you think that they should have an office in Gwydyr House, as happened with the Scottish Parliament?
Mrs Gillan: They have an office in Gwydyr House. It is on the ground floor and it is a very nicely appointed office.

Q530 Karen Lumley: Do they use it?
Mrs Gillan: I am not aware of whether they do. They can come into the reception and go to their office without coming into any other part of the building, so I am not aware of the frequency with which they use it. It is a very nice office.

Q531 Chair: Come, come Secretary of State. You must have an idea. I know they do not have to knock on your door to get in, but surely records are kept.
Mrs Gillan: I will ask whether the office keeps a record of how often the office is used.[2] It is a very nice office. They are of course welcome to come and

2 See Ev 222

use the facilities in Gwydyr House any time that they want to, provided that it does not interrupt the business of the Department. They are very welcome guests.

Q532 Nia Griffith: Lord Green touched on taxation a little while back. I do not know whether Dr Cable could tell us whether he thinks there are features of the current UK taxation regime which are particularly attractive to investments. Looking ahead, would you see any practical way in which anything might be different in Wales—in other words, might there be a different taxation regime? How could that work in actual practice, and would there be any advantage to business from that?

Vince Cable: We have taken the view that the basic rate of corporation tax is probably the most important single measure of business competitiveness in terms of taxation, but specific features of the tax regime— such as the patent box and the R&D tax credit—also play into this. In terms of devolved tax powers, I realise that this is a very fraught and difficult area and I know you have a commission at the moment looking into that, so I will not trespass on its conclusions.

Lord Green: It is important to be tax competitive, at the risk of stating the obvious. Broadly speaking, I think the tax offer does seem to be recognised as competitive. Indeed, just objectively, it is on a European scale but, as we all know, there is one country in Europe that offers a significantly lower corporate tax rate. That is an issue for Northern Ireland, but it is not actually an issue in a British context, if that is the right term.

Q533 Geraint Davies: Dr Cable, it obviously is the case that if there is more economic activity, more jobs and more wealth creation in Wales, clearly the Exchequer gets money back or a return on that, but are you aware of any work that has been done on the impact of reducing the Severn bridge tolls on tax revenues and inward investment? Could you perhaps look at such an econometric study, maybe looking at examples around Britain—the Humber bridge and elsewhere in Scotland—to give the Treasury some idea of whether it was worth investing the money to reduce the toll, which is regarded as a tax on trade and investment, to stimulate business activity and to get the money back? It would not be a gift; it would be a bit of investment. Would you be prepared to look at that in your Department?

Vince Cable: I am not aware of any work. If any work was done, it would be by the Department for Transport, but we can certainly put that to them. We are looking at tolling more generally—not in the context of bridges specifically, but in terms of new road developments. You have seen the autumn statement reference to the A14, which is basically applying a basic economic principle that that is one way of getting new investment going. In terms of the impact of toll bridges, I think you will really have to put that to my colleague Justine Greening.

Q534 Geraint Davies: But would you be prepared to encourage the commissioning of that work? Obviously, it would be of critical value to the South

Wales economy, could pay back a positive profit to the Treasury and make a lot of difference. You have got the power to influence these sort of things in other Departments, haven't you?

Vince Cable: I do not think I do on this particular point. I am always happy to do interesting research, but I am not aware that I can do very much on this one.

Q535 Chair: Is it not the case that the Treasury is looking at subsidising the Humber bridge and keeping down increases on the Humber?

Vince Cable: Yes.

Q536 Chair: Therefore, doesn't Mr Davies have a point here—that if it is good enough for the Humber, it might be good enough for the Severn as well?

Vince Cable: Yes. This is a very difficult subject. There is an issue in Edinburgh as well—this has become a very major political issue. It may be that there is a role for somebody to do a comparative study. I do not think that that is for me, but I think somebody could probably usefully do it.

Mrs Gillan: Can I just make two points which might be helpful? First, I think you could ask the DFT and the Treasury what the financial situation is on the Humber bridge, because I do not think it is directly comparable to the situation on the Severn bridge and to the tolls and the contractual situation there, which takes us up to 2017. Secondly, as you know, this is being looked at, as I said earlier on, in the context of the autumn financial statement, with improvements to the road network as well.

Q537 Jessica Morden: I wasn't going to ask about the Severn bridge but, seeing as the opportunity has arisen, could I quickly ask the Secretary of State for Wales about it? The Chancellor seemed to insinuate last week, when I asked him a question after the autumn statement, that when the bridges came back into the Government's control he was looking at spending the tolling money on the infrastructure and, as you mentioned earlier, on improving the M4 corridor. Does that mean that any calls for the tolls to be reduced are not being heard because any money collected will go off?

Mrs Gillan: No, Ms Morden. I think it means that we are at the very early stages of these negotiations, and I would not want to prejudice them by trying to elaborate any further. I think that the situation is clear until 2017. It is quite obvious that we are looking at the road infrastructure. We have asked the Welsh Government what contribution they would make to improving the M4 corridor, and I think that discussions will take place moving forward on that basis, but I think that the message has been clearly heard.

Q538 Geraint Davies: Moving on, but related to that, on enterprise zones, I think that the Government spend £200 million in England on 24 schemes— around £10 million a scheme—yet all of Wales has £10 million. So we will have an enterprise zone in Bristol with almost the size of the whole budget for Wales, alongside this penal tax on trade and investment, which is the toll we talked about earlier, and yet we want to revive the south Wales economy. What does Dr Cable think about that as a sort of stranglehold on inward investment and trade? Don't you think that something should be done to reduce the costs on the Severn bridge, and not invest enormous amounts in the gateway to Wales, in Bristol, which is basically stopping investment crossing the border?

Vince Cable: I can see you're pushing me very hard to take bridges into my empire, and I am trying to resist the temptation—

Geraint Davies: Building bridges!

Vince Cable: I'm afraid I can't really help you on the bridge issue. I was under the impression that the choice of enterprise zone was down to the Welsh Assembly Government, was it not?

Q539 Geraint Davies: I am simply making the point that they have only £10 million to spend across Wales, when one of these enterprise zones, in Bristol, would have what the entirety of Wales has. In terms of the strategic development of the south Wales economy, wouldn't you agree that that is very harmful?

Vince Cable: Not necessarily, no. I don't see it as a zero-sum game. If Bristol is able to develop as a very successful growth pole in the south-west of England, I would have thought that that would have benefits for Wales. There are a lot of overlaps through the supply chains, which I would have thought would have developed. I don't see it entirely in the negative way that you do. Isn't it the job of the Welsh Assembly Government to decide their own priorities regarding where the enterprise zones should be and how they should be configured? We would not want to trespass on their rights in that respect.

Q540 Geraint Davies: But isn't there a danger of a sort of bidding war across the border, with one side with many more armaments than the other? As I said, Wales has £10 million to spread across the whole country. We will probably have that much planted on the gateway alongside this bridge.

Vince Cable: You keep coming back to the toll bridge, and I'm afraid I'll have to keep passing on that.

Q541 Geraint Davies: I don't know whether Lord Green has a view on whether that will have a negative or positive impact on inward investment in Wales.

Lord Green: I don't. I don't know enough. In my various travels in the past number of months I have never heard anyone mention the toll on the Severn bridge at all, let alone suggest that it was a material fact in their investment decision making.

Q542 Geraint Davies: So, Dr Cable, do you feel that it's fair to have this great big enterprise zone in the doorway to Wales?

Vince Cable: It is perfectly fair, yes.

Chair: Good, that's a great short answer. Jonathan Edwards.

Q543 Jonathan Edwards: Let's try this another way. All the experience in the history of enterprise zones is that they suck wealth in from all other areas, so isn't there a danger that this massive enterprise zone in Bristol will have a hugely negative impact on the south Wales economy? What are you going to do to safeguard the current jobs and firms that we have in Wales?

Vince Cable: One of the lessons of the 1980s was a partial conclusion along the lines you have suggested—that enterprise zones as they were constructed then had the effect simply of encouraging firms to move from one part of the UK to somewhere nearby. There were some successes—London docklands was one, and I think Sunderland was another—and one of the conclusions that we have drawn from that is that enterprise zones are much more likely to be successful if they attract inward investors from overseas. Certainly, having talked to Bristol council—10 days ago, I think—that is clearly the focus of its energies, and it is not at the expense of anyone.

Q544 Guto Bebb: My question is to the Secretary of State for Wales, again regarding enterprise zones. I know that the Secretary of State has to be extremely careful because of the respect agenda, but does she not share a degree of concern that six or seven months down the line we have seen no detail as to how the Welsh Assembly is going to implement enterprise zones in a Welsh context? All we have had is an announcement of geographical areas, for example Anglesey, which was warmly welcomed by the Assembly Member Ieuan Wyn Jones.

Mrs Gillan: Mr Bebb, this was raised with me at Welsh oral questions the other day. I have been as encouraging as I can, because I felt, being responsible for the Wales Office, that the enterprise zones in England had got a real head start, although I must acknowledge that the Welsh Government were also waiting for the position on capital allowances, which I think is now becoming clearer. I felt, however, that that had not prevented the announcements of more detail on the English enterprise zones from being announced. I was encouraged, and I politely said that I hoped the Welsh Government would get a wiggle on, because I have always felt that there was a danger of England getting ahead, and I think that that has happened in certain instances. I do not want to see that happen; I want to see Wales get ahead. I want them to be worried on the English side of the border in Bristol.

Q545 Geraint Davies: I want to ask Lord Green about inward investment. You mentioned the inward investment telescope coming down through China, the UK, Wales and Swansea. To what extent do you think there should be a focus on getting inward investment into Wales out of London? Once multinationals or investors have arrived in London, should we be saying, "Look, with the cost of salaries, the cost of property and the whole density of population, why don't you come to a quality-of-life location where you can look out over the sea while you are on your PC in Swansea, reading a poem?" What opportunities do you think there are in reaching out from Wales across to London—or even Cardiff, in the case of Swansea—and pulling people in, rather than reaching out across the globe?

Lord Green: I think it is a very important point. There are many examples where companies have set up a European or UK headquarters in London and have done business in London, then have gradually moved out various aspects of their activity to other parts of the country. There must be opportunities to ensure that the case for Wales is properly made to those companies. That speaks to the importance of engaging with the European head offices of those companies in London and talking to them about the various things you have just mentioned. We need to talk to them about the reason why, both on cost and on cultural and lifestyle grounds, it would be a good option for them to think about investing at least part of their operations in Wales.

Q546 Chair: I wonder whether the Secretary of State for Wales can enlighten me on the Welsh investment strategic partnership, which I understand was a deal struck with Babcock and Brown to deliver 375,000 square feet of high-quality office space for inward investors coming into Wales, because that was identified as the problem holding back inward investment. I wonder whether that was ever discussed with the Secretary of State for Wales—it obviously took place before her time—and whether as a result of spending that money and developing that office space lots of private companies flocked to Wales. I have not been able to find out from the Welsh Assembly, unfortunately, so I wondered whether you might be able to help me out with that.

Mrs Gillan: Chairman, at this stage, I am not able to help you out on that, but if I can write to the Committee with an answer on that, I would be delighted to do so.[3]

Chair: Absolutely. Thank you very much. Are there any further questions?

Q547 Jessica Morden: In one part of the inquiry, we have been examining public sector investment in Wales. Newport has obviously benefited in the past from civil service jobs being relocated. What assessment have you made with the Treasury of how many of the 300,000 additional public sector job losses running up to 2016 will happen in Wales?

Mrs Gillan: My views, as well as the views of the previous Secretary of State for Wales, are well known: Wales is too heavily dependent on jobs in the public sector. One of the reasons why I am so keen on growth in the private sector and inward investment is so that we can reduce that dependence on the public sector. That is something we should all look at.

Q548 Jessica Morden: With the forecast that more public sector jobs will be lost, how many of those do you expect to be in Wales?

Mrs Gillan: I have looked at all the comments that have been made on this, but I think that at this stage we do not know where the economy is going to go and what other areas the Welsh Government will cut in terms of public sector jobs. I am unsighted on that. As a large number of the public sector jobs in Wales

are entirely dependent on the Welsh Government, it would not be right for me to predict any cuts that they may be making or have made already.

Q549 Geraint Davies: Let me follow that up. Would both Secretaries of State accept that private sector growth and job creation, to a large extent, depend on the spending power of the public sector and public servants? Public servants are going to see a 0%, 0% and 1%, 1% increase in pay, which is an aggregate reduction in real income of 16% over four years, so we will have less money to spend in the private sector and the public sector will have fewer contracts to give, too. How will that impact on private sector growth and inward investment, given that there is less consumption and investment from the public sector? Perhaps Dr Cable could answer first.

Vince Cable: That is a slightly complicated way of saying that there is an issue of aggregate demand.

Geraint Davies: Exactly.

Vince Cable: It is obviously true that in order to attract investment, you need demand. As you know, the Government's strategy is to deal with the fiscal deficit, because we think that is fundamental to confidence, while at the same time trying to sustain demand through monetary policy, interest rates, credit easing, quantitative easing—

Q550 Geraint Davies: I guess what I was getting at is that in places like Swansea, and in Wales more generally, 40% at the moment is public sector. Although we all want to see private sector growth, could any more support be provided to help the public sector to enable the private sector to grow more quickly; or is it the same for everybody, irrespective of where you start?

Vince Cable: In England, we have the Regional Growth Fund, which is designed to address exactly that question. Where there is a disproportionate loss of public sector jobs, the fund is ready to put in additional Government capital to support private enterprise growth in those areas. I would guess that it is very much down to the Welsh Government to use their own instruments. They have a growth capital fund, I think, and a repayable, interest-free loan scheme. They might want to look at how the English Regional Growth Fund operates, because it is designed to address the problem you raise.

Chair: Thank you very much, Dr Cable. There may be others here who suspect that the public sector is actually dependent on the private sector for growth, but that is an interesting discussion that we do not have time for and it does not quite—

Q551 Geraint Davies: I thought that the Secretary of State might want to respond.

Chair: If she wishes to, that is fine.

Mrs Gillan: I think Dr Cable said it all. A lot of these levers are with the Welsh Government. They have just received a large amount of capital allocation—£216.2 million—and it is up to them how they spend it. There are no reasons why they should not consider that.

Chair: Thank you all very much indeed for coming along.

---

[3]   See Ev 222

Written evidence

Written evidence submitted by Dr John Ball, Swansea University

INTRODUCTION

The timing of the Committee's investigation is fortuitous. The extended and much publicised success in attracting inward investment to Wales—especially FDI—has been steadily declining over the past decade, as other regions and nations have competed vigorously for investment. Furthermore, many of the organisations attracted to Wales during earlier investment phases have ceased to trade or withdrawn to areas providing different incentives, often cheaper labour costs. In addition, the National Assembly has pursued policies—it has to be said half heartedly—to encourage enterprise and indigenous business growth with little attempt to link policies with inward investment, past or future.

Much of the evidence provided for the Committee's inquiry, such as levels of investment, will directly address the five areas of investigation laid out in the Committee's original announcement and indeed, is likely to be repetitive. The purpose of this brief memorandum therefore is to draw the Committee's attention to past practices, advantages and limitations but also to suggest ways in which inward investment policy might successfully be directed.

The memorandum is presented in four sections:

— A review of the fundamental aims of regional policy.

— A brief discussion on the role of inward investment in achieving these aims.

— A review of the potential for increased investment together with a critique of past activities.

— A discussion on the conditions necessary to attract inward investment, subdivided into taxation, the production mandate and the need to address competitiveness.

1. REGIONAL POLICY

Before inquiring into direct investment in Wales, it is worth re-emphasising the aims of regional policy, of which inward investment is one instrument:

— The *regional problem* is conventionally associated with the terminal decline of traditional industry found in the regions and is invariably referred to by one of its principal characteristics, that of unemployment. It is attributed to two fundamental weaknesses.

— Many regions have inherited an unfavourable industrial structure as a result of the industries upon which regional economies grew. In addition, the problem is seen as locational. The regions do not provide suitable locations for new industry and firms attracted to the regions are often subject to cost and other disadvantages. Of the two, the inherited industrial structure has been seen as the important determinant in the lack of economic growth.

— To address the above problems, the main aims of regional policy have been twofold: the provision of employment and the diversification of the existing industrial structure to encourage self sustaining growth.

— In reality, policy instruments have mainly been aimed at the former, to the detriment of the latter, and it is this emphasis that has led to criticism of the policy's main instrument, inward investment. In employment provision terms, active regional policy has been successful, without it, the situation in Wales would have been worse in terms of unemployment, out-migration, economic diversification and alternative job opportunities.

2. THE ROLE OF INWARD INVESTMENT

Although there are questions about the long term success of inward investment in resolving the continued decline of the Welsh economy—indeed it is argued that this success has in many ways had the opposite effect—it retains an important role for a number of reasons:

— a major source of employment;

— the introduction of new skills and technology to the receiving region;

— has a substantial multiplier effect;

— encouragement of local suppliers; and

— becomes a long term strategic asset as a basis for economic growth.

3. POTENTIAL FOR INCREASED INVESTMENT

Although successful in quantitative terms, previous inward investment has been only partially successful in achieving the aims of regional policy and is discussed in the following section. That is not to say that inward investment has no role to play, on the contrary, correct and appropriate investment can provide important economic stimulus. The important lesson for future activity is not to repeat the mistakes of the past and the challenge therefore is to strike a balance between employment provision and growth sectors.

3.1 *Inward Investment Assessment*

Although successful in creating employment (which became and to some extent remains, the over-riding motive), inward investment as a major instrument of regional policy, has many shortcomings. Success in employment provision has served to reduce the possibility of long term growth that inward investment is supposed to provide:

— Many of the investing businesses attracted to the regions diversified the industrial base but did little to encourage the technical, managerial or skill base; a pre-condition for successful economic growth.

— Financial inducements—invariably grants—have been the main instrument used and on occasions have supported projects with limited employment prospects, or which would have been undertaken without subsidy.

— Fundamentally, no attempt was made to differentiate between efficient and non-efficient firms, or those with products in a growth sector or on the quality of employment offered.

— The major criticism was that Wales became a "branch plant" economy; inward investment became synonymous with external ownership, low skilled employment, standard end of life cycle products, mature technologies and restricted management opportunities.

— The last decade or so has shown that many of these branch plants were temporary and did little to encourage long term change.

Almost half a century of attracting inward investment has resulted in large employers providing much needed employment, thereby fulfilling to some extent one aim of regional policy. But wealth creation and economic development do not arise solely from the provision of employment. In reality, success in creating employment has served to depress longer-term development because the skills required have not always been appropriate. An important policy assumption is that inward investment has a substantial multiplier effect in encouraging local businesses to supply goods and services, thus increasing the effectiveness of the original investment:

— The reality is that this often does not happen, managerial functions, especially purchasing, inventory and product development, remained outside Wales.

— Suppliers exist, but in *economic* space not in *geographic* space.

— Manufacturers of products at the end of the life cycle are driven by cost. This means for many of these products Wales has been competing against much lower labour costs in Eastern Europe and much of the rest of the world.

— More recent industrial policy in Wales has focused on products in sectors such as motor vehicles and consumer electronics, which are not growth sectors and for which there is *derived* demand; products incorporated into other manufactured goods sold under a variety of international brands. Local suppliers capable of supplying components invariably compete on price, since end of life cycle products are extremely price sensitive.

4. Conditions Necessary to Attract Inward Investment

Whilst it is recognised that the need significantly to improve education standards, skills levels and transport infrastructure are matters for the Assembly, any inquiry into inward investment cannot ignore their vital importance to investors. There remain serious concerns about standards of education and the level of skills available to incoming investors to Wales and these need urgently to be addressed. There is also the vexed question of transport infrastructure, not least the M4 in south Wales, notably the tolls at the Severn Bridge, access to valley communities and poor communications by rail and air. All these need urgent attention and have been discussed *ad infinitum*.

Despite criticism of previous inward investment, lessons have been learned and the development of appropriate incentives and policies can ensure that future investment plays a full part in economic development.

However, so far as attraction of investment is concerned; and recognising international competition for such investment, original and innovative policies are required.

4.1 *Taxation*

— Whatever powers may or may not accrue in the future to the National Assembly, attractive tax regimes are being used by regions and states competing for the same investment and to be able to compete, the use of such incentives must be addressed.

— Taxation based economic development has been remarkably successful in other parts of Europe and its use in tackling the urgent needs of the Welsh economy needs to be addressed. Tax incentives in many forms—although principally corporation tax—have proved successful in many European states, and in a lesson for the UK, *within* states, such as Catalonia in Spain. Low levels of corporation tax have been used as a principal tool of economic development in Ireland, which at 12.5% is the lowest rate and although currently there are serious sovereign debt problems, there has been no reduction in inward flowing investment.

— Carefully targeted corporation tax incentives are attractive for the investing business because they are, by definition, profitable and seeking to reduce their tax liability. For the receiving region, tax incentives are internal to the firm and consequently the bureaucracy associated with traditional incentives is reduced and the need to prove "additionality" and job creation is removed.

— Incentives other than corporation tax are an important instrument of policy, including lower taxation on business that export or which re-invest profits in new products or technology.

— Research has shown an unexpected effect of reducing corporate tax. A cut in corporation tax leads to an increase in employees' earnings. This seems perverse, but with higher profits, capital in the form of innovation and technology is substituted for labour and consequently, there develops a need for employees to develop greater skills.

Within the UK there is the perceived danger that different taxation incentives, albeit limited in application and approach, will result in some regions gaining an unfair advantage. However, addressing the use of taxation is recognition of the need to address the continued decline of the Welsh economy. The concept of regional taxation within the UK is not a new idea, indeed the concept of a universal UK wide tax system is a myth:

— The Selective Employment Tax of the 1960s taxed services and re-used the tax take to support manufacturing and was in reality, given the industrial structure of the UK at the time, a *de facto* regional tax.

— Traditional instruments of economic development—grant aid and regional selective assistance—were regionally based and reflected the re-distribution of taxation, although not in name.

— Similarly, differences in capital allowances over time and used to encourage investment in regional manufacturing areas is by definition, a tax incentive.

— Fiscal transfers by HM Treasury from one part of the UK to another again represent a *de facto* taxation difference.

— Council taxes differ by region and the concept of local income tax to replace council tax enjoys growing, if limited support.

4.2 *The Production Mandate*

In spite of the advantages argued for taxation based incentives that are particularly attractive to footloose inward investors, there is always the danger of competing with other regions and nations with a race to the bottom. Noting criticism of the partial success of past inward investment, courage must be shown in efforts to attract investment and incentives, in addition to financial, should be offered on the basis of the "*production mandate*" concept:

— Incentives remain available, but are offered on the basis of the amount of "mandate" (local autonomy) given to local management.

— The mandate applies to the amount of autonomy to purchase, recruit, and undertake training, research, product development and innovation at the receiving local site.

— If there is insufficient mandate, then incentives are reduced or withdrawn.

— Although the current investigation is concerned with FDI, there is a wider case for the mandate to be applied to *all* incoming investors including incoming multiple retailers and service sector organisations.

— Philosophically, the production mandate approach would represent a fundamental difference from the major criticism of past policy that any employment was acceptable.

4.3 *International Competitiveness:*

In its announcement of this inquiry, the Committee made specific reference to the potential for increased investment, both in traditional sectors and emerging sectors. Future inward investment must avoid the errors of the past and be part of an over arching, coherent economic development policy aimed at attracting investors capable of global reach:

— Economic growth partly emanates from identifying and building upon *existing* strengths. The inability to understand this simple idea has been a constant failing of policy.

— Inward investment must be in sectors that reflect the real level of skills within the economy and the need for, and ability to develop, local suppliers.

— There are distinct skills with the Welsh economy, notably (but not only) manufacturing and engineering, which in many ways are two sides of the same coin. These should form the basis of policy in attracting investors requiring engineering skills.

— There is too great an emphasis on voguish high tech sectors, software or "fashionable" sectors such as financial services. The reality is that aside from competition from the rest of the world, Wales simply does not have the skill levels needed.

— There must be careful analysis of inward investors in emerging sectors to seek a match with skills—to a great extent some energy sectors do require traditional engineering skills.

— A fundamental weakness of the Welsh economy has been the failure to produce final demand products (not necessarily in "traditional" engineering) and the search for such sectors must be a priority.

— Any re-location of government offices should be resisted; the Welsh economy is already over reliant on the public sector.

March 2011

Written evidence submitted by Professor Emeritus Peter Gripaios, University of Plymouth

SUMMARY

— Both inward to the UK and outward FDI by UK businesses were increasing up to 2008, after which there was a fall due to recession.

— However, in recent years, FDI in manufacturing into the UK has been falling, a process which looks likely to continue.

— Attracting FDI has been seen as an important tool of economic restructuring in the UK and its constituent regions.

— Wales has been very reliant on attracting in assembly line manufacturing operations, but despite many headline successes, the Welsh economy remains in the doldrums. Indeed, Wales has dropped to the bottom of the UK economic regional league table.

— It has already suffered some high profile losses of FDI and looks very vulnerable to future restructuring.

— From now on, there should be less reliance on attracting low grade manufacturing jobs.

— There should also be less reliance on financial incentives and more on the underlying factors which would make Wales an attractive location for knowledge based industry.

— The same factors would help improve entrepreneurship and creativity.

TEXT

1. The total level of FDI in the UK at the end of 2009 was £654 billion (ONS, 2011). This compared with £1,030 billion of investment abroad by UK companies. Both figures showed a small decline relative to a year earlier reflecting the impact of recession. In general, however, the trend in all advanced economies over recent decades has been one of increased foreign ownership, a trend referred to as globalisation.

2. There are many reasons why this has occurred including expansion, access to markets in specific trading blocks, cost reduction and a desire to reduce exchange rate risk by matching production to sales in specific areas. In cases, such as the City of London considerable FDI has been attracted because of the importance of agglomeration effects in the financial sector.

3. Much FDI is, therefore, a natural outcome of liberalisation and de-regulation in specific countries and trading blocs and more generally of multi-national agreements on World Trade.

4. In the UK, London has been a major beneficiary. In 2007, it had 14,821 (20.8%) of the 71,185 foreign owned companies in England (WM Enterprise 2010). The South East had 18.5%, the East of England 10% and the South West, 9.3%. The latter had the fastest growth of foreign owned businesses from 2004–07 (56.2%).

5. In total then, nearly 60% of foreign owned businesses in England were in the relatively prosperous "south". Figures published by the Welsh Assembly Government (WAG 2010) suggest that the number of "foreign owned enterprises active in Wales" is smaller than that in any English region. There were around 1,000 in 2007, rising to 1,100 in 2009 and falling back to 1,000 in 2010. They employed around 139,000 people in 2010, 11,000 fewer than in the peak year, 2009.

6. The attraction of FDI has been considered an important tool in restructuring the British economy over the long term and particularly since the de-industrialisation of the 1970s. Policy makers were attracted by the fact that new manufacturing and services jobs would replace those being lost in "heavy" industry and by the possibility that new more efficient production methods and management practices in foreign owned plants would spread to indigenous ones. There was also the hope that, over time, higher order functions in, for example, design and research and development would be devolved to the UK from the country in which the head office of the business was located.

7. Great efforts were made in the problem regions to get as much of the incoming FDI as possible. The concentration here was on manufacturing industries, the hope being that new blue collar jobs would replace the ones being lost in the mines, the steel works, the ship yards and other traditional industries. Huge grants and other allowances were on offer to get foreign owned businesses to the UK and to specific regions. In Wales, in particular, this seemed until very recently to be very much **the** tool of restructuring and development

and the Principality was successful in attracting in numerous headline manufacturing assembly line operations. As the potential supply of these began to dry up in the last decade, increasing attention was focused on safeguarding what had already come in.

8. In total some 13.7% of Welsh employees now work for foreign owned businesses suggesting that the policy has been successful (WAG 2010). Arguably, however, it has been a short term palliative rather than a long run solution and the dangers of long run over reliance on a specific policy lever are becoming ever more demonstrable.

9. Too many of the new jobs have involved low paid assembly line work and have failed to replace the relatively well paid blue collar male jobs lost from the mines and steel works. Moreover, many of the new jobs have been in different locations to the old, meaning considerable structural unemployment and huge levels of multiple deprivation in parts of West Wales and the Valleys. Finally, Wales has not been successful in attracting foreign owned, higher order manufacturing business functions and there is little evidence of significant spin off.

10. The same points apply to DDI in manufacturing and services. In financial services, for example, Wales has tended to attract call centre and back office work rather than Head and Regional Office functions. Cardiff, for example, though the striking success story in Wales, seems to have lost out in nearly all respects to nearby Bristol (Gripaios, 1997).

11. The long term evidence is provided by both the level and decline in GVA per capita in Wales relative to the UK in total (ONS, 2010). In 2009, the figure for Wales was 74% of the national one, the lowest of all regions of the UK. It had declined from 84.4% of the UK in 1989 and 77.4% in 1999. That compares with 91% in the adjacent South West, while the figure for the Cardiff and Vale and Glamorgan sub region at 111% is 21% less than that of the City of Bristol.

12. Wales also shows up badly in terms of unemployment rates, index of multiple deprivation, median earnings and house prices and it all looks like getting worse both during the recession and longer term. UK figures demonstrate that the type of FDI that Wales has concentrated on is the type that is going. Indeed, UK manufacturing FDI fell by 14.9% from the end of 2008 to the same time a year later (ONS, 2011).

13. There is no breakdown by region but the loss of FDI must have contributed to the fact that GVA in Welsh manufacturing fell by 2.8% over 2008–09 (ONS, 2010). There have been some highly publicised losses since then and it is much more than a temporary recession. Quite simply, easy come footloose manufacturing operations are also easy go and both the UK and Wales have become too expensive for routine manufacturing in the light of competition from lower cost new entrants to the EU and, further afield, China and other developing countries.

14. Wales, therefore, faces another period of extensive restructuring and that will be exacerbated by its heavy reliance on public expenditure at a time when this is being savagely cut. Moreover, EU Structural Funding could largely disappear in 2013.

15. There is, of course, no easy solution and there are plenty of other regions in the UK, Europe, USA and Japan facing many of the same problems.

16. Of course, it would be sensible to try and keep as much existing FDI as possible and to attract new high quality FDI, ideally across a range of economic activities. Arguably, less reliance should be put on financial incentives and much more than in the past on creating the conditions in which business will wish to locate in Wales. Those conditions are also necessary to engender more indigenous entrepreneurship and creativity. Better infrastructure but, more importantly, better education and aspiration are likely to be fundamental in this.

February 2011

REFERENCES

Gripaios P (1997) The Welsh Economy: An Outside Perspective, Contemporary Wales, Vol 10, University of Wales Press.

ONS (2011) Foreign Direct Investment, MA4 Business Monitor 2009.

ONS (2010) Regional, Sub-Regional and Local Gross Value Added 2009.

WAG (2010) Size Analysis of Welsh Business 2010.

WM Enterprise (2010) Inward Investment and International Trade Projects Interim Evaluation (2004–09), South West of England Regional Development Agency.

Written evidence submitted by Professor David Pickernell, University of Glamorgan

SUMMARY

— Wales's relatively successful period of inward investment attraction during the 1980s and 1990s was accompanied by a degree of knowledge and innovation transfer that positively impacted on wage rates and demand for higher skilled labour.

— Even after the more recent reductions in inward investment flows, is still relatively successful in its inward investment attraction, though the focus has now switched to services (such as distribution) rather than manufacturing, and even within manufacturing there has been a change in focus from electronics and towards transport-related sectors.

— The reasons for location also seem to have shifted, away from grants per se, and towards the availability of skilled labour and key infrastructure, factors which can also be seen as important in retaining long-term inward investors.

— The reduced public resources likely to be available for inward investment specifically and economic development generally increase the importance of linking inward investment attraction policy with indigenous firm development and entrepreneurship, a linkage that has not been maximised in the recent past.

— The need to improve the innovation performance of the Welsh economy generally also suggests that policies related to institutions such as universities, which can act as attractors to high value adding inward investors and creators (and supporters) of high growth indigenous businesses, need to be more closely integrated.

— In this way, potential policy resource conflicts (eg between inward investment attraction and entrepreneurship promotion that are likely to have occurred in the past) may be reduced, and greater policy synergy obtained.

1. During the 1980s Wales regularly gained three to four times the share of the inward investment and associated jobs coming to the UK that one would expect given its population (Hill and Munday, 1992). In the early 1990s, foreign manufacturing accounted for a greater proportion (25%) of employment in Welsh manufacturing than both the North and North West of England and was on a par with Scotland (Driffield and Taylor, 2000). From the late 1980s to early 1990s, new technology and knowledge transferred into the Welsh economy by inward investors was also seen to increase the demand for skilled labour and wages, though with much less effect on structural unemployment (Driffield and Taylor, 2000).

2. More recently, however, the environment for attracting large-scale investment has changed. Wales has lost large portions of its foreign manufacturing employment and output, particularly to China, South East Asia and Central and Eastern Europe (Evans et al, 2008). For example, from the 171 foreign-owned site closures in Wales that Evans et al (2008) identified as having occurred between 1998 and 2008, nearly 31,000 jobs had been lost, mainly in production (including leather and textiles), though a number of financial call centres had also closed.

3. These other parts of the world can combine much lower labour costs with increasing education and skills levels (Evans et al, 2008), as well as growing market potential, making it difficult for Wales to compete for inward investment focused on production cost minimisation alone. Nevertheless, the UK as a whole has still attracted more inflows than outflows since 2004 (Evans et al, 2008), and the UK still ranks highly as an attractive location for FDI. The recent analysis of Evans et al (2008) also shows that Wales, for 2006–07, attracted over 9% of the new employment in FDI projects in the UK as a whole, remaining a disproportionately large share compared with its population, though less so than in previous years.

4. Employment in foreign firms in Wales, however, particularly in manufacturing, has been falling, from 75,000 in 2003 to 72,000 in 2006 (Evans et al, 2008), with it forecast to continue falling, though increases in FDI in distribution are also expected to continue (inward investors in distribution and services currently employing around 10,000 people). The overall trends since the beginning of the 21st century have, therefore, been for decreasing FDI and employment in manufacturing generally, and increases in lower value added financial services, and more specifically distribution.

5. Broadly, therefore, FDI-based employment in manufacturing is likely to have peaked, and future overall employment growth is unlikely (Evans et al, 2008). It still remains, however, an important part of manufacturing in Wales, accounting for 42% of total employment in this sector. This represents an increasing proportion of total manufacturing employment, explained by the faster decline in manufacturing employment in Wales generally over the past decade.

6. The highest (and increasing) concentrations of inward investors remain in automotive and transport equipment, and also (although declining proportionately) in electrical and optical equipment and chemicals (Evans et al, 2008). Hi-technology Automotive and Aerospace sectors have, therefore, been much less affected than other sectors, due to a combination of the relatively buoyant nature of their markets, close networked relationships with customers and suppliers, and less pronounced cost advantages of competitor locations. This indicates some possible factors upon which Welsh policy could focus upon in attraction of future FDI.

7. It also needs to be recognised that, as Cooke *et al* (2003) illustrate, FDI located in Wales up to the start of the new millennium was contributing disproportionately positively to an otherwise relatively (compared to the UK as a whole) weak Welsh innovation performance. This trend has continued. Inward investors in Wales are much more likely to be employed in high tech production and activities than their indigenous counterparts and there has also been strong increase in the proportion of inward investors undertaking R&D activities over the past decade (Evans *et al*, 2008). To an extent, however, this may also indicate the exiting from Wales of FDI that did not undertake R&D activity in Wales to lower cost locations. Merger/acquisition activity (eg Broughton) where previously UK owned companies with R&D activities have been acquired by foreign owners may also play a part in this result.

8. The exiting from Wales of a significant number of inward investors can be seen, to an extent to be linked to the way in which inward investment tended to be attracted in the past. For example, the strongest contributory factor for FDI locating in Wales during the 1980s and 1990s was the availability of government grants and subsidies facilitating the initial location process (Huggins, 2001).

9. This also illustrates the important role played by the Welsh Assembly Government and the UK Government policy in attracting foreign investment in the past. FDI also continues, however, to be disproportionately located in the South-East and (increasingly) North-East of Wales, for reasons Evans *et al*, (2008) have linked to available infrastructure, local consumers, supply of skilled labour and wider (UK and EU) market access.

10. This raises a crucial point regarding future attraction strategies, particularly given that Wales has lost its competitive advantage in terms of low cost labour, and grant availability is likely to be increasingly squeezed. The North Wales position is increasingly tied up with the Aerospace industry via the Airbus facility at Broughton, whilst the experience in South Wales has been one of closures in the electronics and automotive industries and expansions in distribution (most notably Amazon) services in particular.

11. The most recent investments, however, were more focused on the availability of productive and skilled labour, because of the trend of bringing in more technologically advanced products (Evans *et al*, 2008). Conversely, lower multiplier effects created by FDI attracted into the services sector (Evans *et al*, 2008) in Wales may also call into question the appropriateness of this approach in maximizing the benefits from the resources given.

12. The issue of the opportunity cost of resources can also be seen to be of relevance. The level of public sector investment in Wales in economic development policy resources following the Comprehensive Spending Review in October is also likely to reduce the resources available to attract FDI, or require other strategic priorities, such as those linked to indigenous business development, to be financially squeezed to provide the necessary resources.

13. This raises two important questions. One concerns the opportunity cost in terms of resources of attracting FDI relative to policies that promote indigenous entrepreneurship. The other concerns how one might best leverage scarce resources to maximise their benefit.

14. Brooksbank *et al* (2001), for example, highlighted at the turn of the millennium the increased importance placed on entrepreneurship and skills development in the Welsh Objective One Programme, but also raised the potential difficulties in resourcing this new policy, given the requirements to continue resourcing inward investors, an issue also discussed in Brooksbank and Pickernell (2001).

15. The knowledge spillover theory of entrepreneurship, however, (Audretsch and Keilbach, 2007), highlights the benefits to be derived from explicitly linking inward investment policy with indigenous firm development activities, by showing the potential for knowledge and technology brought into a region by inward investors to "spill over" into the economy more generally and to be exploited by local entrepreneurs. Acs *et al* (2007) illustrate, however, that whilst Ireland was relatively successful in this regard, Wales was has been much less so. This is particularly because it can be seen to have focused more exclusively on inward investment up until the later 1990s when attracting it became more difficult, and then switched its focus to indigenous development (Morgan, 2007), rather than coordinating the two policies more closely.

16. The potential for increased investment in Wales in emerging sectors including IT and energy is also likely, however, to depend on the extent to which Wales also generates attractive conditions for indigenous businesses as well as international ones, given the innovation focus of these industries. There can be a particularly strong role for the government via innovation, through the triple helix of government, industry-institution interaction, and emphasises the importance of network and collaborative activities between these three groups of stakeholders (Etzkowitz and Leyesdorff, 2000). Cooke (2003) also highlights that successful, faster growing "core" regions are more likely to have "entrepreneurial" innovation systems, whilst more economically slow growing and geographically peripheral areas (such as Wales) tend to have "institutional" ones, with a stronger role played by government.

17. The role of institutions such as universities is also, therefore, likely to be of importance here, in generating knowledge and acting as a conduit for knowledge generated elsewhere, disseminating knowledge, and also generating new businesses and opportunities (Pickernell *et al* 2008, Pickernell *et al*, 2009), in areas such as energy and IT, that can be exploited both by indigenous firms and also through collaboration with

inward investors. In this way the attractiveness of Wales as a location to inward investors in sectors focused upon by government can be increased.

18. Given the constrained resource situation, it is likely that policy will require a "bricolaged" approach. This involves using existing resources for new purposes, recombining existing resources and "making do" to provide novel solutions (Baker and Nelson, 2005). As such, it can be seen as potentially relevant with regard to policies related to education and skills, but also key infrastructure developments (including road, rail and air links, as well as telecommunications).

19. The effectiveness of co-operation between various government agencies and indeed between government, other institutions, and private business, is therefore likely to be crucial in the future, to maximise the effectiveness of the resources utilised and to link more effectively inward investment and indigenous firm development policy.

20. In this way, potential policy resource conflicts (eg between inward investment attraction and entrepreneurship promotion that are likely to have occurred in the past) may be reduced, and greater policy synergy obtained.

REFERENCES

Acs, Z, Brooksbank, D, O'Gorman, C, Pickernell, D, and Terjesen, S, (2007), The Knowledge Spillover Theory of Entrepreneurship and Foreign Direct Investment Jena Economic Research Paper No 2007–059. Available at SSRN:
http://ssrn.com/abstract=1022928

Audretsch, D and Keilbach, M (2007) "The Theory of Knowledge Spillover Entrepreneurship", *Journal of Management Studies*, 44(7): 1242–1254.

Baker, T and Nelson, R (2005) Creating Something from Nothing: Resource Construction Through Entrepreneurial Bricolage, *Administrative Science Quarterly* 50 (3): 329–366.

Brooksbank, D and Pickernell, D (2001) "Changing the Name of the Game? RSA, Indigenous and Inward Investors, and the National Assembly for Wales", *Regional Studies*, 35(3): 271–277.

Brooksbank, D, Clifton, N, and Jones-Evans, D, and Pickernell, D (2001) "The End of the Beginning? Welsh Regional policy and Objective One", *European Planning Studies*, 9(2): 255–274.

Cooke, P, Heidenreich, M & Braczyk, H (eds) (2003) Regional Innovation Systems (2nd Edition), London, Routledge.

Driffield, N, and Taylor, K (2000) FDI and the Labour Market: A review of the evidence and the policy implications, Oxford Review of Economic Policy, 16 (3): 90–103.

Etzkowitz, H and Leyesdorff, L (2000) The dynamics of innovation: from National Systems and "Mode 2" to a Triple Helix of university-industry-government relations, *Research Policy*, 29: 109–123.

Evans, P, Holtz, R, and Roberts, A (2008) Empirical investigation of FDI in Wales, Welsh Assembly Government Research Unit, Cardiff,
(last accessed 14/02/2011)

Hill, S, and Munday, M, (1992) The UK Regional Distribution of Foreign Direct Investment: Analysis and Determinants, *Regional Studies,* 26 (6): 535–544.

Huggins, R, (2001) Embedding inward investment through workforce development: experiences in Wales" *Environment and Planning C: Government and Policy* **19**(6): 833–848.

Morgan, K (1997) The Learning Region: Institutions, Innovation and Regional Renewal, *Regional Studies,* 31(5): 491–503.

Pickernell, D, Packham, G, Thomas, B, and Keast, R (2008) University Challenge? Innovation Policy and SMEs in Welsh Economic Development Policy: Towards a New Framework, *International Journal of Entrepreneurship and Innovation,* 9 (1): 51–62.

Pickernell, D, Clifton, N and Senyard, J, (2009) Think Global, Act Local ? Universities, SMEs, and Innovation Frameworks*, Industry and Higher Education*, 23 (2) 79–89.

February 2011

Written evidence submitted by CBI Wales

SUMMARY

This submission deals principally with the fifth issue highlighted in the Committee's call for evidence: the conditions necessary to attract foreign investors to Wales. We cover the following points:

— The continued importance of FDI to Wales and why this is not an either/or choice between FDI and indigenous company growth.

— The key issues considered by businesses when making investment decisions.

— How the business perception of the UK, compared to its competitors, is changing for key factors.

— Government enablers/blockers to increased business investment and how government in Wales might be able to influence some of these.

— Once an attractive business environment is understood, the importance of an effective process for seeking and delivering inward investment projects.

FOREIGN DIRECT INVESTMENT (FDI)

1. We welcome the decision by the Committee to examine the conditions for inward investment into Wales and recent performance. FDI remains of critical importance to the Welsh economy, for the potential for further investment and job creation, but especially given the important installed base of inward investment companies in Wales, and the importance of ensuring their long-term commitment.

2. The debate about FDI in Wales has a tendency to get simplified, wrongly, into a policy choice between attracting inward investment and supporting indigenous Welsh businesses. This is not helpful and the CBI does not recognise this as a choice that needs to be made. We need to accept that as a result of previous FDI success non-Welsh headquartered companies underpin the economies of many of our towns and cities, and encouraging these companies to re-invest will be critical. The CBI's SME members regard these externally owned businesses as key customers, and as important to the economic health of communities across Wales.

3. But this is not to advocate an economic policy solely based on attracting FDI. It is clear that we also need to encourage the development and success of Welsh headquartered businesses as they will tend to be more strongly anchored into the Welsh economy. The good news is that a focus on an intrinsically attractive business environment will support both categories of companies. This needs to be the starting point for governments, whether at a European, UK, Welsh or local level. Interventionist economic development tools can then be deployed selectively to supplement this supportive business environment, and these may well be different for FDI and indigenous enterprises.

4. The retention of existing inward investors faces the challenge of existing factories and premises becoming slowly obsolete. The golden age of inward investment in Wales was 20–25 years ago and the average lifespan of a production unit might be 30–40 years. A number of our earlier inward investors may therefore be facing significant investment requirements to refurbish/re-provision their facilities in the coming years, and we need to be aware of the potential for this to become a catalyst for closure.

KEY ISSUES FOR BUSINESSES IN MAKING INVESTMENT DECISIONS

5. Four key questions dominate business thinking when making investment decisions:

— Is there a market?

— Do we have enough certainty to make an investment and secure a return?

— Is the cost right?

— Do we have the capability?

6. However, discussions on investment are always more granular than this so that, for example, "cost" is considered in its widest sense, including in terms of accessing finance and skills, the amount of tax to pay, grants and other incentives available etc; "certainty" relates not just to certainty about the potential for sales of a new innovation resulting from an investment, but certainty in the wider political and business environment around policy and regulatory changes, long-term planning and whether changes can be predicted. "Capability" is often considered in terms of R&D, skills, supply chain networks and links into the innovation landscape. For many businesses, the UK is recognised as only a small "market" compared to the potential offered by China, India and others—although there is much the UK can do to position itself more effectively with a strategic vision for the future and coherent activity to make progress in realizing the vision with business.

7. Policy changes having a positive impact on these four key factors are likely to be the most influential on future business investment decisions.

KEY FACTORS FOR ATTRACTING INVESTMENT

8. Given the need to increase business investment generally, as one of the few drivers of economic growth available to us in the short to medium term, the CBI has over the past six months engaged in a widespread

dialogue with its members across the UK on the factors that will promote investment by them in this country. We will produce a report in early April on the results, but this section highlights some of the key findings.

9. The World Economic Forum ranks the UK highly in its global competitiveness ranking—currently 12th out of 138 countries assessed. Their index covers a range of factors including innovation and business sophistication, efficiency enhancers (eg labour market efficiency, financial markets, higher education and technological readiness) and more basic requirements (eg macroeconomics, infrastructure, and primary education). This relatively high ranking, coupled with time zone and language advantages, helps to explain why UNCTAD has consistently placed the UK in the top 10 for inward flows of FDI over the last decade and in the top five since 2004.

10. However, as part of our project we asked CBI members how the attractiveness of the UK for business investment has changed relative to other countries, compared to 10 years ago. Members told us that the UK has improved its relative attractiveness in respect of labour relations and the flexibility of work practices, has remained broadly stable for access to markets and quality of life, but has declined in many other areas:

In increasing order of relative decline:

> Availability of trained/skilled workforce.
> Infrastructure.
> Political and economic stability.
> Exchange rate risk.
> Ability to attract internationally mobile key staff.
> Availability of land, planning restrictions.
> Availability of grants/loans.
> Business taxation levels.
> Nature/level of regulation.
> Personal taxation levels.

11. Of particular concern here is that the UK is seen as declining in relative attractiveness in both business and personal taxation, which have a relatively high importance rating for investment decisions (business taxation 7.5/10, personal taxation 6.5/10).

12. From its work the CBI has been able to assess company views on the issues that matter for investment in the UK, and separate them into those that could deliver a step change in investment, those that currently actively dissuade investment, less important factors that nonetheless could act as drivers, and lastly those that currently work in our favour and which we need to maintain.

SUMMARY OF BUSINESS INVESTMENT BLOCKERS AND DRIVERS

Getting these right could create a step change in investment intentions	Currently blocking business investment	Getting these right should also drive business investment	Currently an important driver of investment and position needs to be maintained
Vision and ambition for the UK	Lack of long term policy certainty	Universities—IP and skills for business	Science base R&D and innovation
Stimulating new market activity	50p tax rate	Clusters	English language
Public procurement	Regulation and legislation	Future entrepreneurship skills	Cultural and quality of life aspects
Business tax targeted to encourage investment	Lack of appropriate skills		
Infrastructure resilience	Planning "mood music" from government and media		

ATTRACTING FDI TO WALES

13. The above factors are those that we believe will be critical to encouraging FDI to the UK, indeed to encouraging UK headquartered companies to increase investment in this country, rather than settling for lower growth or investing overseas. It follows that these will be the same factors that will inform potential investors on Wales' attractiveness as an investment location, and if these factors differ in Wales, either due to their being inherently local (eg skills base) or due to their being the result of government policy in devolved fields (eg planning, certain aspects of regulation, infrastructure) then Wales outperforming or underperforming other UK locations will go some way to explaining differing FDI performance levels.

14. And if we relate these policy factors to the questions posed in paragraph 5 of this paper, then it becomes clear how government in Wales can influence decisions.

> — *Is there a market?* FDI into Wales will never take place only to serve a Welsh market, so ease of access to the wider UK, European and other markets will be critical. This highlights transport and communications infrastructure

— *Do we have enough certainty to make an investment and secure a return?* Is there a track record of consistency in policy making, and how will devolution affect the regulatory and legislative environment in which a company will have to operate its investment? Can local government assistance, eg with planning, reduce the uncertainty involved in implementing an investment? Is the mood music right—do we give out the message that government wants FDI, values its international companies, and wants to work in partnership to mutual benefit?

— *Is the cost right?* Can the costs of establishing the investment be influenced by government decisions around policy, construction, support, incentives? Can government in Wales lower ongoing operational costs?

— *Do we have the capability?* Can government influence the supply chain dynamics, the R&D and innovation landscape to make Wales a more attractive option?

15. Having put in place the appropriate business environment, the activity of seeking and winning FDI then needs to be considered. In the past this has been a Welsh strength but recent reports (eg Massey 2009) have questioned whether the WAG approach is as effective as it could be. I hear frequent reports from existing FDI companies in Wales which confirm that they receive excellent assistance from WAG officials. But others active in the promotion of inward investment into Wales (accountancy firms, property agents) comment on a reduced focus in this area. This is a complex picture where disentangling the effects of UK/Welsh policy environment, political emphasis on differing economic development priorities, and operational delivery, is extremely difficult.

CONCLUSION

16. When framed in this way it seems clear that there is much that the UK government, and governments in Wales (WAG and local authorities) can do to influence future flows of FDI, both from new companies and those already present in Wales. However, the world is much more complex than it was when Wales led the UK in FDI performance. A ready supply of low cost labour, premises and incentives is no longer sufficient.

17. Government needs to consider those factors which form necessary conditions to business investment, both by indigenous companies and inward investors, and put them in place (remove the policy blockers). It can then seek to differentiate itself by addressing the enablers to outperform. And it needs to focus on delivery and outcomes, which in the past has been a Welsh strength.

March 2011

Written evidence submitted by Cardiff Business Partnership

INTRODUCTION

1. Funding channelled into Wales by national governments from the 1930's to 1990's attempted to create the economic conditions for prosperity by underwriting inward investment directly and indirectly, funding large scale public industrial/employment estates; housing and new town development and providing major infrastructure such as road and rail bridges. Regeneration programmes meanwhile tended to follow local authority boundaries, or were based on groupings of local authority areas.

WALES AND ECONOMIC STRATEGY

2. Proposals for a National Economic Development Strategy prepared in July 1999 stated that it will be the vehicle for setting the strategic priorities for the economic policies and programmes of the Assembly. It stated that the Assembly had an unique opportunity to take the programmes it has inherited, alongside the significant contribution of the new European funds, and shape them to provide a consistent and concerted impact on our future prosperity. It further stated in 1999 that Europe offered a window of opportunity to achieve new levels of prosperity in the whole of Wales. The key policies and priorities outlined focused on getting the best out of the unique opportunities for development over the period 2000–10. Separate action programme were intended to detail the specific measures necessary to implement European programmes in particular regions of Wales.

3. More importantly, it stated that by 2010, Wales wished to see a renewed Welsh economy based on: high and appropriate skill levels; higher levels of participation; strong representation in growth sectors; innovation; an export culture; added value; higher quality jobs; the highest quality of the natural environment. This economic transformation it stated must increase levels of employment and activity, raise earnings, and increase the quality of life, health and opportunity for all. In 1999 it set Targets GDP to reach: this failed to take place. It is now time to reconsider matters.

THE ECONOMY TODAY

4. Due to the poor nature of the economy in Wales (compared to other regions of the UK) there is a constant call to bring back the likes of the WDA—"Welsh Development Agency" as an economic development driver. Wales needs to now explore what is good about economic intervention by governments as well as the challenges. However:

— Wales had the lowest proportion of exporting companies by UK region in 2006–07, some 2.1% of Welsh businesses. The value of Welsh exports fell from £10.6 billion to £9 billion between 2008–09. *(UWIC, NS)*

— Manufacturing as a proportion of Welsh GDP has fallen from 38% in 1995 to 17% in 2007. In 1980, total employment in basic metals and metal production alone was around 77,000 people, or 6.6% of the working population. *(ONS, Steel Communities Study vol II)*

— Output from biotechnology, pharmaceuticals and telecommunications fell in Wales 2008–9, but rose at a UK level. *(Cited in the IWA response to the Economic Renewal Programme)*

— Wales now ranks last in the UK Competitiveness Index, on 83.9% of the UK average. *(Centre for International Competitiveness)*

— Spend on R&D is 60% of the UK average. *(Centre for International Competitiveness)*

— In the 1990s, pre-recession levels of UK GDP were not regained until three years later. Pre-recession levels of employment were not regained for eight years. *(Assembly Members' Research Service)*

5. Long term unemployed in Wales in the four years to June 2010 rose sharply over the 12 months from June 2009, from around 21% to 28.2% of all those unemployed, overtaking the UK rate of 28%.

6. The youth unemployment rate in Wales also rose sharply, from just under 15% of 16–24-year-olds in June 2008 to 21.7% in June last year, up on the UK average for that time of 19.5%. *(Annual Population Survey, NS)*

7. Four of the 10 districts for highest benefit claimant rates in 2009 are in Wales: Blaenau Gwent (26.7% of the working population), Merthyr Tydfil (26.5%), Neath Port Talbot (22.6%) and Rhondda Cynon Taff (22.5%). Caerphilly (22.1%) is 11th.

8. Welsh GDP against the UK average currently stands at around 75%. It has been falling steadily for over a century and, save an increase during the 1960s to a high of around 88% in 1970, Welsh GDP has been falling since the 1890s, when it peaked at around 95%. London, by contrast, has never fallen below 120% and currently stands at just over 150%. *(Regional GDP in Britain, 1871–1911 & Scottish Journal of Political Economy)*

9. In 2006, Wales was listed as ninth in a table of older industrial regions in Europe, with a GDP per capita of 24,000. This compares Noord-Brabant in the Netherlands, which was on 33,400. *(EU Statistical Unit)*

INWARD INVESTMENT CHALLENGES

10. The Welsh economy was brittle going in to the recession it fears the worse coming out with the loss of major inward investment corporations such as Bosch, Visteon, TRW and Hoover from the economy. Between 1983 and 1997 the WDA (it took responsibility for inward investment in 1983) recorded a number of inward investment projects—estimated to be about 855—from overseas. Investment brought new ways of working and capital expenditure. Instead of seeing what these corporates achieved in Wales and invested commentators who should know better sometimes look on in disbelief that corporations like our heavy industry do not stay in one place forever. Business is globally fleet of foot. We are arguably no longer seen as a place to easily invest because we fail to reach out and compete.

11. To increase competitiveness in economic development targets are essential to measure success or failure. Others measure us but we seem not to wish to do this therefore we figure poorly in UK and European leagues in economic development and it becomes a surprise or a political tennis match ensues with no conclusion or real solutions arrived at. The Welsh Development Agency was established in 1976 under the WDA Act 1975. The purpose of the Agency was to further the economic development of Wales; to promote industrial efficiency; and to further the improvement of the environment, and to promote the development of communities throughout Wales. It had targets which provided focus to staff and its independent Board. There is currently no economic target to measure success in economic development in Wales. Inward Investment is the only economic performance that is reported upon as it is UK report to Parliament but there is no target set.

THE IMPORTANCE OF THE CAPITAL TO THE ECONOMY OF WALES AND FUTURE INVESTMENT

12. Wales' competitiveness is reliant upon both indigenous and foreign investment. Indigenous businesses, as much as the local workforce itself, can benefit from increased foreign direct investment in the city.

13. Despite being the envy of other places in Wales, Cardiff has experienced economic growth over the last 10 years. It boasts buildings that are distinctive and public money was spent wisely on the Millennium Stadium in the City Centre and the Millennium Centre in the Bay.

14. Much of Wales delights in the fact that Cardiff now boasts a growing European Core City and the highest growth in private sector employment over the last 10 years of all UK Core Cities.

15. In the early 1900s, Cardiff controlled the global market for coal, its docks were the world's largest exporter, and the city's Coal Exchange set the world price. In recent times, Cardiff's economy has since become more diverse but remains equally ambitious. Heavy industry has given way to a transformed economy, with dynamic knowledge driven sectors competing effectively at the highest level.

16. European Cities of the Future Awards February 2008—The Financial Times' Foreign Direct Investment magazine, ranked Cardiff as 7th in list of top 50 European cities of the future. Cardiff is also ranked the 7th most attractive city in Europe as a destination for Foreign Direct Investment.

17. Cardiff is an established and thriving international business location. For over 30 years, international companies from all over the world have been attracted to Cardiff by its skilled labour pool, competitive cost base and strategic position close to London.

18. Cardiff has transformed its economy into a modern and competitive knowledge based economy. The city has an above average number of people employed in knowledge based sectors with the greatest opportunities for growth in Biosciences, ICT and the Creative Industries.

19. Cardiff has a strong cluster of around 100 bioscience related companies and organisations and Cardiff University has a growing international reputation for research expertise in bioscience related disciplines. Major international companies like GE Healthcare (employing over 1,000 people locally), Shaw Healthcare, Bio Trace and Cogent, compliment an innovative small firm sector attracted by the University and the 2,500 local students and 500 doctorates in bioscience related disciplines.

EMPLOYMENT BY SIZE BAND IN CARDIFF

Source: Annual Business Inquiry

20. Together these organisations represent much of the Cardiff's workforce. Analysis of the Annual Business Inquiry for Cardiff reveals that over half of those employed in Cardiff can be accounted for by less than 5% of the total number of workplaces. The remainder of those working in the city are spread amongst around 12,000 businesses or organisations. These organisations are also as vital for small businesses as they are for employment. Many of the city's SMEs are reliant upon the large organizations for businesses, and as such it is vital that the city's top corporate, investment and entrepreneurial firms flourish in order to help maintain a competitive SME base in Cardiff.

21. In terms of economic impact, there is a growing understanding of the role that large companies have on the region. A study by Aston University further emphasised that large local companies are the biggest drivers of economic growth in cities. The study found that companies with more than 200 employees were the biggest investors within the city, demanding that policymakers develop a new approach to private sector engagement.

22. The figures in Wales are compelling. In 2006 for example, 41% of business sector employment was accounted for by large enterprises (those with 250 or more employees), compared to 43% for the UK as a whole. This compares with a figure of 32% for micro businesses (0–9 employees), which account for 32% of Welsh business sector employment.

23. Larger domestic companies make a significant economic contribution. Investment by these companies will have the biggest impact on both productivity and employment. Enterprises active in Wales with 250 or more employees accounted for 55% of total turnover in Wales, compared to 52 per cent for the UK as a whole. They also represent an opportunity to deliver the city's aspirations around skills, social inclusion and improved environmental performance.

24. Cardiff's competitiveness has helped it to generate some 40,000 jobs for the Welsh economy according to Annual Business Inquiry data for the period 1998–2008. That's almost three quarters of the total jobs growth for South East Wales. These jobs have benefited the whole City region.

NUMBER OF PEOPLE COMMUTING OUT OF THE AUTHORITY TO:

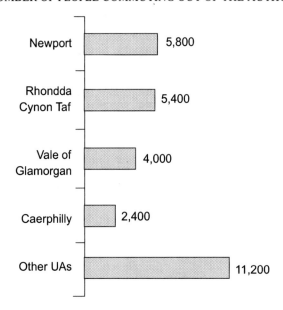

NUMBER OF PEOPLE COMMUTING INTO THE AUTHORITY FROM:

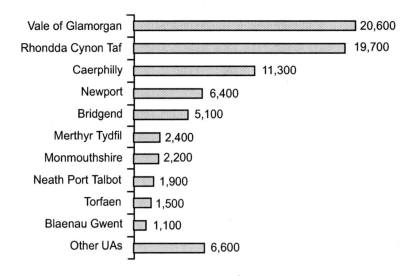

CONCLUSION

25. The Cardiff Business Partnership is committed to maintaining and developing Cardiff's position as a leading city, not just in the UK context but worldwide. We've seen the city successfully navigate the hangover of deindustrialisation to become a modern knowledge-based economy in recent years, but we need to make sure we can make that next step. In a worldwide context we consistently see cities such as Copenhagen, Helsinki and Zurich figure prominently in competitiveness and quality of life leagues, and there is no reason why Cardiff should not also be featuring and continuing to be the engine and shop window of economic growth for Wales.

March 2011

House of Commons

Welsh Affairs Committee

Inward Investment in Wales: Government Response to the Committee's Eighth Report of Session 2010–12

Second Special Report of Session 2012–13

Ordered by the House of Commons
to be printed 21 May 2012

HC 125
Published on 20 June 2012
by authority of the House of Commons
London: The Stationery Office Limited
£0.00

The Welsh Affairs Committee

The Welsh Affairs Committee is appointed by the House of Commons to examine the expenditure, administration, and policy of the Office of the Secretary of State for Wales (including relations with the National Assembly for Wales).

Current membership

David T.C. Davies MP *(Conservative, Monmouth) (Chair)*
Stuart Andrew MP *(Conservative, Pudsey)*
Guto Bebb MP *(Conservative, Aberconwy)*
Geraint Davies MP *(Labour, Swansea West)*
Jonathan Edwards MP *(Plaid Cymru, Carmarthen East and Dinefwr)*
Nia Griffith MP *(Labour, Llanelli)*
Mrs Siân C. James MP *(Labour, Swansea East)*
Susan Elan Jones MP *(Labour, Clwyd South)*
Karen Lumley MP *(Conservative, Redditch)*
Jessica Morden MP *(Labour, Newport East)*
Mr Robin Walker MP *(Conservative, Worcester)*
Mr Mark Williams MP *(Liberal Democrat, Ceredigion)*

Powers

The Committee is one of the departmental select committees, the powers of which are set out in House of Commons Standing Orders, principally in SO No 152. These are available on the internet via www.parliament.uk

Publications

The Reports and evidence of the Committee are published by The Stationery Office by Order of the House. All publications of the Committee (including press notices) are on the internet at www.parliament.uk/welshcom

The Reports of the Committee, the formal minutes relating to that report, oral evidence taken and some or all written evidence are available in printed volumes.

Additional written evidence may be published on the internet only.

Committee staff

The current staff of the Committee is Adrian Jenner (Clerk), Anwen Rees (Committee Specialist), Lori Verwaerde (Senior Committee Assistant), Dabinder Rai (Committee Assistant), Ravi Abhayaratne (Committee Support Assistant) and Jessica Bridges-Palmer (Media Officer).

Contacts

All correspondence should be addressed to the Clerk of the Welsh Affairs Committee, House of Commons, 7 Millbank, London SW1P 3JA. The telephone number for general enquiries is 020 7219 3264; and the Committee's email address is welshcom@parliament.uk

Second Special Report

The Committee published its Eighth Report of Session 2010–12 Inward Investment in Wales on 21 February 2012. The Government response was received on 14 May 2012 and is published as an Appendix to this Special Report.

Appendix: Government Response

Introduction

Below is the Government's response to the Welsh Affairs Committee's report on "Inward Investment in Wales", which was published on 21 February 2012.

The Government welcomes the Committee's Report, which is both comprehensive and wide ranging. In particular, the Government shares the Committee's starting point, which is that all relevant parties need to work together to boost both amounts and levels of inward investment into Wales. The relative decline in the proportion of inward investment to the UK that comes to Wales shows just how important this is to the Welsh economy.

The Committee's inquiry has investigated how well Government departments in Whitehall and the Welsh Government have worked together to bring investment into Wales, and highlights the Government's commitment and concern about investment performance and economic growth in Wales.

The Committee's Report focused on 3 key issues that it feels are central to levels of inward investment in Wales: education; transport; and the international profile of Wales. In our response to the recommendations that follow, we demonstrate the steps we are taking to ensure that Wales is promoted as an ideal location for inward investment. These include for example:

- Improving collaboration between the UK Government and the Welsh Government on the development of Wales's profile so that its strengths and capabilities are calibrated and Wales's assets are presented in the best possible light for international investors;

- Investing in infrastructure as a priority for supporting economic growth in Wales and the development of an efficient transport network that will create job opportunities throughout Wales. We are in the process of electrifying the line between London and Cardiff and continue to work with the Welsh Government on the possible electrification of the Great Western Main Line to Swansea and the Valleys lines around Cardiff, so that wider transport links between Wales and the rest of the UK are strengthened; and

- Encouraging improved links between business and education, so that a better educated and a more employable generation of young people is created, with suitable skills for future careers. We want better collaboration between businesses and universities so that more relevant provision for undergraduates and post-graduates is developed to meet the needs of business. Universities should be active partners in the economy, assisting companies on development of new ideas into commercial and marketable products and services that will benefit Wales.

More detail on these issues is set out in the responses that follow. These focus on areas which are directly within the power of UK Government Ministers. As the Committee notes, other bodies, notably the Welsh Government—through their responsibility for economic development—will also have a key role to play. As also noted by the Committee, there needs to be close engagement between Ministers based in both London and Cardiff if Wales is to reach past levels of inward investment. The lack of close co-operation, for instance, on recent trade missions by the Welsh Government, is therefore disappointing and the Government hopes that a more joined-up approach (as takes place in Scotland and Northern Ireland) can be adopted for the good of Wales in relation to future visits to major trading partners.

The response below only covers those recommendations directly addressed to the UK Government. The responses submitted by other bodies, including the Welsh Government, will also be read with great interest.

Her Majesty's Government Response to the recommendations

Development of Inward Investment in Wales

1. In the early 1990s, Wales was one of the top performing areas of the UK for attracting inward investment. The country benefited from the employment and economic well-being that inward investment brought, as more traditional industries declined. However, by 2009, the country had become one of the worst performing areas of the UK and much of the economic benefit of earlier investment had disappeared. (Paragraph 18)

We have answered recommendations 1 & 2 together (see below).

2. Wales was slow to adapt to the changed conditions for attracting inward investment. In particular, successive governments reacted too slowly to the emerging competition from Eastern Europe and Asia. In addition, Wales's competitiveness compared with other areas of the UK deteriorated markedly. The UK Government and the Welsh Government must work together to reverse this decline. (Paragraph 19)

The UK Government recognises the relative decline in attracting inward investment into Wales and is keen to work with all relevant bodies to help address this. We agree with the Committee that more work is required both across Whitehall and by the Welsh Government to create an environment that encourages companies to invest in Wales. While the Government recognises the wider challenges (and opportunities) that emerging markets can provide, there is also an urgent need to address the relative decline in the proportion of UK inward investment projects coming to Wales. It will be important that lessons are learned from other parts of the UK, particularly Scotland and Northern Ireland which also deal with a balance of devolved and reserved matters.

High quality infrastructure plays an essential role in attracting investors and stimulating the growth that is needed for the recovery of the Welsh economy. The Government has already announced the electrification of the rail line to Cardiff as well as significant (£57m) investment in broadband. We will not stop there: we are working with the Welsh Government to develop the business case for extending electrification of the Great Western Mainline to Swansea and also investing in enhancements to the M4 corridor. We have also announced our intention to move on the electrification of the Valleys lines around Cardiff depending on the outcome of ongoing discussions with the Welsh Government.

The Government, in particular UKTI, continues to work with overseas representatives and the Welsh Government to promote Wales as an investment destination. The services provided by UKTI are available across the UK, including Wales, and following suggestions from the Wales Office, UKTI has recently offered to second an additional staff member to the Welsh Government to enhance co-operation on what Wales has to offer inward investors.

The UK Government takes every opportunity to promote Wales as an ideal location for investment so that the long term prospects of the Welsh economy can be improved. Since June 2010, the Secretary of State for Wales has met with, and made representations to, delegations from Taiwan, China, Turkey, Japan and Russia and launched the first ever trade mission of Welsh businesses to Bangladesh, led by the Wales Bangladesh Chamber of Commerce.

The 2012 budget announcement provided a much needed boost for enterprise and business in Wales by reducing the rate of corporation tax by 1% over each of the next 3 years, providing funding for capital allowances in the Enterprise Zone in Deeside and a commitment to delivering ultra-fast broadband to Cardiff for up to 10,000 businesses.

As noted in the introduction, the UK Government stands ready to work more closely with the Welsh Government to promote Wales as an investment destination. In particular, the Government looks forward to a joint approach being more commonly adopted on contacts with potential investors to avoid duplication and ensure investors understand the support that can be offered by both Government's on investment decisions.

Both the Secretary of State for Wales and Lord Green have offered to take part in future joint missions with Welsh Government ministers to promote Wales as an investment destination as part of the overall UK offer.

3. Traditional approaches, such as grants and low labour costs, can no longer be relied upon to attract inward investors. The development of the knowledge economy has changed how countries attract investment from overseas. The Welsh Government must think innovatively about how to exploit this opportunity and develop a cogent economic strategy to maximise potential gains. In addition to developing domestic business growth, the Welsh Government must reassert the importance of inward investment in its economic policy. (Paragraph 25)

This is a matter for the Welsh Government, who may wish to respond.

Education

4. Failure to improve the skills of young people in key areas will contribute to continued economic decline in Wales. We recommend that the UK Government and the Welsh Government renew their efforts to promote science and engineering in Wales. In particular, both Governments must address negative perceptions among young people of science subjects and should promote links between businesses and schools from the earliest possible age. (Paragraph 34)

Education is a devolved matter in Wales and the Welsh Government may wish to respond on the work it is doing in this area. The Department for Business, Innovation and Skills (BIS), however, funds STEMNET, a UK-wide organisation, whose purpose is to ensure that all young people, regardless of background, are encouraged to understand the benefits of Science, Technology, Engineering and Mathematics (STEM) in their lives, and the career opportunities to which these subjects can lead.

STEMNET's STEM Ambassadors programme has created a unique nationwide network of around 25,000 CRB checked STEM Ambassadors from science, engineering and technical companies or academia, who work with schools across the UK. The Ambassadors both raise awareness amongst children of the range of careers that science and technical qualifications offer and provide stimulating scientific activities to increase their interest in STEM subjects. In return, the initiative provides valued CPD opportunities for the STEM Ambassadors concerned.

The Schools White Paper, 'The Importance of Teaching', set out the UK Government's commitment to continue to provide additional support for the uptake of science. In June 2011 the Secretary of State for Education announced that the Government would be investing up to £135m over the current spending review period to support this aim.

The work of the ESTnet network of technology organisations has also been valuable in highlighting the skills needs of innovative businesses in Wales.

5. We welcome and recognise the work that is currently undertaken by companies to engage with schools. This must be encouraged and expanded. We recommend that the Welsh Government place more emphasis in the school curriculum on the importance of business and industry, including trying to locate a higher proportion of work experience placements within them. The future economy of Wales depends on a well educated and highly-skilled workforce. (Paragraph 35)

Education is a devolved matter in Wales and the Welsh Government may wish to respond on this area. For its part, the UK Government prioritises developing strong links between business and education. Our guiding principle for strong employer links is that decisions should be made locally by schools, supported by local funding and subject to local accountability, with much less central control.

The Education and Employers Taskforce was established in 2008 by a group of business leaders in collaboration with education leaders, intermediaries and central Government, to work with employers and education, and to support the development of a better educated and more employable generation of young people.[1]

As the Taskforce has grown and become self sustainable, the Department of Education no longer provides funding; however, it continues to maintain a strong relationship.

Further and Higher Education

6. Partnership working between universities and industry will play a crucial role in Wales's future prospects and is a key factor in attracting companies to Wales. We believe that there is an urgent need to tailor university courses to business needs in Wales. We welcome the work that has been undertaken at institutions such as Swansea University, Bangor University and Glyndŵr University, and the links they are developing with major multinationals such as Tata, Rolls Royce and Airbus. The Welsh Government should explore how these schemes could be emulated at other universities. (Paragraph 44)

Professor Sir Tim Wilson's independent review of Business-University engagement, launched last month, calls for universities to be at the heart of the economy in order to promote growth in the UK and improve the employability of our graduates. While the review is oriented towards English higher education, many of the analyses and recommendations will be relevant to the higher education systems and businesses within the devolved administrations.

The review's recommendations provide a roadmap for improving collaboration and increasing the ability of universities to meet the needs of businesses. A range of recommendations are set out, aimed at producing graduates with knowledge and skills relevant to their future careers, and provide opportunities for students to integrate work and enterprise experience and study. A key aim of the recommendations is to engage businesses more closely in developing relevant provision for undergraduates and post-graduates.

The review also specifically welcomes the kite marking of HE courses by a number of Sector Skills Councils (SSC). BIS announced in the Autumn Statement that it would provide support for a group of STEM-focused SSCs to facilitate the kite marking of STEM degree courses in order to signal which ones best prepare students for employment in particular sectors.

The need for improved linkages between business and universities has been a key theme of meetings of the Secretary of State for Wales' Business Advisory Group. This group, which brings together representatives from the universities sector and Welsh businesses, shares the Committee's concern and agrees with the recommendation for university courses to be tailored to the needs of Welsh businesses. The group has helped to facilitate contacts between Welsh companies and universities, notably during a meeting dedicated to research and innovation in Wales, attended by the Minister for Universities and Science.

7. We heard evidence that Wales has a poor record in capturing research funding. In addition, much of the knowledge gained from research is lost because it is not used in a

---

1 http://www.educationandemployers.org

practical sense. There is a clear need to ensure that research capabilities are matched by the ability to change ideas into new and innovative products and services for the market place. We urge the UK Government to make it clear how it proposes to close this "innovation gap" and to ensure the future prosperity of the Welsh economy. (Paragraph 50)

In December 2011, the Government published its Innovation and Research Strategy for Growth following consultation with a wide range of partners, including the Welsh Government and representatives from the Welsh academic and business communities.

This is a UK-wide Strategy which contains proposals across a number of policy areas including competition, finance, regulation, infrastructure and procurement to ensure the UK maintains and strengthens its position as one of the world's most innovative economies.

Amongst the measures announced in the Strategy are £75 million of additional funding to support innovative SMEs including the relaunch of the SMART Research and Development Awards programme and the expansion of the Small Business Research Initiative; an increase in the level of support available under Research and Development Tax Credits; and £25 million investment in large scale demonstrator projects. All of these measures are designed to assist companies throughout the UK in developing new ideas into commercial and marketable products and services.

The Technology Strategy Board (TSB) also works with the Welsh Government and with companies in Wales, and its support programmes are available to businesses across the UK. In particular, the TSB has worked closely with the Welsh Government to support sectors of significant importance to the Welsh economy including Digital and ICT; Low Carbon; Health and Biosciences; and Advanced Engineering and Manufacture.

The TSB is also currently working to establish a national network of 'Catapult' Technology and Innovation Centres to help UK companies successfully exploit commercial opportunities from new and emerging technologies with large global potential.

8. The European Convergence Programme has proved to be a valuable investment route for Welsh universities. However, universities in Wales must not limit themselves to focusing only on Convergence funding and must examine wider opportunities for securing European funding. They must work to maximise the value from funding across all R&D income streams and look to take advantage of all European funding opportunities. (Paragraph 51)

This is a matter for the Welsh Government working in partnership with Universities in Wales.

9. We welcome the collaborative approach that has been increasingly adopted by Welsh universities. We encourage them to continue to pursue this approach, not only within Wales but also to develop successful partnerships with overseas institutions. (Paragraph 52)

This is a matter for the Welsh Government working in partnership with Universities in Wales. They may wish to respond.

10. We welcome the work that is being done by Welsh universities internationally and encourage them to develop this further. There is a real opportunity to use alumni to increase awareness of Welsh universities and the work they produce, and to help develop links between industry and government with Welsh universities. (Paragraph 56)

This is ultimately a matter for Higher Education Institutions to consider and we encourage universities to maximise the potential of their alumni networks for building stronger international and national links. The Welsh Government may also wish to respond on this matter.

11. UK Trade & Investment (UKTI) must ensure it is aware of the potential offered by universities in Wales and that it communicates these to prospective inward investors. We call on UKTI to clarify how it aims to support the work done by Welsh universities. (Paragraph 57)

UKTI recognises the importance of the universities in Wales in framing the offer that Wales makes to potential inward investors.

UKTI, working with the Wales Office, has increased its knowledge of UK capabilities and, as mentioned above, will be seconding a member of staff to the Welsh Government to enhance mutual understanding. UKTI is using this engagement to help short-list locations in response to enquiries from investors. This requires a comprehensive understanding of what is available in Wales, including university and research capacity. In addition UKTI deploys a group of specialists with technology and sector expertise whose remit is to understand, in-depth, the UK's research strengths and to help potential inward investors understand them. We would expect these specialists to draw on strengths in Welsh Universities and centres of excellence in this task.

Finally, UKTI Chief Executive Nick Baird recently met the Vice Chancellor of Swansea University to discuss the many opportunities that are likely to emanate from their investment in the Institute of Life Sciences.

Transport Infrastructure

12. We are concerned by evidence that the quality of transport links in Mid and North Wales and the connectivity between the rest of Wales and England deters overseas investment in parts of Wales. We welcome the strong East-West focus in the Welsh Government's new transport plan. We intend to conduct an inquiry into transport connectivity between Wales and the rest of the UK and the Republic of Ireland during this Parliament. (Paragraph 61)

This is primarily a matter for the Welsh Government to respond to. The UK Government however welcomes the Committee's commitment to conduct an inquiry into transport connectivity between Wales and the rest of the UK and Republic of Ireland.

As noted above, the Government for its part is committed to investing in the infrastructure that Wales needs to attract inward investors. The rail improvements mentioned in the introduction will help improve connectivity, particularly with key markets in London and the south-east of England and improvements, such as up-grading broadband coverage on the A470, announced in the 2012 Budget, will further improve the service that investors receive.

13. We welcome the Government's commitment to the electrification of the Great Western Main Line to Cardiff. We believe a strong economic case has been made for electrification of the line to Swansea and we welcome and support the Secretary of State for Wales in calling for it to happen. We call on the Government to announce plans to extend electrification of the Great Western Main Line to Swansea at the earliest opportunity. We also welcome the Secretary of State's commitment to develop a business case for the electrification of the South Wales Valleys lines. (Paragraph 64)

The Government will continue to work with the Welsh Government to consider electrification of the Great Western Main Line to Swansea and the Welsh Valley lines, subject to value for money and agreement on financing details. Decisions for the period 2014-2019 are expected to be announced in the summer.

14. The Great Western franchise will be renewed in 2013 for a period of 15 years. We call on the Welsh Government and the Wales Office to use the opportunity provided by the franchise negotiations to ensure the greater frequency of train services between England and Wales, so that opportunities for attracting inward investment are maximised. (Paragraph 65)

The Welsh Government have been actively participating in the Greater Western Refranchising Consultation. A consultation event in Swansea on 26 March was well attended and featured some constructive debate. The UK Government now has a clear understanding of the Welsh Government's priorities for the new franchise and are considering these, along with other consultation responses. This will help to inform the detailed specification for inclusion in the Invitation to Tender.

15. Currently the maximum gauge clearance accommodates some mainland European gauge vehicles but does not maximise the traffic potential. We call on the Government to consider enhancing the gauge to W12, which would enable Wales to compete for new freight traffic and would allow the movement of additional European rail traffic. We also call on the Government to ensure that railway lines are maintained to route availability standards. (Paragraph 68)

Network Rail is likely to have funding for the development of schemes in Control Period 5 (2014 to 2019) and has identified a number of potential freight schemes in the Initial Industry Plan, including gauge clearance of the Great Western Main Line. These could be developed under the Strategic Freight Network subject to available funding.

16. We call on the UK Government and the Welsh Government to recognise the importance of ports to the economy of Wales. Both the UK and Welsh Governments should, in their responses to this Report, set out how they are promoting investment in this area. (Paragraph 71)

The UK Government recognises the importance of ports to the economy of Wales, and of the rest of the United Kingdom. Milford Haven is the UK's leading port for liquid bulks and thus a vital part of our national infrastructure. Other Welsh ports provide important links to Ireland and are significant for various commodities. Ports (whether in company, trust or municipal ownership) operate in a free market environment and have proven their ability to invest for growth and to adapt flexibly to changing patterns of demand. The Department for Transport will continue to work in close liaison with the Wales Office and Welsh Government in relation to the development planning framework, inland infrastructure, trans-European networks and other areas where UK Government can encourage and facilitate enterprise by and at ports.

17. We have heard evidence that poor transport infrastructure can have a detrimental effect on the levels of inward investment. Transport infrastructure has been underfunded by the UK Government and the Welsh Government for a number of years. While we recognise the UK Government's commitment to reducing the national deficit, transport infrastructure spending should not be considered less important than other areas of spending. The UK Government and the Welsh Government must not consider reductions in infrastructure spending as an easy means of deficit reduction. (Paragraph 72)

The Chancellor has made clear that investment in infrastructure is a priority in supporting national economic recovery. The National Infrastructure Plan, published in November 2011, set out for the first time over 500 infrastructure projects that the Government wants to see built over the next decade and beyond, including forty priority infrastructure projects and programmes overseen by a cabinet committee chaired by the Chief Secretary to the Treasury. The importance of transport infrastructure was reflected in the 2010 Spending Review settlement which secured investment in important projects such as high speed rail, support for ultra-low carbon cars and for some major road building programmes. The priority given to transport investment in last year's Autumn Statement - £1 billion of new investment by Network Rail, over £1 billion of investment on the strategic road network and £500 million for local schemes—reaffirms the importance the Government places on an efficient transport network which supports economic growth and creates opportunities across the country.

18. The UK Government and the Welsh Government must look creatively at ways to fund infrastructure projects. We call on the UK Government and the Welsh Government to examine how European Convergence Funding can be used to fund transport infrastructure improvements in Wales. (Paragraph 73)

Decisions on the use of European Convergence Funding in Wales are primarily a matter for the Welsh Government, though the Secretary of State for Wales recently discussed the need for convergence funding to deliver projects that result in economic growth both in Wales and across the EU with the EU Commissioner for Regional Policy.

More generally, UKTI's Strategic Relations Team, working with the Welsh Government, are helping to attract financial investment from key overseas institutional investors (such as Sovereign Wealth funds and pension funds) into priority areas, including priority infrastructure projects and programmes.

UKTI's particular role is to focus on managing relationships with key funds in order to ensure that we have a clear sense of their investment appetite, that the right propositions are put to them, and that high-level/political relationships are coordinated effectively.

The current funding round for the Structural Funds is from 2007 to 2013. The Regulations concerning the Structural Funds for 2014–2020 are currently being negotiated. On spending on transport infrastructure, the current draft Regulation on the European Regional Development Fund (ERDF) states that investing funds in transport infrastructure may be considered in a 'less developed region' (or a convergence region in the current regulation). The West Wales and the Valleys region may be considered a 'less developed region' in the 2014–2020 round of SCFs, in which case there will be scope to continue to invest ERDF funding in transport infrastructure in this region. However, spending on transport infrastructure is not proposed in 'more developed regions' in the draft new regulation (termed competitiveness regions in current regulation). East Wales is currently categorised as a competitive region and is likely to remain in this category in the 2014–2020 round of Structural Funds, therefore there will be no potential to invest ERDF funding in transport infrastructure in this region.

Management of the Structural Funds in Wales is devolved to the Welsh Government. Allocation of ERDF funding will be subject to meeting the regulatory requirements of the 2014 –2020 funding round: the nature of these requirements is also part of the Structural Funds 2014–2020 negotiations.

Promoting Wales Abroad

19. We call on the Government to set out how it intends to re-balance the UK economy and how it will work with the Welsh Government to attract inward investment into Wales. (Paragraph 80)

UKTI recognises the need for a close working relationship with the Welsh Government in order to help Wales attract inward investment. UKTI and the Welsh Government have signed a Memorandum of Understanding, which sets out clearly the responsibilities on both partners in terms of cooperative working and information sharing.

This should help achieve improvements in the delivery of Foreign Direct Investment (FDI) into the UK, resulting in more and higher quality inward investment projects for the UK as a whole. In addition, the new service will help the trade and investment teams in Wales to attract and retain investments.

In practice, this joint working has the following elements:

- UKTI will ensure that the strengths and capabilities of Wales are covered in the offers presented to appropriate potential inward investors. UKTI is already working closely with the Welsh Government to ensure that the strengths and capabilities that Wales has to offer are fully relayed to them and understood. A thorough understanding of what Wales can offer will help enable UKTI to present Wales's assets in the best possible light as part of the UK proposition, or in support of a Wales-only offer;

- UKTI provides the Welsh Government with the outline details of active projects they receive. Additionally, UKTI passes on any prospective projects that have stated a preference for Wales or a Wales-based offer. UKTI also works with the Welsh Government to ensure that they are fully engaged in relevant projects as they develop and will give feedback on every project when the Welsh Government expresses an interest in bidding, regardless of the outcome;

- UKTI also makes available a monthly report on projects and successes for Wales, which allows the Welsh Office and the Welsh Government to monitor progress and check back with UKTI on any project detail that they require;

- UKTI shares with the Welsh Government its portfolio of existing investors, with the Welsh Government participating fully in any national virtual teams established around particular companies. Managing relationships with existing investors is key to the UK's national success. We need joint engagement to support these companies;

- The Government, through its process of Strategic Relationship Management, works particularly closely with key investors. There are a number of major investors in Wales included in the Strategic Relations list of investors that are considered 'anchor' companies in the UK and Wales; these include Ford, Toyota, Tata, EON, RWE, GE, Johnson and Johnson and EADS. Ministers from across the UK Government play an active role in building and maintaining our relationship with these companies; and

- UKTI already have an experienced FDI manager in Wales for two days a week. Gareth John (an ex Board director of the WDA) has a remit to work with the Welsh Government to help integrate the new FDI delivery processes with UKTI and to also advocate the new arrangements across a wide range of Welsh stakeholders at a more local level. In addition, as mentioned above, UKTI will work with the Welsh Government on seconding an additional official into the WG team.

Also, UKTI ensures that companies are made aware of all commercially sensible location options and will always suggest Wales as a location if it represents a sound business proposition for the potential investor. However, it is recognised that final location decisions are for the investor to make.

UKTI's overseas network provides support to visits by Welsh Ministers and their own delegations and has recently supported the First Minister's visits to New Zealand, China, the United States and India. The level of support will often depend on whether the Welsh Government has its own representation in-country.

UKTI also worked closely with the Wales Office and the Welsh Government to ensure the success of the UK China Joint Economic and Trade Commission (JETCO) meeting which was held in Cardiff in December, which included an accompanying high level business delegation.

20. We are concerned that the Welsh Government has no dedicated trade promotion agency. Evidence suggests that the international recognition of Wales has suffered and that investment opportunities have been missed. We recommend a greater emphasis within the Welsh Government on the need to promote inward investment and job creation in Wales, with a dedicated and focused team for this purpose. (Paragraph 89)

This is a matter for the Welsh Government, though the Government would welcome any measures that would raise the profile of Wales as an investment destination.

21. Wales operates in a competitive global environment. The Welsh Government must market Wales on the international stage more vigorously and must develop a clear narrative about the benefits of Wales that can be promoted to overseas markets. These

include a growing university-industry partnership and innovation built on existing industries such as, aerospace, life sciences, manufacturing, specialist steel and tourism. In addition, Wales provides an attractive quality of life to prospective investors, with its coast and countryside and a rich cultural history. (Paragraph 90)

This is a matter for the Welsh Government, who may wish to respond.

22. Overseas offices provide an opportunity for Wales to market itself abroad. There has been some upheaval in their locations and numbers in the past few years. This has been unfortunate and there should now be some stability in order for them to gain a visible profile in their host countries. In addition, the offices must be made more accountable and must ensure that they utilise their resources effectively. We call on the Welsh Government to publish a review of the operation of these offices and to provide a clear analysis of their effectiveness. (Paragraph 96)

This is a matter for the Welsh Government, who may wish to respond.

23. There is merit in the argument that the offices should be co-located with UKTI offices. Co-location would enable the Welsh Government to utilise the strengths and capabilities of UKTI. We recommend that the Welsh Government pursue this suggestion with UKTI. (Paragraph 97)

The Government agrees with the Committee on the principles of co-location, notably due to the potential for efficiency savings and for greater engagement with the wider UK offer. As a result, the Welsh Government has an open invitation to discuss this option in any markets where UKTI has a presence and where it is practical to do so.

In recent years, the Welsh Government has co-located its US team with the British Consulate in New York and more recently it has a member of staff in the British High Commission in New Delhi, as well as already in the British Embassy in Dubai. UKTI understands that the Welsh Government has no immediate plans to establish a presence elsewhere, but, as above, there is an open invitation for the further co-location, where appropriate.

24. We are very disappointed that the Business Minister for Wales chose not to give evidence to this inquiry. The Minister's decision was a grave discourtesy to the Committee and to Parliament. (Paragraph 101)

This is a matter for the Welsh Government, who may wish to respond.

25. Wales does not have sufficient resources to work alone in attracting inward investment to Wales nor the advantages that UKTI has in terms of resources and networks. With UKTI under new leadership, the Welsh Government must take this opportunity to re-engage with politicians and officials in the UK Government to maximise opportunities to attract inward investment to Wales and so improve the long-term prospects of the Welsh economy. (Paragraph 102)

Please see the response to recommendation 23, above. As stated elsewhere, the Government remains committed to closer engagement that will benefit Wales.

Looking Forward

26. We have heard concerns regarding the Welsh Government's economic sectoral approach. We call for the approach to be reviewed after a sufficient period of time. (Paragraph 104)

This is a matter for the Welsh Government, who may wish to respond.

27. The abolition of the Welsh Development Agency has reduced Wales's visibility in the global market place. Nearly five years on from its abolition, the WDA brand remains one of the most recognisable of all Welsh brands. The Welsh Government must urgently consider how existing recognition of the WDA brand can be used to improve and increase Wales's global identity. (Paragraph 113)

This is a matter for the Welsh Government, who may wish to respond.

28. We repeat our call for the establishment of a dedicated trade promotion agency, either sitting within the Welsh Government or as a private sector vehicle working in collaboration with the Welsh Government to drive inward investment projects into Wales. Such a body should have a mix of skills with an emphasis on private sector experience. (Paragraph 114)

This is a matter for the Welsh Government, who may wish to respond.

29. The independent Commission on Devolution in Wales will examine the devolution of fiscal powers to the National Assembly for Wales. We urge the Commission to consider the evidence submitted to our inquiry on this matter. The Committee will monitor closely the work of the Commission in this area during this Parliament. (Paragraph 120)

It is a matter for the Commission itself to decide what evidence to consider during its inquiry, but as the terms of reference make clear the Commission is consulting widely as it undertakes its work and will make recommendations which are likely to have a wide degree of support, both in Wales and more widely. The Government would expect the Commission to take into account the evidence submitted to the inquiry in the course of its work, and trust that the Committee has already brought this to the Commission's attention.

30. We welcome the decision of the Welsh Government to establish enterprise zones in Wales. The make-up and focus of the enterprise zones will clearly be a determinant of their success. Some nine months since the Chancellor's announcement, the Welsh Government has provided little detail of its plans. We urge the Welsh Government to clarify, without delay, how and by when it plans to implement enterprise zones. (Paragraph 124)

This is primarily a matter for the Welsh Government. However, the Government recognises the attraction that the benefits offered by Enterprise Zones in England can have on investors, and that more detailed information on the benefits that will be offered within Welsh Enterprise Zones is made available as quickly as possible. For its part, the Government was pleased to announce that enhanced capital allowances will be available to projects within the Deeside Enterprise Zone and looks forward to receiving business cases from the Welsh Government in relation to other Welsh zones.

APPENDIX 1

PURE R&D INVESTMENT PROJECTS (OPERATIONS SET UP FOR RESEARCH)

Region	2000	2001	2002	2003	2004	2005	2006	2007	2008	2009	Total
Wales	2	1	2	2	5	1	2	6	5	3	29
Scotland	9	7	3	4	8	10	12	16	9	14	92
UK	47	39	27	28	48	54	47	63	65	68	486

Source: Extract European Investment Monitor 19% going to Scotland 6% going to Wales

NUMBER OF R&D FDI PROJECTS

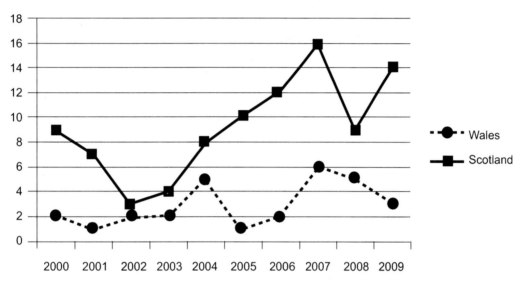

Source: Dr Andrew Crawley, Cardiff Business Partnership Research Fellow, Cardiff Business School

FOREIGN DIRECT INVESTMENT ACROSS THE UK (BY NUMBER OF PROJECTS)

Region	2000	2001	2002	2003	2004	2005	2006	2007	2008	2009	Total
Scotland	55	35	25	39	64	33	62	69	53	51	486
Wales	35	19	27	42	35	13	16	22	35	20	264
UK	574	370	369	453	563	559	685	713	686	678	5,650
Wales's %	6	5	7	9	6	2	2	3	5	3	4.70
Scotland's %	10	9	7	9	11	6	9	10	8	8	9

Source: Ernst & Young's European Investment Monitor (Dr Andrew Crawley's % Calculations)

Written evidence submitted by Swansea University

1. INTRODUCTION

Wales has 4.9% of the UK population, but only 1.6% of UK industrial R&D. To improve this key performance indicator for a Knowledge Economy, it is essential to attract large companies to Wales: 97.5% of industrial R&D is in large companies, which also tend to pay higher wages than SMEs, and will therefore help to tackle Wales' low wage economy problems.

High-tech clusters tend to include a range of different sized companies operating in symbiotic relationship with each other. Larger companies cascade quality standards and high value-added activities down supply chains. To create high-tech clusters, it is important for the Higher Education and Public sectors to engage proactively in the development of supply chains, and to attract investment from large companies.

Swansea University is engaging with this process and specifically positions itself as a research intensive university promoting the region's, and more generally the Welsh, economy through taking a lead in stimulating investment and within the context of developing a Knowledge Economy.

1.1 *Context*

Cities Outlook 2011, published by the Centre for Cities in January 2011, identifies "five vulnerable cities which may not feel the full benefit of national economic recovery for some time", due to their reliance on public sector employment and consequent susceptibility to Government spending cuts.

The report includes Swansea as one of the five vulnerable cities:

— Claimant count Nov 2010: 3.2% (17/64).

— Employment rate Jul 2009 to Jun 2010: 64.8% (58/63).

— Potential job losses in public sector by 2014–15: 2.9% (2/63).

— Residents with no qualifications 2009: 16.1% (51/63).

— Business stock per 10,000 population 2009: 249.2 (44.64).

There is clearly an urgent need for Swansea to provide employment opportunities outside the public sector. This can in large part be achieved through the development of high-tech and high-value added, skills-based jobs alongside the creation of a vibrant, knowledge-based local economy.

The *No City Left Behind* report by The Work Foundation (July 2010) notes that:

"The government faces the challenge of reducing public sector spending while stimulating growth in the private sector. As it does this, it needs to address the structural challenge of replacing the UK's overdependence on debt, financial services, the City and the public sector with a private sector driven, technology led recovery."

The report subsequently notes that "Growth over the next 10 years will be driven by knowledge-based industries and jobs will increasingly demand high level skills. This means universities and the further education sector will play a crucial role in the recovery."

In particular, the document highlights that low carbon industries and high-tech and high-value added networked services will be two of the sectors crucial for economic growth over the next decade, and it identifies universities as "a valuable source of knowledge and innovation which can benefit start-ups and existing local businesses, whilst close linkages with businesses are also very valuable to universities."

The *Impact of Higher Education Institutions on Regional Economies* research brief series produced by the IMPACT initiative (supported by the Economic and Social Research Council in partnership with the Scottish Funding Council, Department for Employment and Learning in Northern Ireland, the Higher Education Funding Council for England, and the Higher Education Funding Council for Wales) notes that:

1. There is evidence that firms locate their R&D facilities close to world-class rated university departments, and that innovative firms located nearer to university departments are more likely to engage with higher education institutions.

2. Firms are six times more likely to produce innovative products if they collaborate with an HEI

3. Firms are five times more likely to produce innovative processes if they collaborate with an HEI.

4. Collaboration between universities and firms has a significant positive effect on organisational innovation.

5. Wales has the lowest levels of knowledge interaction in general but when Welsh firms use universities and other types of collaborative partner, they seem to value them more, even if their actual impact is more marginal.

6. HEIs are still considered poor collaborative partners for firms and poor providers of information. However, when collaboration occurs, the university has a significant influence on the firm's innovative performance.

The IMPACT briefing document further notes that Wales has been less successful in the establishment of networks and that university commercialisation income and activity is less well distributed. (Cardiff and Swansea Universities received more than two-thirds of total income.)

The report shows that Wales ranks lowest in the UK in terms of HEIs sourcing their commercialisation income from within the region, has the lowest proportion of firms engaged in knowledge-based activities, and has relatively low levels of investment in research and innovation—which restricts economic growth.

Whilst not dissenting from this evidence, in recent years Swansea University has made exceptional progress in addressing this historic deficit through progressing quantum leap projects, and refreshing and reviewing its strategy for developing and delivering a broad range of knowledge transfer activities. At the same time the University has employed all the conventional HE mechanisms for supporting a Knowledge Economy:

— providing skilled graduates;

— undertaking collaborative research with industry;

— supporting existing companies and businesses through consultancy and skills development;

— teaching entrepreneurship and innovation skills;

— generating spin-out companies to exploit university IP; and

— encouraging graduates to create start-up companies.

1.2 *Swansea University strengths and strategic directions*

There are five universities and two other higher education institutions in the West Wales and the Valleys Convergence region, but more than 50% of the world-leading and internationally excellent Science, Technology, Engineering, and Mathematics (STEM) research activity is concentrated in Swansea University (2008 Research Assessment Exercise (RAE2008)).

The results of the RAE2008 demonstrate unequivocally that Swansea University is fast achieving its ambition to be a world-class, research-led university. The quality of its Civil Engineering research ranked second in the UK; Engineering as a whole is eighth. Computer Science and Medicine performed well, and there were successes in many other areas, including Business, Law, Economics, Social Sciences, and the Arts and Humanities. Overall, Swansea enjoyed the largest increase in internationally excellent research in the whole of the UK. Swansea University's research income has grown significantly in recent years, and the University attracted a record £65 million in research grants awarded in the 2009–10 academic year. The University's research base is now a significant driver of Knowledge Economy activity, and is supported by an ambitious "Strategic Directions" strategy that focuses on:

— incremental growth, investing against business plans and diverting resources to the most successful areas; and

— strategic ("quantum leap") initiatives, attracting external funding for large new academic developments with the critical mass and level of funding to have a significant impact on the University's profile.

There is ample evidence that world-class and world-leading research has more potential for creating wealth than work which aspires to more modest, national, levels of excellence. For example:

"Unsurprisingly, R&D-based and venture-backed companies locate around high-quality research universities to a far greater extent than around lower-quality research universities." *(The Race to the Top, A Review of Government's Science and Innovation Policies, Lord Sainsbury, October 2007).*

"European growth has been disappointing for the last 30 years but policymakers have only recently started to realise that Europe's growth performance is intimately linked with the research performance of its universities" *(Why reform Europe's universities? Bruegelpolicybrief 2007/04).*

This is entirely consistent with the emphasis placed upon research in the University's Mission Statement, and is the focus which underpins the University's commitment to strengthening and growing the Knowledge Economy.

2. Swansea University's Strategy in Growing a Knowledge Economy

Swansea University is a research-led university of international quality, with a clear commitment to using its strengths to make a substantial and positive impact regionally. It is a powerhouse for growth in the regional economy, which stems from its historic strengths in science and technology and the fact that, from its foundation in 1920, the University has enjoyed close collaboration with industry.

The University has been a significant recipient of EU Structural Funds, which have been deployed to support major research projects and to ensure that the University uses its research and teaching strengths, and its mature industrial links, to support the economy of the region.

The primary aim of EU Structural Funds has been to help create vibrant, self-sustaining, knowledge-led economies in the less prosperous regions of Europe and thereby reduce spatial inequalities. The focus is upon R&D, innovation, and high-level skills underpinning an effective, wealth-creating private sector. There is overwhelming evidence that Wales has not yet achieved this transformation and might be eligible for a fourth round of Structural Funding from 2013.

2.1 *High-tech cluster development*

The University has adopted an holistic approach to knowledge transfer activities, with greater strategic focus and ambition. It is working to become a European exemplar of good practice for HE driving the development of a modern knowledge economy, and is implementing strategies that will strengthen significantly the economy of South West Wales through applying research to three broad academic areas: Engineering, Computer Science and Telecommunications, and Life Science and Medicine.

These areas offer real potential for supporting cluster development of high-technology companies. It is estimated that more than 75% of industrial R&D in the UK is in industrial sectors which link directly to these three areas.

The University's Knowledge Economy strategy focuses explicitly upon promoting the development of these high-technology clusters. This is the "market standard" approach to promoting the development of a modern knowledge economy. For example, it is a key feature of the acclaimed Barcelona economic renewal strategy;

it is an approach adopted by the Welsh Assembly Government; it was recommended to the City and County of Swansea by consultants SQW, and is included in the Swansea 2020 Economic Regeneration Strategy.

The University's research strengths in these areas will lead to the development of a portfolio of postgraduate, high-level skills courses, many developed and taught in collaboration with partner companies, that address the skills needs of the corresponding industrial sectors and provide "fast-stream" routes to leadership positions. They will also attract industrial R&D to the region through targeting of large companies which already work with the University or which might derive significant advantages by working with the University.

An essential complementary development is the further strengthening of the School of Business and Economics, creating a thriving, "full service" management school. Knowledge Economy companies will not derive full market benefit from scientific and technical innovation without the appropriate organisational and leadership skills.

UNIVERSITY RESEARCH SUPPORTING INDUSTRIAL CLUSTERS

A new, 70-acre Bay Science and Innovation Campus will facilitate a step change in the University's interaction with industry. This campus will provide an intensive, open-innovation environment by inter-mingling industrial R&D, academic research, and postgraduate students. The campus will also be designed to facilitate the growth of high-technology clusters in the region by including consultancy, access to business support, and incubator facilities. (See section 3 for further information.)

2.2 Economic regeneration

Despite growing emphasis on developing knowledge economies, universities have not always been the policy makers' first choice as agents for change. There are still common, and not totally unjustified, perceptions of universities as passive organisations, slow to change, and not firmly rooted in the "real world". This position is not unique to the UK. For example, Canada has to contend with a relatively low base of industrial R&D (as in Wales) and was reported to have turned somewhat grudgingly to higher education:

> "Whereas countries like the USA and Japan are developing a knowledge-based economy by stimulating industrial research and development, in Canada, the industrial research and development infrastructure is so small, the government was forced to turn to university scientists to transform the economy" *(McGill Reporter, November 18, 1999)*.

There are, of course, recognised associations between the presence of major research universities and a flourishing technology enterprise within specific geographical areas. Examples include Silicon Valley, Massachusett's Route 128, North Carolina's research triangle, and, closer to home, the Cambridge effect. However it has become clear that the influence of universities on regional economies is far more extensive:

> "Universities and specialized research centres are the driving force behind innovation in nearly every region" *(Clusters of Innovation National Report, USA Council on Competitiveness, Washington DC, 2001)*

2.3 *Improving performance*

International evidence indicates that both the quality and scale of research determine a university's potential for driving change:

> "There is a correlation between [research] quality and impact ... it is possible to have high quality without much impact, but it is highly unlikely to have much impact without high quality" *(The Wealth of a Nation: An Evaluation of Engineering Research in the UK, EPSRC).*

> "Without a large research base, even highly engaged universities are not able to exert enough impact to make a difference in a regional economy" *(Universities and the Development of Industry Clusters, 2004. Report prepared for Economic Development Administration, US Department of Commerce by the Carnegie Mellon Center for Economic Development).*

Wales is disadvantaged by an historical deficit in STEM research and, until recently, it could be argued that only Cardiff University had the scale of high quality research which the evidence indicates to be necessary (circa £50million/annum research spend).

As has been pointed out Swansea University has benefitted significantly from EU Convergence Funding. The Cluster model described in section 2.2 above demonstrates the approach that the University is taking in delivering high-technology and high-value added knowledge transfer activities. Although the cluster strategy is being delivered primarily through three broad academic areas, it is intended to be fully inclusive, involving every part of the University. This is important because the traditional boundaries between academic disciplines are usually unhelpful in addressing the challenges facing the public or private sector, including high-technology companies.

The Knowledge Economy Strategic Framework recognises that a campus environment is particularly conducive to cross-cutting, interdisciplinary links. Mechanisms for encouraging the formation of multidisciplinary research teams are already under development in the University. These mechanisms will be further enhanced to ensure that the academic areas identified for driving cluster development can both inform and draw upon academic strengths across the whole University. An important example is the multidisciplinary group researching Ageing. This group has already demonstrated substantial potential for generating innovative, wealth-creating solutions by linking social science with medical engineering and ICT. A successful, representative example of the University's implementation of its strategy is the Institute of Life Science.

2.4 *The Institute of Life Science*

The Institute of Life Science (ILS) is a £52 million, purpose-built facility strategically located between the College of Medicine and Singleton Hospital, part of the Abertawe Bro Morgannwg University Health Board. This facility has been made possible through a unique collaboration between IBM, Swansea University and the Welsh Assembly Government.

The emphasis at the ILS is on high quality inter- and multi-disciplinary research into areas such as cancer, diabetes and obesity, neurological disorders and hospital-acquired infections. ILS activity is focused on discovering radical ways to treat disease and deliver healthcare. Its state-of-the art laboratories are complemented by a unique supercomputing infrastructure centred on Blue C. One of the very few supercomputers in the world dedicated to life science research, Blue C has a permanent home at Swansea University as part of a high-profile collaboration with IBM.

Life science is recognised as one of the most fertile sources of technology transfer in the world, giving the ILS the potential to create significant economic wealth. Opportunities are arising from areas such as research collaboration, intellectual property licensing, spinout companies and inward investment and, in readiness for these, the ILS is well equipped. With state-of-the-art laboratories and a dedicated Business Development Centre, the focus is on building long-term commercial-academic links and making first-class medical progress to take medical advances from the laboratory into hospitals, surgeries and homes.

ILS Outputs

Audited figures reported to WEFO in February 2009 show unequivocally that the ILS is delivering against its objectives and is having measurable impact on the Knowledge Economy:

	Achieved Feb 2009	*% of target achieved Feb 09*	*Forecast to 2012**
New jobs created	207	105	607
Companies advised in R&D/Innovation	135	100	435
New companies created	22	105	32
Increase in turnover	£14.7m	101	£34.71m
Collaborative research projects	32	110	62
New patents/trademarks	20	100	35

*on target as of September 2010

ILS2

The second phase of the ILS project has seen the development of ILS2, a £30 million state-of-the-art research centre. The new seven-storey, 6,000 square metre building is currently under construction. It will house clinical research and play a major role in developing new products and services for the healthcare industry. It will triple the space available to grow related businesses.

2.5 Case Study: Boots Centre for Innovation

ILS is home to the Boots Centre for Innovation, which was established to help researchers and entrepreneurs to develop new products. The Centre, backed by a Regional Selective Assistance grant from the Welsh Assembly Government, is using the facilities and expertise of the ILS to assist the innovators to develop new products for Alliance Boots plc in areas as diverse as pain relief, skin treatments, diabetes, and healthy ageing.

Pioneering researchers and innovative small businesses are able to bring promising ideas to the Boots Centre in Swansea to obtain scientific expertise, business know-how and financial backing.

They are able to work with the Centre's specialist staff to turn those ideas into valuable new products, and a partnership between Alliance Boots plc and venture capitalists Longbow Capital LLP offers entrepreneurs access to investment funding.

Under one of the most trusted brands in the UK, the Boots Centre for Innovation offers a direct route into close to 2,500 Boots stores across the UK and the possibility of international distribution. Researchers and entrepreneurs therefore have ready access to expert producers and developers, together with an exceptional route to the health and beauty market.

2.6 Attracting investment

Providing a vibrant environment that fosters good research and skills development has enabled Swansea University to develop and deliver new projects that stimulate links with industry. In turn, this facilitates an enabling environment that encourages the growth of a supportive infrastructure. Accessing a broad range of funding opportunites, including Convergence and Research Council support, stimulates further economic opportunities that cohere to Welsh Assembly and UK Government objectives to create jobs, grow the skills base, and to attract inward investment from large companies that support broad supply chains.

2.7 Case Study: The Sustainable Product Engineering Centre for Innovative Functional Industrial Coatings (SPECIFIC)

The Engineering and Physical Sciences Research Council (EPSRC) and the Technology Strategy Board has provided financial support for a new Innovation and Knowledge Centre based at Swansea University.

The £20 million *Sustainable Product Engineering Centre for Innovative Functional Industrial Coatings* (SPECIFIC) aims to transform buildings into "power stations" through the rapid commercialisation of functional coatings on steel and glass in the areas of energy capture, storage and release. The ambitious target of the SPECIFIC academic and industrial partnership is to generate a portfolio of products which, by 2020, will generate over one third of the UK's requirement for renewable energy.

In the UK there are more than four billion square metres of roofs and facades forming the building envelope. Most of this could potentially be used for harvesting solar energy and yet it covers less than 1.8% of the UK land area. The vision for SPECIFIC is to develop affordable large area solar collectors which can replace standard roofs and generate over one third of the UK's total target renewable energy by 2020 (10.8 GW peak and 19 TWh) reducing CO_2 output by six million tonnes per year.

This will be achieved with an annual production of 20 million m^2 by 2020 equating to less than 0.5% of the available roof and wall area. SPECIFIC will realise this by quickly developing practical functional coated materials on metals and glass that can be manufactured by industry in large volumes to produce, store and release energy at point of use. These products will be suitable for fitting on both new and existing buildings, which is important since 50% of the UKs current CO_2 emissions come from the built environment.

The key focus for SPECIFIC will be to accelerate the commercialisation of IP, knowledge and expertise held between the University partners (Swansea, ICL, Bath, Strathclyde, Glyndwr, and Bangor) and UK based industry in three key areas of electricity generation from solar energy (photovoltaics), heat generation (solar thermal) and storage/controlled release. The combination of functionality will be achieved through applying functional coatings to metal and glass surfaces. Critical to this success is the active involvement in the Centre of the global steel giant Tata and the global glass manufacturer Pilkington. These two materials dominate the facings of the building stock and are surfaces which can be engineered.

SPECIFIC is a unique business opportunity bridging a technology gap, delivering affordable novel macro-scale micro-generation, making a major contribution to UK renewable energy targets and creating a new export opportunity for off grid power in the developing world. It will ultimately generate thousands of high technology jobs within a green manufacturing sector, creating a sustainable international centre of excellence in functional coatings where multi-sector applications are developed for next generation manufacturing.

The Welsh Assembly Government is supporting the project in recognition of its strategic nature and its potential economic impact.

2.8 *Convergence funding projects*

Further examples of how Swansea University has accessed convergence funding to support knowledge economy and knowledge transfer activities targeted at meeting employers' needs include:

Steel Training Research and Innovation Partnership (STRIP): a £7 million initiative that involves Cardiff, Bangor, and Glyndwr Universities. STRIP will specifically supply demand led flexible credit based training addressing higher level skills gaps to enable the creation of next generation high level employees equipped with expertise in new technology, essential for increasing productivity, minimising environmental impact and with the capacity to develop novel products essential for the creation of a sustainable steel industry in Wales. The project will also maintain vital strategic partnerships with the Welsh steel industry, expand the collaboration within the supply chain to larger numbers of companies, and act as a catalyst for larger clusters of research activity in key areas of advanced manufacturing and energy.

Feedback from the steel industry shows that:

— global market changes have caused significant decline and, in a number of situations, the death of heavy industry in the UK. Even so, the UK still has a thriving and economically crucial engineering sector;

— the sector is experiencing serious difficulties in recruiting engineering graduates, a situation which is five times greater than in other industry sectors;

— the consequent skill shortage has hindered economic development within the sector;

— 29% of companies are unable to expand because they lack skilled people;

— new technology and advancement in engineering practices has seen demand shift towards employees with high skills levels; and

— 26% of engineering companies now go abroad for the skilled people they need.

ArROW—Aerospace Research Organisation Wales: an £8 million initiative that involves six other universities in Wales. ArROW aims to set up a national organisation based on collaboration between the universities that will work in a distributed way to lead, co-ordinate and drive forward aerospace research in Wales, increasing research capacity and applying that resource to improving industrial competitiveness.

Feedback from the aerospace industry shows that:

— high level skills are a key requirement. Over 30% of employees in the sector are educated to degree standard or equivalent, and more than 11% are involved in research and development;

— formal engineering qualifications need to be combined with transferable skills such as project management, presentations, report writing, and working and contributing to a team; and

— increasingly, engineering skills shortages are forcing companies to look offshore for workers, and there is genuine demand for "home grown" highly skilled engineers.

Software Alliance Wales (SAW): a £13 million initiative over five years, involving four other Welsh HEIs. The aim of the initiative is to support the development of a vibrant software industry in Wales by setting up a network for software developers in Wales, supporting the network with a strong CPD programme, and setting up an Accreditation Centre for the benchmarking of Welsh Computing and ICT companies.

Advanced SusTainable ManUfacturing Technologies (ASTUTE): a £25 million initiative involving every HE Institution in Wales that has an interest in advanced manufacturing and associated technologies. The project will support firms to invest in, and utilise outcomes of R&D, develop new and improved products and processes, and enhance collaborative research initiatives between HE institutions and firms.

2.9 *Reviewing Knowledge Economy projects*

However, while quality and scale of research may be a necessary condition for transformational impact, it is certainly not sufficient on its own. Swansea University keeps its knowledge economy projects (particularly those funded by the EU) under informal internal review to identify the interventions that are most successful. The major lessons from the review are not about operational detail.

It is clear that, if the University is to become a genuine powerhouse for the regional economy, it must progress beyond the conventional piecemeal engagements in knowledge transfer to a holistic approach with greater strategic focus and ambition. It also had to become more pro-active in its engagements with large companies. Large companies are under-represented in Wales but they build supply chains, have access to global markets, and, with about 97.5% of industrial R&D in the UK, they drive innovation.

The following table highlights the areas that are perceived to work well in Knowledge Economy projects linked to the higher education sector.

Strategic for the University and included explicitly in the University's Strategic Plan	Develops capacity in the HEI with full governance approval—a strong guarantee of sustainability.
Contains a research capacity development element	Academics are measured on their research credentials in RAE and REF. Peer esteem is mainly research. The larger the research component and longer the project duration the better.
Links with large business	Large business has many challenging and strategic problems which are not readily solved by competent professionals. They have financial resource to pay for the work. The problems are not usually short term—this fits with academic timescales of semesters and academic years. Academic can interweave this kind of work with their other duties.
Scale of project	HEIs and large business come into their own when projects get potentially very large. Both have significant internal resource. HEIs are good at getting large initiatives moving but need the private sector to take over the initiative longer term as the project moves towards commercialisation or implementation.
Projects led by academics with good interpersonal and leadership skills, who understand the broad ethos of business, have an aptitude for project delivery, and an ability to recruit the talented team essential for project delivery.	As in the private sector, this is a limited resource. Avoid using existing staff just because they are there.
Projects led by academics who have a well developed research team infrastructure	This buys the academic time to properly interact with project stakeholders.
Projects with a capital element in them	HEI building infrastructure is poor. HEIs need to replace equipment and facilities and keep up to date.
Projects where the academics have access to an effective technology transfer team.	
Projects which have a long timescale	These are usually delivered better because lift-off and closedown phases are a smaller proportion of the project. The mainstream part can be treated as "business as usual" using existing HEI administration and infrastructure.
SME engagement where this engagement can be coordinated by the technology transfer team which defers to academia where a difficult issue arises.	Many SME problems are small and can be resolved by the technology transfer team themselves. Many technology transfer teams include STEM PhDs and MBAs. A large number of small quick turnaround problems from SMEs is a disruption for academics who have to deliver mainstream RCUK research, and have teaching duties and student support issues.

Where HEI, SME and Large Company engagement is predicated by real need	Examples: — Large Co is developing a platform product but needs SME systems delivers. — Large Co cannot cope with market demand and wishes to subcontract service to SMEs. — Large Co needs University R&D and maintenance, support, and ongoing product development from a range of SMEs because large co does not have the resource to do everything, and needs to access the marketing window quickly. — Large Co has a skills shortage but this resides in SMEs that receive subcontract work — Large Co wants to outsource non strategic work, which is of strategic interest to the SMEs — HEI is looking to licence IP to SMEs to lever them into large co supply chain — SMEs form an industrial cluster to take on contracts of greater size from large co
Projects where the number of partners is limited and where financial accountability and leadership is clear from the outset.	Managing relationships and conflicts are very time consuming. Different organisations have different priorities and view risks in different ways. Skills imbalance can be more easily addressed with fewer partners. There is also less risk of one partner not treating the project seriously because it is less strategic for them.
Projects in which Government, Business and Higher Education are mutually self supporting.	Where each partner puts its best and most influential people into the team with a view to bring their organisations inherent strengths to bear on project delivery and long term sustainability and economic growth. This represents a key skills and priorities issue for each of the partners.

3. THE BAY SCIENCE AND INNOVATION CAMPUS

Although growth of the Knowledge Economy is a major part of the Welsh Assembly Government's economic strategy, Wales overall has one of the lowest (and currently declining) levels of commercial R&D activity in the UK. There is strong evidence that, where leading academic expertise exists, knowledge intensive companies will co-locate their activities.

A new Bay Science and Innovation Campus is being developed by Swansea University, which will provide a catalyst for collaborative research dealing with key WAG Knowledge Economy clusters with other research intensive Universities.

Economic development will be secured through spin-outs, spin-ins, R&D and consultancy support, and supply chain synergies. The intention is that this regional spread of economic activity will be facilitated by a regional infrastructure of local KE centres. Such a knowledge network provides the asset base for the identification, assimilation and exploitation of new knowledge and along with land, capital and labour will provide a key factor in economic production.

In particular, the Bay Campus provides the opportunity not just to increase the scale of research collaborations but to become the principal driver for further multinational enterprise (MNE) Knowledge Economy inward investment to SW Wales and beyond. This in turn will multiply local supply chain opportunities for regional small medium enterprises (SMEs).

3.1 The vision

The total cost of the project for phase 1 is £200 million, with significant private sector investment together with public sector support, facilitated by BP's gifting of its land to the University as part of the company's strategy of exiting the region with honour.

The University estimates that Phase 1 of the Bay Campus will bring in additional research income of £22 million per annum by 2020 (£97.5 million cumulative). Using comparative data from similar projects, this would be expected to create 332 extra jobs per annum by 2020 (1,463 cumulative) in the field of industrial collaborative research, and lever many more economic outputs, including support for SMEs, commercial income, spin out SME's, indirect regional jobs and expenditure creating an estimated £3 billion of additional regional impact over 10 years.

The Bay Science and Innovation Campus will also draw together the range of expertise located within universities and further education institutions delivering joint foundation degrees, to provide training and skills development opportunities to all levels of the workforce via employer-related learning routes, and working with the National Science Academy.

Projects already committed to the Bay Campus include the EPSRC-backed industry partnership with Rolls-Royce (the SMART project), which will require over 2,000 square metres of the campus. The remaining additional space will be fully committed by Campus opening in (2014). The provision of additional space and the open innovation design of the Innovation Hub will maximise applied research and commercialisation growth.

3.2 The Innovation Hub

The Bay Science and Innovation Campus is an exemplary project that will deliver against the new HE agenda of promoting innovation within the region and beyond in line with economic renewal objectives, and which will stimulate significant investment opportunities.

The core of the project is the Innovation Hub, which has been uniquely designed to provide an intensive, open-innovation environment to maximise the growth of collaborative research with industry in specific high-tech clusters (Advanced Engineering, Digital Economy and Low Carbon) where the University's Engineering College has established strengths.

Cluster	Sub cluster areas	Examples of MNEs and SMEs the university currently works with within the clusters
Digital Economy	— Wireless Communications — Communications — High Performance Computing	BT, Nokia, Alcatel-Lucent, EADS, BAE Systems , Orange, Vodafone, BBC, Fujitsu, Huawei, 3KT, NEC, Nortel, Phillips, Samsung, Thales, Toshiba, Microsoft and Orange.
Low Carbon	— Sustainable Building — Marine Renewables — Vehicles — Climate Change Adaption and Environmental Engineering	Corus and Rolls Royce, Npower Renewables, Enfis, Eon UK, Eco2/ Tidal energy Ltd, Wave Dragon Wales Ltd, Severn Tidal Power Group, Halcrow, Crown Estates, BAE Systems, Toyota, Hitachi, Mikrotechnik, Austria MicroSystems, ABB, Dialog Seminconductor, Diodes Zetex Semiconductor Plc, X-Fab UK Ltd, Aviza, Semelab, International Rectifier, Vishay Siliconex, Magnox North and, Phillips and Marks and Spencer.
Advanced Engineering	— Materials — Aerospace — Nanotechnology — Autonomous Systems — Printing and Coating — Visualisation — Ultra Efficient Lighting	Airbus/EADS, Timet, Corus Strip Products, Corus Colors, Corus Packaging plus, Testing Solutions Wales, BASF, Akzo Nobel, Wedge Group Galvanizing, Qineti Q, Cogent Power, Crown Cork and Seal, Dyesol UK, Heckett Multiserv, Rolls Royce (SMART), Corus, TWI Wales, Newport Galvanisers, Rocckfield Software Ltd, EADs, Airbus, Rolls Royce, Timet, Thales, Quintiq, Agfa, Asahi, BAe, Corus, Dow Corning, Kodak, Sun Chemicals, Innovia, Philips, SCA Trelleborg, Markes International, Cardinal Packaging, IBM, SERCO, SGI, Airbus UK, EADS, Royal Mint, Qinetig, Matra Bae Dynamics, Delcam, Boeing, Toyota, BMW, Honda and Blitiz Games.

The Innovation Hub co-locates both Multi-National Enterprises (MNEs) and Small and Medium sized Enterprises (SMEs) engaged in knowledge economy R&D together with the research capabilities of the University' College of Engineering, and the School of Business and Economics.

The design of the Innovation Hub will facilitate an open innovation environment involving the co-location of personnel from MNEs and SMEs with academic members of staff and also EngDoc and other applied postgraduate research students. This approach will significantly enhance Wales' ability to attract the Research and Development activities of global companies, even those not already present in Wales, as evidence demonstrates that for such companies proximity to the best available academic research expertise is the major location-driving factor.

Each Cluster area will deliver the following outputs:

— full integration of collaborative industrial and academic environment;

— increased productivity of companies in the cluster;

— increased research funding;

— strategic platform for joint programmes within education (FE and HE), research and innovation;

— stimulating new businesses in the cluster;

— creation of industry centres of excellence including standards setting;

— creation of Cluster Forums;

— increase in industry research partners;

— attraction and retention of companies to the region;

— raising the profile of Wales and the region;

— SME Development as a result of the supply chain effect within each cluster;

— increased National and International collaboration;

— links with other Science Parks/ Innovation Campuses;

— skills development along the skills continuum from workforce to EngD;

— increased IP output and value;

— retention of graduates in the area; and

— sustainability of Convergence projects and maximisation of outputs.

The Innovation Hub integrates fully academic and industry personnel and is at the highest end of the partnership continuum.

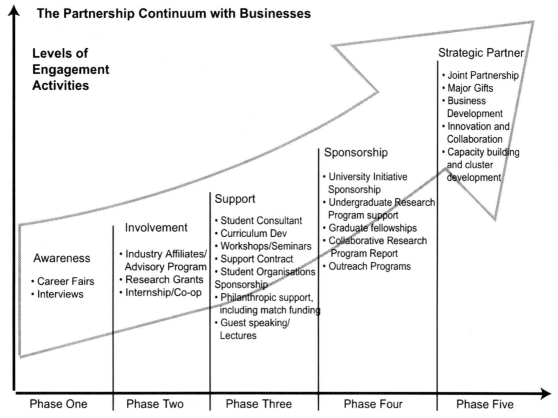

At present the College of Engineering and business collaboration is at various stages along the continuum. With the transformation of the temporary measures into the full Innovation Hub, engagement with industry will move to Stage 5 (as evidenced by the example of the Swansea Materials Research and Testing (SMART) company described below).

3.3 *Case Study: The Swansea Materials Research and Testing Company*

An early example of the way in which the Innovation Hub will engage MNEs in Knowledge Economy activities is the Swansea Materials Research and Testing Company, which demonstrates the potential for commercialising the output of Innovation Hub activity.

Funding for a strong research input has been secured through significant research council involvement from the Engineering and Physical Sciences Research Council (EPSRC) which has made £50 million available over a 10 year period to Swansea University and its collaborating University partners with Rolls Royce namely the Universities of Birmingham and Cambridge.

The company has started trading and it is expected that overall income flows (research, training and commercial) into the region will increase from currently around £1 million a year to nearly £5 million a year as a result of this venture. Swansea University will be replicating this model of working with the EPSRC, for example with Corus in the context of developing new materials and manufacturing processes to accelerate the commercialisation of photovoltaic modules for low cost-based, dye-sensitised solar cells.

Research shows that the establishment of areas of research strength supported by effective commercialisation strategies stimulates the formation of clusters of activity, bringing together research funding, spin out formation, supply chain establishment, and venture capital funding. This creates impact through new business formation, employment, procurement and requires coordinated support to deliver the workforce skills required and the SME up-skilling.

Increased major business involvement, increased research funding and increased SME collaboration will lead to an increased level of spin out companies from the HE/FE sector. More of these will be successful as a result of increased professionalism in their support.

The following table demonstrates the outputs enabled by the extra space provided for the initiative:

	Pre 2010	*Post Innovation campus*
People:	— Three academic staff	— minimum five academic staff
	— 8 post docs	— minimum 12 post docs
	— one FTE administrator	— professional marketing, finance and HR team
	— one FTE technician	— ~10 full time trained professional technicians
	— minimal technician pool	— increased technicians frees up post docs to concentrate on research
Facilities:	— Cramped/old fashioned laboratories with poor environmental performance and regular power disruptions	— purpose built/"showpiece" laboratories
		— enhanced environmental performance
	— University Quality management system	— Un-interrupted power supplies
	— 24 creep machines	— Purpose designed training suite
	— 18 universal rigs	— 55 universal rigs
Finance:	consultancy income ~£75K per annum (UWS Ventures) generic EPSRC income ~£200K per annum. TSB core partner income ~£200k per annum	commercial income £1.5M per annum (SMART) EPSRC Partnership £2M per annum HEFCW Chair funding £600K significant increase in R-R TSB sub-contracts ~£1 million per annum

The co-location of the College of Engineering and the School of Business and Economics will have a synergistic effect enabling the Innovation Hub to provide both technical and professional support for commercialisation.

3.4 *Skills and FE/HE collaboration*

A key feature of the Innovation Hub will be the collaboration between HEIs and FEIs in the region and across Wales. The University's discussions with businesses revealed the critical need to:

1. enhance skills training for their existing and future staff;

2. ensure an appropriately skilled workforce across all levels of job activity; and

3. ensure there is an appropriate skills pipeline within the region.

As a regional project, the Bay Science and Innovation Campus will draw together the range of expertise located within universities and Further Education Institutions to provide training and skills development opportunities to all levels of the workforce in South West Wales through traditional undergraduate, masters, postgraduate and postdoctoral training, links with FE (Foundation degrees, pathways to learning) and workforce skills in collaboration with FE and business, particularly SMEs. This will involve developing employer-related learning routes.

The Innovation Hub will be designed as a STEM showcase in order to inspire and excite children and adults about STEM and its industry applications. The Innovation Hub will be designed with viewing windows and platforms in order to make the science more accessible to visitors.

Facilities will be shared, as part of longstanding applied research collaboration, with other Welsh HEIs as identified below:

Cluster	Welsh HEI collaborators
Digital Economy	All Welsh HEIs
Low Carbon	Cardiff University, Glamorgan University, Aberystwyth University, Swansea Metropolitan University, Glyndwr University, University of Wales Institute Cardiff, University of Wales Newport and Bangor University
Advanced Engineering	Cardiff University, Aberystwyth University, Bangor University, Swansea Metropolitan University, Glyndwr University, University of Wales Institute Cardiff and University of Wales Newport.

3.5 *Economic and regional impact*

The development of the Bay Science and Innovation campus is a key part of the wider regeneration of Swansea Bay which has been made possible by the decision of BP to remediate its remaining industrial estate in the region and return it to beneficial community use. This will lead to the creation of the Coed Darcy Urban village, the Bay campus and the Baglan industrial development area. The campus is a key catalyst to creating value in the entire Swansea Bay area through its central location and its ability to trigger higher value business activity and therefore jobs than would otherwise be the case.

The development will also connect Swansea and Neath Port Talbot, aligning with the strategy for Swansea Bay.

Economic Impact Analysis for the Bay Science and Innovation Campus project indicates potential for around £3 billion of economic impact over a 10 year period, including the effects of construction activity. The initiative is projected to result in direct and indirect creation of around 3,000 new jobs. The impact arises from:

— growth in research income, resultant employment of academic staff and postgraduate students, creation of IP and licencing;

— creation of business initiatives with major international companies;

— development and growth of SME based supply chains around those anchor projects and through a range of collaborative links with the campus; and

— creation of spin out companies from campus research.

By the end of September 2009, Swansea University had been granted 34 patents through the delivery of world class and internationally recognised collaborative research projects. During the same period, the University supported many businesses and start-ups in the Swansea area—resulting in 28 spin-out firms, employing 71 people, and active after three years of trading.

It is projected that the University will create a minimum of seven high growth spin out companies a year and 14 low growth spin outs a year when the campus is fully operational because of the increase in research activity and the number of postgraduate students.

4. CONCLUSIONS

This document demonstrates that Swansea University has a clear commitment to using its research strengths and increasingly effective links with industry to make a substantial and positive impact regionally.

The University's Knowledge Economy strategy is focused on the development of three high-technology clusters, which will provide significant opportunities for economic growth, and job and wealth creation. Key to the success of this activity is the formation of multidisciplinary research teams able to undertake high-quality work in a range of cross-cutting themes.

Examples of where the University's research strengths and industry links have yielded significant success in terms of Knowledge Economy and Knowledge Transfer activity include:

— the Institute of Life Science;

— the Boots Centre for Innovation;

— the Sustainable Product Engineering Centre for Innovative Functional Industrial Coatings; and

— the *Swansea Materials Research and Testing* Company.

The Bay Science and Innovation Campus (and the integral Innovation Hub) will provide a major focus for HE collaboration with industry in Wales, and will stimulate a wide range of large-scale inward investment opportunities.

Swansea University's position as a research intensive university therefore enables it to take a lead in attracting investment to the region, and within the context of a flourishing Knowledge Economy.

March 2011

Written evidence submitted by e-skills UK

SUMMARY

This document is the e-skills UK written input to the Welsh Affairs Committee on Inward Investment in Wales and outlines existing and potential future skills issues in the IT sector which will need to be addressed in order to attract new companies to Wales.

e-skills UK is the SSC for Business and Information Technology covering software, internet and web, IT services, Telecommunications and business change.

Our Strategic Plan for Wales sets out a coherent skills strategy to (a) Inspire Future Talent, (b) Support IT & Telecoms Professionals and (c) Campaign for the IT nation.

ICT is an economic priority sector in Wales, employing 39,000 people. Software, Computer Games and Electronic publishing industries are also part of the Creative industries.

The sector is predicted to grow strongly to 2019 with employment growth at 1.21% per annum, nearly five times faster than the average for Wales.

Over 3,000 new entrants to the IT & Telecoms professional workforce are needed in Wales each year to meet projected growth and replacement requirements.

IT related Higher Education remains an important source of talent for the sector's labour force requirements. However, the pipeline of future talent is compromised by issues related to IT education and uptake in schools and colleges. A pervasive gender imbalance in IT education and in the sector remains, restricting the available labour pool.

We need to: encourage young people to consider and parents, teachers and careers advisors to promote relevant further study and a career path in IT; promote opportunities in the sector; provide relevant qualifications, CPD for teachers and viable alternatives to HE.

In the short term, to address the immediate skills needs of the sector and encourage inward investment we need to: attract talented individuals; support retraining and upskilling; and develop accessible, excellent training opportunities.

1.0 INTRODUCTION

1.1 As the SSC for Business and Information Technology, e-skills UK works on behalf of employers to ensure the UK has the technology skills it needs to succeed in a global digital economy. Our work covers software, internet and web, IT services, Telecommunications and business change. e-skills UK takes the lead on the IT-related skills needs of business leaders and managers and of individual workers in all sectors (IT users).

1.2 We are an employer-led, not-for-profit company, and were rated as 'outstanding' in the re-licensing review of all SSCs by the National Audit Office (NAO) and UKCES. We bring together employers, educators and government to address the technology-related skills issues no one party can solve on its own and provide advice, services and programmes that have a measurable impact on IT related skills development in the UK. The membership of the Employer Board for Wales can be found in Annex A.

1.3 Our strategic plan for Wales sets out a coherent skills strategy that enables the nation to create the skills needed for a digital economy and to derive maximum benefit from the power of technology to transform competitiveness and productivity. We work with partner organisations to deliver on three strategic objectives to ensure Wales is world class in delivering maximum value from technology both in business and in society more widely:

1. *Inspire future talent*: To motivate talented students to pursue IT & Telecoms related careers, and better prepare all young people for work in a technology-enabled world.

2. *Support IT & Telecoms professionals*: Develop the IT & Telecoms professional skills pool as the best in the world for deriving business benefit from digital technology.

3. *Campaign for the IT nation*: Promote the compelling benefits of increased IT capability to organisations and individuals in every sector across the UK economy.

1.4 Our response sets out the evidence base, briefly outlining the importance of the sector in Wales and the nature of current and future skills issues in Wales. We conclude with some recommended solutions for consideration in relation to addressing these issues.

2.0 SUMMARY OF IT SKILLS ISSUES

2.1 *Technology is key to Wales and the rest of the UK's economic revival*

Technology is the key ingredient for global competitiveness in the private sector and for efficiency in the public sector. The IT & Telecoms industry in Wales currently delivers an annual GVA contribution in excess of £1.2 billion, 5% of the total Wales economy and is recognised as a key sector for economic renewal.

2.2 *The importance of IT employment, now and in the future*

There are more than 112,000 IT & Telecoms workplaces in Wales—84% of these are services orientated and two thirds of employees (67%) are based in small or medium sized companies.

Overall 39,000 people work in IT & Telecoms in Wales. 16,000 people are directly employed in the IT & Telecoms industry itself and 23,000 people work in IT & Telecoms professional roles in other sectors of the economy.

Globalisation means that IT & Telecoms work in Wales is increasingly focussed on higher value, highly skilled roles. Growth in the sector is predicted to continue strongly to 2019 with employment in the IT industry expected to grow at 1.21% per annum, nearly five times faster than the predicted average employment growth for Wales. Over 17,000 new IT & Telecoms professionals are needed in Wales over the next five years to meet projected growth and replacement requirements.

2.3 *IT skills demand indicates potential areas for concern*

Despite weaknesses in the economy, demand for IT & Telecoms professionals in Wales has risen by around 13% over the past year, currently averaging about 900 advertised positions a quarter. Around two in three (60%) of IT & Telecoms recent positions advertised by employers in Wales were for Systems Design or Systems Development. The most commonly advertised job specific, technical skills required by employers in Wales were: SQL, .NET, C#, SQL Server, ASP, JavaScript, Java, PHP, HTTP and Visual Basic.

General shortfalls in the skills of individuals applying for IT & Telecoms positions appear relatively common place particularly in respect of business skills, higher level technical skills and sector knowledge/experience. And although skills shortages[1] are currently at a relatively low level, they are most likely to be reported by recruiters that are medium to large in size or operating the IT & Telecoms industry itself.

Such shortages are reported to result in delayed recruitment and an increase in advertising and recruitment spend. In the longer term, skills and recruitment issues often lead to: delays in developing new products and services, difficulties introducing technological change and a loss of business or orders to competitors.

2.4 *IT skills development and education*

IT related Higher Education remains an important source of talent for the sector's labour force requirements. In contrast to the rest of the UK, the number of applicants to Computing degree courses in Wales has been rising since 2004 but females account for only 16% of people on Computing related degrees.

In 2008–09 there were 1,275 Computing degree qualifiers[2] from Higher Education Institutes in Wales. However, 40% of new graduate entrants to IT & Telecoms occupations are from degree disciplines other than Computing.

There was a 13% decline in the number of people "in learning" on FE IT professional courses between 2008 and 2009 and the majority of learning is below Level 3, the accepted entry level for IT & Telecoms occupations. And, whilst the number of people taking the less industry-relevant ICT A-level has increased, A-level Computing in Wales has seen a 63% drop in entrants since 2004.

3.0 SOLUTIONS TO DEVELOP FUTURE TALENT AND MEET CURRENT DEMAND FOR SKILLS

3.1 There are major issues with IT-related education in schools and with the uptake of IT-related subjects in higher education. These are seriously compromising the pipeline of future talent. e-skills UK research shows students' experience of IT at Key Stage 4 is a major factor in the decrease in IT-related education at school and in FE. Although university applications for Computing are rising in Wales (but not at the same rate as for all subjects), a pervasive gender imbalance remains.

---

[1] Specifically where employers report vacancies are hard to fill because of a lack of candidates with the required skills, qualifications or experience.

[2] Including post-graduate qualifiers.

3.2 e-skills UK is supporting economic growth in Wales by strengthening the pipeline of talent in the Economic priority renewal sectors as defined by WAG. ICT and the Creative industries (which include Software, Computer Games and Electronic publishing) are strategically important in terms of economic recovery, future potential and inward investment.

3.3 In order to encourage young people, parents, teachers and careers advisors to consider relevant further study and a career path in IT we need to:

— Promote the sector as a high growth, high skill sector with excellent earning potential and career prospects for young people and adults.

— Ensure that IT-related qualifications and curriculum in Wales are valued by industry and delivered by quality higher and further education providers.

— Continue to strengthen links between employers and universities and FE and training providers

— Ensure teachers have access to relevant CPD in order to deliver an industry endorsed curriculum.

— Embed Computing within the STEM agenda, capitalising on rising applications to Computing in Wales.

— Develop apprenticeship pathways with colleges and employers as a viable alternative to higher education.

— Develop in partnership with Universities relevant, employer led degrees and foundation degrees that blend technology and business skills.

— Incentivise schools, colleges and universities to deliver qualifications relevant to the priority sectors including ICT.

3.4 To address the immediate skills needs of the sector and encourage inward investment in the near future we need to:

— Attract talented individuals from other occupations into the sector to fill areas in demand such as Systems Design and Systems Development.

— Support retraining and upskilling particularly in programming languages.

— Developing excellent training opportunities for individuals in the sector and new companies who want to invest in Wales.

March 2011

Annex A

WALES EMPLOYER BOARD LIST

Ronan Miles	Director of Collaborative Solutions Practice, BT Client Services	BT
Chris Goldoni	Director	Cardiff Financial Partnership
Penny Copner	Coordinator	Care sector
Richard Sheppard	Director	Draig Technology
Mike Greenway	Senior Commercial Consultant	EADS
Alan Pound	Wales Manager	Fujitsu
David L Morgan	Delivery Manager	HP Services
Ian Clark	Engineering Operations Manager & Head of Configuration Management	General Dynamics
Cenydd Burden	Head of EMEA Client Services	Mitel
Christine Bamford	Director of OD	NLIAH
Jo Preece	Wales Manager	Steria
Greg Jones	Head of Corporate Services	DFTSSC
Terry Killer	Skills Manager	Microsoft

Gwyn Thomas	CIO	Welsh Assembly Government
Rick Cooper	Director Alactel-Lucent University	Alcatel Lucent
Nia Davies	Policy Officer	Federation of Small Business

Written evidence submitted by Energy & Utility Skills (EU Skills) and the National Skills Academy for Power (the Skills Academy)

1. INTRODUCTION

1.1. EU Skills is the Sector Skills Council for the gas, power, waste management and water industries.

1.2. The Skills Academy was established in 2010 to transform the future of skills and competence delivery across the UK power industry; addressing the critical skills challenges faced now and in the future through targeted investment and collaboration. Employers, through the Skills Academy, now take a national approach to skills needs and related provision to identify gaps and avoid duplication.

1.3. For the purposes of this submission the "energy sector" includes the activities of all forms of electricity generation (ie combustion and renewable/low carbon—but excluding nuclear), the transmission and regional distribution of electricity and gas, and metering operations.

1.4. EU Skills' own research estimates that around 12,000 people are employed in these activities within Wales.

1.5. These activities are carried out by around 100 employers. These range from large asset owning companies to smaller, more specialised contractor companies.

1.6. The transmission and distribution activities of the sector operate on a regional monopoly basis and are subject to economic regulation by Ofgem. The generation and metering aspects of the sector are open, competitive markets.

2. SUMMARY

2.1. Much of today's energy infrastructure is decades old and was designed to meet the energy demands of a centralised system. If the energy demands of the future are to be met, this infrastructure will need to be significantly upgraded and expanded to meet the requirements of a more distributed energy system. Ensuring the availability of the skills needed to implement this investment should be central to both the government's and industry's plans.

2.2. It is clear that new technologies will play a key role in the generation of energy in a low carbon future. Wind energy is leading the way with rapid growth occurring over the past two to three years and with significant opportunities becoming available over the coming years. The challenge will be for the supply of skills to keep up with demand.

2.3. Skills shortages are reported across the energy sector now. Occupations which are key to the development of the industry over the coming years include technical skills (in relation to the design, build, installation and operation of plant and equipment), project management, environmental impact analysis and product/business development skills. The development of a workforce with strong STEM skills will be crucial.

3. CURRENT SKILLS SHORTAGES

3.1. Decarbonising the power industry and security of supply are major driving forces behind the energy industry. However, as there appears to be uncertainty as to how the market will develop over the coming years, in terms of the timing and location of nuclear, fossil or renewable energy opportunities in Wales, current investment activity is sluggish.

3.2. Over the medium-term, fossil-fuelled power stations (such as Aberthaw and others on the north east coast of Wales) will continue to be required, and with the development and deployment of clean coal technologies (eg carbon capture and storage) new skills will be required.

3.3. With energy demands increasing and production of energy coming from a wider variety of sources and from an increasing number of locations (eg offshore wind developments off the coast of north Wales), the transmission and distribution infrastructure is in need of significant updating and expansion if it is to meet our needs over the next 40+ years.

3.4. The occupations that are currently recognised as being in shortage in the UK's electricity generation and transmission and distribution industries by the Migration Advisory Committee are listed in Annex 1.

3.5. Energy production from wind and marine technologies is a rapidly developing market. As a result of the rapid growth experienced over the last two to three years, employers are reporting difficulties in recruiting the skills they need to develop their businesses further. Skill shortages currently affect around one-in-four UK wind and marine energy employers (over half of the larger employers are affected), with the principle skills in shortage relating to the technical skills needed to design, build, install and operate plant and equipment, project management, environmental impact analysis and product/business development skills.

3.6. The occupations that are currently being reported as being hard-to-fill in the UK's wind and marine energy industry are listed in Annex 2.

3.7. The production of biogas (biomethane) through anaerobic digestion processes and the generation of heat and electricity from energy from waste (EfW) systems are still in their infancy in terms of commercial activity, although largescale projects are being developed (eg Covanta Energy's planned plant in Merthyr Tydfil). These are highly complex operations that require high levels of engineering, science and technical skills in areas such as thermal engineering, process engineering, project management, environmental impact analysis, and various business development roles.

3.8. Due to the lack of gas mains infrastructure in Wales, particularly in rural areas, it is expected that there will be significant potential in Wales for domestic gas engineers to diversify into the installation and maintenance of all the main micro-generation technologies (eg solar, photovoltaic, etc). The Welsh Assembly Government's *Developing Low Carbon Skills* project, which EU Skills is involved in, and the British Gas Green Skills Training Centre in Tredegar aim to support the development of this new and expanding market.

3.9. The advent of new technologies and the lack of certainty in the market is leading to skills gaps in the existing workforce as the industry continually adjusts its plans based on the latest developments and policies. More clarity of opportunity and stability are needed.

3.10. Moreover, over the last two years, the impact of the economic recession has had an effect on skills investment generally across the energy sector. This, coupled with continued uncertainty as to the direction and pace of the future energy mix, has continued to constrain investment in long-term skills develop activities; particularly in terms of apprenticeship and graduate in-take.

3.11. The drive to decarbonise the energy sector is now a global phenomenon. The demand for technical knowledge and experience has created a worldwide market for skills. This creates both opportunities and challenges for the energy sector in Wales—while having the potential to attract new investors into the area, we will also have to work harder to upskill and retain our skilled workforce in the face of global competition.

3.12. The sector, and UK engineering in general, has an aging workforce. EU Skills' Workforce Planning Model predicts that the number of retirements will continue to increase year-on-year until the early 2020s.

3.13. The number of UK-domiciled HE students accepted onto electronic and electrical engineering has decreased by over 40% since 2001–02. In 2008/9, HESA data shows that only 22 Wales-domiciled HE students entered employment in the energy sector in Wales. While this number may not be 100% accurate due to the nature of the data collection, it gives an idea of the scale of the challenge ahead.

4. Current Activities in Wales of EU Skills and the Skills Academy

4.1. EU Skills (through the Skills Academy) has established a number of industry network and skills provider groups to help facilitate a co-ordinated response to the current and future skills challenges that the power sector is facing. It has also developed a sector value proposition and launched the Think Power initiative to attract young people into a career in the power industry.

4.2. EU Skills is currently working with Wales & West Utilities and their principle contractors to identify the recruitment and skills needs of the gas distribution network in Wales over the next 15 years. Using our Workforce Planning Model we will be able to assess potential demands based on a number of different scenarios for the industry.

4.3. The data already held within the Workforce Planning Model for power and gas industries is in the process of being refreshed and updated. We are also applying the model to aspects of the renewable energy and metering industries and also looking to involve contracting organisations as well.

4.4. EU Skills and the Skills Academy has embarked on a programme of foresight research which will identify the drivers of skills in the power industry and to aid our understanding of how skills demands may change based on various industry growth scenarios. During 2011–12 we will apply this technique to the other aspects of the energy and utility sector.

4.5. Work is currently on-going to develop a power sector HE Strategy for implementation in the autumn of 2011.

4.6. In response to the ERP's priority sectors, EU Skills, in collaboration with the Skills Academy has established a Power Forum in Wales. This is being led by our Skills Director in Wales, who also works directly with employers, stakeholders and skills providers to deliver bespoke solutions to specific issues (eg promoting

WAG initiatives to energy sector employers, developing appropriate delivery mechanisms for power sector apprenticeships and supporting Coleg Llandrillo's energy-focused Foundation Degree).

4.7. The Cross-Sector Low Carbon Steering Group seeks to address the requirement raised by the Environmental Audit Committee and become the authoritative voice on strategic cross-cutting low carbon skills issues for Government and other stakeholders. The Group acts as a catalyst for the actions required to deliver solutions that will ensure the UK has the skills they need now and in the future.

4.8. The Gas Network Policy Forum was established in order to facilitate collaboration between all of the UK's network asset owners to ensure that safety standards, training, competence recognition and registration could be achieved on a consistent basis. This approach also facilitates the transfer of people between the networks with minimal additional cost. Wales & West Utilities are a founder member of this group and continue to play a full role.

4.9. The Energy & Utility Skills Register was created to enable employers to record the skills, capabilities and permits held by their employees and supply chain contractors. It has grown over the last ten years into one of the most sophisticated databases used by any sector and, being web based, enables the monitoring of competence on-line. Wales & West Utilities and National Grid use the EUSR for both their own employees and those of their contractors'.

5. POLICY RECOMMENDATIONS

5.1. If investment in the energy industry is to be forthcoming, there needs to be greater understanding and certainty of the future energy mix. Once the preferred energy mix has been set, appropriate incentives need to be put in place so that the market has clear sight of the opportunities open to them. Delays in this area will hold up skills investment and shorten the time available for employers and skills providers to respond when it does happen.

5.2. The planning process for the development of new facilities needs to be freed-up; particularly wind farms and other renewable energy sites. This creates another point of uncertainty for the market which means that skills development often starts too late in the process.

5.3. STEM skills are crucial to the successful development of the energy sector. More needs to be done to promote the opportunities afforded by careers in technical and engineering roles. The decline in single subject science (eg physics, chemistry, etc) in schools and decreases in the number of Wales (and UK)-domiciled HE electrical engineering graduates are major contributing factors to the skills shortages currently being reported across the sector.

5.4. The energy sector in Wales is a vibrant and growing sector of the economy. Sector intelligence needs to be produced and communicated to those that provide career information, advice and guidance. EU Skills and the Skills Academy are leading the way in producing this sector intelligence; basing it on bespoke research and employer engagement, and not on nationally produced employment estimates which do not accurately reflect to future dynamics of the energy sector.

5.5. The two key pools of labour are young people and adults looking to change careers (perhaps because of redundancy in another sector). Therefore, EU Skills and the Skills Academy are developing clear career pathways and are looking to communicate these at appropriate points in the system.

March 2011

Annex 1

SKILLS SHORTAGES IN THE UK ELECTRICITY INDUSTRY (INCLUDING WITHIN WALES) THAT ARE RECOGNISED BY THE MIGRATION ADVISORY COMMITTEE

Power Generation
— Project Manager
— Station Manager
— Shift/Group Leader
— Project Civil Engineer
— Mechanical Engineer
— Electrical Engineer
— Project Control Engineer
— Control & Instrumentation Engineer
— Assistant Engineer
— Plant Process Engineer
— Production Controller

Power Transmission and Distribution
— Project Manager
— Site Manager
— Power System Engineer
— Control Engineer
— Protection Engineer
— Design Engineer
— Planning/Development Engineer
— Quality, Health, Safety and Environment (QHSE) Engineer
— Project Engineer
— Proposals Engineer
— Commissioning Engineer
— Overhead Linesworker
— Site Supervisor

Annex 2

OCCUPATIONS PROVING HARD-TO-FILL IN THE WIND AND MARINE ENERGY INDUSTRY (BY TECHNOLOGY TYPE), 2010

The table below summarises the occupations reported as being hard-to-fill by wind and marine employers in 2010. Where occupations are in **bold**, they are reported as being hard-to-fill in two or more of the technology types.

Onshore Wind	Offshore wind	Marine
Aerodynamics-Mechanical Engineer	**Aerodynamics-Mechanical Engineer**	**Aerodynamics-Mechanical Engineer**
		Business Administrator
Commercial Stock Trader		
	Business Development Manager	
	Commercial Manager	**Commercial Manager**
Construction Management	**Construction Management**	**Construction Management**
		Consultancy Project Manager
	Contracts Manager	**Contracts Manager**
Designer		
	Driller	
Ecologist	**Ecologist**	**Ecologist**
Electrical Engineer	**Electrical Engineer**	**Electrical Engineer**
	Electrical Design Engineer	**Electrical Design Engineer**
Electrician		
Electronic Engineer		
		Engineering Manager
Environmental Consultant		**Environmental Consultant**
Environmental Impact Assessment Manager	**Environmental Impact Assessment Manager**	**Environmental Impact Assessment Manager**
	Environmental Development Officer	
Field Service/ Installation Engineer		
Financial Analyst		
	Geophysical Surveyor	**Geophysical Surveyor**
	Geo-Technical Engineer	**Geo-Technical Engineer**
	Head of Off-shore Renewables	
Health and Safety Manager	**Health and Safety Manager**	**Health and Safety Manager**
	Hydraulic Engineer	**Hydraulic Engineer**
	Hydro-Dynamic Modeling Engineer	**Hydro-Dynamic Modeling Engineer**
	Hydrographic surveyor	**Hydrographic Surveyor**
IT Project Manager	**IT Project Manager**	**IT Project Managers**
	Lawyer (specific to energy issues)	
Managerial Positions	**Managerial Positions**	
		Manufacturing Manager
Mechanical Engineer	**Mechanical Engineer**	**Mechanical Engineer**
Noise Assessor	**Noise Assessor**	**Noise Assessor**
		Offshore Construction
	Off-Shore Structural Engineer	**Off-Shore Structural Engineer**
	Offshore Superintendent	**Offshore Superintendent**
Ornithologist	**Ornithologist**	**Ornithologist**

Onshore Wind	Offshore wind	Marine
Planner	**Planner**	**Planner**
Power Systems Engineer	**Power Systems Engineer**	**Power Systems Engineer**
PR and Communications Experts		
Project Developer	**Project Developer**	**Project Developer**
	Project Engineer	**Senior Project Engineer**
Project Managers (Engineering-based; degree qualified)	**Project Managers (Engineering-based; degree qualified)**	**Project Managers (Engineering-based; degree qualified)**
QHSE Manager	**QHSE Manager**	**QHSE Manager**
	Renewable Development Specialist Managers	**Renewable Development Specialist Manager**
Technical Consultant		
Software Engineer	**Software Engineer**	**Software Engineer**
	Specialist Riggers	**Specialist Rigger**
	Specialist Scientists	**Specialist Scientists**
Structural Engineers (with knowledge of composite, aerodynamics—need a Masters degree as a minimum)	**Structural Design Engineer**	**Structural Design Engineer**
		Sub-Sea Designer
	Supervisors	**Supervisors**
		Senior Technologists (research and development)
Technical Planner	**Technical Planner**	**Technical Planner**
Technical Sales	**Technical Sales**	**Technical Sales**
Sales Manager		
Turbine Loads Analyst		
Wind Turbine Structural Designer	**Wind Turbine Structural Designer**	
Wind Turbine Technician	**Wind Turbine Technician**	**Wind Turbine Technician**
Windpower Engineer	**Windpower Engineer**	**Windpower Engineer**
Wind Development Professional		**Wind Development Professional**

Written evidence submitted by Wm Morrison Supermarkets plc

MORRISONS KEY FACTS

— 4th largest UK Supermarket in the UK.

— 2nd largest Fresh Food Manufacturer in the UK.

— 5th largest overall food manufacturer.

— Every week, nearly 12 million customers pass through our doors.

— We employ 132,000 colleagues across our retail and manufacturing businesses.

— 6,000 employed in Wales in 25 stores.

— £16.5 billion turnover annually.

— 439 stores, two new stores in Wales due this year creating circa 450 new jobs.

SUMMARY

— We believe passionately in developing the skills of our colleagues and that the investment involved helps us to achieve greater success and provide stable and lasting careers.

— We believe the Retail sector plays a major part in the Welsh economy and should be a key consideration for future development of the skills base.

— We would encourage all retailers to follow our lead in putting skills development at the forefront of their business strategies.

— We believe that consistency and simplicity are crucial aspects of any and all programmes put in place to support the development of skills in Wales. If engrained in processes, both these elements will help successful implementation and create a lasting effect.

— Regular changes to programmes and procedures are not helpful and can divert employers' attention from the task of building the skills base of their organisation. Consistency builds understanding, reduces costs of implementation and administrative burdens.

— We would like to see the breadth and depth of skills within the Retail industry fully recognised.

— We believe that investments in skills development should consider how we develop and enhance service skills in the economy as well as supporting traditional craft skills development.

INTRODUCTION

1. We are proud of every one of our 6,000 colleagues employed in our 25 stores in Wales, and want to continue our investment in the country. Last year we were pleased to confirm that Farmers Boy (a wholly owned subsidary of Morrisons) had entered into an agreement to acquire a majority interest in a food manufacturing site at Deeside, expanding our food manufacturing into Wales.

2. Because we only source fresh British beef, pork, lamb and poultry, we are also big customers of the farmers in Wales, purchasing thousands of heads of cattle and sheep to be processed through our own abattoirs and meat manufacturing plants.

3. We believe that anyone who has the right attitude can work in retail. We hire our colleagues for their attitude, and then we train them with the skills they need.

4. We believe passionately that every one of our colleagues has talent and we therefore invest heavily in developing their skills. We believe greater skills engender greater confidence, greater efficiency and greater levels of service to our customers. Skills are a point of difference for us. Our business prides itself on the freshness of our product, our belief in traditional food skills such as baking and butchery, and the ability of our colleagues to serve our customers well through great training and excellent product knowledge.

THE MORRISONS ACADEMY

5. Our skills development framework continually evolves and we refer to it as our Fresh Food "Academy".

6. Our Academy provides award winning skills development at all levels throughout the business:
   (a) Basic Skills Training for New Entrants.
   (b) QCF level 2 qualifications in Retail Skills for all colleagues.
   (c) Management Development Training from "Shop Floor to Top Floor".
   (d) Young Starters Management Training Scheme.
   (e) Craft Apprenticeships in Bakery and Butchery.
   (f) Modern Retail Apprenticeships.
   (g) Foundation Degrees.
   (h) Pre registration Pharmacist Training.
   (i) Advanced Senior Management Development including MBAs.

7. We work with a variety of learning providers including external assessors of our vocational qualification programmes, colleges for our apprenticeships and the University of Bradford and Leeds Metropolitan University for our degree level, senior management and leadership programmes.

8. Our Apprenticeship programme is well established and has been running for 14 years. We recognised the vital nature of bakery and butchery skills to our business and invested in these programmes against the trend. We currently have 260 apprentices employed on the programme. So far 1,300 colleagues have successfully completed an apprenticeship with us. The programme lasts nine months and apprentices spend four weeks of the programme attending specialist craft food colleges across the country. We currently have 10 of these apprentices in our Welsh stores.

9. Our apprentices have become a key factor in being able to develop the skills we need to successfully grow our business for the long term.

QCF Level Two in Retail Skills

10. Our ambition is to accredit 100,000 colleagues with the level 2 qualification by the end of 2011. It is open to everyone. So far 50,000 colleagues have started on the programme and 24,500 have successfully completed to date. We believe this is the largest programme of its kind in the UK.

11. The programme is mapped against our internal skills development programmes and builds enhanced specialist skills and knowledge for our colleagues and ultimately the benefit of our customers. It takes 26 weeks for a new starter to complete the qualification and a learning provider carries out external assessment and verification of the training and learning.

12. For a large number of our colleagues this is the first qualification they have ever received and it is a significant source of pride and motivation for them and the business. In Wales we have 2,241 colleagues on the programme and of these 1,875 have already successfully achieved their qualification.

13. We currently have 6,500 colleagues on the Modern apprenticeship programme—731 of these are in our Welsh stores. Colleagues can move onto this scheme once they have completed their QCF level 2.

14. We provide a structured investment in skills which we believe makes us successful and this in turn provides excellent career opportunities and job security for our colleagues.

15. Recently Leeds Metropolitan University conducted research into what makes our best people the success that they are. It concluded that our structured approach to developing skills and providing opportunities for colleagues to build their careers has been crucial.

16. One third of our senior manager group (director level) began their careers on the shop floor. In our Retail Division the percentage of store managers being promoted from the shop floor is up to 95%.

17. In the last year we promoted 3,500 people to a higher level role in our business. We believe in growing our own talent, and are convinced the investment in the skills development needed to do this is money well spent. We also believe providing strong and stable employment opportunities is good for the local communities in which our stores and factories are based.

The experience in Wales

18. There is limited funding in Wales to access. However, this is only available to Welsh Training Providers. There is unfortunately, very little provision of both Bakery and Meat training in Wales. For those providers that do offer it, it is not viable for them to take on our relatively small number of colleagues from Welsh stores. Consequently, we have been using colleges in England to train them.

19. The small numbers of colleagues who are put forward for the programme are therefore spread out over several colleges as the funding is not applicable. The colleges put our Welsh colleagues through free of charge and we absorb the cost of transport and accommodation.

RECOMMENDATIONS

20. We would ask that the practice of restricting funding to Welsh providers is only used when a provider is available, and when it is economically viable for them to provide that training. We believe that the funding should follow the candidate, and not the training provider. Given our difficulties in locating a viable solution in Wales our priority must be to offer the training to our colleagues, even if this has to happen in England.

21. We would ask that members of both the UK Parliament and the Welsh Assembly do all they can to promote the worth of retail jobs, both to the economy, and to the individual employee. As mentioned, 95% of our store managers start their career on the shop floor, often in part time roles whilst in education. Store managers look after a workforce often in excess of 300 people, as well as a business with a turnover of close to £50 million per annum. There are few part time jobs where people can develop as quickly and as successfully as retail.

March 2011

Written evidence submitted by Professor Stuart Cole

BASIC HYPOTHESIS

The hypothesis generally put forward is one of: improved journey times, capacity and connectivity (regional, national and global) will improve competitiveness.

Wales competes with many other parts of the European Union for inward investment. Our competitors were once limited to other "western" European countries where labour, production and land costs were not dissimilar to those in Wales.

Wales' now competes with "eastern" European states such as Poland, Lithuania, and Czech Republic where labour costs are as low as 25% of wage rates in Wales.

The entry of those former Soviet Union states into the European Union ended arrangements present in some of them where any inward investor was required to have a domestic partner. The ending of this restriction has made investment even more attractive to inward investors. EU grants (Convergence Fund sourced) are available as they are in parts of Wales.

However these countries do not only have labour cost advantages. They are also adjacent to the so called "golden banana" of Europe—the high GDP area and major consumer market which curves from Milan to south east England via western Germany and Benelux.

Our transport facilities therefore have to be able to help overcome the cost differentials and distances from these markets by become ultra-efficient and influence competitiveness for inward investment as discussed below.

WHICH PARTS OF WALES?

Both the Welsh and UK governments have to consider all options in achieving the best for the future of economic activity in Wales. They are therefore mindful of the impact transport forces both positive and negative on the economies of north, mid and south Wales.

RECEIVED BELIEF

There is a generally held view that transport will increase the chances (probabilities or possibilities) that inward investment or inward tourism will take place because a country or region becomes more competitive compared with other similar locations. This is the view generally put forward by the development agencies of areas wishing to attract investors. The criteria used in such promotional material included journey times (usually by motorway but also by rail if there were good rail freight facilities or if there was a fast train service) and the ability to achieve "just in time" delivery windows.

The A55 investment across north Wales in the 1980s was described by the Secretary of State at the time, Mr Peter Walker, as the "corridor of opportunity". It was this new *Expressway* that would give north Wales particularly the north west of Wales this new opportunity to attract the providers of jobs (ie the inward investors)—be they tourists or manufacturing/service industries.

These transport links and the criteria attached have now been converted into the new "connectivity".

The Ministerial Advisory Group (MAG, 2009) also had a concern about congestion on motorways and major roads and its impact on costs. This involved "restoring capacity and reliability to the east west corridors in south and north Wales that link our key economic concentrations with the rest of the UK and the wider global economy" (pp33–35 Chapter 5 Transport and the Economy).

The MAG also recommended (p38) providing additional domestic connectivity in the priority east—west corridors and in particular, the electrification of the south Wales to London main line to reduce journey times and improve reliability.

MODIFIED VIEW

There is however, also a view that the provision of high quality transport links (efficient connectivity) is not a guarantor of increased competitiveness but is a pre requisite (DETR 1999; Cole 1998, 2005). Without this efficient connectivity it can be hard to "sell" an area in the inward investment job creation market.

The argument that good transport leads to inward investment is not fully proven. Indeed there have been many instances where the building of a new airport has not brought in large numbers of tourists or where a new road or railway has not led to inward investment.

However the absence of such infrastructure has prevented or severely slowed down inward investment or economic regeneration. The conclusion therefore can only be that good transport links for a country such as Wales (on the periphery of Europe) are a pre-requisite, if employment is to grow through inward investment. Manufacturing industry requires the need to deliver on a day to day basis. Inward tourism, a major employer in Wales, has to be competitive in accessibility terms. Ironically those who demand that level of accessibility also come to Wales to enjoy the peace and quiet and beautiful scenery, unhindered by the congestion and pollution (much of it caused by the motor car) of their urban lives. Transport should therefore be a driver of, not a response to, inward investment and subsequent economic growth.

Transport infrastructure—an essential pre-requisite to inward investment?

There is a body of opinion which argues that the availability and reliability of transport links are seen by business as important in achieving high levels of efficiency. Transport infrastructure can play an important part in attracting inward investment, serving more peripheral areas and encouraging economic regeneration.

However there is a potential conflict between business benefits from, for example, increasing, the size of the rail network (in terms of kilometres of track or frequency of trains), and environmental interests which have taken an opposing view. Indeed, the pollution and environmental consequences of new rail (or road) construction, or an enhanced use of either mode, at particular locations can act as a disincentive to economic activity. This may be illustrated by the visual impact of the Channel Tunnel Rail Link (CTRL—HS 1) seen as environmentally negative; but positive in terms of modal split (air to rail) and for journey times between London and Paris.

The view supporting transport infrastructure investment however points to the effects of good quality transport links on competitiveness, on how transport (and congestion) affects costs and the extent to which new infrastructure has reduced costs. The relative weight which companies put on the level of transport costs and the predictability of transport times and schedules will determine how new infrastructure affects business investment and location decisions. This is the link between traffic growth, transport investment in rail or road and inward investment.

In an annual survey for Lloyds Bank/Black Horse Insurance based on responses from 1,000 companies in Great Britain asking which factors were considered the most important in determining the location of industrial or commercial premises. The transport element consistently ranked in the "top 4" overall.

Transport infrastructure investment is not linked to inward investment/economic growth

A number of studies however have demonstrated a lack of a convincing association between transport investment and inward investment. The importance of transport as *the* location determinant has been questioned by European governments who concluded that transport is a secondary consideration in company strategy when deciding where to locate their activities. Other costs, particularly labour, are more of an influence, because transport only accounts for 3–5% of total production costs for many industrial sectors. In 12 countries surveyed, a road link between a developed area and an underdeveloped location improved the traffic flow in two directions and entailed (in a region such as north Wales) a risk of competition from outside and a draining of resources and potential loss of jobs.

One example of this negative move followed the completion of the high quality south Wales road corridor from St Clears in Carmarthenshire to the Severn Bridge. The dual carriageway Expressway (A40/A48) and the M4 Motorway did encourage inward investment. However its construction, coupled with new methods of milk production led to the closure of dairy/creamery facilities at Whitland, St Clears and Carmarthen. Shorter journey times and just in time production saw the bulk haulage of chilled milk from west Wales to a large scale production facility in Gloucestershire processing Welsh and west country milk nearer to the markets of the English west midlands, south east Wales and London and south east England and achieving lower costs of production through economies of scale.

CONCLUSION—SO WHAT ARE THE WIDER ECONOMIC BENEFITS?

Without rail electrification to Bristol, Cardiff and Swansea there will be no additional capacity and there will be a loss of the wider economic benefits in particular employment and economic regeneration in south Wales and the Valleys. If the High Speed Rail 2 to the north of England is built Cardiff will not just be competing with Bristol but also with several other great cities such as Sheffield, Leeds and Birmingham (please see Case Studies 1 and 2 below).

The absence of such infrastructure has prevented or severely slowed down economic growth or economic regeneration. The conclusion therefore can only be that good transport links for Wales (on the periphery of Europe) are a pre-requisite, if employment is to grow through economic regeneration. Manufacturing industry requires the need to deliver on a day to day basis. Inward tourism, a major employer in Wales, has to be competitive in accessibility terms. Transport should therefore be a driver of, not a response to, economic development. The redevelopment of Lille, an old coal mining area gives an indication of the power of transport.

The French Government (SNCF, 2003) determined that the criteria for high speed rail investment would be:

— environmental benefits;

— employment benefits from inward investment;

— commercial elements (such as the decentralisation of economic development, transfer from other modes leading to reduced congestion and overcrowding on roads and other train services, and the decentralisation of public sector employment from Paris); and

— reduced journey time.

The Welsh Transport Planning and Appraisal Guidance (WelTAG) has similar criteria for evaluating road and rail investment particularly in respect of the wider economic benefits. WelTAG also examines impacts on:

— Population age and gender profiles.

— Employment/unemployment.

— Income levels.

— Index of deprivation.

— Regional Gross domestic product.

— Level of economic activity

— Car ownership levels.

— Transport mode distribution.

This reflects the view that *the provision of high quality transport links (efficient connectivity) is not a guarantor of increased competitiveness but is a pre requisite.* Without this efficient connectivity it can be hard to "sell" an area in the job creation market.

These conclusions are illustrated in the case studies below

CASE STUDY 1

INTERNATIONAL COMPETITIVENESS IN THE EUROPEAN CONTEXT

The investment appraisal techniques for new TGV train services in France incorporate employment impacts. However a report indicated that infrastructure does not automatically have positive effects on local development and anyway those events are themselves affected by local influences. The Paris–Lyon TGV service produced considerable journey time savings but did not affect the pattern of economic activity. While some firms in Lyon were able to penetrate the Paris market, industrial and commercial organisations in the French capital began seeing Lyon "as a remote suburb, so that the two areas merge and increase further the peripheral status of the Lyon region" (SNCF, 2003).

Three examples may be considered—Lille (northern France), Lyon (Central France) and Cologne (Germany).

Lille

It was on the basis of the above criteria that the decision was made to route the TGV Nord from Paris to the Channel Tunnel via Lille at the heart of a key (but declining) industrial area, rather than the more direct originally planned route via Amiens.

The rationale was the potential for economic regeneration of an area heavily dependent on industry including coal mining and cotton processing with high unemployment but which had potential to be an international city. The development of the *Lille Europe Centre*, a major commercial centre with offices hotels and a large modern retail centre, built on the site of a military barracks followed the construction of a new station, Lille Europe, reserved for TGV high speed rail services. The frontage has a public park and provides a link to the old city centre which in turn has benefited in economic terms. That investment, in the early 1990s, represented an additional E500m over the direct rail route. The routes to Brussels and Amsterdam were in consequence also diverted via Lille.

In subsequent years further programmes of substantial new building of offices, public housing and a major conference and events hall form part of the long term development plans for the railway station environs. Cotton mills buildings have generated employment through their occupation by local universities while some of the latter's buildings have been converted into regional head offices for multinational companies.

Further expansion is now envisaged by redeveloping a disused railway goods yard with further regeneration in other parts of the conurbation through modernised former industrial buildings.

This has made Lille the fourth most accessible city in a benchmarking research report (EIUA, 2006) comparing Cardiff with other European cities. The report rated Cardiff 34 out of the 51 in terms of connectivity by rail, just above the EU average. As the figure below shows in the sample, it is a position not commensurate with what would be expected of a competitive international capital.

Figure 1

RAIL CONNECTIVITY—CARDIFF'S PLACE IN EUROPE

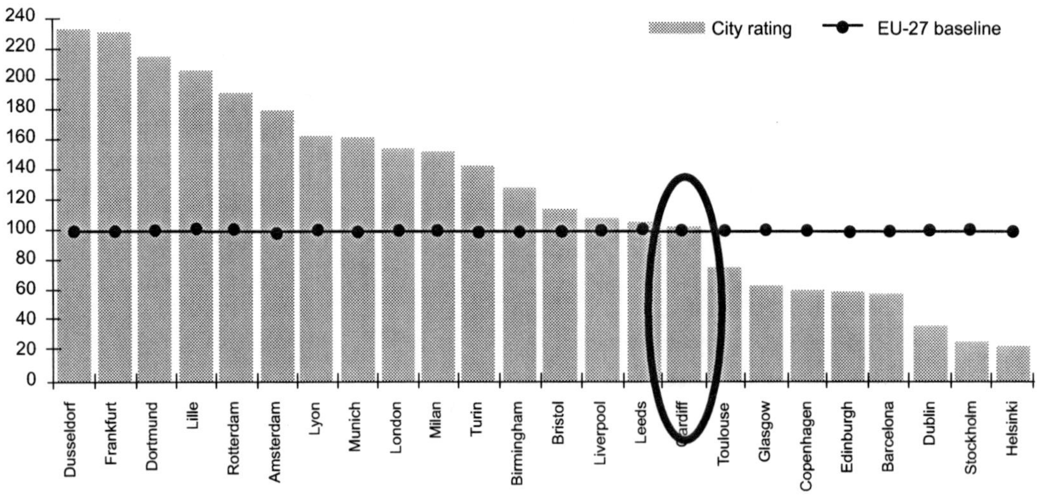

The report also concluded that Cardiff has poor accessibility by air, ranked 47 out of 51 EU cities in the recent EU Urban Audit. The chart below presents a sample of European cities, where Cardiff is next to last. Improved links with London would vastly increase the number of international flight destinations that are realistically available to Cardiff, significantly improving its international.

Lyon

A new TGV station, Lyon part—Dieu was built because of land constraints at the original station and is now a key part of an emerging commercial district. There has been relocation to this new area at a scale which has created its own momentum thus attracting further developments (a form of local agglomeration).

The urban public transport system including the VAL has been developed to enable better access to the new station. New hotels have been built adjacent to the station enhancing an already popular tourist destination but also suggesting that tourists prefer hotels close to their place of arrival.

Cologne

Similar consideration to the French criteria was given by German authorities planning (in 1988) the Brussels–Cologne–Frankfurt high speed corridors. This led to a rebuild of the railway station and the redevelopment of the adjacent "Cologne Fairground" sites to include offices, hotels, and housing. This is seen together with the high speed train access as putting Cologne in a strong position to attract major international events. The station is also a key hub for regional and local public transport services and is linked to the historic centre of the city by pedestrian ways thus extending its economic impact in spatial terms.

CASE STUDY 2

THE ECONOMIC IMPACT OF HIGH SPEED 2 (HS 2)

A series of reports (Sheffield *et al*, 2009; Northern Way, 2009; Arup, 2009; MVA, 2008; Greenguage 21, 2006) has been produced all of which point to the key outputs resulting from the construction of a high speed rail route through different areas in the north of England. The primary output effects identified are:

— Differing rail investment: Impact on economic disparity.

— Removing connectivity constraints between the area and London.

— Potential productivity benefits.

— Substantially reduced journey times/Capacity increases on the existing network to match forecast growth in freight and passenger movement.

— Network accessibility between classic and High Speed railway services.

— Standard transport benefits.

— Supporting sustainable economic growth.

— Appraisal techniques to evaluate the impacts.

— Wider economic benefits (WEB's).

— Agglomeration effects.

Differing rail investment: Impact on economic disparity

The Great Western Main Line corridor running from Carmarthenshire to Slough, (Figure 1) with a population of 4.5 million people currently with economic output at £92 billion is bigger than the individual regional economies of West Midlands, Yorkshire and Humberside the East Midlands, the North East and Northern Ireland. However when the HS 2 corridor is measured in terms of economic output, it is more than twice the size of the total Welsh economy.

Figure 2

THE CORRIDOR IN QUESTION—GREAT WESTERN MAIN LINE CORRIDOR

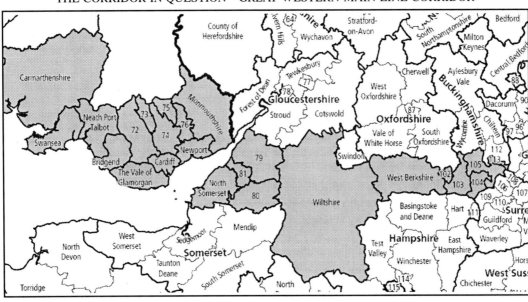

The corridor's location and accessibility to London currently results in its being a competitive and sustainable location with ICT, aerospace and the creative industries as key employment sectors enabling it to be ranked the 4th UK region after south east England, London and eastern England.

A report (Greengauge 21, 2010) assessed the economic impacts of a High Speed Rail (HSR) network which included full specification 320kph HSR links serving most of the UK, but only a 200 kph HSR line between London, Bristol and Cardiff (ie the proposed electrification scheme with line speed increases but on the existing track).

KPMG, the accounting firm, estimated that this network could boost national (UK) annual Gross value Added (GVA) in 2040 by between £17 billion and £29 billion contributing between 25,000 and 42,000 additional jobs in Britain through more productive businesses offering higher wages and attracting additional people into the labour market.

These figures exclude the benefits that south west England and south Wales would gain from a full specification 320kph HSR link, which showed other regions having a significant positive impact upon jobs and economic output.

The report indicated that by merely having a 200kph HSR link, south Wales and south west England could experience a loss of GVA growth in the range of between £2.0 billion and £5.1 billion per annum and a loss of between 49,000 to 149,000 jobs due to lost competitiveness.

These figures demonstrate how a partial "national" HSR network (DfT, 2010) is likely to lead to uneven economic development with central and northern England prospering at the expense of south Wales and the south west of England. A preferred HSR network serving each UK core city and its surrounding region would ensure that the UK economy as a whole can remain globally competitive, and can develop in a sustainable and equitable way.

This is further evidenced from the reports referred to above the outputs from which are summarised below

Removing connectivity constraints between the area and London

This is often seen as the most important benefit to be derived from high speed rail. London is without doubt one of Europe's most important financial centres and it is therefore potentially beneficial for the south Wales economy. Indeed there is considerable emphasis in the report on the benefits for London and Britain's other core cities—in the main the large English conurbations.

Leeds and Sheffield see a fast link to "the national hub of London and international gateways such as Heathrow" as essential particularly as the north east of England and Yorkshire have no direct air links (Sheffield *et al*, 2009; Northern Way, 2009). The East Midlands also sees the HSR as providing links into key international gateways (Arup, 2009) and also supporting business clustering and the development of key sectors of the economy

In their view the constraints affecting connectivity to London has impaired their ability to maximise economic potential. However apparently contradicting that position, they do claim a high rate of economic growth based on knowledge industries.

The benefits to Nottingham, Derby and Leicester are not limited to those for regular commuters as in Kent for example. In the view of the East Midlands RDA, London is at the centre of a "mega" city extending to Swindon, Northampton, Peterborough and Bournemouth with a population of 18.5 million. This is driven by the concentration of activity in central London in the key world city sectors of financial and business services, government and corporate headquarters, creative and cultural tourism and major public services. Many of these activities in law, accounting and business services (strong growth sectors) have been displaced into other centres in outer London and cities where there is a good rail connection. The view taken is that the three English east midlands cities could become part of this "functional economic area" strengthening the economic base providing such services for local as well as London clientele (Arup, 2009).

Potential productivity benefits

Faster journeys on high speed lines achieve productivity benefits in themselves through reduced journey times but bring additional benefits for freight and passenger users on the existing tracks through relieving capacity constraints (Northern Way 2009)

Substantially reduced journey times/Capacity increases on the existing network to match forecast growth in freight and passenger movement

Extra capacity is required to support forecast passenger growth thus reducing the journey times between London and other major centres (Sheffield *et al* 2009). High speed rail could reduce journey times to London from Leeds by up to 30 minutes and from Sheffield by up to 45 minutes. Enhancements to the East Coast Main Line alone will not achieve this for freight and passenger traffic (Northern Way, 2009).

Several of the reports agree that the forecast rate of growth in rail passenger and freight traffic over the next 20 years cannot be catered for with the existing network. HSR will provide that increase on an incremental basis relieving initially those routes from London to Birmingham (and Reading which is not mentioned in any of the north—south proposals).

May 2011

References

MAG (2003) Phase 2 Report on Transport, Ministerial Advisory Group, Welsh Government, Cardiff.

SNCF (2003), Rapport D'Activite Etats Financiers, Societe Nationale des Chemins de Fer, Paris.

EIUA (2006) Cardiff—A Competitive European City? a report by Professor Michael Parkinson and Jay Karecha, (European Institute for Urban Affairs, 2006). *This benchmarked Cardiff against other leading cities in the UK and Europe and considered the factors impinging on future competitiveness.*

Greengauge 21 (2010) Greengauge 21's *Fast Forward* report (September 2010) based on a report by KPMG in January 2010, (*The Fast Forward HSR network included full specification 320kph HSR links serving most of the UK, but only a 200 kph HSR line between London, Bristol and Cardiff*).

Sheffield *et al* (2009) The Case for High Speed Rail—Sheffield, Leeds, Yorkshire. Report by Metro, South Yorkshire PTE, Arup, Volterra.

Northern Way (2009), Transforming our economy and our community—Speed Rail for the North. Moving Forward: The Northern Way. Report by One North East/Northwest RDA.

Arup (2009) The Case for High Speed Rail to the Three Cities. Report for East Midlands RDA (This area covers the Derby, Leicester and Nottingham city regions).

MVA (2008) Appendix J regional and Wider Economic Benefits. Report for Greenguage 21 (MVA and Systra).

Greenguage 21 (2006) Manifesto: The High Speed Rail Initiative. www. Greenguage21.net

DfT (2010) High Speed Rail, Cmnd 7827, HMSO, London (*Primary report of the team led by Sir David Rowlands to evaluate a "national" high speed rail network. Wales and the west of England are completely excluded*)

DETR (1999) Transport and the Economy, the Standing Advisory Committee on Trunk Road Assessment (SACTRA), Department of Environment, Transport and Regions.

Cole, S (1998, 2005) Applied Transport economics (2nd, 3rd editions) Kogan Page, London.

Written evidence submitted by Owens (Road Services) Ltd

1. Owens (Road Services) Ltd is appreciative for the opportunity to be selected to give evidence to the Welsh Affairs Select Committee inquiry into *Inward Investment in Wales (infrastructure)*. We will call upon our 40 years experiences as a haulage company working in Wales with depots in Llanelli, Port Talbot, Bridgend, Newport and Droitwich in the Midlands.

2. Road infrastructure is the bloodline that connects all modes of transportation in Wales, to the rest of the UK and beyond.

3. A fit for purpose road infrastructure, which is both reliable and free flowing is a vital component for business when making a decision to invest or expand in Wales, this important aspect is fundamental in securing future growth for Wales.

4. Of course it is vitally important for the Welsh Economy to indentify the reasons for the down fall in investment however once recognised they need to be acted on to ensure that Wales comes out of this recession better off with a foundation in place to encourage new business opportunities.

5. Wales has two routes, which form part of the Trans European Network [TENs] The M4 Motorway leading on to the A48 and on to the A40 in the south of the country and the A55 in the North. Both Routes are important trade routes that link Ireland to Wales with England and the rest of Europe.

6. The Severn Bridge tolling structure acts as a hindrance to South Wales investment, company's which locate in this region will have to pay the ever increasing toll to transport goods between England and Wales. Vehicle operators which pay these tolls must recoup this additional cost from its customers, the knock on effect of this means that Welsh companies which compete for work in England are doing so with an additional cost to bear, one which their competitors in the Southwest of England do not, this therefore will be a factor for business when looking at where they are able to gain most benefit when relocating or establishing sites.

7. Reliability of the Network through congestion is a major concern not only for Wales, but also for the UK in general. Congestion means longer and less predictable journey times and wasted fuel sitting in traffic that is stationary or slow moving. This is unsustainable as vehicle operators are increasingly paying more to operate their vehicle with fuel now representing a third of all operating costs.

8. In recent years, we have seen major infrastructure projects cancelled by the Welsh Assembly Government (WAG). For example in July 2009 we had the announcement by the Transport Minister for Wales, Ieuan Wyn Jones, that the M4 relief road was to be cancelled due to rising costs, additionally this was followed by the announcement that the connection to the Wales International Airport by means of a dual carriageway from the M4, would also be scrapped. The decision to scrap both of these projects made by the Welsh Assembly Government shows a complete lack of understanding and consideration for the future economic growth of the Nation.

9. The M4, around the Bryn Glas tunnels is one of the most congested parts of the road network in Wales; at peak flow, traffic volumes exceed the capacity of this stretch of road by up to 105%.[3] The Welsh Assembly Government has rightly looked at this problem unfortunately, as we have already highlighted, these plans were scrapped in 2009 with consultants the only winner.

10. The alternative to the aforementioned M4 relief road is the upgrading of the Newport Southern Distribution Road, linking up with the dual carriageway through Llanwern Steel Works Site. Although an alternative, this will reduce peak traffic flows by an estimated 10% on the M4. However, by the time this project is scheduled for completion, traffic volumes are predicted to increase by the same amount, which will again leave the M4 Bryn Glass tunnels stretch of the M4 at peak capacity or beyond.

11. In 2009, the M4 was closed on two occasions around the Bryn Glas tunnels area by the police for fatal road traffic incidents. On both occasions, the M4 was closed for in excess of eight hours. The whole road network ground to a halt as far as Cardiff and up the Valleys reaching the A465 heads of the Valleys road. On both occasions, the financial loss to Owens (Road Services) Ltd exceeded an estimated £20,000 in back log of work and redeliveries as customers could not get to their places of work. It is therefore imperative that this important European route is brought up to an international standard and all routes off the motorway network, which have been recognised as alternatives in emergencies, are fit for purpose.

12. Owens Roads Services reserve judgement on issues appertaining to rail, sea and airport freight movement. However, it is only right and proper to highlight the importance of connectivity to these vital areas of the supply chain. Therefore, an improvement to road infrastructure that connects these areas to the main trade routes is vital.

13. Having the correct rest facilities for HGV drivers is not only a Welsh Assembly concern but also that of the UK Government. Due to regulations that govern the minimum rest requirements of drivers, it is important that rest areas are developed, and are fit for purpose. Rest facilities must offer good secure parking, facilities to wash and eat, any future planning applications for industrial parks, must consider the requirement to offer these services.

---

[3] Traffic Wales.

14. The Welsh Assembly Government must show joined up thinking in relation to road infrastructure with the rest of the UK.

15. As an organisation, we are fully aware of the spending reductions placed upon WAG; however, this should not be used as the reason for lack of investment, but smarter investment in projects that will benefit the Welsh economy as a whole. It is important therefore, the WAG talks to the logistics sector to identify the priorities, some of which are highlighted in this submission.

16. As an active member of both the Freight Transport Association [FTA] and the Road Haulage Association [RHA], we ask that both WAG and Westminster work closely with sector trade associations, such as the Freight Transport Association [FTA] and the Road Haulage Association [RHA] who represents the needs of the freight industry.

May 2011

Written evidence submitted by Milford Haven Port Authority

SUMMARY

— Milford Haven Port Authority is the statutory harbour authority for the port of Milford Haven. It is an independent commercial entity generating turnover of £27.8 million and Profit Before Tax of £7.1 million.

— This submission focuses on the role and benefits of infrastructure investment.

— Whilst it is acknowledged that there are important categories of infrastructure besides ports and energy installations, this submission asserts that ports and energy offer the best opportunity for creating inward investment hubs with strong commercial logic and momentum.

— Milford Haven is the largest port in Wales, and the third largest in the UK. In fact, Milford Haven handles over 70% of all Welsh port traffic—more than twice as much as all other Welsh ports combined and is the UK's leading energy port. Activities include oil and gas, ferries, fishing, cruise, ship repair and marine engineering, and marine leisure.

— Milford Haven has attracted over £2 billion of direct inward investment over the past five years, creating over 300 permanent high skill jobs and substantial levels of associated economic activity.

— The level of investment activity at Milford Haven has been driven by four factors:

  — The port's exceptional depth of water—over 17 million at all states of tide—permitting operational scale and lower cost/lower impact logistics.

  — Quick access to Atlantic trade routes unimpeded by locks.

  — Established and new infrastructure links (5GW electrical grid capacity, gas and fuel pipelines, and rail access).

  — The availability of brownfield sites with existing jetties that reduced the regulatory process time for various approvals.

— Milford Haven is planning a new £multi-million national centre for processing and redistribution of biomass fuels which will be underpinned by the same features—depth of water, location and inland grid and rail links. As the UK's leading energy port Milford Haven is also the ideal location for the construction of new power stations.

— Whilst it would be desirable to comment more generally on infrastructure as a driver for inward investment, it is hard to avoid the established dominance of Milford Haven as a port and centre for the energy industry based on the port's depth of water, its established linkages, the clustering of relevant skills including engineering, the opportunities available, and the levels of recent investment which prove the thesis. No apology is made therefore for the emphasis given to Milford Haven in this submission.

— The one major potential deterrent to similar levels of future inward investment is the complexity and risk of the consenting process, and the experience of the current operators in their attempts to run their operations cost effectively in the face of monolithic systems of regulation driven by self perpetuating bureaucracies. Irrespective of whether major projects have been successfully implemented, there is a substantial risk that Wales in particular (and the UK in general) is developing a growing reputation as a costly and difficult environment in which to manage an established complex operation, and that obtaining consents for major development entails exceptionally high amounts cost, time, and reputational risk to be worth contemplating when compared with the choice of allocating capital to alternative jurisdictions.

— The narrative at the political level may sound encouraging towards inward investment, but is always offset by other discourse focused on regulation and control, the practical effect of which is to block or delay development, impose cost and reduce sustainability.

— The Milford Haven story exemplifies the opportunities inherent in a port focused infrastructure development strategy. The creation of a conducive industrial and development zoning around ports, with comprehensive support for new links—coastal shipping, pipelines, transmission lines, interconnectors, railways, roads and IT—will create the strongest possible private-sector-led inward investment dynamic.

1.0 MILFORD HAVEN PORT

1.1 Since 2007, the Port has attracted over £2 billion of Inward Investment, based on three internationally significant projects:

— Construction of the South Hook LNG terminal.

— Construction of the Dragon LNG terminal.

— Construction of the Pembroke RWE gas-fired powerstation.

1.2 These investments are in addition to substantial new investment by Murco Petroleum in 2010 to increase the capacity of its Pembrokeshire refinery, over £40 million of capital investment by SEM Logistics to upgrade the UK's largest petroleum products storage facility located adjacent to Dragon at Waterston, and over $750 million being invested by Valero to acquire the Pembroke refinery from Chevron. The Chevron transaction of course represents an investment exit as well as an entry.

1.3 These investments were not stimulated or aided by grant funding, but are all based on the commercial logic associated with sound infrastructure investment:

— It is the deep water available within the port (17m+ at all states of tide) that allow the use of large vessels with commensurately lower shipping costs per tonne of cargo moved. It is axiomatic that this also means lower emissions per tonne of cargo moved.

— The port is connected to the market place via the electricity grid and the petroleum products pipeline running from Milford Haven to Birmingham and Manchester. These long established inland links were augmented, in connection with the development of the LNG terminals, by the construction by TRANSCO of a new gas pipeline.

— The recent developments were also based on the availability of appropriate sites.

1.4 In 2010, the Port of Milford Haven had a throughput of 42.9 million tonnes of cargo, principally energy product in the form of LNG and oil products, but also including approximately 1m tonnes of RoRo cargo and 325,000 passengers on the Irish Ferries service from Pembroke Dock Ferry Terminal (owned by MHPA) to Rosslare, as well as the largest volume of fish in any Welsh port.

1.5 This cargo throughput makes Milford Haven Port the third largest port in the UK and represents over 70% of the total seaborne cargo movements for Wales. Milford Haven Port is therefore pre-eminent within Wales, and is the UK's major energy gateway.

1.6 The established infrastructure in the form of berths, pipeline and grid connections, allied with the Port's exceptional depth of water and established skill base is likely to make the Port area a key site for continued inward investment.

2.0 LINKAGES

2.1 The RWE Power Station at Pembroke would not be a viable proposition without the security of supply afforded by the LNG terminals. Equally its go-ahead was dependent on the pre-existence of the unused 400kVA spur and sub-station, essentially lying dormant since the closure of the previous oil-fired power station.

2.2 The fuel and LNG complex at Waterston also houses the new 48MW Milford Energy Cogeneration plant. Taking gas feed from the adjacent LNG complex, it provides electricity to the National Grid, and also provides heat and electricity to the adjacent LNG regassification Dragon LNG terminal. This configuration has succeeded in making the Milford Energy plant possibly the UK's most efficient power station. The thermal efficiency to be derived from regassifying product from −167°c itself makes the case for the creation of additional high efficiency power stations associated with these terminals.

2.3 The LNG berths at South Hook and Dragon are not operating at full capacity. Productivity of the entire gas and fuel product logistics chains would be enhanced (meeting the demand with relatively lower environmental impact) by achieving more intensive utilisation of the berth structures and other infrastructure. The overall pressure for increased sustainability and productivity is likely to make Pembrokeshire an attractive, if not essential location for investment in additional new electricity generating capacity.

2.4 Investment in new under-sea electricity connections from Pembrokeshire to Anglesey and from Pembrokeshire to Ireland will spur additional inward investment into value added operations within Wales and lead to the desired intensification of use of existing marine infrastructure.

2.5 The presence of the refineries, and indeed the gas terminals, has sustained a substantial cluster of high skill engineering companies which have gone on to compete in international markets for other fabrication projects. This successful sector, itself leading to the sustainable employment of over 500 highly skilled technicians, would be jeopardised were the refineries to close.

2.6 The revenues generated by the Milford Haven Port Authority from the consequential growth in shipping activity are enabling MHPA to make its own substantial plans for an investment programme in new and related commercial sectors. These plans include:

— Investment to develop Milford Docks into a regional centre for the marine leisure and fishing industries—Milford Docks is the largest fishing port in Wales and contains a 328 berth marina.

— Investment to support the expansion of Pembroke Port's boat building, ship repair, and other marine engineering businesses. Crucially this involves providing construction and assembly areas for participants in the renewable energy sector (tidal and wind).

— Investment to develop a new deep water facility to create a national facility for the handling of biomass as a key step to enable this sector to develop on a commercial basis.

3.0 EMPLOYMENT AND ECONOMIC CONTRIBUTION

3.1 MHPA has commissioned from Cardiff University an employment and economic impact study in relation to the Port of Milford Haven. It is expected to be available later in the year and to show that the port is directly responsible for over 2,000 high skill jobs in Pembrokeshire.

3.2 MHPA and the terminals based on the Haven spend over £100 million on supplies and services within the Welsh economy.

3.3 The Construction of the two LNG terminals and Pembrokeshire Power Station created over 3,400 construction jobs (short term) at peak.

4.0 GOVERNMENT AND POLICY INPUTS

4.1 Milford Haven Port can be taken as a case study for drawing general conclusions about Infrastructure as a key driver for Inward Investment and job creation within Wales: Milford Haven is not just another port, it is the pre-eminent port in Wales handling 70% (as stated) of Wales' port throughput. The scope for Milford Haven with its substantial depth of water to attract Inward Investment is fully proven. The Investment over recent years has been driven entirely by sound commercial judgements based on the beneficial impact the use of the Port and its associated infrastructure (which includes the electricity and energy pipelines) can have on the major players' global logistics chains.

4.2 As such it should receive a specific focus from government. The key input from government to make these projects happen has been the policy support and, simplistically, the granting of relevant planning and other consents within acceptable timeframes.

4.3 In some respects the investment is happening despite rather than because of government efforts. Inward Investors are driven by fear, as well hope. Regardless of the successes, any and all negative stories—eg about the complexity and timeframe required for securing a consent, day to day frustrations in connection with regulation and inspection, including the issue of standard operational licenses, the tone of political discourse and policy and all other negative encounters with the state in the broadest possible sense—can all too easily result in international companies deciding to invest their money in more supportive jurisdictions. Milford Haven Port, and all ports in Wales, are not only in competition with nearby ports but with all the major ports in Europe and elsewhere in the world.

4.4 For example, the current message in relation to the installation of a second gas pipeline connecting Milford Haven to the inland market place is that it will take seven years to deliver. If this timescale was instead two years, there would already be matching inward investment plans for the construction of additional berth capacity and tank storage.

4.5 As a further illustration, WAG's recent consultation document on the evolution of Marine Spatial Planning listed the relevant European Legislation and existing Welsh plans policies and strategies (to which the Welsh Marine Spatial Plan will duly be added) and went on to make the questionable assertion that the final outcome of the work they are doing in 2011 to 2012 would be a *clear* set of national priorities.[4] The list of consequential UK legislation is equally daunting.

4.6 The consenting framework is overly complex, and of itself imposes massive risk in terms of:

— The difficulty of bringing together a site, a plan, a customer contractual commitment, lending and finance commitments, and holding this matrix together for years whilst pursuing all necessary consents.

— The cash cost and risk of planning and obtaining all necessary consents.

— Reputational risk.

---

[4] The relevant extracts are available here—pp 22–23 and pp 26–27
http://wales.gov.uk/docs/desh/consultation/110216marineconsultationen.pdf

4.7 Inward Investors can only embark on such projects having first obtained absolute security in relation to a site, via ownership or an option.

4.8 Policy should therefore be directed towards defining inward investment zones where consent can be made progressively more straightforward and investors are able to focus on specific large scale and general purpose sites.

4.9 This is essentially what ports and airports are.

5.0 SUSTAINABLE DEVELOPMENT

5.1 Objections to any port development will always be based on the local impact. This must be set against the role of a sustainable port development in reducing the cost and environmental impact of the entire logistics chain using the port.

5.2 This is particularly the case for Milford Haven with commensurate environmental benefits:

— With depth of water enabling the use of larger ships, the cost and emissions for every tonne of cargo shipped is reduced.

— Users of the port are able to operate on a very large scale.

— The port is well located for the onwards coastwise shipment of processed product to other ports in the UK and Europe and for shipment to the United States.

— The total impact, in terms of reduced cost of energy and security of supply have a significant impact on the competitiveness and sustainability of the UK economy.

— The piled jetty structures prevalent in the Haven and which would be required for further inward investment opportunities do not impede the flow of water and have negligible discernable impact on the local marine habitats particularly by reference to natural waterway dynamics; to the extent there is any impact, this is more than offset by the wider environmental benefits of a more productive logistics chain stretching from the point of origin of the cargo through to the proverbial light switch.

5.3 Locating value-adding operations away from ports inevitably introduces a substantial and permanent deviation penalty on manufacturers. This has led to the growing support for the principle of "port-centric logistics". An important factor underpinning this dynamic is that the port is usually the point of contractual delivery by the supplier to the customer for many cargo shipments. This means that ports (and, by implication, airports) are a natural point in the overall logistics chain for receivers to inspect their cargos and begin the process of adding value.

5.4 In addition to pipeline, rail and electricity links, Milford Haven needs effective communication links. This is essential if professional management functions are to be co-located with the installations themselves. The motorway/dual carriageway road network stops 30 miles short at St Clears, mainline rail services stop at Swansea, and the IT network is under-invested, offering insufficient bandwith and speed.

6.0 CONCLUSION

6.1 Ports and their associated transport links have consistently proven their ability to be the leading driver of substantial Inward Investment.

6.2 The logic we imply for ports is as relevant for other types of key infrastructure investment (airports, roads, railways, IT), but the key feature of ports is that they constitute a natural development zone for value added activity. Handling over 70% of Wales sea-borne cargoes and offering 17 million operational depth of water at all states of tide, Milford Haven is particularly important in this regard.

6.3 Port Centric Logistics is a key driver for establishing logistics chains with lower overall environmental impacts.

6.4 The impressive inward Investments in Milford Haven in recent years have all occurred without grant support, although that is not to deny that grant support is sometimes essential, particularly if such grants are available in rival jurisdictions.

6.5 The one step we look for to stimulate further inward investment into ports generally and Milford Haven in particular is a fully supportive fast track, and vastly simplified planning, consenting and regulatory environment. There is no balance in the current position, and there is no other single outcome that would have a greater and more profound impact on the scope for Infrastructure Investment to drive the Welsh economy.

May 2011

Supplementary written evidence submitted by Milford Haven Port Authority

I would like to thank you and your committee for the opportunity to appear before your committee earlier this week. I found it a very useful and informative discussion, and hope you found us strongly supportive of the work you are doing to investigate the issues relating to Inward Investment into Wales.

I would like to offer one final thought for the consideration of the committee. Infrastructure underpins everything. It ultimately is what drives growth in productivity and provides the ability for individuals and commercial operators to link to service providers, customers and job markets. There was nothing wrong, in my view, with the policy of Predict and Provide as it led directly to continuous investment in infrastructure in an entirely constructive way. This point was emphasised in the discussion by the various comments that it is incredibly difficult to make a commercial justification for investment, as commercial criteria require there to be a guaranteed or nearly guaranteed demand. Predict and Provide on the other hand leads to investment which at that point in time cannot be wholly justified, but requires something of a leap of faith. However the inevitable consequence is that it stimulates productivity growth and consequently boosts the economy in a very broad and fundamental way. This encapsulates the core driver of economic growth in the entirety of the post war period, whether you are talking about roads, railways, Telecoms and IT and, indeed, ports.

There could be no better use of sparse funds than to put them into infrastructure. Other issues such as skills are quickly sorted out and addressed by companies once they have taken a decision to invest, but the one thing companies cannot deliver and look to government to provide is the core infrastructure to support their trading.

In any event, it was a great pleasure to have the opportunity to participate in the discussion, and I look forward to the final report with great interest. Please pass on my thanks to your committee colleagues, and allow me to extend an open invitation to come and find out for themselves what Milford Haven is about whenever time allows.

May 2011

Written evidence submitted by Sir Roger Jones OBE

Despite being probably the best known and most effective Industrial Development Agency in Europe, the Welsh Assembly Government saw fit to disband the WDA in 2006, and transfer its functions to the Civil Service in Wales. My pleadings at the time went unheeded. I stated publicly that it would take three years for WAG to realise its mistake, a further three years to decide what to do and three more years to implement change. This would sentence Wales to nearly 10 years in the wilderness in terms of industrial development. To this day, I stand by my prediction. We have seen expenditure in excess of £100 million per annum that has produced next to nothing in the form of outcomes.

Why did this happen? I hold that it was political expediency. A rivalry amongst political leaders as to who could best deliver the "bonfire of the quangos" precipitated this summary action. The single factor which differentiates the public and private sectors is the propensity to take risks. The Public sector is risk averse, as is the majority of its hierarchy. A profit is nothing more than a reward for taking a risk. If the system demands a completeness of information prior to a decision, it will probably take too long and the opportunity will have passed.

The WDA was successful because it insulated politicians and civil servants from risk. In its heyday, probably 50% of its employees were inward facing, providing levels of comfort at the interface with Government. The other half were managing the interface with the private sector. Simplistically and possibly accurately, the public sector were seen as the wealth destroyers and the private sector as wealth creators. In the post-WDA era, it became evident that the management controls which were applied made the interface with the wealth creators dysfunctional.

The WDA was far from perfect. There were areas of dysfunctionality particularly in overseas representation, mostly due to poor selection of individuals for overseas positions. The imperative to have a spread of offices in all continents was flawed. The concept of being a "one stop shop" for all industries was flawed. There was insufficient selectivity in the technologies sought, and poor integration with Universities in Wales despite some heroic efforts. There was too much emphasis on the role of grants. It is the availability of skills and markets that create job.

On reflection, the absence of a strategic vision at Ministerial level was debilitating. The driver was the safety of the civil service position, not the outcomes in terms of wealth creation. The Board of the WDA was never able to transcend the relative inexperience of its paymasters.

What might be done to secure the improvements that the Welsh Nation so desperately deserve. Trapped with GDP per capita at around 75% of UK average, the status quo is not acceptable. Some kind of arm's length agency is essential if Industrial Development is to be achieved. This has to be in position by the time the economy starts to recover.

Without resurrecting the WDA, there is an opportunity to start again with a smaller, more focused and independent body. This should be controlled by a private sector board with strong trade union representation, for without new skills the transition of the economy will be impossible. The Board will set strategy and evaluate outcomes.

The functions to be covered by the new organisation are as follows:

(A) global technology tracking with close liaison with Welsh Universities;

(B) knowledge of investment sources and finance;

(C) knowledge of Manufacturing and skills in Quality Assurance;

(D) experience in selecting target technologies (energy, life sciences and high added value tourism);

(E) capacity and flexibility to follow other leads;

(F) limited overseas representation but to include BRIC and development of remote networking for liaison with international contacts;

(G) leading edge interactive web representation, which provides real access to appropriate personnel;

(H) high level internal audit;

(I) competent HR to attract key players from competitors;

(J) effective marketing and brand creation; and

(K) limited regional representation in Wales.

These functions would be represented on the Management Board. Interface with Welsh Government would be via the Main Board. This would limit the scope for micromanagement and introduction of new initiatives by the civil service. Success will be achieved only by limiting the dead hand of public sector control. However the Board would be fully accountable to the Government of Wales and would report with whatever frequency that was required.

If the above functionality is broadly acceptable, it would be worked up into a structure and format, capable of being fully costed. My estimate is that much could be achieved with an annual expenditure of £50 million, to include £10 million initial marketing spend.

June 2011

Written evidence submitted by Airbus

COMPANY PROFILE

— Airbus is a global company, the world's leading aircraft manufacturer. Airbus consistently captures approximately half of all orders for airliners with more than 100 seats. In 2010, Airbus achieved a 50.7% share of the global market. Airbus in the UK is world-renowned for its centres of excellence for both wing design, integration and manufacture.

— Airbus has two UK sites located at Filton, near Bristol, and Broughton, in North Wales. Its total combined workforce is around 10,000 people. These sites are responsible for wing research and technology development, wing design, manufacture, management of the wing supply chain and wing integration. The two sites are also responsible for fuel systems and landing gear integration.

— The Broughton factory is widely acknowledged to lead the world in the manufacture of large civil aircraft wings. The principal focus at Broughton is on high value adding tasks that include the long-bed machining of large-scale components, such as wing skins, or panels, and stringers, which are used to fasten the skins together. The site is also responsible for the assembly and equipping of complete wings.

— Any audit of UK technological performance would rank the Airbus wing technology developed over the last three decades as among the country's most significant achievements. This has given the UK and Europe a lead in wing technology that has played a major role in the market success of Airbus.

— Airbus is a wholly owned subsidiary of EADS (European Aerospace and Defence Systems). EADS employs around 116,000 people worldwide and has over 70 production sites in places like France, Germany, Spain, United States, China and Australia.

AIRBUS IN WALES

The Broughton based factory has a long history. In 1935, the Government unveiled the "Shadow Factory Scheme", designed to move vital industries to remote areas in the North of the country. In 1937, the Broughton site was chosen to build a plant capable of producing Wellington bombers, thanks to clear, year round test flying conditions.

This factory was financed by the Government, but was leased to and managed by Vickers-Armstrongs Chester.

Since then, the factory has passed successively from Vickers-Armstrongs to de Havilland, Hawker Siddeley, British Aerospace, and BAe systems. In 2001, Airbus was formally incorporated into a joint stock company, with BAe Systems owning a 20% share, and EADS owning the further 80%. In 2005 BAe Systems sold its 20% share to EADS and Airbus became a wholly owned subsidiary. Since 1971, over 6000 Airbus wing sets have been produced at Broughton.

Today, the Broughton site employs over 6,000 people (permanent and temporary), more than half of whom live in Wales. Its annual salary bill to Welsh resident employees is around £100 million per annum. Airbus provides its employees with secure, long term employment. For example 30% of employees have 15 years or more experience and 10% with 25 years or more experience within the company.

The 700 acre site has seen significant inward investment. Excluding R&D, Airbus has invested over £1.86 billion into the Broughton site during the last 10 years, to create a state-of-the-art, high tech, innovative and modern facility.

A number of key suppliers are based in or near the Airbus site in Broughton. Businesses such as Metal Improvement Company, Electroimpact and Hawker Beechcraft all have a manufacturing presence on site. Aerotech and Gardner both have facilities based on the adjacent business park, which was established with the support of the Welsh Government.

It is estimated that as a result of the supply chain impact, in addition to the 6,000 directly employed Broughton workforce, a further 2,000 people are employed by suppliers to Airbus, located on, or in close proximity to the Broughton site.

Thus, Flintshire is recognised by many as the "engine" of the North Wales economy and has established Airbus as a key component of the wider UK economy. To that end, Airbus' Welsh supply chain is also worth nearly £121 million per annum.

Airbus is currently in the preliminary stages of enhancing its engineering skills base at Broughton. Indeed, 25 fully qualified engineers have started at Broughton since January 2011, with a planned recruitment of a further 25 before the end of the year.

Skills in Wales

Airbus currently employs almost 400 apprentices at its Broughton site, with a further 20 based in Filton. Not only is the scheme recognised internally (70% of senior managers at Airbus started their careers as apprentices), but also externally. For example, the Sector Skills Council for Science, Engineering and Manufacturing Technologies (Semta) recognised the Airbus apprenticeship as a "model progression route".

Due to the high tech nature of the industry in which Airbus operates, training and skills support is a fundamental part of business activity. Therefore, Airbus has developed close relationships with a number of universities and further education colleges in order to ensure that the workforce is equipped with the correct skills set for current, and future business needs. Typically, all first year apprentices will attend Deeside College, where tuition and training costs are provided by the Work Based Learning and Further Education budget from the Welsh Assembly Government. Partnerships between Airbus and local education institutes, such as Glyndŵr University, allow for the progression from foundation degrees, to Masters degrees, and eventually full Chartership.

In 2009–10, in order to provide flexibility for potential market downturns and thus a shortage in immediate full time employment opportunities within Airbus, the company worked with the Welsh Assembly Government and trade unions to extend the apprenticeship period by one year. This allowed Airbus to equip trainees with the new skills sets needed for the A350 XWB programme.

The craft and higher apprenticeship represents an individual investment of £55,000 and £75,000 respectively, over a period of three years.

Airbus also operates a two-year graduate programme which employs around 60 graduates each year. The company is in The Times Top 100 Graduate Employers.

The research relationship between Airbus and UK-based universities is very strong. The company has research and development links with 35 UK universities, including Bath, Bristol, Cranfield, Imperial, Cardiff and Glyndŵr. The main mechanisms for partnership with universities include: direct research contracts; sponsorship of PhDs; support to university bids for funding from the Engineering and Physical Sciences Research Council (EPSRC); as well as inclusion of Universities in TSB and EU supported collaborations.

In January 2011, the aerospace market had improved so much that against the background of improved market conditions the business was able to award permanent Airbus contracts to 770 former Blue Arrow employees, who had formed the basis of the complementary workforce at Broughton. Unite the union commented on the announcement "Unite is pleased to have reached an arrangement with Airbus, which will see 770 Blue Arrow workers offered permanent Airbus employment. We hope the new labour agreement will ultimately result in more permanent Airbus jobs in future."

Skills development of its workforce is key to Airbus' success. Operators training to work on the A350XWB will pass through demo boxes. A demo box is a full scale representation of a jig that Airbus would use in a production environment. They allow Airbus to trial new manufacturing and tooling techniques as they provide an accurate representation of what one might expect when production starts.

Last year Broughton spent over 71,000 man hours training its employees. Excluding apprentices, this represents an investment of around one million pounds.

RELATIONSHIP WITH GOVERNMENT

Airbus has a strong relationship with the UK and Welsh Government's, and is committed to maintaining this. Through site visits, Airbus management aims to provide key government stakeholders with up to date information regarding latest orders, economic impact and employment figures. Cabinet and Shadow Cabinet ministers, MPs and AMs have all visited Broughton in recent months.

Recently, the Rt. Hon. George Osborne MP visited Airbus and said:

"Airbus is incredibly important to the UK economy, and is one of the best companies in the whole of the UK. What's great is the enthusiasm amongst apprentices and their self confidence that they are doing the right thing, not just for their career, but also in making a valuable contribution to the broader economy".

The week before, the Rt. Hon. Ed Balls MP visited and said:

"Lessons should be learnt from Airbus—It is an example of a business that invests in skills". This kind of cross party support is essential to Airbus.

The Business, Innovation and Skills Department (BIS) is the primary interface for corporate issues with Airbus. Regular meetings and site visits ensure all issues are aired. Airbus often provides BIS and UKTI with updates on key sales campaigns around the world and the Government regularly shares information on sales missions being co-ordinated. Over the last few years this process has been tightened up and Airbus is always keen to find when Ministers are on visits to other countries as far in advance as possible. This gives Airbus the opportunity to provide a briefing or facilitate events or visits. Other governments share the planning of their Ministers more extensively.

With the expansion of aerospace manufacturing elsewhere in the world, the support provided by the UKTI will be even more significant.

Repayable Launch Investment, which was provided for the A320, A330/340 and A380 projects, is an income generator for the UK taxpayer. On the A320 programme for example, repayments by the company have already been more than three times the amount initially provided by the Government.

Airbus represents itself in a number of government forums, including the Welsh Business Advisory Group and the BIS Skills and Retention Group.

There is also an Airbus presence in a number of trade bodies, which include the Aerospace Leadership Council, the Technology Strategy Board, the CBI, Semta, ADS, and the Aerospace Sector Strategy Group (Semta/ADS). Airbus senior management tend to play a prominent role in these groups, often acting as a Chairman or board members.

Airbus has been awarded "Anchor Company" status by the Welsh Government. Whereas the term is not a formal designation, it is used to recognise high-growth businesses with a significant corporate presence in Wales. This entitles Airbus to a high level, strategic relationship with the Welsh Government, resulting in a close cooperation between the public and private sector.

Within this context, Gareth Jenkins, Advanced Materials and Manufacturing Sector Chair, recently visited the Advanced Composite Training and Development Centre in Broughton to view the site at first hand and gain an appreciation of some of the business issues faced.

Broughton is located in a "Tier 2 Assisted Area". This has enabled Airbus to secure support for some major capital investment projects.

Airbus values its close relationship with the UK and Welsh Governments, and is mindful of being a prime recipient of Welsh Government support. However due to the current economic climate, and the changes highlighted in the Welsh Government's "One Wales Agreement", Airbus will be keeping a watchful eye on how the new policies develop.

June 2011

Written evidence submitted by GE Aviation, Wales

BACKGROUND

Every two seconds a GE powered aircraft takes off somewhere in the world.

Over 1,350 people work at the GE Aviation site in Nantgarw, just outside Cardiff in South Wales, overhauling and repairing a range of engine product types and associated components. Today, GE Aviation in Nantgarw occupies 1.2 million square feet of workshop space and handles more than 400 engines a year in its two state of the art test facilities that ensure the engine can go into service immediately once back to the customer. Over the past three years, export earnings have nearly doubled totalling over $1.9 billion.

The highly skilled workforce, which in 2010 expanded to include 100 engineering apprentices and 42 interns for finance, commercial and engineering roles, need only 45 days to completely overhaul an engine. GE Aviation Wales supports Emirates, Continental, Etihad, and a range of other global customers.

The business overhauls the following engines:

— the GE90—the world's most powerful aircraft engine, weighing 18,260 lbs and measuring 135″ in diameter;

— the complete range of CFM56 engines: the world's most popular aircraft engine with nearly 18,000 in operation worldwide; and

— the GP7000, the engine that powers the new Airbus A380.

WHAT HAPPENS TO THE ENGINES?

On receipt, each engine is internally inspected. Then the engine is disassembled—first of all into modules and then right down to individual piece parts. Each part of the engine is then cleaned and then inspected for serviceability using various methods, involving magnetic particles, fluorescent dyes, X-rays and other technologies.

Parts are then repaired or replaced via GE Aviation's global specialist repair network. Once these processes have been completed the engine is rebuilt, into modules and then the complete engine. Once built the engine is then tested before being re-installed to an aircraft.

CORPORATE SOCIAL RESPONSIBILITY

GE Aviation Wales has a strong culture of volunteering with hundreds of employees engaged in working with local schools, or taking part in activities such as the GE Welsh 3 Peaks Challenge, which raised over £200,000 for local charities in 2010.

GE Aviation has also achieved the Global Star Award for world class health, safety and environmental performance—over half the employees are active throughout the site promoting safety and environmental standards. The business has also recently been awarded the Carbon Trust Standard, reflecting the achievements in carbon reduction.

The business is also a key sponsor and organiser of Gemau Cymru. A schools' Olympic Games in Wales which is designed to be a lasting legacy of the 2012 Olympic Games.

QUEEN'S AWARD FOR ENTERPRISE IN INTERNATIONAL TRADE

GE Aviation Wales have been awarded the Queen's Award for Enterprise in International Trade 2011 after three years of continued success for the site which is the biggest GE facility in the UK, and one of the biggest employers in Wales.

The site has seen substantial growth in terms of employee numbers and earnings over the past three years. The site's managing director, Adrian Button, said; "The top four markets for our work at GE Aviation Wales are the Middle East, North and South America and China. We are delighted to receive the Queen's Award—a recognition that is testament to the dedication, success and outstanding contributions of the entire team."

WHY WALES?

As an anchor company, GE Aviation Wales has a strong and productive relationship with the Welsh Government. Although we do have some reservations regarding the composition and role of the sector panels (for example, there do not appear to be any aerospace representatives when this is widely regarded as a key sector in Wales) we are very keen to continue to play an active part in helping to promote inward investment.

Naturally we are very interested to see what economic strategy generally will emerge from the new administration and, in particular, what relationships are proposed with schools and universities to ensure that business is provided with the relevant education and skills that it needs to prosper.

The reasons for GE Aviation investing in Wales are clear.

People: the availability of a skilled workforce;

Infrastructure: accessible links to Europe and the Rest of the World;

Training: strong links with universities and academia; and

Government Support: without Welsh Government support the GE90 product would not have been brought to Wales. It is key that this support continues in order for the business to secure further investment for future expansion into additional products.

June 2011

Written evidence submitted by Professor Siân Hope, Bangor University

INTRODUCTION AND AIM

This document aims to place Bangor University in its socioeconomic context both at a regional and city level, discuss the history of inward investment in this part of Wales, an area that has not experienced the large scale influx and outflow of international corporations, and to discuss the economic impact and role Bangor University can and does play as one of the largest employers in the area. Finally the research strategy of the university is outlined, with a number of key projects highlighted—projects that have a direct impact on interactions with enterprises and a possible bearing on future inward investment to the region.

SOCIOECONOMIC CONTEXT

1. Bangor University is located in North West Wales, an area that is rural in nature with a number of towns and small villages where the economy is largely dependent on traditional agriculture and service sector industries with a small representation in production industries.[5]

2. There are trends towards an aging population with outward migration of people aged 20–29, inward migration of older groups (50–64 years old), and a diminishing birth rate. Outward migration of young people is a particular problem for Anglesey.

3. The University straddles the border of the counties of Gwynedd and Anglesey, within a region attracting EU Convergence structural funds. GVA data for Gwynedd show an area which is not monetarily successful but relatively robust compared to other areas in "West Wales and the Valleys".[6]

4. In 2008, mean GVA/head was £13.7k in Gwynedd and £11.3k in Anglesey, ranked 10th and 22nd (lowest) respectively. The Welsh average was £15.2k, and the joint highest £22.2k (Cardiff and Vale of Glamorgan).[7]

5. Within Gwynedd, this GVA gap can be explained largely by lower value-added employment whereas in Anglesey it is a combination of this, together with lower employment rate and a higher proportion of workers who commute out of the locality for work.

6. Unlike North East Wales which has a relatively high number of large employers, the North West economy is dominated by small and micro businesses. Of the 6,250 VAT/PAYE registered enterprises in Gwynedd, 85% are micro-businesses employing <10 and only 15 enterprises employ 250 or more. The picture is similar in Anglesey. By contrast, of its 12,035 units, Cardiff has 110 large enterprises, with 10 of them employing 1,000 or more.

7. Whilst the lack of large inward investment projects has meant that this region has been less heavily impacted by large scale redundancies, the north of Anglesey has been heavily impacted by the closure of Anglesey Aluminium in 2009 with the loss of over 500 jobs, and expects to be further impacted when Wylfa nuclear power station ceases generation in late 2012.

8. In 2010 Horizon Nuclear announced that the existing Wylfa site was its preferred location for a new build and it is intended that the six-year construction period would commence immediately planning permission is awarded. This is estimated to generate around 5,000 construction jobs.

9. The eventual operation and maintenance of the proposed 3,300 Megawatt station from 2020 would generate an initial 800 permanent jobs rising to about 1,000 and would bring in about £8 billion to the local economy. Clearly this is a very important development for North West Wales, Bangor University and local Further Education establishments.

10. A recently-launched strategy, "Anglesey Energy Island", which seeks to capitalise on the above developments and on the diversity of renewable energy opportunities afforded by wind, tidal and biomass, is supported by local stakeholders including Anglesey and Gwynedd Councils, the Welsh Government and Bangor University.

---

[5] Office of National Statistics (2006) Workplace employment in Wales by industry, 2001–04 (as cited in Convergence Operational Programme—ERDF 2007–13).

[6] Trends in Gwynedd, Gwynedd Council Research and Information Unit, September 2010. (p8).

[7] Op Cit (p17).

11. The university is located in an area designated the "Môn a Menai Hub" in the Wales Spatial Plan (WSP).[8] Bangor is a key settlement which is of importance to Gwynedd and Anglesey, and a socioeconomic hub for the region.

12. The WSP states a vision for Môn a Menai as "a high-quality natural and physical environment supporting a cultural and knowledge-based economy that will help the area to maintain and enhance its distinctive character, retain and attract back young people and sustain the Welsh language."[9]

13. The area is firmly bilingual. Gwynedd has the highest numbers of Welsh speakers in Wales (83%), with Anglesey a close second (79%).[10]

14. The proximity of the university is important to the Môn a Menai spatial strategy which cites the following as one of its aims:

— Developing an outward-looking and confident knowledge based economy, with particular emphasis on bio-sciences, geosciences, environmental goods and services, marine science, medical technology, renewable energy, nuclear decommissioning technologies and creative industries, recognising the key role Bangor University has in supporting this and seeking to ensure that the benefits are derived across the region.

15. Bangor University is also important to Gwynedd Council's economic strategy (2010–13) which has within it the following aims:

— To co-operate with Bangor University and the Betsi Cadwaladr University Health Board in order to prepare plans to establish a Medical and Technology Campus in Bangor. This would instigate the growth of business clusters in the fields of health and technology.

— Co-operate with Anglesey County Council in order to agree on a programme to maximise the benefit to the economy of the North West through the new development of Wylfa B and the decommissioning process.

— The impending end of power generation at Wylfa in Anglesey and the end of phase one decommissioning of Trawsfynydd in Gwynedd could further widen the existing gap in economic performance as measured by gross value added (GVA) between the region and the rest of Wales. However job creation potential could be achieved via extended and new low-carbon power generation in the Eryri and Môn Spatial Plan Area.

16. The proportion of full time jobs in Gwynedd is lower than in Wales and the UK, with employment in the service sector much higher (86% of all jobs in 2008). The economy in NW Wales is dominated by the public sector, especially within Gwynedd, which has a much higher level of employment in Public Administration, Education and Health (37% total in 2008, compared with 33% all Wales).

17. The UK government cuts to public services are only just beginning to take effect, and have not yet had widespread impact. However, uncertainty around HE funding has led to recruitment freezes within the university itself.

18. Self-employment is also important in N Wales, and traditional sectors such as agriculture are declining slightly. Diversification is becoming increasingly important.

History of Inward Investment in NW Wales

19. The past 20 years have seen few large inward investment projects of note; however, it could be argued that the few exceptions have been of a high quality, and unlike other parts of Wales which have in the past evidenced a "branch plant economy", those companies that have invested in NW Wales have demonstrated a long term commitment to the area. Examples are healthcare diagnostics provider Siemens, which has a base in Llanberis employing around 600 staff, and which recently took the decision to invest in and expand this plant in preference to the larger site in Los Angeles, and RWE-NPower, which operates a number of wind farms on Anglesey and is currently planning to build the new Wylfa nuclear power station (through a joint venture with E:ON known as "Horizon Nuclear").

20. Bangor University's relationship with Siemens has been informal, indirect and primarily in regard to provision of graduate level employees to the company. The Llanberis site is largely focused on manufacturing, quality assurance, technical support and distribution, with no new product research and development taking place. There is therefore less scope for a relationship based on a research driven interaction, although discussions have taken place in relation to executive management training through the university's Management Centre.

21. In passing, it should be noted that Siemens has produced or helped catalyse a number of small spin-out ventures that are still operating in North West Wales, all within the medical technology and precision engineering sectors, and who were in some cases part of the supply chain for Siemens. This has been an

8   http://wales.gov.uk/about/programmeforgovernment/strategy/spatial/?lang=en (accessed 27 May 2011).
9   Peoples, Places, Futures: The Wales Spatial Plan Update 2008.
10 Welsh Language Board, Language Use Surveys 2004–06 (2008).

example of a successful large enterprise creating new opportunities for predominantly local individuals, who have seized the entrepreneurial opportunity afforded them.

22. On a smaller scale, Bangor University has been instrumental in attracting software and technology-based companies to the area through the Technium CAST building based on Parc Menai, a business park located to the west of Bangor. A gaming company chose Bangor as a location for both international support and software development because of the availability of suitable business accommodation, a ready supply of qualified graduates (software and languages) and the prospect of a relationship with the university's School of Computer Science.

23. The university, through its membership of Anglesey Energy Island, is strengthening existing relationships with Magnox North Sites and with Horizon Nuclear in regard to future opportunities for knowledge exchange and accredited programmes.

24. An inward investment project that has also had links with the university School of Computer Science is The Book People. The company provides employment for around 400 in Bangor and it should be noted that the company does not fit neatly into any of the six priority sectors targeted for support by the Welsh Government. Concern has been expressed that companies who do not see themselves as fitting the six sectors may be put off from considering Wales as an inward investment destination.

25. Those with direct experience of managing inward investment in NW Wales have stated that the presence of the university, even where there is no pre-existing or direct R&D relationship, is nevertheless an important influencing factor in terms of a company's decision to relocate to the region, for the following reasons:

— the availability of qualified, graduate level recruits;

— availability of and access to business and academic networks;

— as a potential collaborator for future interactions;

— as a provider of post-experience training (eg management and leadership);

— as a cultural and civic hub (eg music and entertainment, conferences, accommodation); and

— as a potential future employer for family members (particularly important in North West Wales, where high grade employment opportunities may be scarce in other organisations).

BANGOR UNIVERSITY AS AN ECONOMIC DRIVER

26. The university is the second largest employer in Gwynedd, and the university clearly has a profound effect as a driver of the local economy. This effect will be greater than for a university located in a large urban centre.

27. In a region where there have been comparatively few large inward investment projects, Bangor's most important contribution to socioeconomic wellbeing is to act as an economic engine, beyond the simple question of research "impact".

28. Bangor and its hinterland including Menai Bridge on Anglesey have a population of around 18,000 and this does not include the majority of 11,500 students who are present during the university semester. Whilst acknowledging the sometimes negative social impacts of such large numbers in a small city, clearly in terms of spend in the local economy, there is a huge benefit.

29. A discussion paper[11] by Michael Porter[12] of Harvard Business School, considers the health of the regional economy as being inextricably linked to the health of the colleges and universities located therein. According to Porter, universities bring about disproportionate benefits to the regional economy through a number of key factors identified below. These benefits can be further enhanced by taking a number of cost-effective steps (identified below).

30. Porter states: "To best manage Higher Education's role and fully leverage the surrounding economy to improve their own competitive position, university leaders need to understand the composition of the regional economy, and where the university can contribute ... HE needs to take a leadership role ... in developing/ executing a regional economic plan that addresses weaknesses in the general business environment. With a strategic approach, HE can have a major impact on regional economic revitalisation—without massive new funding."

31. The importance of traded clusters is discussed, citing California's wine cluster as an example, which has grown as a result of a combination of environment, skills availability, infrastructure and local government investment. It is intertwined with California's agricultural, tourism and processed food clusters, as well as having links with educational and governmental bodies, trade and export, and advocacy groups. Ensuring the vitality of clusters, and improving the environment for new, related clusters, is essential to regional and economic development.

[11] Colleges and universities and Regional Economic Development: A strategic perspective., Forum for the Future, 2007.
[12] Michael Eugene Porter is the Bishop William Lawrence University Professor at Harvard Business School. He is a leading authority on company strategy and the competitiveness of nations and regions. Michael Porter's work is recognized in many governments, corporations and academic circles globally. He chairs Harvard Business School's program dedicated for newly appointed CEOs of very large corporations (Source; Wikipedia, accessed 30 May 2011).

32. He further states that "universities can and do play an essential role in this process, and the *education and knowledge creation* cluster is a major traded cluster in its own right."

33. The paper suggests *six* distinct areas of influence where HE can contribute effectively to the local economy:

  (a) as an employer;

  (b) as a purchaser;

  (c) as an estates/property developer;

  (d) as a workforce developer;

  (e) as an adviser and network builder; and

  (f) as a technology transfer vehicle and business incubator.

34. *Employer*—how much labour comes from a local labour pool? A centralised, coordinated effort to hire locally builds stronger economic ties to surrounding communities, and generates political capital as well.

35. Research into the Economic and Social Impact of Bangor University carried out in December 2009[13] indicates that there are 2,800 individuals employed in education in the Bangor area. Bangor University has a total staff of around 2,200, of which only 600 are academic. Therefore nearly three quarters of Bangor staff are administration and support positions, and the university accounts for 78% of all employment in this sector locally.

36. In terms of impact, the Cambridge study estimates that the university supports a further 200 indirect jobs in Bangor, 2,400 in North Wales and 3,600 in UK.

37. Through the Gwynedd Local Service Board (LSB) we have begun to streamline aspects such as shared recruitment between member organisations (such as Gwynedd Council, Health Board and others), and have also considered aspects such as specialist skills-sharing between members. This reduces costs and may help retain skills in the area.

38. *Purchaser*—Universities have substantial spending power—Bangor has an annual turnover of £125 million. How much of this is spent centrally on procurement of goods and services locally? This is direct spending. Indirect spending from staff, student and visitors (conference, parents etc.) also helps contribute substantially to the local economy.

39. A number of studies and methodologies exist to carry out economic impact studies of spend in the local economy. Both Universities UK and Strathclyde University have published models which differ in complexity and usability.

40. As a rural university, there is a greater degree of "leakage" of spend from the area than in more urban settings. This is because the goods, services or professional skills are not always available in the locality. An example is to be found in the area of professional legal services. Large projects often resort to companies in Manchester, Liverpool or Birmingham for specialist advice. Latterly however, it has been encouraging to note that some mid-sized legal and accountancy firms have sought to increase their local presence, partly as a consequence of the university's existence, and in recognition of the above need.

41. Various estimates exist for the multiplier which can be applied to Bangor University's spend in the local economy. Some years ago a specific exercise was carried out by Cardiff University's Welsh Economy Research Unit (WERU)[14] in regard to the economic impact of Bangor University and a figure of 1.38 was calculated. This was lower than the average for Wales (1.56) because of the leakage noted above. This means that every £1 spent by the university is worth £1.38 to the local economy.

42. Professor Dermot Cahill of Bangor Law School has already contributed substantially to the debate in Wales regarding public sector procurement, both from a supply and a demand perspective. The Barriers Report, which he co-authored for WAG in 2009, has led to Value Wales redesigning the approach to pre-qualification questionnaires, thereby making it easier for small indigenous business to compete for public sector contracts.

43. Prof Cahill was involved in a recent INTERREG project "Tenderwise" which identified barriers for SMEs wishing to sell to the public sector, and is leading a new €3.7 million project "Winning in Tendering" aims to transform and improve the experience of SMEs when engaging in such tendering exercises.

44. *Estates Developer*—large capital projects have a real impact locally. Taking account the economic interests of the local community is a win-win strategy that can transform communities and benefit institutions alike.

45. Recently Bangor upgraded its student accommodation in a £30 million redevelopment, and the £41 million PONTIO Arts and Innovation Centre project opening in 2013 is an example of one such capital project that has levered in considerable external funds to the city. This iconic project would almost certainly not have

---

[13] Assessing the Local Economic and Social Impact of a University, Professor Barry Moore, Centre for Business Research, University of Cambridge and PACEC, December 2009.

[14] The Local Economic Impact of Bangor University, Welsh Economy Research Unit, University of Wales, Cardiff and John Treble, University of Wales, Bangor,1999.

been undertaken by the private sector. The university needs to be clear when communicating with local stakeholders that this venture would not otherwise happen, were it not for (a) substantial support by EU and the Welsh Government, and (b) the university's credibility as a delivery vehicle for such a complex project.

46. In the mid term there are also plans for a Clinical Research Facility, which will see both estates development and additional income and expertise levered into the North West Wales economy.

47. A case study of PONTIO is presented below, outlining its socioeconomic impacts as discussed in this section.

48. *Workforce Developer*—universities can develop executive and CPD programmes to serve regional clusters, and better align existing programmes with those fields where there are local undergraduate and graduate hiring needs. Do we know well enough our regional clusters and the economic make up of the area?

49. Research on labour supply and demand and workforce development best practice are helpful (eg Energy Island, Nuclear, Environmental Goods and Services, Creative Industries, etc). The university's Management Centre is a delivery vehicle for this sort of activity as are new programmes around Enterprise by Design (see below). The "entrepreneurship as a career choice" message plays well to a sub-region composed predominantly of micro and small businesses, where self employment features large.

50. *Advisor and Network Builder*—Business advisory programmes that channel faculty and student know-how to business are the most common type of college and university engagement. In addition, sitting on and facilitating networks and forums, hosting Business Clubs, consultancy research drawing on academic expertise are also very important contributors.

51. Bangor has a well-recognised history of interaction with the Small to Medium Enterprises on a regional basis. Programmes such as the Aber-Bangor Skills Centre, GO (Graduate Opportunity) Wales, The WISE network and Synnwyr Busnes-Business Sense (sustainability for business), are all good examples. Bangor has used structural funds to assist in business engagement in regard to specific sectors—SEACAMS aims to bring together businesses from the marine environment sector with the expertise of the university.

52. There are also executive leadership training programmes such as the LEAD programme aimed at growth businesses locally, and other training which is part-funded by structural funds. In addition, the Bangor University Business Club is hosted and facilitated by the Management Centre, a venue which offers higher level executive management and leadership training as well as high quality meeting spaces and conference facilities.

53. *Technology Transfer and Incubation*—Universities have a crucial role in developing technology and catalysing its commercialisation. They also have a critical role to play in operating incubators.

54. In regard to Knowledge Transfer, Bangor has always enjoyed a great deal of success in the area of Knowledge Transfer Partnerships (KTP, formerly Teaching Company Scheme). It has consistently been in the top 10 of UK universities and secured first place in the DTI best KTP award of 2007 with a Computer Science KTP (Vision Support). It was also the first to broker a KTP in the Arts (music), with a local music company, Sain Studios, whose business was greatly enhanced by knowledge transfer, creating new graduate level employment and increased turnover. At this time, Bangor is celebrating its 100th KTP, and is strengthening its links with the Technology Strategy Board on a number of levels.

55. Again, the PONTIO project has a clear role to play in regard to provision of space, equipment and expertise for development of collaborative research projects, interdisciplinary design, new venture creation and hosting, through its pre-incubation spaces, as will the Clinical Research Facility.

56. Bangor is a key player in a number of other technology transfer projects, such as the Low Carbon Research Institute (LCRI) where Bangor is focusing on dye-sensitised solar cells. Also the Software Alliance Wales (SAW) project and ASTUTE—an advanced manufacturing and materials project.

57. Note that there is *no direct mention* of "research with impact" in the above list, although it is implied within a number of the points mentioned above. A recent article in the Times Higher Education Supplement by Professor Drew Faust, President of Harvard University, argues that it is dangerous to see Higher Education *only* as a driver of economic growth. She warns that the insistence on having to demonstrate "impact" can favour conventional risk-free proposals at the expense of less predictable, more ambitious and possibly paradigm-shifting endeavours. She also notes that the Chinese Universities are looking to expand their output in the humanities, when other nations are scaling back on this.[15]

58. Impact should not be the sole aim of all new research. There is continuing importance for both blue skies research, and "softer" arts and humanities research to take place, because the former is the bedrock of knowledge, and market demand is not always best placed to anticipate disruptive change, and in regard to the latter, in order to imagine new future scenarios we need to foster the ability to imagine a world different from our own—understanding where we have come from is a powerful tool in this.

59. A final benefit of the university as a force for socioeconomic good is that unlike many inward investment projects, the university is here for the long term, and is not about to depart for new pastures when economic

---

[15] http://www.timeshighereducation.co.uk/story.asp?storyCode=412387&sectioncode=26 (Article dated 8 July 2010. Accessed 30 May 2011).

conditions become less favourable, and therefore is a potentially safer investment within a peripheral area such as North West Wales.

CASE STUDY

PONTIO and its contribution to meeting the economic outputs listed above

60. PONTIO (Welsh "to bridge") is an Arts and Innovation Centre that will link Bangor University and the wider North Wales region, by bringing the life of the university out into public arena, whilst engaging that wider public through rich and varied arts programme, delivered within a state-of-the-art performance facility. The iconic building will be a showcase for the research strengths of Bangor University, and break down barriers of access to higher education for visitors.

61. The project will engage specifically with regional SMEs by providing interdisciplinary skills and facilities to encourage the generation and development of new products and processes. PONTIO will be a centre for interdisciplinary Design and Enterprise in collaboration with business, aiming at addressing real life business global challenges. The building will provide new learning spaces, including social learning spaces for new forms of teaching delivery, as well as "pre-incubation" space to host new ventures.

62. In addition, the building will offer two performance theatres, lecture theatres, a cinema, an innovation hub including design studio, a fully immersive audiovisual studio, bars, restaurants and showcasing/ exhibition space.

63. PONTIO will contribute to the region's economy in a number of ways, both directly and indirectly, estimated through econometric multipliers to be in the region of £15 million annually:

— Through a capital construction project worth over £41 million, generating spend in the local construction supply chain.

— Through the operational turnover of the centre, as a result of commercial activities.

— Through an estimated 95 new posts created over a five year period.

— Through increased research grant and other funding capture leading to increased spend in the local economy.

— Through new businesses created, and concomitant commercial activities.

— Through additional staff and students attracted to Bangor university.

— Through increased visitor numbers and spend in the local economy.

64. By working with companies and individuals, it is anticipated that a number of new products, processes and services will be developed through collaborative R&D projects, leading to increased employment, with creation of high net-worth local opportunities, increased sales, improved business processes, more employable graduates, and graduates who see entrepreneurship and business ownership as a career path—which in turn helps to retain highly skilled individuals in North Wales. It will also increase the university's profile and image with large corporate organisations, attract visiting academics, and enticing businesses seeking to make an inward investment in the North Wales region.

BANGOR UNIVERSITY KNOWLEDGE ECONOMY STRATEGY (2008–13): WORKING GLOBALLY — IMPACTING LOCALLY

65. The third mission plan 2007–13 for Bangor University is based on two core products: research and graduates—and there are three cornerstones to activity that drives the knowledge economy (KE):

— Feeding the KE—eg our graduates and related postgraduate activity/CPD.

— Growing the KE—through such activities as KTPs and collaborative industrial/business activity, focusing on the sectors relating to health and technology, energy and environment; the establishment of a Medical School.

— Regenerating the economy—through our commercial IP portfolio including spinout companies (from staff and students), attracting global R&D for inward investment and capital development programmes.

66. This puts in place the mechanisms to implement the elements of the strategic plan for the university which relate to the Knowledge Economy.

67. *Knowledge Clusters:* The university will be the main driver of the KE for the region. Building on our links with business and industry, we will make a step change in our approach to partnering with large corporates, linking clusters using an open innovation approach.

68. *Research Strengths Applied to Industry:* The strategy focuses on industry-led, demand-driven research based on excellence at the university. The particular areas which support this approach are high-tech clusters encompassing Health and Behavioural Sciences, Computer Science and Electronics, Medicine, including Bioscience and Chemistry. Other sectors relevant to the Welsh and NW Wales economy are also supported, for example, in Geoscience and Marine Sectors.

69. *Leadership, Commercial Law and IP:* Underpinning all of this activity is the role played by our Business and Law Schools in developing "know how" in the clusters. The intention is to expand on the work of the Business School and the Management Centre.

70. *Creation of Research and Industry Clusters:* Research teams will be clustered together to maximise their contribution to the region's KE. Cluster groups will include: medical health and behavioural sciences; medical health technologies in computing and electronics; natural and material sciences.

71. *Skills:* All our academic disciplines have impact upon higher level skills, but in particular, CPD for teachers, trainers and careers professionals in science, technology and innovation; specific CPD, Continuing Education and re-training for key sectors alongside Sector Skills Councils will be a feature of our skills strategy and this will be demand-led from industry and business.

72. *Delivery:* Cluster champions will be appointed to support the link between the demand from the industry clusters for research and graduates and the applied research in the university. At the heart of the strategy is the strengthening of Bangor's research capacity; establishing long term strategic collaborations within Wales and internationally; and substantially upgrading and renewing its estate with world-class new developments (such as PONTIO) to support the region and build international profile.

73. *The 21st Century Challenge:* The university plans to be known as an exemplar of best practice for its KE engagement and aims to make its partnerships self-funding by 2013 (when EU Convergence Funding ceases). The university will develop its role as a major hub to continue to support the Wales Spatial Plan and the Môn a Menai Spatial Area plans. Two major university initiatives will be part of the key drivers for the region's KE: the PONTIO Arts and Innovation Centre as described in the case study above, and the Clinical Research Facility (CRF).

74. *CRF Outline:* The CRF will focus on four research areas:

— Medical Imaging, Visualisation and Haptics (artificial touch).

— Health technologies.

— Clinical Trials and Health Economics.

— Primary Care.

75. There is a demonstrated need for a Clinical Research Facility in North West Wales:

— There is a competitive gap with other more prosperous regions across Wales and the UK.

— There is an economic gap and need for sustainability.

— Betsi Cadwaladr University Health Board is the only health board in the country without a CRF.

— The University is in need of further research outlets for application and advancement in this field.

76. There will be a number of clear benefits in terms of the KE in NW Wales:

— Improvement in recruitment and retention of staff, clinical students and researchers.

— Greater potential for spin out and spin off businesses.

— Greater collaboration with the Health Board.

— Capitalisation on availability of improved infrastructure and hardware (JANET, Fibrespeed, High Performance Computing Wales, RIVIC—Research Institute for VIsual Computing).

— A greater chance to compete internationally and attract inward investment business.

77. With the appointment of a new Vice Chancellor, the commitment to working with businesses and the public sector across health, engineering, agriculture, forestry and the wider environment in Wales and beyond has been further strengthened. Bangor leads on the Convergence funded KESS programme which supports PhD and MRes programmes jointly with Business, building on a successful programme of ESF funded PhDs in the previous Objective 1 round of funding.

78. The measurable aims of the research strategy are as follows:

— Aim to have >90% academic staff highly research active and REF returnable whilst increasing quality and increasing the number of returnable staff by at least 25% to over 350.

— Invest in areas of research success in terms of quality and areas where Bangor's physical and cultural environment allows it to make a unique contribution.

— Build on the success of the 125 Anniversary Studentship scheme and the WEFO funded KESS partnerships, research postgraduate student numbers will be expanded by 25%.

— Increase Research Council income by 25% through supporting individual schools and colleges and HEFCW funded reconfiguration and collaborations projects to meet targets set.

— Provide a supportive structure to enhance the exchange of knowledge with businesses and other organisations to enable innovation by strengthening engagement thereby delivering added value.

79. Measures used will be:

— Numbers of research postgraduate students per staff FTE.

— Number and proportion of high quality research staff.

— Research Council Income, success rate and per staff FTE.

— Engagements with business and public sector organisations as measured by HEBCIS.

— Active spinout companies.

BANGOR UNIVERSITY RESEARCH GRANT CAPTURE

Source	2007–08	2008–09	2009–10	2010–11 to date
Europe	£827,460	£4,195,813	£21,541,065	£10,814,454
KTP	£198,087	£544,256	£543,171	£345,701
Overseas	£424,371	£321,813	£380,738	£1,177,650
Research Councils	£5,667,764	£2,822,502	£6,444,699	£1,178,468
UK Charity	£460,586	£969,771	£1,232,947	£489,867
UK Government	£3,648,580	£5,831,202	£6,350,468	£6,656,334
UK Industry	£401,223	£306,371	£780,681	£187,060
UK Other	£156,139	£645,051	£719,765	£243,187
Totals Grants	£11,784,210	£15,636,779	£37,993,534	£21,092,721

KEY BANGOR PROGRAMMES DRIVING THE LOCAL ECONOMY

Project	Description
SEACAMS (Sustainable Expansion of the Applied Coastal and Marine Sectors)	Joint EU finded project between Bangor, Swansea and Aberystwyth. Knowledge Exchange within the Marine Environmental clusters in North Wales.
Knowledge Transfer Partnerships	Supported by Technology Strategy Board, Bangor is celebrating its 100th KTP, and has a number of award winning projects to its name, including the first in the creative industries/arts.
Enterprise by Design	A pilot programme that aims to bring students and academics together from different disciplines, and to work collaboratively with industry on real-world challenges. Feeds into PONTIO.
Inventorium	An INTERREG funded programme of events, activities leading to ideas sharing and creating a repository of ideas in the digital arena. Feeds into PONTIO.
PONTIO	See above.
Clinical Research Facility	See above.
Management Centre	An executive and post-experience training and conference centre, offering meeting rooms and hosting Bangor University Business Club.
KESS (Knowledge Economy Skills Scholarships)	Knowledge Economy Skills Scholarships (KESS) is a major European Convergence programme led by Bangor University on behalf of the HE sector in Wales. Benefiting from European Social Funds (ESF), KESS will support collaborative research projects (Research Masters and PhD) with external partners based in the Convergence area of Wales (West Wales and the Valleys). KESS will run from 2009 until 2014 and will provide 400+ PhD and Masters places.
Aber Bangor Skills Centre	Led by Bangor University, the A-BSC opens the door to a wide range of training opportunities for the business community of Mid and North Wales and works towards advancing the Knowledge Economy of Wales.
GO Wales	Provision of students to Welsh based SMEs.
B-Enterprising	A programme which provides students at Bangor University and graduates in Wales with a range of services to help develop their enterprise skills or to support them in starting a new business.

Project	Description
RIVIC (Research Institute of Visual Computing)	The, RIVIC, is the amalgamation of research programmes between the computer science departments in Aberystwyth, Bangor, Cardiff and Swansea Universities. With a mission to: — Bring Wales to the forefront of visual computing research. — Promote long term and sustainable collaborations between Welsh HEIs. — Support excellence in computer science education. — Develop industrial research and knowledge exploitation and engagement.
HPC (high performance Computing) Wales	High Performance Computing Wales (HPC Wales) is a £40 million five-year project to give businesses and universities involved in commercially focused research across Wales access to the most advanced and evolving computing technology available.
LCRI (Low Carbon Research Institute)	The Institute was set up to unite and promote energy research in Wales, UK to help deliver a low carbon future. The multidisciplinary LCRI aims to support the energy sector, UK and globally, to develop low carbon generation, storage, distribution and end use technologies, and to offer policy advice.
BioComposites (BC)	BC has been at the forefront of research, development and the commercial application of bio-based alternatives to synthetic materials in manufacturing and industry. BC offers businesses the knowledge and technical means to put alternative materials into practice, lowering costs, increasing productivity and making activities more environmentally and socially responsible.
WISE (Welsh Institute for Sustainable Resources) Network	Provides an easy-to-access, friendly "front door" for companies to access all of the sustainability and environmental expertise across three institutions of Aberystwyth, Bangor and Swansea. As a result of the WISE Network, almost 500 companies have been able to both increase their financial success, and reduce their environmental impact.
Synnwyr Busnes Business Sense	A specialist support service on sustainable development, working with businesses and other organisations, in Wales and beyond, with a network of experts located across Wales. Aim to help businesses learn more about what sustainability means for them.
Food Dudes Programme	A psychology-based behaviour change programme around helping children to make sensible food choices, that has been successfully rolled out in 1,590 primary schools in the Republic of Ireland and is being piloted in UK schools.
IMSCaR (Institute of Medical and Social Care Research)	IMSCaR aims to enhance the health and welfare of the people of Wales, the UK and the rest of the world through Research in Medicine, Health Issues and Social Care. It has worked extensively with the private care home sector to improve the offering for older people and dementia sufferers, and impacting on the business profile of such homes.

80. A number of other business supporting projects are in the process of development, supported by a variety of funding mechanisms.

June 2011

Written evidence submitted by Glyndŵr University

EXECUTIVE SUMMARY

— Glyndŵr University undertakes an extensive range of international activities aimed at promoting Wales overseas in order to attract greater inward investment into the University and the wider community in North Wales and the country as a whole.

— Significant benefits accrue to the University and the region as a result of inward investment. These benefits are not restricted to financial, but also include academic, reputational, social and political benefits.

— In particular the University and region benefit from Glyndŵr University's extensive academic links with other universities across the world.

— The University's preferred way of working is through developing strong partnerships which give it a flexible critical mass.

— Crucial to the University's success is continuing governmental support at both Welsh and UK levels.

Introduction

1. Glyndŵr University exists to promote the economic and social development of its region and the country. It seeks to achieve this by creating an environment in which businesses and communities will prosper, providing employment and social cohesion. Many of its activities are aimed at local employers but the University has long recognised the importance of attracting investment from outside the region to provide a valuable stimulus financial or otherwise to the economy. Consequently the University has been active across the UK and internationally promoting its expertise and facilities available to any potential investor and explaining the benefits of such an investment.

2. The University has always endeavoured to ensure that it is outward looking as it believes considerable benefit can be brought to Wales by its interaction with the rest of the world. This idea was one of the fundamental principles adopted by the University when it was established in 2008 as it had been to its predecessor organisations since 1887.

3. This evidence intends to show the extent of the University's activities in attracting inward investment, how that interaction with the rest of the world has brought benefit to North Wales and to the University, and the role of the Welsh and UK Governments in its success. It also offers a few suggestions as to how that could be improved from the point of view of the University.

How Glyndŵr University Contributes to Inward Iinvestment

4. It is widely recognised that universities play an integral role in the economic development of a region. Governments in Westminster and Cardiff and organisation such as the CBI consistently praise the work and potential of universities working in collaboration with industry to contribute to economic prosperity. In particular universities can contribute through providing access to academic expertise as well as specialised equipment and facilities. In addition the universities help to create a skilled workforce which is a vital component in an attractive environment for businesses.

Research

5. One of the main ways Glyndŵr University is able to bring inward investment into North Wales is through the research being undertaken at the University. This research is often of the highest international standards and the presence of the academic expertise and technology transfer infrastructure within the University makes the region particularly attractive to international companies eager to expend their operations.

6. The University undertakes focused specialised research, building on the expertise that exists within the University and for which there is an existing market. New areas of research are only introduced where they are related to existing research areas.

7. The areas of research undertaken at Glyndŵr University are closely linked to taught curriculum areas. For example, new MSc and MRes in Composites are linked to composites research, the MRes in Polymer Science and Technology is linked to hydrocolloids research and research in the Centre for Applied Internet Research is linked to the MSc in Computer Networking.

8. For over 30 years Glyndŵr University has been one of the world's leading centres for research into hydrocolloids and polymers. These are naturally occurring materials which are soluble in water and are used to control the properties of the substance. For example they can thicken, gell or stabilise the product or can add flavour. Although they are mainly used in the food industry they can also be used in wound dressing and as food packaging. Throughout those thirty years the University has been the host of a biennial international conference on food and stabilisers.

9. In 2003 a contract was signed with the Japanese food company San Ei Gen to establish a specialised research centre within the University called the Glyn O Phillips Hydrocolloid Research Centre. This centre has undertaken hydrocolloid testing work on contracts signed with a large number of international food and drink companies. The contract with San Ei Gen was renewed in 2009 for a further three years and negotiations are under way into further developments of the centre. The value of the contract to date has been in the region of £1.6 million.

10. A high profile research project currently being undertaken by the University at its St Asaph site, Optic Glyndŵr, is work on the largest telescope in the world. The Extra Large Telescope (ELT) is funded by the European Southern Observatory and will start operating in South America from 2018.

11. Glyndŵr University's role within the project is in the preparation of the mirrors. The project requires the mirrors to be polished to an accuracy of 20 microns. The current phase is for the production of six prototype mirrors to the required accuracy and within the specified timescale. The value of this prototype stage is €5 million. The final contract would require the production of 1,148 mirrors (approximately four a week) and the value of the full contract could be approximately €200 million to the North Wales economy.

12. Currently the project led by Glyndŵr University involves two industrial and two university partners Qioptiq (St Asaph), Zeeko (Leicestershire), University College London and Cranfield University. Other companies have been involved in various aspects of the work including the construction of the necessary test tower. Most of these were from mainland Europe as no UK companies were able to meet the specification. As a result of this project a new sister company to Zeeko has been established, Zeeko Research Ltd, with its headquarters in St Asaph.

13. Were the final contract to be awarded to the North Wales consortium there would need to be a new production facility, probably of the same size as the existing Optic Glyndŵr building. The detailed specification for the new building is still being prepared. It is estimated that there would be 40 new jobs within the facility with many more supporting the work in the wider area. Further jobs would be created with new contracts that would naturally follow from this pioneering development. Indeed enquiries are already starting to be made from around the world concerning future projects.

14. Policy decisions by the UK Government can have important consequences on the success of activities such as the ESO project. For example the relationship of the UK Government towards individual pan European organisations may affect the attitude of those organisations towards UK based partners. In addition the University believes the UK Government can be of considerable assistance in ensuring the political environment is sufficiently amenable to allow the University to compete for such contracts. More details of the role of the Government are given on paragraphs 44–52 below.

15. The complexities of this project have drawn considerable interest around the world and the ESO official in charge of the project has described the science involved at Optic Glyndŵr as "the best in the world outside the military." It has also attracted the attention of the US Air Force and NASA, both of which have visited the facility.

16. The University is engaged in many other international research projects on a smaller scale. One example of this is the Easyline + project which was aimed at supporting the elderly to enable them to remain independent in their own homes for longer. This would be facilitated by the use of computerised support and a remote monitoring facility. The project involved industrial and university partners from across the European Union.

Impact

17. The most obvious initial impact of the University's research is in the income it brings to the University. In the financial year 2009–10 the University's research activities attracted funding worth nearly £2.5 million.

18. Within the wider community the creation and securing of employment is an important result of the research. One recent example shows the value to the region of having a university based within it. The University was approached by Wrexham Council for assistance in securing investment in the town by a Chinese owned company. A visit was arranged to the campus and the company representatives were shown the facilities and example of the research and undergraduate and postgraduate work undertaken there. As a result of the visit the company has decided to establish a major facility in the town. The University understands that negotiations are continuing as to the finer details and that an announcement will be made shortly.

19. Much of the research also results in the creation of clusters of related industries. The most obvious example is the creation and maintenance of the opto-electronic industry cluster centred on the work at Optic Glyndŵr in St Asaph. Another growing cluster is in the creative industries in Wrexham, based around the University's new Centre for the Creative Industries which includes the BBC's new Wrexham studio.

20. The importance of these clusters in securing a local supply chain was underlined by recent events at Toyota which had to shut down its Deeside operations temporarily as a result of the interruption to their Japanese supplies following the recent earthquake and tsunami.

21. Although the direct link between the investment and the benefits to the local companies may not be immediately obvious, the effect is real as the expertise generated at the University as a result of inward investment is made available to local businesses through government schemes such as KTP and the KTC. This is an example of the vertical spillover described in the UKTI Inward Investment Evaluation Case Studies (2009). However, as the UKTI report says these are considerable difficulties in quantifying the financial benefits of all aspects of spillover.

Skilled workforce

22. The development of a skilled workforce is an important part of the University's contribution to attracting inward investment. In many cases the potential for the workforce is apparent as a result of existing or previous industrial involvement in the area. This potential is then built on by the Welsh Government and local authorities seeking out new businesses and the University is approached to see if the package can be made more attractive by including workforce development proposals.

23. The skilled workforce may be centred on expertise retained within the University, such as the hydrocolloid centre at Glyndŵr University, or it may extend to the development of a larger skilled workforce, with allied businesses, such as being created at Airbus in Broughton by the collaboration between the University and the company.

24. It is not possible to quantify accurately the value of this contribution towards attracting inward investment. Although the University does collect information of graduate employment within six months of the graduate leaving the University, this data does not include information on the financial background of the employer or any parent company. However with 50% of graduates staying in the region with around the same number working in the private sector, in particular the Health Service, it is believed that the contribution of its graduates to the local economy is extensive.

Educational links and Contracts

25. The University has established a considerable number of important international educational links. These are with universities either which have a role within their countries similar to that which Glyndŵr University plays within Wales or which have been attracted by Glyndŵr's particular expertise and wish to lend their support to the development of the University.

Russia

26. One example of the latter group is the Bauman Moscow State Technical University. This is one of the premier technical universities in Russia and played an integral part in the development of the Soviet and later Russian space programmes. Their rocket scientists have been impressed by the expertise that exists in Glyndŵr University has in composite materials and they hope that the collaboration with Glyndŵr University may allow the greater use of composites in space travel. This collaboration has taken the form of international composite conferences held at Glyndŵr University, a number of staff development programmes for the Bauman staff, joint PhD programmes and joint research, particularly supporting research into composites and associated technologies. The principal value of this collaboration is in raising the profile of Glyndŵr University and North Wales within highly influential international scientific circles.

Vietnam

27. A contract signed in May 2011 between Glyndŵr University and the Vietnam Media Corporation, in the presence of the Prime Minister of Vietnam, will bring benefits to both countries. Under the contract, which is worth five million pounds over the next five years, the University will provide training for the Vietnamese television company both in Vietnam and in Wales. This will support the employment of additional staff by the University. It is an important development for both Wales and Vietnam. A recent ceremony held by Glyndŵr University in Vietnam to confer a Visiting Professorship on Dr Thai Minh Tan was broadcast to an estimated audience of 37 million.

Malaysia

28. A similar contract for teacher training in Malaysia is expected to be announced shortly. This will allow the University to retain some of its staff who would otherwise have lost their jobs following the decision of the Higher Education Funding Council to withdraw teacher training from Glyndŵr University.

China

29. Glyndŵr University has established links with a number of Chinese universities especially the South Western University for Nationalities (SWUN) which caters for the minority nationalities within China, especially the Tibetan population. The Vice-Chancellor of Glyndŵr University was recently in Sichuan at the invitation of SWUN to celebrate its sixtieth anniversary. As part of the celebrations Professor Scott addressed a 10,000 strong audience in a sports stadium, the only foreign representative accorded that honour. A television interview was shown to an estimated 100 million audience in Sichuan. This and other Chinese links are important factors in influencing Chinese based businesses to invest in Wales.

REASONS FOR GLYNDŴR UNIVERSITY SUCCESS

30. Despite having been a university for only three years, Glyndŵr has established a good name for itself internationally. It believes this is the result of its dedication to providing a high quality and personal service.

31. However good the quality of the product it can only attract new business if potential customers and partners know of its record. The University has therefore invested considerable resources into obtaining good contacts. This is the result of extensive work being undertaken by the University's International Office and through their local contacts.

32. Once a contract has been awarded and successfully performed the reputation of the University is enhanced and further work may arise. In addition contracts have been won through the word of mouth of former students who have enjoyed their time considerably at the University and have recommended the University to influential figures at home.

EFFECT ON GLYNDŴR UNIVERSITY

33. The principal effect on the University of its international contacts are financial. The direct contribution to the University's turnover for the year 2009–10 was in excess of four million pounds.

34. A non-tangible benefit, although one of considerable important is the enhancement of the University's research reputation. The work being undertaken in hydrocolloids and optics have won the University considerable international recognition, which can also favourably influence the University's wider international reputation.

35. Successful international links also often produce an increase in the number of international students interested in studying at the University. Some of these will be the direct result of the link, through sponsorship deals with the partners others will become aware of the University through its own promotional activities in country as a result of the link.

36. The University's higher profile internationally also means that it is easier to recruit highly qualified staff to posts within the University. Recent years have seen an increase in the number of staff coming to the University from overseas, particularly Russia and China.

INFLUENCES ON GLYNDŴR UNIVERSITY

37. The University is conscious of its own capacity to continue to expand its international activities. However, by collaborating with international partners it is bringing considerably more to the economy of North Wales than a university many times its size could without these important links. At the heart of the University's operations is its extensive network of partners. These allow the University to undertake considerably more work than would be possible otherwise.

38. The role of government is vital to the continuing to attract inward investment into Wales. The government's strategy in this is set out in a number of documents and policies most noticeably the *Economic Renewal; a new direction*. In that document the government states its priorities including the industrial sectors considered vital to economic prosperity and the specific priority areas in which government intervention is most important.

39. As a result the University has adapted its own strategies and operations to reflect these priorities and to allow it support the economic development of the Government.

40. The six priority sectors set by the Government include:

— *the creative industries*, in which the University has invested considerably including in the new Centre for the Creative Industries;

— *ICT*, where the University has undertaken important research through its Centre for Applied Internet Research and elsewhere;

— *energy and environmental*, in which the University's Centre for Solar Energy Research is undertaking important research work in collaboration with a number of industrial partners, including Sharp;

— *advanced materials and manufacturing*, as seen in the University's collaboration with Airbus on composite materials.

41. It also states that five priority areas which include:

— *investing in high quality and sustainable infrastructure*: the University is working on a number of projects to improve the infrastructure or overcome some of the problems inherent in the existing system;

— *making Wales a more attractive place to do business*: the University has long provided the public sector with many employees, including nurses and social workers who contribute to social cohesion and the welfare of society, which also benefits from its extensive cultural programmes;

— *broadening the skills base*: this is done not only at degree and postgraduate levels but also through professional and knowledge transfer programmes; and

— *encouraging innovation*: this is integral to the University's academic programmes and is co-ordinated by a dedicated unit within the University, the Centre for Entrepreneurial Learning.

ROLE OF INWARD INVESTMENT ON WALES

42. The University would agree with the findings of the UKTI Inward Investment Evaluation Case Studies (2009) which argued that decisions on the location of investments are more likely to be influenced by regional and spatial concerns, in particular the accessibility to expertise, similar businesses and/or a skilled workforce rather than social concerns about the relative wealth of possible areas for investment.

43. The University also agrees with the report that reverse spillover will occur with technology being exported back to the investor's country. However, it believes that this is integral to a university's role and the very nature of education and research. The main office of San Ei Gen in Osaka, for example, has many

graduates of Glyndŵr University among its research staff. The University believes this is beneficial to both the University and the region as it ensures continuing links between Japan and Wales and places North Wales is a good position to receive further investment.

ROLE OF WELSH GOVERNMENT

44. The University believes that the potential to North Wales of the research work being undertaken at St Asaph is considerable. This work has been described by Professor John Harries, Chief Scientific Officer for Wales as the "best research project in Wales". The University believes therefore that the policy of the Welsh Government should be to support such research activities. It is concerned therefore at the increasing pressure applied on the University by the Funding Council to move away from research and concentrate solely on teaching.

45. The Universities tries to take advantage of any scheme operated by the Welsh Government to assist attracting inward investment. One such scheme is the use of trade missions and University staff have used many such missions to countries such as India, Russia, South Africa and South East Asia.

46. Another important factor in attracting investment is the country's transport infrastructure. The location of both the University's facilities at St Asaph and the Northop campus on the A55 has proved attractive to potential investors. Similarly Wrexham proximity to the UK motorway system is also useful.

47. Sometimes the policies of the Welsh Government can make potential investment in certain industries less likely. The opening of discussions and establishing a Norman Borlaug Institute to the Northop campus failed as a result of the Welsh Government's ban on genetically modified crops.

48. The use of Convergence funding can play a major role and many potential inward investors are acutely aware of the geographical extent of the eligible areas. Throughout the discussions with San Ei Gen on the possible relocation of the Glyndŵr University Glyn O Phillips Hydrocolloid Research Centre to Northop, the University was continually being lobbied about moving the facility further West to St Asaph which unlike Northop was in a Convergence area.

ROLE OF UK GOVERNMENT

49. The UK government also has an important role to play in attracting inward investment and the use and support of British embassies can be crucial to a mission's success. During a recent visit by the University's Vice-Chancellor to Russia, the British Embassy in Moscow was highly supportive and influential, effecting vital introductions and providing valuable information.

50. The presence of the UK Minister for Universities to Moscow a few weeks earlier was also of great help. During his visit Mr Willetts had met leading figures from the Bauman Moscow State Technical University who told him of the great benefit to Russia and Wales of the link between Bauman and Glyndŵr University. Mr Willetts then spoke favourably of these links at other meetings and conferences.

51. The UK government also influences the success or otherwise of inward investment projects through its policies. A decision will shortly need to be made by ESO on the awarding of the next stage in the telescope project. Support from the UK government is essential if Wales is to benefit from the project.

52. The new immigration rules introduced in 2011 have caused all universities with a significant international student population, considerable problems as the student profile changes. The imposition of CAS numbers means that the University is having to chose between full-time students enrolled for between one and three years and a visiting postdoctoral student anxious to gain a few months' experience in the University's research centres, with the result that immediate financial considerations may take precedence over longer term prospects of enhanced inward investment.

CONCLUSIONS

53. Glyndŵr University operates on the international stage. All such operations are undertaken in accordance with Welsh Government policy with a view ultimately to benefitting the University and the economy of North Wales. This can be through direct financial sponsorship such as with San Ei Gen, the financing of students or the purchase of services from the University. Alternatively it can be indirect investment including the recruitment of staff from overseas or growing academic collaboration with international universities.

June 2011

Written evidence submitted by Eluned Parrott AM

INTRODUCTION

1. We recognise that the Welsh economy does not exist in a silo, and that Welsh policy-makers need to engender positive working relations with their neighbours in order to deliver a thriving Welsh business sector. By 2009–10, Wales was receiving 4% of the UK's total inward investment, down from 15% in the 1990s.[16] An over-reliance on inward investment meant that the current economic downturn and the one preceding it had a much greater effect on the Welsh economy than other areas, as there was not sufficient home-grown industry to cushion it from a consequent decline in investment. Essentially Wales has been hit twice-over, receiving less of a proportion of the investment pool, when the pool itself is smaller than it was.

2. There are significant concerns about the challenges facing the Welsh economy as it seeks to pull out of recession. The national transport infrastructure is fragile, particularly in places where it interfaces with the English road and rail networks. There are potential clashes of policy between the devolved nations, where a failure to work effectively with colleagues in England, Scotland and Northern Ireland could have potentially devastating effects on Welsh businesses. While policy reflects national boundaries, commerce does not. Failing to co-ordinate economic policy with partners across the UK and Europe could lead to the creation of a destructive competitive cycle.

3. In the past, Wales has been sold to potential investors as a low-cost location to do business in Europe, but as soon as the Eastern Bloc countries joined the EU, this was no longer the case. In fact, I would argue that no part of the UK should be attempting to compete for jobs on price—as a developed economy we cannot compete with countries outside the EU where wages are a fraction of what they are here. Wales needs a new strategy that identifies its key selling points to potential investors, targets new entrants to the European market effectively, and demonstrates to them that Wales is an attractive location to invest.

4. Our vision is that Wales can and should be a strong player within the UK and European economy, but that some major investments and real leadership are likely to be required.

PART 1: OVERCOMING BARRIERS FOR BUSINESSES OPERATING IN WALES

5. During the last wave of inward investment, the barriers to entry in Wales were greatly reduced—mostly as a result of direct government investment in bringing companies to Wales, alongside historically lower wages and property costs. The entry of low-cost Eastern European regions into the European Union, as well as improving infrastructure and skill levels in countries such as India and China, has undermined these advantages. To compound this, there was little apparent effort to supplant these benefits with other competitive advantages. We successfully removed barriers to entry but failed to develop strong barriers to exit.

6. Unfortunately, inward investment into Wales has slowed consistently in recent years as Wales has not adequately identified, developed or promoted its competitive advantages. There is a need to ensure that Wales can compete on grounds other than low wages and property values. Developed economies need to sell on a combination of bases, including the quality of support on offer as well as access to markets, supply chains, skills and research and development expertise. Wales is well-placed in some of these respects, but needs to improve in others.

7. Welsh Liberal Democrats believe an effective infrastructure and strong skills-base is the best way to develop a strong environment for inward investment. These critical attributes will assist in attracting more hi-tech and high-skill businesses to Wales and will create the conditions whereby strong supply and demand chains can grow and prosper.

Areas of infrastructure investment:

Transport

8. Transport infrastructure is critically important. Companies seeking to invest need to be assured that potential staff can access their working locations and meeting points efficiently, and that the freight infrastructure can cope with transporting both supplies and outbound products. A modern and efficient transport infrastructure also sends the subliminal signal that a location is "open for business".

Rail

9. Recent political debate about rail infrastructure has focused on the ongoing review of the business case for electrification to Swansea, however, there are other infrastructure priorities that need attention.

Electrification and modernisation of the Valleys lines:

10. This presents a rare opportunity to stimulate development into South Wales Valleys, areas which rank amongst those most in need of economic development. The UK and Welsh governments must immediately begin substantive work on developing the detailed business case for electrifying these lines and undertake negotiations with Arriva Trains Wales about the provision of new rolling stock.

---

[16] http://wales.gov.uk/topics/businessandeconomy/publications/reviewofibw/?lang=en

11. A series of reports[17] have identified the potential for economic development in the South Wales Valleys if transport improvements can be made. The planned electrification of the Great Western Main Line to South Wales, and the associated engineering works, makes this infrastructure investment cost-effective for the first, and possibly last, time in a generation.

12. The opportunity to electrify the Valleys Lines, however, presents a much larger opportunity to develop a regional transport strategy for South Wales. This should include examining whether additional transport systems could be developed to improve the infrastructure, such as light rail or metro services.

Freight services:

13. The Third Assembly's Enterprise and Learning Committee in January 2010 said that,

> "The only parts of the Welsh rail network that are currently considered part of the Strategic Freight Network are the Great Western Main Line as far as Port Talbot and the Marches Line from Newport to Wrexham and from Chester to Shrewsbury".[18]

14. This clearly places the western half of Wales at a competitive disadvantage, especially as a number of major ports, including Swansea, Milford Haven and Holyhead are excluded from the strategic network. There is also little provision for the development of the freight network in Wales beyond 2014.

15. As the cost of fuel increases, many firms will be looking to reduce the cost of transport by increasing use of rail freight. Inward investment could be stimulated by ensuring that there is an extensive freight network with access to major ports.

16. The UK and Welsh governments should begin by developing a feasibility study and impact assessment of improving freight access to all major ports.

Road

17. Despite efforts to move as much freight as possible onto the rail network, there is still likely to be a significant demand for road haulage. For major inward investors, links to other commercial centres and ports are vital, as are efficient access routes for staff. There should be a strategy for ensuring these roads are well-maintained and able to meet capacity demands. Following recent incidents affecting major routes such as the M4 and A55 corridors, it is also clear that contingency plans for accidents, repairs or emergencies on major routes are not currently adequate.

18. Any road utilisation strategy would need to examine:

(a) Improvements to the M4 corridor and its access points into South-East and South-West England via the M4/M5 and access into the Midlands via the M50,

(b) the need for an M4 relief road at Newport,

(c) Improvements to the A55 corridor and its access points into the North-West and Midlands, as well as additional resting points for heavy goods vehicles, and

(d) Improvements to the A49 route between North and South Wales which straddles the English and Welsh border along the Marches, particularly at pinch-points such as Hereford.

19. Economic impact assessments of the Severn Bridge Tolls are currently being undertaken by both the UK and Welsh governments. It is our expectation that these assessments will demonstrate that there is a significant disincentive to inward investment in Wales (especially when compared to Western England) and we would urge the tolls to be abolished or significantly reduced when they revert to public ownership.

Energy

20. As the cost of fuel rises, we believe that a nation with a modern power infrastructure and a vibrant renewable energy sector will provide significant advantages for inward investors. A modern infrastructure will re-assure investors about the efficiency and reliability of supply, whilst a high percentage of energy being generated from renewable sources will provide evidence of supply and cost security in a volatile energy market.

21. As well as investing in renewable energy, particularly off-shore wind, and modernising some aspects of the transmission network, the UK and Welsh governments can ensure that stability of a low cost energy network is available to investors, through the provision of a balanced energy mix.

22. As the environmental and energy sector has been identified as a key sector for the Welsh economy, there is a need to ensure that the appropriate infrastructure is available to support this. We would ask the UK government to ensure that steps are taken to support this sector, specifically developing the role of feed-in tariffs and resolving the dispute over who is responsible for deep sea ports.

---

[17] For example, Barry, Mark *A Metro for Capital City's Region: Connecting Cardiff, Newport and the Valleys* (Institute of Welsh Affairs, 2011). SEWTA have also expressed their support for the electrification of the South Wales Valleys Lines.

[18] Enterprise and Learning Committee, *Future Railway Infrastructure in Wales* (National Assembly for Wales, 2010).

Digital access

23. Up-to-date and up-to-speed telecommunications access is essential to ensuring that Wales is attractive to inward investment from hi-tech companies. This includes Broadband and 3G, but in many areas of Wales, improvements to mobile phone networks as well. There are two challenges for improving access to these services—the first is to ensure digital access is possible across Wales and the second, to improve the quality of the digital access that is available.

24. The Welsh Government has already committed to improving broadband access, but there is also a need to invest in rolling out 3G mobile phone technology. We have previously also called for work, between the Welsh government, UK Government and internet providers, to develop "wi-fi towns", particularly in rural areas which have previously benefitted from tourism and conferences, such as Llandudno, Aberystwth and Llandrindod Wells. This would ensure that they are able to compete in the modern market.

Skills

25. Many employers[19] are concerned about low skill levels in Wales, which can affect productivity and is therefore a source of competitive disadvantage relative to other areas. Basic skills attainment is 1% lower in Wales than across the UK as a whole, and 4% lower than Scotland. Higher Skills attainment is 3% lower than across the UK and 7% lower than Scotland. Wales is lagging behind at least two of its competitor regions.

26. As previously stated, given that the cost of employing staff in the UK is higher than in many other EU countries, Wales cannot present itself as a low-wage destination for foreign investors. A high-skill-base is a critical element of a quality-led market position for Wales as a business location.

27. It is worth noting that Wales has 17% more HE students per head than in England[20], showing a clear source of competitive advantage in the capacity of Wales to train its population as compared to other areas of the UK. Wales' HE sector also has the potential to offer access to R&D expertise as an additional selling point, subject to the availability of funding for innovation and engagement from the UK Research Councils.

28. Despite attracting people to study in Wales, however, there is currently a skill base which is being lost back to England due to the lack of high-skilled and graduate jobs in Wales. Steps must be taken to break the vicious circle whereby the lack of graduate jobs leads to the loss of skills which, in turn, encourages employers to take skilled jobs elsewhere. Positive steps could include a Wales-specific graduate science programme designed to retain skilled people and send the message to investors that Wales is serious about innovation.

29. Currently Wales's schools are funded by £604 less than schools in England,[21] and this gap has been growing continuously over the last decade. Over the same period, Wales's exam results have fallen behind England's and this gap has also been growing.

30. Wales and England are two education systems with close proximity to each other. If the Welsh education system continues to underperform by comparison with England as a result of underfunding there is a danger that Wales could lose out from having a less highly-skilled workforce, or one that is perceived as being less highly-skilled.

31. Finally, Wales also needs to develop a more comprehensive approach to professional and industrial skills if it is to create a workforce with the right skills for business. We have previously argued for a training grant for companies setting up in Wales to ensure that new companies are able to close the skills gap easily.

PART 2: ATTRACTING BUSINESSES TO WALES

32. For companies abroad looking to invest overseas, it is essential that Wales is marketed as a nation which is open to new and innovative companies and open for economic growth. The Welsh Development Agency, which was abolished in 2004, had a reputation across the world that has not been matched by International Business Wales, its successor. This needs to be addressed. However, we are also concerned that the Welsh government appears unambitious on innovative programmes for economic growth, especially when compared to competitor regions.

Promoting Wales abroad

33. The Welsh government's overseas arm, International Business Wales, ceased to exist as a brand after the publication of *Economic Renewal: A New Direction,* and while a successor organisation is planned, no visible progress has been made to date. However, even when that body is established, there is a danger that the new successor to IBW will suffer from the same problems. Our principal concerns are outlined below.

34. The rationale for the placement and size of overseas offices was not immediately apparent. For obvious reasons, offices were located in those economies that already invest heavily in Wales, but the number of staff

---

[19] For example, Rosser, David, "Why education must be the top priority for the new government" (Western Mail, 11 May 2011). Mr Rosser is the director of CBI Wales.

[20] Independent Commission on Funding and Finance in Wales, *Funding Devolved Government in Wales: Barnett and beyond* (Welsh Assembly Government, 2009) p 50.

[21] http://wales.gov.uk/topics/statistics/headlines/localgov2011/110126/?lang=en

in those locations varied widely. For example, the New York office had 13 members of staff working there, while the office in Germany had just one—despite the fact that Germany is almost as significant an investor as the US is for Wales.

35. Similarly, it did not appear that the government had any ability to alter its overseas activity to reflect changing economic circumstances, nor enough flexibility to enter into arrangements with new and emerging markets. Any overarching policy for the location, size and flexibility of offices was not apparent.

36. It is difficult—if not impossible—to know if particular investments in Wales were secured as a result of the work of the government's overseas arm. There are undoubtedly other factors at play in helping attract foreign investment. The Government however does still have a role to play, but this role needs to be much more visible, transparent and accountable.

37. The issue of IBW underlines that haphazard approach to marketing Wales overseas. There is a real danger that the lack of co-ordination between the UK's nations and regions means the message that the UK is broadcasting to the international business community is a cacophony rather than a chorus. In this, Wales' voice is being lost.

38. There needs to be a more co-ordinated approach to promoting Wales overseas. The UK Government should meet regularly with the Welsh Government to ensure that the bodies that promote Britain overseas, such as the Department for Business, Innovation and Skills and the British Council, recognise and promote Wales effectively as an attractive part of the UK for business investment.

Empowering the Assembly to act

39. Whilst some of the ideas suggested above are within the powers of the National Assembly to deliver on behalf of Wales, they are necessarily dependent on the funding available to it. With this in mind, we suggest three steps that now need to be taken in order for the Assembly to be empowered to act when it is necessary:

Reform of the Barnett Formula

40. The arguments are well-rehearsed, but it is clear to politicians, commentators and the business community in Wales that the Barnett Formula does not, and has never, given Wales the level of funding required to allow it to compete on a level playing field with other areas of the UK. There is an urgent need for reform of this formula, and a move towards a needs-based structure for the funding of Wales and its services.

Allowing borrowing powers

41. From a pragmatic view-point, the Welsh Government needs the power to borrow money in order to give it the flexibility to act to protect the Welsh economy, and Welsh services, in difficult times. It should also be pointed out, however, that from a point of principal, this is a power available to councils across the UK, and there can be no justifiable reason to withhold it from the nation's government.

Corporation Tax

42. Welsh Liberal Democrats have long been advocates of the devolution of powers over corporation tax to the National Assembly and examining the potential of lower corporation tax to attract inward investment to Wales.

43. The Holtham Commission identified the complexities that surround the devolution of taxes, but the potential for a differing rate of corporation tax in Northern Ireland could provide a practical example of how this could work.

Potential policy clashes between England and Wales

44. The nature of devolution is that economic development policy will differ between England and Wales. We support these differences as it will allow Welsh economic problems to be addressed in a unique manner. However, these differences need to be approached in a complementary and not a competitive way.

Enterprise Zones

45. If successful in reaching their aims, the creation of Enterprise Zones on the borders of Wales, in Bristol, Hereford and Liverpool, is likely to have a significant adverse affect on the prospects of towns and cities on the Welsh side of the border to attract inward investment. It may also act to draw existing jobs out of economically vulnerable areas such as Newport, Wrexham and Powys.

46. A likely, and understandable, response from the Welsh Government would be to establish its own Enterprise Zones offering at least equal benefits to those proposed in England. This would be entirely necessary to support the Welsh economy, but opens the possibility of a potential "price-war" developing between the regions of England and Wales facing the border. Steps urgently need to be taken to avoid this situation.

Tax Increment Financing

47. The UK Government has announced its intention to allow local authorities to introduce Tax Increment Financing as part of a new range of powers to allow cities to develop. These have already been used in some parts of Scotland (such as Edinburgh and Aberdeen) to allow major commercial regeneration in urban areas.

48. The Welsh Government has made no progress in allowing TIF for Welsh local authorities, which means that they could be left at a competitive disadvantage if cities across the border are developing at a faster pace.

49. The UK Government needs to publish the process and timescale for this immediately, as well as the mechanism by which it will do this, so that the Welsh Government can develop an appropriate response.

50. It is also worth noting that, should corporation tax be devolved, there is the potential for a high profile policy clash between different nations of the United Kingdom, and there could be a "price war" between them. This may become an important issue soon if the rate of corporation tax in Northern Ireland is lowered.

51. We believe that there should be more regular meetings between the Welsh and UK governments on the subject of economic development, to acknowledge the fact that both governments have roles to play in the economic development in Wales. These meetings should have a published agenda and minutes, to ensure visibility and transparency. Such meetings could help avoid potentially damaging clashes of policy as those outlined above as well as provide a mechanism for monitoring joint initiatives to promote Wales as a business location.

52. The Welsh Government has to ensure that its inaction on either Enterprise Zones or Tax Increment Financing does not give the impression that the government is unconcerned with economic growth or that it lags behind England in economic innovation. Such a reputation would not enhance the attraction of Wales to potential inward investment.

CONCLUSION

53. Inward investment into Wales has declined in the past 20 years and to address this, and to bring inward investment into Wales in greater amounts and a more sustainable manner, we must address fundamental issues. Wales' relatively poor infrastructure and relatively low skills base are a visible source of competitive disadvantage which need to be overcome. As well as this, the UK and Welsh governments need to identify Wales' key selling points, and use them to improve the impression of Wales abroad, showing investors that Wales is a nation in which investment will be rewarded.

August 2011

Written evidence submitted by Nick Ramsay AM

Inward investment is key to promoting and developing the Welsh Business Sector and has been an important part of the Welsh Economy since the 1970s.

It peaked in the mid 1990's when Wales made up close to **15%** of the total inward investment into the UK. Between 1998 and 2008 Inward Investment has steadily fallen to a point in 2009 when only **4%** of the total UK Inward Investment was found in Wales. During this period over 171 foreign owned sites relocated away from Wales, many setting up in Eastern Europe.

The Gross Value Added (GVA) per head measurement of economic output in Wales as a percentage of the UK total has declined between 1999 (**77.3%**) and 2009 (**74.3%**) meaning that output per head has fallen in almost every year over a 10 year period resulting in Wales officially becoming the poorest part of the United Kingdom. It is also worth highlighting that Wales is still to achieve the "at least 90%" target that the Welsh Government set under Rhodri Morgan in 2000.

This trend needs to be turned around. 2010 saw an upturn in the global investment market for the first time since the economic crash of 2008. Wales needs to ensure that it really is "Open for Business" as the Labour Government claimed in this year's Assembly manifesto. The Welsh Conservatives understand this and will continue to put pressure on the Assembly Government to come up with a new strategy, a new focus and a long term commitment to this vitally important source of future investment.

There are a number of ways by which inward investment can be sourced and stimulated.

Earlier this year the Welsh Conservatives led an Assembly debate on Wales' position in the world and developed four key themes as a way of encourage further investment into Wales.

(1) Recognise the key role of tourism in the Welsh economy.

(2) Promote Wales overseas as a whole.

(3) Increase the number of companies exporting from Wales and the value of Welsh exports.

(4) Ensure that further inward investment into Wales is encouraged.

Welsh Conservatives also made the following key points concerning the current position of Wales to help identify how it can remain competitive in comparison to other areas of the UK and similar size nations throughout Europe and the world.

(a) *The Welsh market is small, so Wales needs to look beyond its borders.* Opportunities for tourism promotion, exports and inward investment exist. But they are all too often untapped.

(b) *Tourism supports more than 10% of the Welsh economy.* It deserves to be taken seriously by the Welsh Labour Government. Regular tourism data needs to be published to ensure resources are focused on the most promising markets.

(c) *Repeated Welsh Government re-organisations are taking attention away from the task of selling Wales to the world.* A strong and recognisable brand needs to be built and the Welsh Government should take a lead.

(d) *The Welsh Labour Government must listen to concerns about the abolition of the WDA.* It was recognised across the world and was scrapped at great cost to Wales' brand. Welsh Labour should act to ensure Wales is not in the "industrial wilderness" for a decade, as Sir Roger Jones warned.

Taking each of the themes in turn:

TOURISM

Tourism revenue has fallen over the last six years from close to £1.8 million in 2003 to just over £1.4 million in 2009. Overnight bed stays has also witnessed a downward trend.

Air Travel

— In 2010 passenger numbers at Cardiff Airport fell by 14% compared with 2009.

— In the same period Bristol Airport's passenger numbers grew by almost 2%.

— The airport's market size is a concern. Air France-KLM's General Manager for UK and Ireland said: *"It's all a question of market size and it's this that deters other airlines. To have permanent long-haul flights there has to be a critical mass in order to maintain a profitable service which is not the case at present."*.

— Cardiff Airport's Managing Director, Patrick Duffy, said the Welsh Government must *"step in to address market opportunities"* at Cardiff.

— Martin Evans, of the Chartered Institute of Logistics and Transport and an air transport consultant said: *"...this is not just an issue for the management at Cardiff Airport. This is an issue that has to be addressed by the Assembly Government as well. Cardiff can get an advantage in bringing inbound passengers rather than focusing on the outbound market. You can only get that if the Assembly Government uses its marketing money available to raise awareness of Wales in foreign markets and then they can support the airlines in bringing in new routes and spend time convincing them that the market is there."*

Welsh Conservative policies

— The manifesto pledged to *"boost the marketing of Wales as a destination in the home and international markets"*. Successive Labour-led governments have not marketed Wales in an integrated way. The Welsh Government itself admitted *"a more coherent approach"* was necessary for the Welsh economy.[22]

— Welsh Conservatives proposed to abolish business rates for businesses below £12,000 rateable value and taper relief from £12,001 to £15,000 would help small tourist operators. The last Welsh Government refused to help tourist operators with extra rates relief.[23] Welsh Conservatives have long campaigned for small tourist operators, who are the lifeblood of their local tourist sectors. We were successful in our campaign with Conservative colleagues in the rest of the UK to abolish Labour's planned changes to capital allowances for self-catering properties, which would have devastated the industry.

ENGAGING WITH THE WORLD

— The Welsh market is relatively small. Wales needs partners outside Wales.

— The Institute of Chartered Accountants in England and Wales' Global Enterprise Survey found that, compared with other UK regions Welsh business is less "globally engaged".[24]

— Professor Robert Huggins, UWIC, said: *"Compared with many other regions, Wales barely engages in the global economy."*[25]

---

[22] Economic Renewal Programme, 2010.
[23] Letter from Carl Sargeant, Local Government Minister, to Graham Tayler of the Welsh Association of Self Catering Operators.
[24] ICAEW response to Economic Renewal Programme.
[25] Western Mail, "Rather than being on a spike Wales lies in the economic lowlands", 18 November 2009.

EXPORTS

— Welsh exports have performed reasonably well in the past two years, aided by the low value of the pound. In Q1 2011 almost £3.5 billion of Welsh exports were made, including £1.5 billion to the European Community.

— However, Wales still lags behind similar English regions, such as the south west and north west.[26]

Welsh Conservative policies

— Our manifesto pledges to *"promote Welsh food and drink and other key growth markets like walking, fishing and country sports"*. Wales should seek to promote Welsh produce to strategic locations, such as high-profile shops and delicatessens. Products with particular appeal can be marketed strategically: eg Welsh whisky could be promoted in India, which is the world's largest whisky market.[27]

— We also pledged to establish a Welsh hub in London to help Welsh businesses take advantage of global opportunities. London is a global economic centre, and it is also on Wales' doorstep. A hub would help sell the Welsh economy and culture to the world and feed vital intelligence back to Wales about economic opportunities. Unlike existing Welsh Government overseas offices a Welsh hub could have the specific remit to grow the Welsh economy and increase awareness of Wales abroad.

INWARD INVESTMENT

— Around £7 billion was invested between 1980 and 1995.[28]

— The average number of jobs created per project in Wales from 2003 to 2010 was 173.[29]

— The number of Foreign Direct Investment projects typically varies from year to year:

Region	2004	2005	2006	2007	2008	2009
Wales	35	13	16	22	35	20
Scotland	64	33	62	69	53	51
Northern Ireland	16	18	17	26	19	25

Source: Ernst & Young's European Investment monitor

— The Economic Renewal Programme need to develop "a clearer narrative around the business proposition".[30] It abolished IBW, which was replaced with *"Integrated sector teams... responsible for securing new investment as well as targeted aftercare of existing Foreign Direct Investment so that we can build synergies across the sectors and encourage re-investment."*[31]

— UK Trade and Investment (UKTI) helps UK based companies in the global economy. UKTI treats the UK as a single investment unit and the Welsh Government handles marketing of Wales. The two organisations have a formal mechanism for joint working.[32]

— From 1976 until 2006 the Welsh Development Agency held the remit for inward investment. The WDA was abolished in 2006 and taken "in-house" into the Welsh Government civil service as International Business Wales (IBW). IBW came under fire following the Massey Review into its activities.

— A report by *Oxford Intelligence* into the life science industry conducted a "spontaneous awareness of development agencies" survey and found the WDA came joint second with UKTI, despite its being inactive for more than five years.[33]

— *Sir Roger Jones, a former WDA chief executive,* criticised the WDA's abolition in June 2011. He acknowledged that the WDA was "far from perfect".[34] However, he said: *"I stated publicly that it would take three years for the Welsh Government to realise its mistake, a further three years to decide what to do and three more years to implement change. This would sentence Wales to nearly 10 years in the wilderness in terms of industrial development. To this day, I stand by my prediction. We have seen expenditure in excess of £100 million per annum that has produced next to nothing in the form of outcomes."*

---

[26] HGM Revenue and Customs, June 2011 update.

[27] BBC News, May 2007.

[28] UK Department for Business, Innovation and Skills, Paper to Welsh Affairs Committee, February 2011.

[29] FT, fDi Markets Monitor, 2011.

[30] Economic Renewal Programme, p 16.

[31] Economic Renewal Programme, p 41.

[32] UK Department for Business, Innovation and Skills, Paper to Welsh Affairs Committee, February 2011.

[33] Oxford Intelligence, The MedTech Report 2011, International Investment Strategies and Location Benchmarking Study, June 2011.

[34] Evidence submitted to Welsh Affairs Committee by Sir Roger Jones, June 2011.

Enterprise Zones

The successful identification and implementation of Enterprise Zones is central to the economic prosperity of Wales.

The Westminster Government recently announced new Enterprise Zones as part of David Cameron's wish to *"do everything we can to make Britain the best place in the world to start and grow a business"*. He went on to say *"Enterprise zones are a major step towards delivering this—cutting business taxes, easing planning restrictions and giving business the tools they need to invest and expand. These new enterprise zones will be trailblazers for growth, jobs and prosperity throughout the country."*

Whilst the Welsh Conservatives welcome such zones, concern exists that forming Enterprise Zones in areas such as Hereford, Bristol, The Black Country, Cheshire and Liverpool, all close to the Welsh Border, may have a negative impact on the economic competitiveness in the neighbouring areas in Wales. Welsh Conservatives are calling on the Welsh Government to form similar zones in border counties/communities of Wales.

Shadow Minister for Business, Nick Ramsay AM has accused the Welsh Government of *"dragging their feet"* and *"failing to put forward plans for a single enterprise zone in Wales despite putting forward a policy to do so last March."*

The manifesto for the Assembly Election committed the Welsh Conservatives to creating at least four Enterprise Zones in Wales.

September 2011

Written evidence submitted by Admiral Group Plc

INTRODUCTION

Admiral is the UK's second largest car insurer, selling car insurance almost exclusively via the internet, under a number of different brand names.

We came to Cardiff as a brand new company in August 1992 and started trading in January 1993, with around 50 employees on day one. We now employ just over 4,000 people in Cardiff, Swansea and Newport. Cardiff is the headquarters for the UK and for our wider international operations (Spain, Italy, France, India, Canada and the U.S.). Everything we do, we do in South Wales—from entry level customer service, through to highly trained technical insurance sales, specialist I.T. and marketing functions, to the senior management of the company. Our current annual wage bill is in the order of £70 million, and we will award staff in South Wales shares to a (current) value of circa £30 million during 2011.

LOCATION CRITERIA

Generally, car insurance is a much commoditised, low margin, business and success requires tight expense control. In that context, the availability of a substantial pool of relatively affordable staff and relatively cheap office space were important criteria.

The management team, who were based within, or within commuting distance of, London, realised this would require some or all of them to relocate given the cost of any operation within or around the M25.

The parent company, Hayter Brockbank, itself headquartered in the City, were keen that the operation chose a cost-effective location, but were also insistent that the operation should be within 2 hours travel time from London. They stipulated this constraint in order to reduce the time burden on their management team supervising this new, majority-owned subsidiary.

As well as the two key criteria of cost-efficiency and 2 hour proximity to London, the management team were also interested in the potential for grant support from candidate locations. Hayter Brockbank was not a large operation and had very rationally structured the financing of Admiral in such a way that it could afford to close down the operation early, without major loss, if results proved disappointing.

The management team was sensitive to the appeal of grant support, not as a material contributor to the long-term health of the operation, but as a possible way of giving ourselves a cushion to adapt the model in the event of early disappointment; of essentially buying a second roll of the dice. With these criteria in mind, we went to the economic development departments of a number of cities which were within 2 hours of London and which were likely to be competitive on cost. The cities contacted included, amongst others, Folkestone, Brighton, Corby, Leeds and of course, Cardiff. We explained that we were a financial services start-up, hoping to employ 50 staff initially, rising according to our business plan to circa 250 at the end of three years. We asked if they could tell us why we should locate in their city.

SELLING ADMIRAL ON CARDIFF

From the outset of the process, Cardiff stood out in terms of their enthusiasm to secure Admiral as an inward investor. Almost all the cities approached wrote to us with generic reasons to choose them and invited us to visit their city. Only one came to us in South London and presented to us, Paul Gorin from the economic development section of South Glamorgan Council. He then invited us to come to Cardiff—the first of five or six visits before we committed to Cardiff—and he arranged introductions to a number of public and private sector bodies able to help answer questions and provide support. All were positive and enthusiastic advocates of Cardiff and South Wales.

By the end of this process Cardiff had become our preferred location because of its cost competitiveness, its approach as a pleasant place to live, the immediate availability of affordable office space, and, perhaps most importantly at that stage, because of the offer of £1 million grant support. However, there was a major obstacle—the lack of a local pool of skilled senior technical insurance managers to recruit; notably the lack of a car insurance underwriter, a key initial appointment. A candidate had been identified, willing to commit to an inevitably risky start-up, but he was unwilling to relocate to South Wales from the South Coast of England (an area in which a number of car insurers are based). This meant that we had to regretfully tell Paul Gorin that we wouldn't be based in Wales, but rather in Brighton, and that therefore, incidentally, we couldn't accept his invitation to hospitality at Royal Ascot. Paul persuaded us to come to Ascot anyway and to bring the car insurance underwriter too—on which occasion he successfully sold the underwriter on the merits of Cardiff, and we were able to revert to Cardiff.

Admiral did look at other locations in South Wales as well as Cardiff. We visited possible sites in Merthyr and Blackwood. These sites were much less attractive for a number of reasons—smaller labour pools, fewer and more restrictive office space options and, sadly, the fact that they were markedly less attractive places to work and live than Cardiff. The extra travel time from London was also an issue for our parent company.

POSSIBLE LESSONS

We would hesitate to draw definitive conclusions from what was only one company's experience, but below are a few possible "lessons" in terms of how best to attract worthwhile inward investment to Wales.

(a) *Attract businesses that are willing to locate lock, stock and barrel in Wales*

Operations that base their headquarters and senior management in Wales are ultimately potentially more valuable than off-shoots of big companies based elsewhere, fulfilling only a subset of servicing/processing functions for a business where real decision-making power lies elsewhere. Businesses with their hearts and brains in Wales are more likely to offer higher quality, better paid jobs, which last longer. Businesses with only "muscle" in Wales are more likely to withdraw in hard times or if cheaper location options emerge.

(b) *Attract early stage or start-up business to Wales*

Practically speaking, it's hard for large and long-established businesses to re-locate in their entirety, so it possibly makes sense to seek to attract start-up or early stage operations. An advantage of this is that potentially small financial inducements in absolute financial terms can be very influential on the decisions of small, early stage businesses.

A policy of attracting early stage business is, of course, a long game and would require political courage. It would lack the headline grabbing appeal of a big name investment in a big facility, with hundreds of jobs from day one. There'll also inevitably be some failures along the way—start-ups that receive support and subsequently fold.

(c) *Recognise the importance of financial incentives to locate to Wales*

Although there are many very good reasons to come to Wales and it has proved fertile ground for Admiral, there are real barriers to choosing Wales. Cash support is valuable in overcoming these barriers.

(d) *Provide a competent, motivated, and entrepreneurial team devoted to persuading companies to come to Wales*

Without the competence, salesmanship, and determination of Paul Gorin and his colleagues, we would now be located in Brighton. Creating an effective team requires a budget, a degree of autonomy and a certain culture—best defined by what it isn't, namely bureaucratic, risk averse, slow to take decisions.

(e) *Recognise the important role of the quality of infrastructure in attracting inward investment*

Good infrastructure and a good environment in which to live and work are important in attracting inward investment and in helping existing Welsh companies to flourish.

Admiral partly came to Cardiff because it was reasonably accessible from London for our funders. Since we came to Cardiff, travel to London times have increased by 10–15 minutes, while a number of competitor cities have seen travel to London times reduce over the period. Cardiff will fall further behind if high speed train investments bring the Midlands and North West of England relatively "closer" to London.

Admiral now operates in six countries beyond the UK. The problems of convenient access are heightened once a Cardiff-based business begins to operate on an international scale. The bulk of our international travel is conducted through Bristol or Heathrow, given the limited services operating through Cardiff.

June 2011

Written evidence submitted by UKTI and Wales Office

INTRODUCTION

This evidence is provided by the UK Government. UK Trade & Investment (UKTI) is the government department with lead national responsibility for trade and investment. The Trade and Investment team at the Welsh Assembly Government (formerly International Business Wales) has lead responsibility for marketing Wales to foreign investors. The two organisations work together closely to promote the UK and Wales to potential investors.

UK Trade & Investment (UKTI) is the government department that helps UK-based companies succeed in the global economy and assists overseas companies to bring their high quality investment to the UK. UKTI has two parent departments: the Department for Business, Innovation and Skills (BIS), and the Foreign and Commonwealth Office (FCO). UKTI has staff in British Embassies, High Commissions and Consulates-General in 96 markets, including 33 that focus on attracting high quality inward investment into the UK. UKTI also works in close partnership with the Ministry of Defence (MOD), drawing employees and associated running costs from both parent departments, as well as employees on loan from the MOD. UKTI also has its own stream of programme funding.

Wales has a history of performing well in attracting inward investment in comparison to the rest of the UK, attracting substantially more than its population share of new and safeguarded jobs in the early to mid-1990s. That figure has fallen over the last 10 to 15 years to something equating more closely to a population share.

Wales has a number of benefits to offer potential investors, some of which are set out below:

— **Skills:** Wales long traditions of expertise in a number of sectors, including engineering and manufacturing while more recently, it has developed capabilities in areas such as IT, financial and professional services.

— **Proximity to UK hubs and European Marketplace:** As well as being a destination in itself, Wales offers easy access to London as a financial centre and offers good transport links to the rest of the UK and Europe.

— **Property:** Property in Wales is competitively priced in comparison with the rest of the UK.

— **Exceptional quality of life:** Wales offers easy access to stunning landscapes and beautiful beaches as well as exceptional cultural and sports facilities.

The evidence presents the Government's view of inward investment in Wales as it currently stands and examines the changing future investment landscape. We understand that the Welsh Assembly Government will be submitting its own evidence to this enquiry and so we will only examine devolved aspects of attracting inward investment briefly.

The evidence presented in the memorandum covers:

— The current position, in particular examining the most recent inward investment figures.

— The role of the Trade and Investment team in Welsh Assembly Government (formerly International Business Wales).

— The role of the UK Government in attracting inward investment to Wales with particular attention paid to UKTI.

— The support available to organisations involved in promoting Wales, focussing on support provided by the coalition Government.

— Public sector investment, focussing in particular on recent successes and the relocation of Government departments to Wales.

— Conditions to attract inward investment to Wales, looking in particular at recent coalition Government policy changes in this regard, and at the investment business drivers.

— Conclusion and forward look examining the future roles of the Wales Office and UKTI.

— International Business Development Forum principles and guidelines (Annex A).

— Supporting charts (Annex B).

— Investment examples (Annex C).

This presents an overall picture of a changing landscape amongst the organisations working on attracting inward investment to Wales. Both the Trade and Investment team at the Welsh Assembly Government and UKTI will undergo programmes of substantial change in the coming months that may affect the support infrastructure for potential inward investors.

Again, we would expect the Welsh Assembly Government to address the changes set out in their Economic Renewal Programme in more detail in their evidence.

The Wales Office will also play an important role in both promoting Wales as an investment destination, engaging with international organisations and facilitating cross-Government working on inward investment. Wales Office Ministers and officials have already put this into motion but this work is at an early stage. The Secretary of State for Wales has already met with the Government's Trade Advisor, Lord Brittan and a meeting with the new Trade Minister will take place soon after his appointment in January to further progress this work. In addition, the Secretary of State for Wales has set up a Business Advisory Group in order to gather information from businesses and academics in Wales about the state of the Welsh economy, including the conditions necessary for successfully attracting inward investment.

1. CONTEXT

1.1 Historically, Wales has performed well in attracting inward investment with around £7 billion invested between 1980 and 1995. By the mid-1990s, inward investment in Wales had begun to fall, with 11.8% of new and safeguarded jobs in the UK going to Wales in 1992 but only 5.6% of jobs going to Wales by the middle of that decade.

1.2 A detailed analysis of inward investment in Wales over the last five years is included at **Annex B** along with headline data for the past 20 years, country breakdown data from 1990–91 and full sector breakdown data from 1998–99. Tracked over the past five years, Wales' share of the total number of UK investment projects has ranged between 3.4% and 4.6%. In 2009–10, 65 of the total number of 1619 investment projects in the UK went to Wales—4 % of the total. These figures are broadly in line with Wales' share of regional GVA[35], which according to ONS was 4% in 2008.

1.3 Significantly, though, Wales receives a higher proportion of jobs from inward investment projects with these shares varying from between 3.4% in 2008–09 to 7.8% in 2006–07. This suggests that Wales generally attracts larger investment projects that deliver more jobs.

1.4 According to UKTI data, of the 12 geographic areas, made up of the three Devolved Administrations and nine English Regions, in 2009–10 Wales ranked 4th in the UK for attracting new FDI related jobs (see 2.1).

1.5 UKTI FDI project and job statistics are based on:

— information provided by the company at the time of the announcement of the decision to invest in the UK; and

— the investing companies' best estimates of capital expenditure and jobs created/safeguarded in the first three years.

The figures do not take account of subsequent developments.

1.6 There is no requirement for investors to notify UKTI of new investment projects, and so the figures only include those projects where UKTI and/or a partner organisation, such as International Business Wales, were involved, or which have otherwise come to our notice.

1.7 There are already a number of large international companies based in Wales including Amazon, Airbus, Ford and Toyota with around 500 international companies in total, basing themselves in Wales.

The Welsh Development Agency

1.8 Pre-devolution, attracting inward investment into Wales fell within the remit of the Welsh Development Agency (WDA) under the old Welsh Office. The WDA was set up in 1976 to encourage business development and investment in Wales.

1.9 Employing several hundred workers, the WDA was one of Wales' most significant employers with a network of offices worldwide to supplement its Welsh base. Following devolution, the WDA became an Assembly Sponsored Public Body

1.10 Prior to its abolition in April 2006, the WDA was credited with creating thousands of jobs and securing billions of pounds in investment. In addition, the WDA has been credited by some with creating a brand that was recognisable worldwide which may have contributed to its inward investment successes.

1.11 It should be noted, though, that as per paragraph 1.1 above, the number of jobs generated by inward investment during the organisation's tenure did fluctuate. Figures for the mid-1990s, for example, are comparable with recent years during which International Business Wales had taken over the WDA's remit with regard to inward investment.

---

[35] Gross value added is the difference between the value of goods and services produced (output) and the cost of raw materials and other input which are used in production (intermediate consumption); that is, the value added by any unit engaged in production. This is calculated gross of any deductions for depreciation or consumption of fixed capital. Regional gross value added (GVA) is estimated at current basic prices and comprises gross domestic product (GDP) less taxes (plus subsidies) on products. Taxes on products are taxes that are payable per unit of some good or service produced or transacted. Examples include value-added tax and excise duties. Subsidies are payments made to producers by the government or institutions of the European Union to influence production.

1.12 The WDA was merged with the Welsh Assembly Government in April 2006 with its network of international offices falling under the remit of International Business Wales.

International Business Wales

1.13 International Business Wales (IBW) has provided a similar international network to the WDA in order to promote Wales as an inward investment destination. It currently has offices in 13 countries, including three locations in China—Beijing, Shanghai and Hong Kong. Other offices are located in Germany, India, Australia, the United Arab Emirates and the United States. IBW also maintains an office in London in order to encourage inward investment from both foreign and UK companies based in London and the South East.

1.14 In the summer of 2009, IBW took its largest ever trade mission to the United States with 80 companies attending the Smithsonian celebrations in Washington DC to showcase Wales and its products.

1.15 International Business Wales is also responsible for promoting Welsh businesses overseas and as with inward investment its efforts seem to have born fruit over the last decade. Total Welsh exports rose by 47% from 1999 to 2009 with exports to non-EU nations rising by 167% in the same period. For the UK as a whole, exports rose by just over 32% in the same period.

1.16 More recently, IBW has faced occasional criticism, such as through the Massey report published last year. In July this year, the Welsh Assembly Government took the decision to merge the organisation with the Department for Economy and Transport.

2. CURRENT POSITION

Inward Investment to Wales: Overview of the current position

2.1 Wales is the 6th most attractive destination for inward investment projects in the UK and attracts between 2 to 9% of all projects, averaging 4.7% over 10-years. However, according to fDi Markets[36] the average number of jobs created per project in Wales from 2003 to 2010 was 173. This compares to the UK average of 105. In 2009–10 Wales was ranked 4th most successful geographical area for attracting new FDI related jobs.

Table 1

FOREIGN DIRECT INVESTMENT ACROSS THE UK'S NATIONS AND REGIONS (BY NUMBER OF PROJECTS)

Region	2000	2001	2002	2003	2004	2005	2006	2007	2008	2009	Total
South East (1)	281	168	169	169	242	287	379	410	342	346	2,793
Scotland	55	35	25	39	64	33	62	69	53	51	486
West Midlands	48	31	17	32	46	43	49	54	37	51	408
North	17	11	34	46	50	49	31	42	37	39	356
North West	39	20	10	33	28	27	37	26	51	37	308
Wales	**35**	**19**	**27**	**42**	**35**	**13**	**16**	**22**	**35**	**20**	**264**
South West	27	9	31	28	22	20	23	9	29	32	230
Yorkshire & Humber	27	23	15	25	24	17	14	16	22	42	225
East Anglia	15	16	18	5	25	30	28	29	30	19	215
Northern Ireland	20	21	13	10	16	18	17	26	19	25	185
East Midlands	10	17	10	24	11	22	29	10	31	16	180
Total	**574**	**370**	**369**	**453**	**563**	**559**	**685**	**713**	**686**	**678**[37]	**5,650**
Wales's %	**6%**	**5%**	**7%**	**9%**	**6%**	**2%**	**2%**	**3%**	**5%**	**3%**	**4.7%**

(1) includes London.

Source: Ernst & Young's European Investment Monitor.

Table 2

INWARD INVESTMENT—NEW JOBS IN EACH OF LAST 10 YEARS

Year	UK	New Jobs Wales	%	Ranking against the UK's 12 geographic areas
2000–01	71,488	4,520	6.3%	7
2001–02	34,087	3,872	11.3%	1
2002–03	34,396	4,083	11.8%	3

[36] Crossborder—Investment Monitor.
[37] UKTI recorded data shows total UK investment for 2009–10 as 1,619. EIM and UKTI have different methodologies for collecting data and Annex D explaines the methodologies employed.

| | | *New Jobs* | | |
Year	UK	Wales	%	*Ranking against the UK's 12 geographic areas*
2003–04	25,463	4,064	15.9%	1
2004–05	39,592	2,593	6.5%	9
2005–06	34,077	3,132	9.2%	6
2006–07	36,526	3,379	9.3%	4
2007–08	45,051	3,743	8.3%	6
2008–09	35,111	2,185	6.2%	7
2009–10	53,358	3,431	6.4%	4

Source: UKTI data.

2.3 Wales has also sustained its inward investment performance through the economic downturn better than the UK as a whole. Overall investment into the UK in 2009–10 fell by 7% on the previous year while investment into Wales rose by 8%. The number of jobs associated with that investment showed that while UK job numbers were up 20% on the previous year, job numbers in Wales almost tripled (see Table 2).

Table 3

UKTI RECORDED SUCCESSES IN THE UK BY INVESTMENT TYPE—2008–09 AND 2009–10

Year	Project Type	*No of Projects*	*No of New Jobs*	*No of Safeguarded Jobs*	*Total No of Associated Jobs*
2008–09	Acquisitions, Mergers & JV's	457	719	21,882	22,601
	Expansion	460	15,975	20,222	36,197
	New	827	18,417	1,325	19,742
	TOTALS	**1,744**	**35,111**	**43,429**	**78,540**

Year	Project Type	*No of Projects*	*No of New Jobs*	*No of Safeguarded Jobs*	*Total No of Associated Jobs*
2009–10	Acquisitions, Mergers & JV's	225	1,153	9,844	10,997
	Expansion	544	17,435	29,391	46,826
	New	850	34,770	1,753	36,523
	TOTALS	**1,619**	**53,358**	**40,988**	**94,346**

UKTI RECORDED SUCCESSES IN WALES BY INVESTMENT TYPE—2008–09 AND 2009–10

Year	Project Type	*No of Projects*	*No of New Jobs*	*No of Safeguarded Jobs*	*Total No of Associated Jobs*
2008–09	Acquisitions, Mergers & JV's	12	75	329	404
	Expansion	18	589	200	789
	New	30	1,521	0	1,521
	TOTALS	**60**	**2,185**	**529**	**2,714**

Year	Project Type	*No of Projects*	*No of New Jobs*	*No of Safeguarded Jobs*	*Total No of Associated Jobs*
2009–10	Acquisitions, Mergers & JV's	3	13	67	80
	Expansion	34	1,467	3,864	5,331
	New	28	1,951	0	1,951
	TOTALS	**65**	**3,431**	**3,931**	**7,362**

Source: UKTI data.

2.4 Of the 65 projects recorded by UKTI for Wales: 63 were assisted and two landed without any government assistance: (UKTI assisted: three (8%); UKTI working with WAG assisted: 15 (24%) and WAG assisted: 45 (71%)). Therefore, UKTI was involved in 18 projects, or 29%, of the total projects assisted.

Foreign Direct Investment in 2009: The Global, European and UK Context

2.5 The UNCTAD World Investment Report 2010 valued global Foreign Direct Investment (FDI) inward flows in 2009 at US$1,114 billion, a decrease from the previous year (US$1,770 billion). The UK and its competitors were not immune from the downturn in FDI Flows. The flow of inward FDI into the UK in 2009 was US$45.6 billion, a decrease from the previous year (US$96.9 billion).

2.6 However in relative terms, and against the backdrop of reduced global FDI flows and world recession, 2009 was a good year for inward investment to the UK. In 2009, the UK attracted and retained US$1,125 billion of FDI Stock, an increase from the previous year[38]. Within the UK, Wales performed relatively better than average: overall investment into the UK in 2009–10 fell by 7% on the previous year while investment into Wales rose by 8%. The number of jobs associated with that investment showed that while UK job numbers were up 20% on the previous year, job numbers in Wales almost tripled.

2.7 The number of FDI projects in Europe fell by 11% to 3303 in 2009, and FDI generated 16 % fewer jobs in the same period[39]. According to Ernst & Young, the UK was the top country in Europe in 2009 in respect of number of FDI projects and job creation, and the most attractive destination in Europe for FDI. Annex 1 for full investment project figures.

Foreign Direct Investment to Wales

2.8 Overall investment into the UK in 2009–10 fell by 7% on the previous year while with 65 projects, investment into Wales rose by 8%. The number of new jobs (3,431) was 57% up on the previous years; the number of safeguarded jobs (3,931) was an impressive 643% up on the previous years and total jobs associated with investment in Wales was 7,362, up some 171% on 2008–09 figures. Table 2 provides statistics on inward investment in Wales and the rest of the UK over the last two years (2008–09 and 2009–10).

2.9 According to fDi Markets[40] the average number of jobs created per project in Wales from 2003 to 2010 was 173. This compares to the UK average of 105. Additionally, Wales attracted an average of 6% R&D over 10 years (Table 3).

Table 4

R&D INVESTMENT PROJECTS ATTRACTED TO WALES

Summary:

—   Wales attracted an average of 6% R&D over 10 years.

Region	2000	2001	2002	2003	2004	2005	2006	2007	2008	2009	Total
South East (UK)	18	14	8	6	12	12	12	15	18	14	129
Scotland	9	7	3	4	8	10	12	16	9	14	92
East Anglia	3	3	5	1	7	10	3	7	9	5	53
Northern Ireland	4	5	2	3	5	6	4	5	5	7	46
North	1	1	3	2	2	3	5	4	7	3	31
Wales	**2**	**1**	**2**	**2**	**5**	**1**	**2**	**6**	**5**	**3**	**29**
North West	2	1	2	4	2	2		3	2	9	27
West Midlands	4	2		1	1	2	1	5	3	8	27
East Midlands		3	1	2	2	3	4	1	2	2	20
South West	2		1	2	1	3	2	1	4		16
Yorkshire & Humber	2	2		1	3	2	2		1	3	16
Total	**47**	**39**	**27**	**28**	**48**	**54**	**47**	**63**	**65**	**68**	**486**
Wales's %											**6%**

Source: European Investment Monitor.

3. UK GOVERNMENT ROLE AND SUPPORT AVAILABLE

UK Government Role

3.1 UK Trade & Investment (UKTI) is the government organisation that helps UK-based companies succeed in the global economy. It tailors its services to the needs of individual businesses to help them maximise their international success. UKTI also helps bring high quality inward investment to the UK's economy, providing support and advice to investors at all stages of their business decision-making.

---

[38] UNCTAD World Investment Report 2010.
[39] Ernst & Young's 2010 European Attractiveness Survey.
[40] Crossborder—Investment Monitor.

Foreign Direct Investment (FDI)—UK and Wales

3.2 UKTI markets the UK as a whole as a destination for FDI, while specific marketing of Wales as a FDI destination rests with the Trade and Investment team in the Welsh Assembly Government (formerly IBW). However, the two organisations work together closely, under an agreed formal mechanism[41], to maximise inward investment successes.

Trade and Investment team in Welsh Assembly Government (formerly International Business Wales)

3.3 International Business Wales was formed in April 2006 by the Welsh Assembly Government to promote trade and attract inward investment, following the merger of Wales Trade International (the trade arm of the Assembly) and the International Division of the Welsh Development Agency (an executive agency responsible for inward investment). The Trade and Investment team in the Welsh Assembly Government receives its own funding for trade and investment activities through the Welsh Assembly Government; and separate funding through the EU Structural Funds Programme. In addition, companies in Wales have access to the majority of UKTI programmes and services (mainly trade-related).

3.4 The Trade and Investment team at the Welsh Assembly Government (formerly International Business Wales) provided a similar international network to the WDA in order to promote Wales as an inward investment destination. It currently has offices in thirteen countries, including three locations in China—Beijing, Shanghai and Hong Kong. Other offices are located in Germany, India, Australia, the United Arab Emirates and the United States. It also maintains an office in London in order to encourage inward investment from both foreign and UK companies based in London and the South East.

3.5 In the summer of 2009, The Trade and Investment team at the Welsh Assembly Government (formerly International Business Wales) took its largest ever trade mission to the United States with 80 companies attending the Smithsonian celebrations in Washington DC to showcase Wales and its products.

3.6 The Trade and Investment team at the Welsh Assembly Government (formerly International Business Wales) is also responsible for promoting Welsh businesses overseas and as with inward investment its efforts seem to have born fruit over the last decade. Total Welsh exports rose by 47% from 1999 to 2009 with exports to non-EU nations rising by 167% in the same period. For the UK as a whole, exports rose by just over 32% in the same period.

3.7 More recently, following the Massey Report, WAG took the decisions to merge IBW with the Department for Economy and Transport.

3.8 The Welsh Assembly Government's Economic Renewal Programme published in July set out, *inter alia*, changes to its delivery of trade and investment services in Wales. It confirmed that business support in future will focus resources on where they can add most value, acting as an enabler of growth for the Welsh economy as a whole, rather than a significant direct deliverer of services to individual businesses. There will be a sector based strategic approach to business support. The key sectors will be ICT; energy and environment; advanced materials; creative industries; life sciences; and financial and professional services. Foreign Direct Investment and Trade will be an integral part of the sectoral approach.

3.9 Under the Economic Renewal Programme, International Business Wales ceased to be a separate function of the Department of Economy & Transport. Instead, integrated sector teams in the Welsh Assembly Government will be responsible for securing new investment, as well as targeted aftercare. Welsh Assembly Government also announced a review of its overseas offices network, which we understand will be concluded by the end of the year.

Potential for Increased Investment in Wales

3.10 Economic development, including trade and investment, is devolved, and the Welsh Assembly Government is submitting to this inquiry.

Collaborative Working UKTI and Wales

3.11 The principles and guidelines (Annex A) of the International Business Development Forum (IBDF), govern the way in which UK Trade & Investment and the English RDAs work together to manage the flow of Foreign Direct Investment (FDI). The Devolved Administrations, including the Trade and Investment team at the Welsh Assembly Government (formerly International Business Wales) have also agreed to co-operate with these arrangements in line with their devolved powers. The overall aim is to maximise the amount of knowledge-driven FDI for the UK, to improve transparency and partnership working, to strengthen the UK Brand, avoid perceptions of wasteful competition and the risk of customer confusion, and to promote the more efficient use of public money across the network.

3.12 The following key client relationship principles govern this work and are designed especially for use with strategically important inward investors with the propensity to make high value investment in the UK

---

[41] The International Business development Forum which brings together UKTI, the trade and investment promotion organisations of the Devolved Administrations and the English regions.

economy. These principles rely on stake holders cooperation. Four key principles for effective Client Relationship Management:

(1) That we make a priority of winning the business for the UK and acting in the national interest;

(2) That we are Client-oriented, ie we put the Client first and adopt a true service ethic towards them;

(3) That we focus on building long term relationships with Clients;

(4) That we maintain transparency across the network with prompt sharing of information whilst respecting Client confidentiality where appropriate in line with the IBDF Guidelines.

3.13 IBDF members operate transparently. Project information is shared through an electronic communications platform allowing the Devolved Administrations of Wales, Scotland and Northern Ireland, and the nine English Regional Development Agencies to see and respond to potential projects. Propositions prepared by the DAs and RDAs for potential projects are collated by UKTI. The final document is delivered to the client, usually, by UKTI overseas.

3.14 The last formal IBDF meeting took place on 28 January 2010 in London, at which International Business Wales participated. Regular teleconferences take place between UKTI and the Devolved Administrations, the most recent being on 3 November 2010, at which the Welsh Assembly Government participated.

Interchange between Trade and Investment team at the Welsh Assembly Government (formerly International Business Wales) and UKTI

3.15 Trade and Investment team at the Welsh Assembly Government (formerly International Business Wales) and UKTI cooperate and foster knowledge transfer through interchange of staff. For example IBW seconded a China inward investment specialist to UKTI for a period of three months in 2009–10.

Training

3.16 Trade and Investment team at the Welsh Assembly Government (formerly International Business Wales) regularly hosts and provides training for members of UKTI's global network to ensure that the national investment messaging accurately reflects Wales offer to investors.

Sectoral Coverage

3.17 UKTI works collaboratively to attract, retain and add value to inward investment for the UK. The Project Teams and their partners work with foreign-owned companies where the UK has a compelling proposition, focussing particularly on assisting the highest value inward investment to enter the UK. The work includes influencing the decision to invest in the UK, development of existing investors' footprints in the UK, and helping to grow existing investors into third markets.

3.18 UKTI currently runs 11 sector support teams, with UKTI Defence & Security Organisation providing additional support for these sectors. UKTI's sector teams include the sectors that feature strongly in Wales (ICT; energy and environment; advanced materials; creative industries; life sciences; and financial and professional services.). All sector support is UK-wide.

3.19 UKTI's sectorally-focused Investment Project Teams work in close collaboration with: UKTI's global operation, other Government Departments, the Devolved Administrations, including the Welsh Assembly Government, the English Regional Development Agencies and private sector experts in virtual teams.

3.20 The virtual teams offer extensive bespoke business and policy expertise and advice (including skills, infrastructure, tax, financial, R&D and sector specialists). Bespoke propositions are developed to help companies make their location decision, and to help them to grow within and from the UK internationally.

4. Public Sector Investment

Public Sector Investment

4.1 Much has been made of the size of the public sector in Wales and its future role in economic growth. In particular, Wales has a relatively high proportion of public sector employment compared to the rest of the UK with 35% of jobs in Wales in 2009 being classed as in public administration, education and health. This equates to 392,246 jobs and is an increase from 328,816 jobs, or 32%, in 2000.

4.2 The corresponding UK statistics show 28% of jobs in public administration, education and health last year, and increase from 24% in 2000. In Scotland in 2009, the corresponding figure was 32% and in Northern Ireland it was 35%, the same as in Wales. This indicates high levels of public sector employment across all three devolved nations but it should not be taken necessarily as an indication of an overlarge public sector.

4.3 The employment level in Wales, according to the latest Labour Market Statistics (July to September) is currently 67.1%, the lowest in the UK, barring Northern Ireland. Therefore, the high rates of public sector employment as a proportion of employee jobs do not necessarily equate to a large public sector. Rather, it indicates a need for the private sector to grow to expand employment.

Civil Service Relocation Programmes

4.4 The Office of Government Commerce (OGC) is responsible for the former administration's relocation programme which committed to relocating a substantial number of public sector activities from London and the South East of England to other parts of the United Kingdom.

4.5 In addition, Ian Smith's Review: *Putting the Front Line First: Smarter Government*, published in March this year, recommended a target of relocating a further 15,000 civil servants over the next five years.

4.6 Up to 31 December 2009, 21,541 posts had been re-located from London and the South East to the rest of the UK. Wales has received 3,629 of these posts and is the third highest receiving location behind the North West (4,794) and Yorkshire and the Humber (4,262). Newport has received the most posts in Wales, with 1,285 having relocated to the city, the majority of posts from the Prison Service and Office for National Statistics (ONS).

Government Investment in Business

4.7 The coalition Government is committed to creating the right conditions for the private sector in Wales to grow, including through inward investment (see Section 6) but we recognise the role that certain targeted public investment in business can deliver. Given the UK's fiscal position, though, we have examined investment decisions made by the previous Government on a case by case basis in order to assess affordability.

4.8 Where affordability can be demonstrated, we have proceeded with investments as planned, with the £340 million of investment in Airbus to develop the new A350XWB aircraft, being a notable example in Wales.

5. Conditions to Attract Investment

Conditions to Attract Inward Investment

5.1 Through the Budget in June and the Comprehensive Spending Review in October, the coalition Government has set out its plans for creating the right business environment for strong and sustainable growth. We intend these measures to encourage inward investment as well as encouraging the expansion of home-grown businesses. UKTI works to ensure that feedback from existing and potential investors is drawn into the policy development process.

5.2 In particular, the budget announced the following key policies to encourage business growth and inward investment through:

— increasing the threshold for employer NICs by £21 a week above indexation—leading to a saving of around £140 million in Wales;

— extending the Enterprise Finance Guarantee Scheme—this has already benefitted 516 businesses in Wales by over £40 million;

— cutting Corporation Tax from 28% to 24% over the next four years and small Companies Corporation Tax from 22% to 20% over the same period with the aim of creating one of the most competitive corporate tax regimes in the G20;

— reducing the costs of regulation with all businesses benefiting from a reduction in red tape including 201,000 SMEs in Wales, and

— repealing the special tax rules for furnished holiday lettings—benefitting an estimated 4,100 individuals in Wales who have income from furnished holiday lettings.

6. Conclusion and Forward Look

6.1 Wales is the 6th most attractive destination for inward investment projects in the UK and attracts between 2 to 9% of all projects, averaging 4.7% over 10-years. However, according to fDi Markets[42] the average number of jobs created per project in Wales from 2003 to 2010 was 173. This compares to the UK average of 105. In 2009–10 Wales was ranked 4th most successful geographical area for attracting new FDI related jobs.

6.2 Wales has also sustained its inward investment performance through the economic downturn better than the UK as a whole. Overall investment into the UK in 2009–10 fell by 7% on the previous year while investment into Wales rose by 8%. The number of jobs associated with that investment showed that while UK job numbers were up 20% on the previous year, job numbers in Wales almost tripled.

6.3 Close joint working already exists between UKTI and the Welsh Assembly Government to ensure the best possible outcome for investment in Wales. The two organisations work closely through fora such as the International Business Development Forum (IBDF) to ensure that our policies are coordinated to the benefit of companies throughout the UK.

---

[42] Crossborder—Investment Monitor.

Annex A

INTERNATIONAL BUSINESS DEVELOPMENT FORUM (IBDF)
INWARD BUSINESS ACTIVITY

PRINCIPLES AND GUIDELINES

The following principles and guidelines have been adopted by the International Business Development Forum and govern the way in which UK Trade & Investment and the English RDAs work together to manage the flow of Foreign Direct Investment (FDI). The Devolved Administrations have also agreed to co-operate with these arrangements in line with their devolved powers. The overall aim of the principles and guidelines is to maximise the amount of knowledge-driven FDI for the UK, to improve transparency and partnership working, to strengthen the UK Brand, avoid perceptions of wasteful competition and the risk of customer confusion, and to promote the more efficient use of public money across the network.

We are keen to focus on client facing principles while avoiding too many detailed rules.

The following are key client relationship principles.

These principles are designed especially for use with **Target Companies**, which have been systematically segmented, and their related projects. These principles will succeed if the different stakeholders demonstrate trust and pragmatism.

Four key principles for effective Client Relationship Management:

(1) That we make a priority of winning the business for the UK and acting in the national interest.

(2) That we are Client-oriented, ie we put the Client first and adopt a true service ethic towards him/her.

(3) That we focus on building long term relationships with Clients.

(4) That we maintain transparency across the network with prompt sharing of information whilst respecting Client confidentiality where appropriate in line with the IBDF Guidelines.

Four related principles for the **Virtual Teams** that will engage with the companies on a case-by-case basis:

(1) We adhere to IBDF Guidelines/Output Measures.

(2) We include within the team all knowledge and expertise that can add value to the Target Client and/or Client's project.

(3) The team works to an agreed engagement strategy with defined roles, developed on a case-by-case basis, including appointing a team leader who will take responsibility for the management of the team, all driven by the Client's needs.(Further advice on the effective operation of Virtual Teams scattered across a range of organisations and countries is available from the R&D Programme team.

(4) The team takes a holistic view of the company from a global perspective.

Note. It is envisaged that the core team responsible for the pursuit of target companies will change its shape when a project emerges. Sub groups may be set up to deal with specific aspects, eg R&D. The key is that the team should respond flexibly according to the emerging opportunities.

But we also need some guidelines on operational aspects of how we work as a network.

GUIDELINES ON OPERATIONAL PROCEDURES

Partnership

(a) There shall be regular meetings of the IBDF and its sub-groups. The sub-groups deal with:

— output measures and benchmarking;

— case handling;

— investor development;

— marketing;

— R&D Programme;

— research; and

— other issues as they arise: eg Task and Finish Group on overseas office review.

(b) Propagation by each organisation of IBDF Principles and Guidelines throughout their network.

(c) The Devolved Administrations to advise UKTI of significant changes in overseas representation, including opening new offices, in recognition of UKTI's wider role in promoting the UK as a whole to foreign investors.

(d) English RDAs to discuss with UKTI proposals for opening new overseas offices for inward investment activity, and to provide UKTI with a business case for prior Ministerial approval.

(e)　Consider option of co-locating (R)DA offices with UKTI inward investment overseas offices where practical and in accordance with FCO procedures. UKTI to ensure that (R)DAs not co-located or not represented in the market are treated fairly.

(f)　Efficient operation of client propositions system, including provision of feedback—in accordance with Service Level Agreement (COP/CHG 14/2005).

(g)　Regular exchange of information on marketing and communications plans and activities.

(h)　Members to continue to develop regional selling points to enable UKTI to best market regions and the UK.

(i)　RDAs to host briefing tours by inward investment officers, whenever practicable.

(j)　RDAs and UKTI to consider options for interchange.

(k)　UKTI will work through (R)DAs on FDI. UKTI will refer any approached from local authorities or other sub-regional bodies (including Multi Area Agreements) to the relevant (R)DA(s), unless there has been prior engagement between UKTI and the RDA to deal direct.

Joint planning overseas

UKTI, RDA and DA overseas teams ("the network") in markets where more than one of these organisations has an office or offices or other representation will ensure joint planning.

Representatives of the organisations concerned will meet before the following financial year to achieve a planning agreement. This may well take the form of an action list. They will look at and reach agreement on:

Overall Approach to Market

(a)　Are network offices best located geographically in the market? Are they all in the same place? Is that a good thing? Or in larger markets should the network collectively achieve a geographical spread?

(b)　To what extent do/should offices specialise in specific sectors? Should there be sector leads? If so, UKTI or an (R)DA?

(c)　Prospects for co-location.

In year activity. Planning agreements must include:

(a)　Targets and any other agreed performance measures.

(b)　Consideration of pooling market research activity and database and data sources, eg location benchmarking tools.

(c)　Systematic look at events planned for the year. To what extent should these be joint events between two or more members of the network? Are locations and event focuses (including sectors) getting the best spread/concentration for the UK?

(d)　Systematic look at PR and marketing activity. Are offices maximising the impact of PR and marketing spend?

(e)　Optimal aftercare arrangements.

(f)　Reinforcing current arrangements—pursuit lists (see Transparency section below).

(g)　Ensuring clarity on roles—eg responsibility for reporting, names of who provide and receive visit reports.

(h)　Provisions for review in year and at year end. This entails review of how the planning arrangements worked; and activity and outputs.

(i)　Use of the UK brand overseas (guidelines to issue).

Those (R)DAs without an office or other representation in those markets covered by this guidance must have an opportunity to comment on the agreed draft plans before sign-off, where they opt to do so.

Overseas teams, on a market-by-market basis, should systematically consider the branding of marketing activity—events, written materials, websites etc with the presumption of use of the "UK" brand. Further branding guidance will be provided. This consideration should be part of the annual planning round, and in-year reviews.

Participation by Devolved Administrations and LDA is at their discretion.

Baselining, measuring, reporting and evaluating overseas inward investment activity

UKTI and RDA HQs, and DAs and LDA if they wish, will benchmark and measure inputs and outputs. There will be quarterly reporting on outputs and annual reporting on inputs.

Under the new arrangements UKTI will ensure common evaluation of UKTI, RDA and perhaps DA overseas inward investment activity. [Further detail being discussed in Overseas Review Implementation Task and Finish Group].

Baseline and measuring

Overseas offices will need to establish baselines for reporting against:

(a) Outputs:

— Number of leads.

— Number of leads passed from one network member to another.

— Number of successes.

— Examples of co-location (ranging from regular hot desking to RDA staff under UKTI overseas team management).

— "Soft" factors—illustrations of closer co-working.

(b) Inputs (Costs):

For UKTI, costs are established by using FCO figures for full costs of staff—ie including overheads—modulated by grade and by country of location and diplomatic mission within country. This will sometimes involve allowing for the fact that many staff have combined trade and investment functions.

RDAs identify the full costs of their overseas offices. As these are inward investment dedicated further refinement should not be required.

Devolved Administrations also identify the full costs of their overseas offices and pro rata them down in proportion in the approximate share of overseas offices activity represented by inward investment.

[nb RDAs and DAs have not yet agreed these arrangements].

Reporting

[The Overseas Review Implementation Task and Finish group is looking at UKTI proposals for expanding the existing quarterly RDA IBDF reporting form and the annual DA form].

Evaluation

UKTI operates the Performance and Impact Monitoring Surveys (PIMS). A third party (OMB) interviews a substantial sample of UKTI's trade and inward investment clients. OMB then produce reports on the value achieved for companies, additionality, and customer perception of quality. PIMS won't reliably attribute the extent of contribution from overseas offices—but can link inward investment successes with leads from overseas, assuming sufficient details of the source of leads are provided to the PIMS research team. And the process will of course currently only cover leads where UKTI has had a role. Most of these will come from UKTI overseas teams, though some could come from (R)DA offices. This will therefore be a component of evaluation, as will RDAs' and DAs' own assessments.

Transparency

(a) Each member will exchange with UKTI inward investment overseas teams, on a strictly one to one confidential basis, their pursuit lists of prospective investors and lists of events. This will help to:

— Avoid confusing potential investors.

— Maximise the potential for combining resource.

Exchange of lists will take place between UKTI inward investment overseas teams and (R)DA overseas representation or (R)DA HQ, where there is not an (R)DA representative in market. Similarly, where there is no UKTI inward investment team in an overseas market, lists should be exchanged with UKTI HQ in London. UKTI (both HQ and Overseas Teams) will not approach a client on a (R)DAs' list without prior consultation. Similarly, (R)DAs will not approach a client on UKTI's list, without prior consultation. An exception to transparency will have to be made if the client insists on anonymity.

(b) Transparent distribution of active projects by UKTI through Docstore as defined below:

— All High Value projects where there has been a request for substantive information—multi-region or single region request;

— All Good Quality projects where there has been a request for substantive information—multi-region or single region request;

— All (R)DA Priority projects.

Cases to be defined as confidential and thus not placed on DocStore should be agreed between relevant stakeholders.

(c) The R&D Programme team will ensure that all initial Account Plans for target companies are shared with BERR Business Relations and with (R)DAs to ensure that they have an opportunity to feed in information about relationships with target companies, especially where these may be at a sensitive stage.

Co-ordinated relationship management of existing inward investors

(a) **Proactive participation** in the (R)DA-chaired National Investor Development Forum; a sub-group of IBDF that meets quarterly; focus on best practice, benchmarking/measuring value-added and greater cross-border cooperation in support of strategic investors.

(b) **Default sharing** of overseas-owned company visit reports generated by R/DAs with UKTI HQ's Investment Policy Section through the existing investor.support@uktradeinvest.gov.uk email inbox. UKTI to disseminate to the relevant members of the Investor Development (ID) network unless otherwise requested by the originator for specific client-confidentiality reasons. UKTI to provide regular feedback also to (R)DAs on the issues raised in their own ID reporting on UK regional issues.

(c) **All members** will feedback to UKTI those policy-related issues raised by clients using the existing "exchange of information" mechanism (see "b" above). UKTI will use this received information to build its "Business Issues" evidence base in support of its policy-influencing objective to improve the UK's business environment for inward investment.

(d) **Sub-regional partners and stakeholders** should likewise be encouraged to reciprocate in sharing their own ID reporting with (R)DAs and UKTI HQ where there are business environment issues relevant to the UK's wider competitiveness.

(e) **All members** establish/update (at least biannually) their respective lists of strategic companies to be relationship managed (with name & contact details of relationship manager) for national distribution round the ID network using BERR's Sector Unit RM Excel spreadsheet. (R)DAs are encouraged to embrace the idea of regional transparency on ID reports, i.e. copying to other strategic regional stakeholders where there is an identifiable mutual interest. However, it is recognised too that, similarly to "b" above, this might not always be possible/desirable for reasons of stated company confidentiality, but not copying should be more the exception than the rule.

(f) **All members** to be receptive (subject to resources and priorities) to suggestions from other stakeholders for companies (esp. inward investors) to be included on their ID company lists.

N.B. These Principles and Guidelines are supplemented by GUIDELINES ON OVERSEAS JOINT INWARD INVESTMENT WORK BETWEEN RDAS, DEVOLVED ADMINISTRATIONS AND UKTI at Annex I

December 2010

Annex I

GUIDELINES ON OVERSEAS JOINT
INWARD INVESTMENT WORK BETWEEN
RDAS, DEVOLVED ADMINISTRATIONS AND UKTI

INTRODUCTION

These Guidelines set out new arrangements for closer working between UKTI, the RDAs and Devolved Administrations (DAs) in key overseas inward investment markets following the Joint Review in 2007 of Overseas Representation, which was published in March 2008. The Guidelines explain the background to and aim of closer working and describe the new procedures covering in-market activity planning, branding, reporting and evaluation, and co-location. They do not replace the IBDF Inward Business Activity Principles and Guidelines, of which they are a part.

BACKGROUND

1. Following a major review including a study and survey by Arthur D Little, RDAs, DAs and UKTI agreed to closer and more co-ordinated working overseas. In all cases, participation by the DAs and LDA in any new UK arrangements will be at their discretion, in keeping with their devolved powers.

Key points in the agreement are:

(i) UKTI will have overall responsibility for co-ordination of the pre-enquiry promotional effort in overseas markets.

   (a) Pre-enquiry promotional effort is defined in this instance as agreeing objectives and targets; promotional activity aimed at lead generation such as networking, lobbying, events, market research and intelligence gathering.

(ii) UKTI will lead the co-ordination of an annual "UK plc" plan for events, marketing and promotion for each agreed market and sector, which will set out the responsibilities, objectives and targets for UKTI and individual RDAs and working with DAs.

   (a) The process will be designed jointly by UKTI, the RDAs and DAs; governing principles will be promulgated to their overseas posts and offices/representatives;

   (b) The process will be a co-ordinated, bottom-up approach in each market;

   (c) It builds upon the principle that UK plc's needs are served best by the UKTI/RDA/DA network overseas.

(iii) UKTI will co-ordinate performance monitoring and evaluation against the plan.

    (a) The overall process will be managed centrally in the UK.

    (b) UKTI, the RDAs and DAs will agree data to be collected and performance measures.

    (c) The parties will evaluate the targets jointly, in a systematic way, at a market level, and report back to their respective headquarters.

    (d) The Peer Review[43] process will be discontinued.

(iv) UKTI and the RDAs will adopt a more consistent approach to UK branding overseas. Discussion will take place in overseas markets between UKTI and the RDAs on how best to brand events and materials in overseas markets. The DA's will also be involved in these discussions.

(v) UKTI and the RDAs will explore the possibility of co-location and procurement of services in overseas markets where this would be cost effective. Discussions will also involve the DAs where appropriate.

    (a) At British Embassy/Consulate General or alternative location;

    (b) UKTI, the RDAs and DAs will work together to minimise issues of space, security and host government policy.

(vi) To achieve full national co-ordination, UKTI, RDAs and DAs will continue to work as delivery partners; sub-regional partners, local authorities and city regions will work through the RDAs and DAs.

(vii) Under revised IBDF Inward Business Activity Principles and Guidelines[44], UKTI, the RDAs and DAs will deal directly with enquiries, sales and aftercare.

AIM

2. This agreement built substantially on and replaced previous arrangements for exchange of pursuit lists, peer review and a degree of common branding. These guidelines implement the agreement. **The overall aim is to minimise the risk of duplication, improve efficiency and transparency and so increase the amount of knowledge-driven FDI won for the UK.** The arrangements need to be as light touch as possible while achieving results. The pre-year planning meeting is key. In addition, in-market teams may or may not want in-year meetings. And, of course, we have agreed to dispense with Stage 1 (in-market) peer reviews and replace Stage 2 with a new lighter touch approach in the UK (IBDF Partners Bi-lateral Reviews).

PLANNING

3. UKTI, RDA and DA overseas teams ("the network") in markets where more than one of these organisations has an office or offices or other representation will ensure joint planning. **The pre-year planning meeting is key.**

4. Representatives of the organisations concerned will meet before the following financial year to achieve a planning agreement. Any RDAs and DAs not currently represented in market must be given with, sufficient notice, the opportunity to participate in, or provide input to, this planning meeting. The in-market plan may well take the form of an action list. The planning meeting should look at and reach agreement on:

Overall Approach to Market

— Are network offices best located geographically in the market? Are they all in the same place? Is that a good thing? Or in larger markets should the network collectively achieve a geographical spread?

— To what extent do/should offices specialise in specific sectors? Should there be sector leads? If so, UKTI or an RDA or DA?

— Prospects for co-location.

In year activity

— Planning agreements must include:

    — arrangements for obtaining views of RDAs and DAs without in market representation, where RDAs or DAs say they want involvement.

    — Targets and any other locally agreed performance measures.

    — Consideration of pooling market research activity and database and data sources, eg location benchmarking tools.

    — a systematic look at events planned for the year. To what extent should these be joint events between two or more members of the network? Are locations and subject matter for events (including sectors) getting the best spread/concentration for the UK?

---

[43] Peer Review was a process, led by UKTI in Posts and in the UK, under which it annually reviewed and evaluated business plans with RDAs and DAs in overseas markets.

[44] UKTI, the RDAs and DAs operate under the principles and guidelines agreed by the International Business Development Forum (IBDF) (the IBDF Inward Business Activity Principles and Guidelines).

— a systematic look at PR and marketing activity. Are organisations maximising the impact of PR and marketing spend?

— looking at optimal aftercare arrangements.

— Reinforcing current arrangements—RDAs, DAs and UKTI teams must share their pursuit lists and active case lists systematically. See para 6 for guidance on the sharing framework.

— ensuring clarity on roles—eg responsibility for reporting, names of who provide and receive visit reports.

— provisions for review in-year and at year end. This entails review of how the planning arrangements worked; and activity and outputs.

5. Those RDAs and DAs not represented in those markets covered by this guidance must have an opportunity to comment on the agreed draft plans before sign-off, where they opt to do so.

6. These arrangements replace the first stage of the former peer review process. These arrangements include the established provisions on exchange of pursuit lists—the following is from the IBDF Inward Business Activity Principles and Guidelines:

Each member will exchange with UKTI inward investment overseas teams, on a strictly one to one confidential basis, their pursuit lists of prospective investors and lists of events. This will help to:

— Avoid confusing potential investors.

— maximise the potential for combining resource.

Exchange of lists will take place between UKTI inward investment overseas teams and (R)DA overseas representation or (R)DA HQ, where there is not an (R)DA representative in market. Similarly, where there is no UKTI inward investment team in an overseas market, lists should be exchanged with UKTI HQ in London. UKTI (both HQ and Overseas Teams) will not approach a client on a (R)DAs' list without prior consultation. Similarly, (R)DAs will not approach a client on UKTI's list, without prior consultation. An exception to transparency will have to be made if the client insists on anonymity.

— UKTI overseas teams will load their active case lists onto DocStore at the end of each quarter no later than end of 3rd week after the quarter.

— (UKTI HQ teams will also load their own version of the active case lists by sector onto DocStore at the end of each quarter and no later than the 3rd week after the quarter).

— UKTI and RDA overseas teams will exchange their pursuit lists on a strictly one to one confidential basis each quarter. Where no local RDA representation exists, the RDA will share their pursuit list on the same basis with the UKTI HQ Investment Sales Teams.

— UKTI HQ teams will share their annual pursuit lists with the network as part of the business planning cycle and provide up to date details of their lists on request to RDA partners no less than twice per year in line with business planning reviews.

— UKTI overseas teams will enter all leads (including early stage leads and developed project enquiries/active cases) in all value bands onto DocStore making exceptions only where the national interest or the client's own confidentiality is concerned.

— UKTI will provide the RDAs with a numeric summary breakdown of the leads generated for their own organisations on a one to one confidential basis twice a year.

BRANDING

7. Overseas teams, on a market-by-market basis, should systematically consider the branding of marketing activity—events, written materials, websites, etc, with the presumption of use of the "UK" Flag identity brand. Please register at www.promotingukbusiness.org.uk to access guidelines on how UKTI, RDAs and DAs can use the UK Flag identity as well as on how to use the "compelling message". You will need to click on the register button and fill in a very simple form.

8. This consideration should be part of the annual planning round, and in-year reviews.

9. Use of the UK Flag identity by DAs and LDA is at their discretion.

BASELINING, MEASURING, REPORTING AND EVALUATING OVERSEAS INWARD INVESTMENT ACTIVITY

SUMMARY

10. UKTI and RDA HQs (and DAs at their discretion) will benchmark and measure:

(a) Inputs.

(b) Outputs.

11. There will be quarterly reporting on outputs. A revised IBDF Output Measures RDA Quarterly Return has been agreed to capture this information. RDAs and DAs will report annually on input costs.

12. Under the new arrangements UKTI will ensure common evaluation of UKTI, RDA and perhaps DA overseas inward investment activity.

Baseline and measuring

13. Overseas offices will need to establish baselines for reporting against:

(a) Outputs:

— Number of leads as per IBDF Inward Business Activity Principles and Guidelines definition.

— Number of leads passed from one network member to another.

— Number of successes.

— Examples of co-location (ranging from regular hot desking to RDA staff under UKTI overseas team management).

— "Soft" factors—illustrations of closer co-working. For quality of service the results of ADL surveys in Canada, France and India and some other markets will be relevant.

(b) Inputs (Costs):

For future evaluation UKTI, RDAs and Devolved Administrations need to be in a position to say what their costs are at that particular point in time, but regular reports on costs are not required as part of the annual in-market planning process.

Evaluation

14. UKTI will have regard to input and output data. Third party (consultancy) evaluation is a prospect. With regard to its own activity. UKTI operates the Performance and Impact Monitoring Surveys (PIMS). These rely on data input by UKTI staff into UKTI's e-CRM system. A third party (OMB) uses this data to interview a substantial sample of UKTI's trade and inward investment clients. OMB then produce reports on the value achieved for companies, additionality, and customer perception of quality. PIMS will not reliably attribute the extent of contribution from overseas offices—but can link inward investment successes with leads from overseas, assuming sufficient details of the source of leads are provided to the PIMS research team. And the process will, of course, currently only cover leads where UKTI has had a role. Most of these will come from UKTI overseas teams, though some could come from RDA and DA offices. This will therefore be a component of evaluations, as will RDAs' and DAs' own assessments. RDAs and DAs agreed in a task and finish group to adopt PIMS subject to agreement on costs.

CO-LOCATION

15. Co-location of partners is encouraged. UKTI will monitor and report on the extent to which this occurs and the forms of co-location deployed, with a view to facilitating further co-location. FCO has issued guidance on co-location within UK diplomatic missions. UKTI has agreed with FCO how RDA costs should be treated.

HQ ROLE

16. UKTI, RDA and DA HQs will provide advice to overseas offices and representatives in line with these guidelines. UKTI and EMDA (as the lead RDA for International Trade and Investment) will collate quarterly reports for the RDAs and present their observations on them to IBDF members. IBDF will discuss these observations and progress on the new overseas arrangements and take any necessary actions—in preparation for a likely review of the arrangements required by the Treasury in due course.

17. Advice on joint overseas working can be sought in UKTI from Andrew Levi and Laura Faulkner.

Annex II

GLOSSARY (SEE MAIN IBDF INWARD BUSINESS ACTIVITY PRINCIPLES AND GUIDELINES FOR FULL DETAILS)

— **Lead**—an early stage enquiry from a potential or existing investor which may subsequently move rapidly to an active case or conversely remain dormant for a period of time depending on the due diligence undertaken/contact with the client.

— **Pursuit**—a potential or existing investor that is being proactively targeted by either UKTI or an RDA with a view to yielding active FDI projects or project wins.

— **Active Case**—an on going discussion regarding a potential FDI project where the project decision date is likely to be within 18 months from the date of initial contact.

— **DocStore**—UKTI's IT communications platform for sharing its project leads and active FDI project case work with the RDA and DA stakeholder network.

Annex B

UKTI—RECORDED FDI TO WALES FOR THE PAST 20 YEARS

Year	No. of Projects	No. of New Jobs	No. of Safeguarded Jobs	Total No. of Jobs
1990–91	62	3,356	5,065	8,421
1991–92	72	5,195	5,634	10,829
1992–93	65	2,382	4,489	6,871
1993–94	64	3,913	2,651	6,564
1994–95	51	3,151	2,084	5,235
1995–96	53	4,429	4,602	9,031
1996–97	45	10,397	2,256	12,653
1997–98	55	4,976	2,479	7,455
1998–99	48	5,591	1,796	7,387
1999–2000	47	4,161	3,636	7,797
2000–01	39	4,520	1,833	6,353
2001–02	61	3,872	3,445	7,317
2002–03	60	4,083	3,696	7,779
2003–04	67	4,064	4,067	8,131
2004–05	56	2,593	1,261	3,854
2005–06	51	3,132	2,072	5,204
2006–07	67	3,379	2,788	6,167
2007–08	68	3,743	1,886	5,629
2008–09	60	2,185	529	2,714
2009–10	65	3,431	3,931	7,362

UKTI FDI project and job statistics are based on:

— information provided by the company at the time of the announcement of the decision to invest in the UK; and

— the investing companies' best estimates of capital expenditure and jobs created/safeguarded in the first three years.

The figures do not take account of subsequent developments.

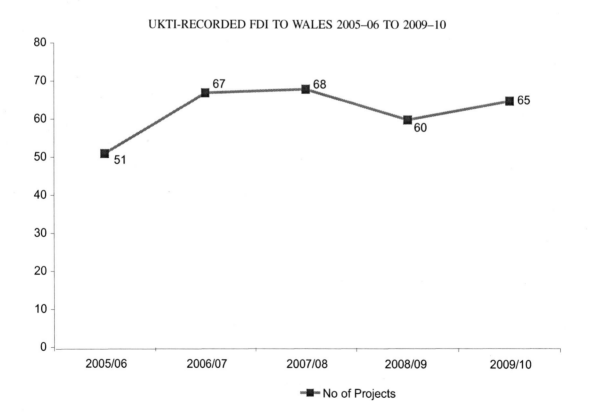

UKTI-RECORDED FDI TO WALES 2005–06 TO 2009–10

Tracked over the past five years, Wales' share of the total number of UK investment projects has ranged between 3.4% and 4.6%. In 2009–10, 65 of the total number of 1619 investment projects in the UK went to

Wales—4 % of the total. These figures are broadly in line with Wales' share of regional GVA[45], which according to ONS was 4% in 2008.

Area breakdown of UKTI-recorded Investment Projects 2009/10

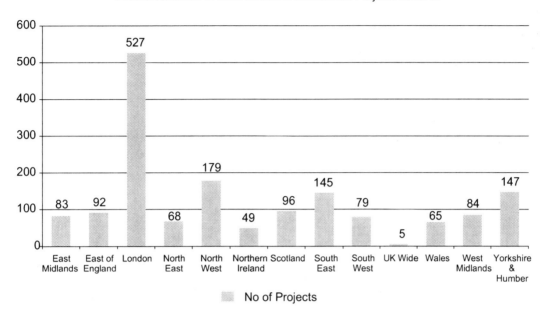

No of Projects

Area breakdown of UKTI - recorded Investment Projects 2009/10

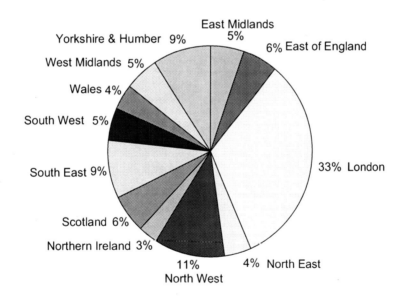

[45] Gross value added is the difference between the value of goods and services produced (output) and the cost of raw materials and other input which are used in production (intermediate consumption); that is, the value added by any unit engaged in production. This is calculated gross of any deductions for depreciation or consumption of fixed capital. Regional gross value added (GVA) is estimated at current basic prices and comprises gross domestic product (GDP) less taxes (plus subsidies) on products. Taxes on products are taxes that are payable per unit of some good or service produced or transacted. Examples include value-added tax and excise duties. Subsidies are payments made to producers by the government or institutions of the European Union to influence production.

UKTI -recorded Total No of Jobs Associated with Investment into Wales
2005/06 - 2009/10

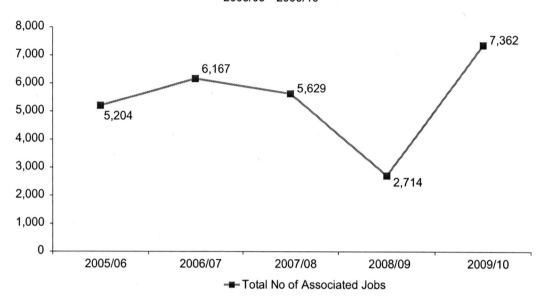

Breakdown of Jobs Associated with UKTI - recorded projects in 2009/10

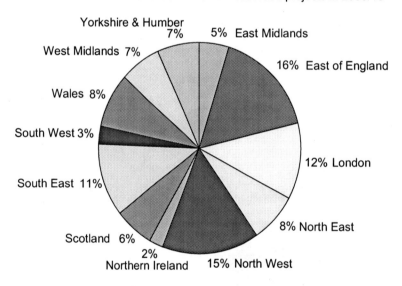

UKTI recorded project successes into Wales by Sector - 2009/10

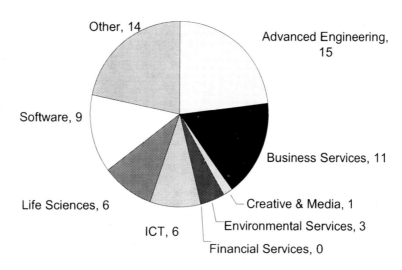

New and Safeguarded Jobs Numbers by Sector for UKTI-recorded investment projects in Wales in 2009/10

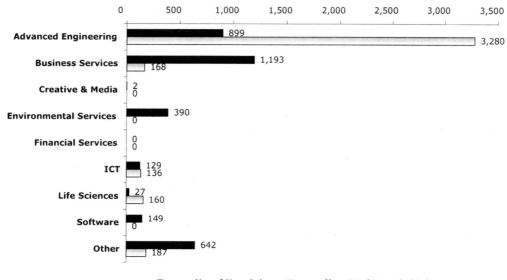

WELSH FDI 2009–10

SECTOR BREAKDOWN

	Number
Aerospace	3
Agriculture, Horticulture And Fisheries	1
Automotive	8
Biotechnology And Pharmaceuticals	2
Business (And Consumer) Services	11
Chemicals	1
Communications	1
Construction	1
Creative And Media	1
Defence	1
Electronics And IT Hardware	5
Environment	3
Food And Drink	3
Healthcare And Medical	4

	Number
Mechanical Electrical And Process Engineering	4
Metals, Minerals & Materials	1
Ports And Logistics	2
Power	3
Software And Computer Services Business To Business (B2B)	9
Textiles, Interior Textiles And Carpets	1
Grand Total	65

COUNTRY BREAKDOWN

	Number
Australia	3
British Virgin Islands	1
Canada	3
China	1
Denmark	2
Finland	2
France	7
Germany	3
Hong Kong (SAR)	1
India	2
Ireland	3
Italy	1
Japan	8
Luxembourg	1
Romania	1
South Africa	2
Taiwan	1
United Arab Emirates	1
United States	22
Grand Total	65

WELSH FDI 2007–08

SECTOR BREAKDOWN

	Number
Aerospace (Civil)	6
Automotive	4
Biotechnology And Pharmaceuticals	8
Business (And Consumer) Services	4
Chemicals	3
Communications	1
Construction	4
Education And Training	3
Electronics And IT Hardware	2
Environment	11
Financial Services	1
Food And Drink	3
Healthcare And Medical	3
Household Goods, Furniture And Furnishings	2
Metals And Minerals	2
Oil And Gas	2
Ports And Logistics	2
Railways	1
Software And Computer Services Business To Business (B2B)	6
Grand Total	68

COUNTRY BREAKDOWN

	Number
Australia	6
Austria	1
Belgium	2
Canada	3
China	2
France	8
Germany	5
India	1
Ireland	8
Israel	1
Italy	1
Japan	7
Mexico	1
Netherlands	4
New Zealand	1
Qatar	1
South Africa	1
Spain	1
Sweden	1
Switzerland	1
Taiwan	1
United Arab Emirates	1
United States	10
Grand Total	68

WELSH FDI 2006–07

SECTOR BREAKDOWN

	Number
Aerospace (Civil)	2
Automotive	8
Biotechnology And Pharmaceuticals	2
Business (And Consumer) Services	6
Chemicals	2
Clothing, Footwear And Fashion	2
Construction	4
Creative And Media	4
Electronics And IT Hardware	6
Environment	6
Financial Services	2
Food And Drink	1
Giftware, Jewellery And Tableware	1
Healthcare And Medical	1
Household Goods, Furniture And Furnishings	2
Marine	1
Mechanical Electrical And Process Engineering	1
Metallurgical Process Plant	1
Metals And Minerals	1
Power	1
Software And Computer Services Business To Business (B2B)	12
Textiles, Interior Textiles And Carpets	1
Grand Total	67

COUNTRY BREAKDOWN

	Number
Australia	4
Belgium	1
Canada	2
China	2
Denmark	3
Estonia	1

	Number
France	6
Germany	4
Hong Kong (SAR)	1
India	3
Ireland	2
Italy	1
Japan	7
Korea (South)	1
New Zealand	1
South Africa	1
Spain	3
Switzerland	1
United States	23
Grand Total	67

WELSH FDI 2005–06

SECTOR BREAKDOWN

	Number
Aerospace (Civil)	3
Automotive	7
Biotechnology And Pharmaceuticals	3
Business (And Consumer) Services	4
Chemicals	1
Construction	1
Electronics And IT Hardware	5
Environment	3
Financial Services	2
Food And Drink	3
Giftware, Jewellery And Tableware	1
Healthcare And Medical	7
Household Goods, Furniture And Furnishings	1
ICT	1
Leisure Industry	1
Metals And Minerals	2
Oil & Gas	3
Software And Computer Services Business To Business (B2B)	1
Textiles, Interior Textiles And Carpets	3
Grand Total	52

COUNTRY BREAKDOWN

	Number
Australia	4
Austria	1
Canada	2
China	4
Finland	1
France	4
Germany	2
India	2
Ireland	4
Italy	2
Jordan	1
Japan	5
Malaysia	1
Norway	1
New Zealand	1
South Africa	2
Sweden	1
United States	14
Grand Total	52

WELSH FDI 2004–05

SECTOR BREAKDOWN

	Number
Aerospace/Avionics	1
Automation Systems	1
Automotive	4
Automotive Components	3
Ceramic Goods	1
Chemicals	1
Construction	2
Electronics—Consumer	1
Electronics—Specialised	2
Engineering	4
Environmental Sers/Prods/Procs	4
Finance	3
Food And Drink	1
Furniture Manufacture	1
Healthcare	3
Horticultural	1
Info/Communications Technology	1
It/Internet Services	2
Leisure Ind/Toys/Sports	4
Managem't & Business	2
Manf. Of Industrial Machinery	1
Metal Products	1
Paper/Packaging Manufacture	2
Pharmaceuticals	1
Plastics	1
Power Generation	2
Retail Services	2
Shared Service Centres	1
Software	1
Telecommunications	1
Textiles, Clothing & Footwear	2
Transport/Storage/Postal	1
Grand Total	58

COUNTRY BREAKDOWN

	Number
Australia	3
Austria	1
Canada	3
Switzerland	1
China	3
France	2
Germany	3
Hong Kong	1
India	1
Ireland	3
Italy	1
Japan	7
Malaysia	1
Netherlands	2
Norway	2
Singapore	1
Spain	3
Sweden	2
Taiwan	1
USA	17
Grand Total	58

WELSH FDI 2003–04

SECTOR BREAKDOWN

	Number
Aerospace/Avionics	2
Automation Systems	2
Automotive	1
Automotive Components	3
Biotechnology	2
Call Centre	2
Chemicals	1
Construction	1
Cosmetic & Beauty Ind. Manf	1
Electronics—Consumer	2
Electronics—Specialised	7
Engineering	2
Environmental Sers/Prods/Procs	2
Finance	3
Food And Drink	3
Furniture Manufacture	1
Health & Safety	1
Healthcare	1
Info/Communications Technology	2
Language Services	1
Leisure Ind/Toys/Sports	1
Managem't & Business	1
Manf. Of Industrial Machinery	2
Metal Products	7
Paper/Packaging Manufacture	4
Pharmaceuticals	2
Plastics	3
Power Generation	2
Retail Services	1
Shipbuilding	1
Software	1
Training	1
Wood & Wood Products	1
Grand Total	67

COUNTRY BREAKDOWN

	Number
Australia	4
Austria	2
Belgium	1
Canada	2
Switzerland	2
China	1
Denmark	2
France	3
Germany	4
Hong Kong	1
India	1
Ireland	3
Israel	1
Italy	5
Japan	4
Netherlands	1
Norway	1
New Zealand	1
Singapore	1
Spain	1
Sweden	3
USA	23
Grand Total	67

WELSH FDI 2002–03

SECTOR BREAKDOWN

	Number
Aerospace/Avionics	1
Agriculture/Fisheries	1
Automotive Components	5
Biotechnology	1
Call Centre	4
Chemicals	1
Electronics—Consumer	2
Electronics—Specialised	3
Engineering	1
Finance	1
Food And Drink	5
Furniture Manufacture	3
Health & Safety	1
Healthcare	1
Info/Communications Technology	1
It H/Ware/Off Machinery & Mauf	1
Managem't & Business	1
Manf. Medical & Surgical Equp	1
Manf. Of Industrial Machinery	4
Metal Products	3
Paper/Packaging Manufacture	6
Pharmaceuticals	2
Plastics	3
Shared Service Centres	1
Software	4
Telecommunications	1
Transport/Storage/Postal	2
Grand Total	60

COUNTRY BREAKDOWN

	Number
Australia	3
Belgium	2
Canada	2
Switzerland	1
China	1
Denmark	1
Finland	1
France	4
Germany	3
Greece	1
Hong Kong	1
India	1
Ireland	4
Israel	1
Italy	4
Japan	2
Kuwait	1
Netherlands	1
Norway	1
Singapore	1
Sweden	1
Thailand	1
Taiwan	1
USA	21
Grand Total	60

WELSH FDI 2001–02

SECTOR BREAKDOWN

	Number
Aerospace/Avionics	3
Automotive Components	10
Call Centre	3
Chemicals	1
Cosmetic & Beauty Ind. Manf	1
Electronics—Consumer	1
Electronics—Specialised	8
Engineering	6
Finance	1
Food And Drink	4
Healthcare	1
Info/Communications Technology	1
It/Internet Services	1
Language Services	1
Leisure Ind/Toys/Sports	1
Manf. Medical & Surgical Equp	2
Manf. Of Industrial Machinery	2
Metal Products	2
Paper/Packaging Manufacture	4
Pharmaceuticals	2
Plastics	1
Telecommunications	3
Textiles, Clothing & Footwear	1
Grand Total	60

COUNTRY BREAKDOWN

	Number
Australia	1
Austria	1
Bermuda	1
Canada	3
Switzerland	1
France	6
Germany	5
Hong Kong	1
Ireland	7
Japan	8
Korea	1
Netherlands	2
Norway	1
Sweden	1
USA	19
South Africa	2
Grand Total	60

WELSH FDI 1999–2000

SECTOR BREAKDOWN

	Number
Automation Systems	1
Automotive	2
Automotive Components	7
Call Centre	2
Chemicals	2
Construction	1
Electronics—Consumer	1
Electronics—Specialised	2
Engineering	2
Food And Drink	4
Healthcare	4

	Number
Leisure Ind/Toys/Sports	1
Machine Tools	1
Metal Products	5
Paper/Packaging Manufacture	4
Pharmaceuticals	1
Power Generation	1
Shared Service Centres	1
Telecommunications	3
Textiles, Clothing & Footwear	1
Training	1
Grand Total	47

COUNTRY BREAKDOWN

	Number
Australia	1
Austria	1
Canada	2
Switzerland	1
France	2
Germany	7
Greece	1
Hong Kong	1
Ireland	3
Italy	2
Japan	7
Spain	1
Taiwan	1
USA	17
Grand Total	47

WELSH FDI 1998–99

SECTOR BREAKDOWN

	Number
Agriculture/Fisheries	1
Automotive	1
Automotive Components	7
Chemicals	4
Electronics—Consumer	1
Electronics—Specialised	5
Engineering	3
Finance	3
Food And Drink	2
Furniture Manufacture	3
Horticultural	1
It/Internet Services	1
Leisure Ind/Toys/Sports	1
Metal Products	1
Minerals	3
Paper/Packaging Manufacture	3
Pharmaceuticals	1
Shared Service Centres	1
Software	1
Textiles, Clothing & Footwear	1
Training	1
Wood & Wood Products	3
Grand Total	48

COUNTRY BREAKDOWN

	Number
Australia	1
Canada	1
Denmark	1
France	3
Germany	6
Hong Kong	1
Ireland	2
Italy	2
Japan	5
Korea	1
Liechtenstein	1
Netherlands	2
Norway	2
Turkey	1
Taiwan	1
USA	18
Grand Total	48

WELSH FDI 1997–98

SECTOR BREAKDOWN

	Number
Not Known	54
Telecommunications	1
Grand Total	55

COUNTRY BREAKDOWN

	Number
Australia	2
Canada	1
Denmark	2
France	3
Germany	7
Ireland	1
Italy	3
Japan	12
Liechtenstein	1
Netherlands	1
Norway	1
Taiwan	1
USA	20
Grand Total	55

WELSH FDI 1996–97

SECTOR BREAKDOWN

	Number
Automotive	1
Not Known	44
Grand Total	45

COUNTRY BREAKDOWN

	Number
Australia	1
Belgium	2
Canada	1
Switzerland	3
Finland	1
France	2

	Number
Germany	2
Ireland	1
Italy	4
Japan	8
Korea	2
Netherlands	2
Singapore	1
Sweden	1
USA	14
Grand Total	45

WELSH FDI 1995–96

SECTOR BREAKDOWN

	Number
Automotive Components	1
Not Known	52
Grand Total	53

COUNTRY BREAKDOWN

	Number
Australia	1
Belgium	3
Canada	1
Denmark	1
France	3
Germany	3
Hong Kong	1
Ireland	1
Italy	4
Japan	6
Korea	2
Norway	1
Singapore	1
Sweden	1
Thailand	1
USA	23
Grand Total	53

WELSH FDI 1994–95

SECTORS UNKNOWN

COUNTRY BREAKDOWN

	Number
Belgium	1
Canada	3
Switzerland	3
Denmark	1
Finland	1
France	1
Germany	5
Ireland	3
Japan	7
Netherlands	1
Norway	2
Sweden	1
Taiwan	1
USA	21
Grand Total	51

WELSH FDI 1993–94

SECTORS UNKNOWN

COUNTRY BREAKDOWN

	Number
Austria	1
Belgium	1
Canada	4
Switzerland	2
France	4
Germany	5
Hong Kong	2
Ireland	5
Italy	2
Japan	10
Liechtenstein	1
Netherland Antilles	1
Netherlands	4
Norway	1
Spain	2
USA	19
Grand Total	64

WELSH FDI 1992–93

SECTORS UNKNOWN

COUNTRY BREAKDOWN

	Number
Australia	2
Belgium	2
Canada	1
Switzerland	4
Denmark	3
France	4
Germany	10
Hong Kong	1
Ireland	2
Italy	3
Japan	2
Liberia	1
Netherlands	4
Spain	1
Sweden	1
USA	24
Grand Total	65

WELSH FDI 1991–92

SECTORS UNKNOWN

COUNTRY BREAKDOWN

	Number
Unknown	1
Australia	2
Belgium	2
Canada	3
Switzerland	1
Cayman Isles	1
Denmark	1
France	5
Germany	12
Ireland	2
Italy	2
Japan	8

	Number
Liechtenstein	2
Netherlands	3
Norway	2
Portugal	1
Singapore	1
Sweden	2
USA	20
South Africa	1
Grand Total	72

Annex C

EXAMPLES OF ASSISTED SUCCESSES

Fillcare, part of Fareva Holdings of France: manufactures and packages hair care and styling products for leading brands creating jobs at its plant, Talbot Green, Rhondda Cynon Taf.

Assistance provided by: UKTI and IBW.

Project start date: 11.08.09/confirmed 03.03.10

Capital Ex: unknown.

Jobs: ~200 over four years.

Grant assistance: £1.9 million (in public domain).

UPM, Finland: materials recovery facility at its UPM Shotton paper mill, Deeside, North Wales.

Assistance provided by: UKTI and IBW.

Project start date: 31.01.09/confirmed 11.03.10.

Capital Ex: £17 million.

Jobs: 160.

Grant assistance: £1.7 million (in public domain).

Payswyft, USA: established its HQ in Cwmbran. To launch the first totally integrated web based service in the UK from this facility.

Assistance provided by: IBW.

Project start date unknown/confirmed 17.05.10.

Capital Ex: unknown.

Jobs: 26 new.

Grant assistance: to the best of our knowledge no grant was given.

Sharp, Japan: electronics company doubling production of solar cell modules at its plant near Wrexham, which currently employs 750 staff.

Assistance provided by: IBW.

Project start date: unknown/confirmed 25.02.10.

Capital Ex: unknown.

Jobs: 103 safeguarded.

Grant assistance: to the best of our knowledge no grant was given.

Annex D

METHODOLOGY

EUROPEAN INVESTMENT MONITOR

The Ernst & Young European Investment Monitor, researched and powered by Oxford Intelligence, is a highly detailed source of information on cross-border investment projects and trends in Europe, dating back to 1997.

The database focuses on investment announcements, the number of new jobs created and, where identifiable, the associated capital investment, thus providing data on FDI in Europe. It allows users to monitor trends, movements in jobs and industries, and identify emerging sectors and cluster development. Projects are identified through the daily monitoring and research of more than 10,000 news sources.

The research team aims to contact directly 70% of the companies undertaking the investment for direct validation purposes. This process of direct verification with the investing company ensures that real investment data is accurately reflected. The employment figures collected by the research team reflect the number of new jobs created at the start-up date of operations, as communicated by the companies during our follow-up interview. In some cases, the only figures that a company can confirm are the total employment numbers over the life of the project. This is carefully noted so that any subsequent job creation from later phases of the project can be cross checked and to avoid double-counting in later years.

The following categories of investment projects are excluded from the EIM:

— M&A or joint ventures (unless these result in new facilities, new jobs created).

— License agreements.

— Retail and leisure facilities, hotels and real estate investments.

— Utility facilities including telecommunications networks, airports, ports or other fixed infrastructure investments.

— Extraction activities (ores, minerals or fuels).

— Portfolio investments (ie, pensions, insurance and financial funds).

— Factory/production replacement investments (eg, a new machine replacing an old one, but not creating any new employment).

— Not-for-profit (eg, charitable foundations, trade associations, governmental bodies).

UK TRADE & INVESTMENT

UKTI is required by Parliament to collate an accurate and comprehensive record of project investment into the UK. It records announced and unannounced project investments, including those from emerging markets and Asia where companies tend to make investments without press notices. Figures remain indicative in nature. Welsh Assembly Government is focused on the attraction on "High Value Jobs" including R&D jobs. Welsh Assembly Government provides information to UKTI based on involved Welsh successes, but does not track all investment eg retail expansion.

Written evidence submitted by the Rt Hon Mrs Cheryl Gillan MP, Secretary of State for Wales

I am writing with regard to your inquiry into Inward Investment in Wales and to supplement the coalition Government's memorandum of written evidence which you have received from Mark Prisk MP.

The Government memorandum provides you with detailed information on how Wales has performed in attracting inward investment. As you know, I value improving that performance as one of the most important factors in driving economic recovery in Wales. Attracting new investment into Wales must be a key strand of our efforts to reverse the economic decline that has afflicted Wales. This will require all parties with a role to play to pull together and I wanted to briefly set out some of the activity I intend to take forward from the Wales Office to encourage more inward investment into Wales.

Since my appointment as Secretary of State, the Wales Office has begun work to look at how we can combine our efforts across government to better facilitate inward investment in Wales. Clearly, we are working in a time of constrained public finances so it is more important than ever that there is effective collaboration at all levels to boost investment in Wales. This has involved engagement with both UKTI and with the Welsh Assembly Government at official level and I have established a regular constructive dialogue with the Deputy First Minister regarding this work.

More immediately, I have recently held the first meeting of my new Business Advisory Group. This brings together business leaders and academics from across Wales to provide me with information on the Welsh economy and in particular, the business environment. The first meeting covered a range of issues, but the members have already given a clear message: they want all parties working together—they do not want devolution to work to Wales' disadvantage when it comes to attracting inward investment. At our next meeting, in March 2011, we intend to discuss inward investment in more detail with a focus on some of the further work that will have been done by then, including the conclusions of your inquiry.

I have also held discussions with Lord Brittan, as the coalition Government's Trade Adviser and I have commissioned work from officials in the Department for Work and Pensions to identify the key factors that drive inward investment. This work will seek to map out the areas of Wales that could benefit most from such investment. It is due to be completed in February and I would be happy to discuss it with the Committee.

Going forward, I will be meeting with the new Trade Minister, Lord Green, to further embed this collaborative agenda and ensure that he is fully aware of the importance of Wales to the work of UKTI.

Given the range of partners involved in decisions on investment within the UK and the additional complexity of the devolution settlement in Wales, I see the Wales Office as having a pivotal role in instilling a collaborative approach that works to the benefit of Wales. The Wales Office also has other advantages to offer, including access to a London base for Welsh businesses (I am happy for Gwydyr House to play a role in attracting business) and influence with government colleagues at cabinet level. Taking forward this new approach is still in the earliest stages, but some important parts of it are already underway.

This is all very much work in progress. Your inquiry is timely in that it will provide a steer that will guide government activity both in London and Cardiff at a time when these issues are being considered anew and new policies formulated.

I hope that this letter gives you an idea of the work that I have started to take forward in the Wales Office and of course, I would be happy to discuss this further as part of oral evidence during the New Year, should the Committee wish me to.

March 2011

Supplementary written evidence submitted by UKTI

Further to Nick Baird's evidence session at Welsh Affairs Committee 8 November 2011:

Q 450 & Q 487: *breakdown of improved performance measures following the use of PA Consulting; a description of how the contract with PA Consulting works and a breakdown of the monies awarded to PA Consulting including performance incentives and what they get paid upfront*

1. Breakdown of improved performance measures following the use of PA Consulting

UKTI is working with PA to:

— develop a more rigorous methodology for qualifying opportunities that come through the investment pipeline;

— introduce additional measures to better understand attrition rates, to monitor and support projects as they move through the project lifecycle, and to identify and support projects in a more flexible way; and

— develop protocols for working as a single, united team, the aim being better experience for client investors.

2. Description of how the contract with PA Consulting works

The new UKTI Inward Investment Service is now responsible for providing inward investment services across England (except London, which has its own arrangements) following the closure of inward investment activities within the Regional Development Agencies. The Investment Services team is delivered jointly by PA Consulting Group, OCO Consulting and British Chambers of Commerce and is responsible for:

— co-ordinating and managing delivery of FDI support for the United Kingdom with prospective foreign direct investors, working with local partners across England, the devolved administrations of Scotland, Wales and Northern Ireland, the Greater London Authority, and the UKTI and wider FDI network;

— provide sufficient geographically dispersed resource to support the FDI delivery arm for England (for this purpose England excludes London—ie the area covered by the Greater London Authority (GLA)); and

— providing direct relationship management and investor development, in association with international, national and local stakeholders (including the Devolved Administrations and London & Partners) to nominated existing investors in the UK as agreed with UKTI.

PA Consulting has been contracted to deliver the following number of successes into the UK for each of 2011–12, 2012–13, and 2013–14. PA is incentivised to deliver the following breakdown of projects:

— High Value and High Value Plus: projects to land in the UK: 286 (stretch target: 315).

— Good Quality: projects to land in the UK: 256.

— All Other Wins: projects to land in the UK: 226.

— Total projects to land in the UK: 768 (stretch target: 797).

The Investment Services Team also has a qualitative target in line with the Performance Impact Monitoring Survey (PIMS) evaluation system.

3. Breakdown of the monies awarded to PA Consulting including performance incentives and what they get paid upfront

UKTI's contract with PA is on a cost-plus basis: all costs incurred by PA Consulting which relate to the delivery of the Investment Services contract are passed through to UKTI on a monthly basis. The performance incentive is broken out as follows:

— 40% of the fee relates to the landing of High Value and High Value Plus project Successes in the UK within the year in question.

— 25% of the fee relates to the landing of Good Quality and Other project Successes in the UK within the year in question.

— 25% will be based upon achieving required quality, satisfaction and impact ratings, based upon the PIMS evaluation system.

— 10% of the fee relates to the stretch target for High Value project Successes landing in the UK.

Q 462 & 469: *expansion on the relationship between UKTI and the Welsh Government, and the outcome of the meeting with Edwina Hart on 24 November*

1. Expansion on the relationship between UKTI and the Welsh Government

— The Welsh Government is able to draw on the resources of UKTI's Trade and Investment teams at diplomatic missions across the world. The Welsh Government is co-located with UKTI in UAE and the US.

— Our delivery team works closely with the Welsh Government, and has a senior member of its team dedicated to Wales.

— The day to day working relationship between UKTI and investment officials within the Department for Business, Enterprise, Technology and Science within the WG is strong and positive.

— Officials in UKTI and the Welsh Government have just signed an MOU that sets out the guiding principles under which we will jointly operate to attract FDI.

— Operationally and strategically there are strong synergies between how UKTI and the Welsh Government's FDI focus:

— Wales currently promotes ICT, Energy and Environment, Advanced Materials and Manufacturing, Creative Industries, Life Sciences and Financial, and Professional Services.

— UKTI lead sectors are Life Sciences, Chemical Food and Drink, High Performance Engineering, Financial & Business Services, ICT, Communications, Electronics, Infrastructure and Environmental sectors.

— The three new Welsh sectors—Tourism, Construction, and Food (including agriculture)—are slightly different to UKTIs focus but can be accommodated.

— UKTI makes available to the Welsh Government the outline details of all active projects received by UKTI.

— Our Investment Services Team delivers investment inquiries to the Welsh Government.

— Depending on the nature of the need and Wales' interest, we will include Welsh locations or capabilities in the response to the company.

— Before this "hub" arrangement we used (and still use) an IT system called "Doc Store" that:

— Promotes openness between investment agencies and allowed us to load up a project's details so partners like the Welsh Government could see the opportunity and "bid" for the project.

— Partners put forward a case for investment in their area using this system and UKTI would then put a UK package forward.

— Under the new system we will have more user friendly and comprehensive pipeline visibility. Our dedicated relationship manager for Wales will also help to ensure that any relevant projects that enter the pipeline are recognised by Welsh Government staff. He will also help to support the interface between WG and UKTI in responding to such opportunities.

— WG officials also have access to UKTI's intranet Connect.

— UKTI was involved in 26% of FDI into Wales in the last five, and last year (2010–11) we were involved in 37%.

— We supported 74 FDI projects in Wales in the last five years.

2. Outcome of the meeting with Minister Edwina Hart on 24 November

— James Price, Director General, Business, Enterprise, Technology and Science in the Welsh Government met UKTI CEO Nick Baird in Wales on 24 November. Nick Baird also visited Swansea University and its Institute of Life Science and *Ortho Clinical Diagnostics* a leading biomedical company (part of Johnson and Johnson).

— It was not possible for Nick Baird to meet Minister Edwina Hart on this occasion as she had a prior engagement elsewhere in Wales.

— SME Summit: event in Wales with intermediaries to promote SME exports to be co-hosted by Minister Edwina Hart and Lord Green.

Q 479: *the number of Welsh representatives on recent trade missions; how are these companies identified and are they put forward by the Welsh Government*

1. Number of Welsh representatives on recent trade missions

— Since January 2010 at least 40 Welsh companies have participated in UKTI's sector based overseas trade missions. There were no Welsh companies as part of the Prime Minister's recent delegation to India.

2. How are these companies identified

— When working on major overseas trade missions, UKTI works hard to alert colleagues across UK and via business associations to reach effectively into local business networks. Contacts and selection for missions vary depending on sector/mission type, fit with competitive advantage of the different UK region/nations, and the sectoral priorities of the devolved national trade and investment agencies.

— When we have expressions of interest for a mission we will consider the company's suitability for the mission in conjunction with business associations and other partners.

— For example, with the PM visit to China late last year we worked with CBBC (China Britain Business Council) and they reached out to businesses in Wales. We will be holding the next JETCO with China in Cardiff.

— Our overseas network always provides support to visits by Welsh Ministers and their own trade delegations.

3. Are they put forward by the Welsh Government?

UKTI welcomes nominations from the Welsh Government, whether directly or via business associations depending on the nature of the mission and fit with Welsh priorities.

Q 480: *how do you avoid different parts of the UK competing against each other*

— UKTI provides a UK-wide and global inward investment service. Our number one priority is to ensure that investment comes to the UK and not a competitor country.

— The Investor Business Development Forum (IBDF) facilitates at strategic level the close relationship that exists between UK Trade & Investment (UKTI), the Devolved Governments and London (represented by London & Partners) on foreign direct investment and trade development activity. The Forum meets approximately every quarter (last meeting September, and next meeting January 2012), and the Welsh Government regularly attends.

— On winning investment, UKTI works in partnership with the devolved government investment partner agencies and London & Partners to provide the best offer to every company, matched against their needs.

— Our approach is driven by company requirements. We help the company to identify the strongest UK location or locations for any given project, helping the project to land rapidly, cost-effectively and sustainably. In our experience the investing company may have an initial preference, often a strong one, but ultimate decisions usually relate primarily to actual financial or commercial drivers.

— To promote fairness and opportunities for all locations, UKTI through our Investment Services Team shares information about potential projects freely across the UK, enabling investment agencies like the Welsh Government to bid in to any opportunity.

You also requested the following information on BETS in Wales:

Please be aware that it is more appropriate for BETS itself to clarify aspects relating to its own operations. The information below accords to UKTI's own understanding so may be inaccurate:

— the new structure of BETS in Wales;

— 2010 the WG Department of Economy & Transport (under the Deputy First Minister), under their new Economic Renewal Programme, took the decision to cease operation of its trade & investment arm—International Business Wales. It announced that in future the focus would be on six key sectors and the new structure would be fully integrated into Sectors and Business, Department for Business, Enterprise, Technology and Science (BETS) in the Welsh Government.

— The six sectors are: ICT; Energy and environment; Advanced materials and manufacturing; Creative industries; Life Sciences; and Financial and professional services.

— Announcement in Summer 2011 of three additional sectors—Tourism, Construction, and Food (including agriculture)—along with six new Enterprise Zones.

— the location of their overseas offices.

At this point in time, the Welsh Government has a small number of overseas offices (three in China, two in India, plus offices in Japan, UAE and the US), and is co-located with UKTI in UAE and the US.

— and a description of the new major projects unit.

We have not yet been provided with this information from the WG.

December 2011

Supplementary written evidence submitted by the Rt Hon Mrs Cheryl Gillan MP, Secretary of State for Wales

I am writing further to my evidence session to the committee inquiry on Inward Investment on 5 December, during which I undertook to provide some additional information in respect of three particular issues.

Firstly, with regard to investors or potential investors I have met, I attach as an annex to this letter, a list of companies and organisations I have met since May 2010 with a view to developing the Welsh economy by securing further inward investment into Wales.

You also asked about the use of Gwydyr House by Welsh Government officials. As I advised the Committee, we have provided the Welsh Government with the use of a well-appointed self contained office in Gwydyr House. Access to the room is controlled but not monitored and so I am unable to provide information on the use of this room by the Welsh Government.

We discussed the use of office space built by the Welsh Government for inward investors. My office has contacted the First Minister's office regarding this matter and I will clarify the position as soon as I receive a response.

I hope that this additional information on these specific points is useful and I look forward to reading the Committee's report when it is published.

Annex

Date	Organisation
Dec 2011	Wales Consular Business Forum
Nov 2011	Valero
Oct 2011	Opening of the Airbus North Factory with the Prime Minister
Oct 2011	TATA Steel
Oct 2011	ESTnet
Sept 2011	Bangladesh Trade Mission Participants
July 2011	National Grid
June 2011	KPMG
June 2011	Swansea Business Club
June 2011	Visit Britain
May 2011	Panasonic UK
May 2011	Airbus, Broughton
May 2011	Turkish Ambassador
May 2011	Japanese Ambassador
May 2011	Valerian International Ltd
April 2011	Representatives of Engineering and Construction Bodies, Civil Engineering Contractors Association (CECA) Wales, Civil Engineers (ICE) Wales Cymru, Association for Consultancy and Engineering (ACE) Wales, Construction Products Association (CPA).
April 2011	Meeting with Representative Chang, from the Republic of China (Taiwan)
April 2011	Cassidian
March 2011	TATA Steel, with the Secretary of State for Business, Innovation and Skills
March 2011	Bridgend Ford
March 2011	Finnish Ambassador
March 2011	General Dynamics
March 2011	US Delegation on Cyber Space
March 2011	RWE
March 2011	Technium Pembroke and Dragon LNG
Feb 2011	Visit to JCB with the Chancellor
Feb 2011	General Dynamics
Jan 2011	Toyota UK
Jan 2011	Lloyds Banking Group
Jan 2011	Axeon
Nov 2010	Wales Bangladesh Chamber of Commerce
Nov 2010	Dr Lyushun Shen at Taiwan Embassy
Nov 2010	Logicalis

Date	Organisation
Oct 2010	(Minister) Russian Delegation
Oct 2010	Westbridge Credit
Oct 2010	Swift Invest Ltd
Sept 2010	Price Waterhouse Coopers
Sept 2010	Lunch with Japanese Ambassador
Sept 2010	Dinner Meeting with Minister Counsellor Zhou Xiaoming, of the Economic and Commercial Counsellor's Office from the Peoples Republic of China
Sept 2010	Covanta
Sept 2010	Metrix
Aug 2010	Sharp Manufacturing UK
Aug 2010	South Hook LNG Ltd
Aug 2010	Ultrapharm Ltd
July 2010	General Dynamics
July 2010	German industry UK
June 2010	G24 Innovations
June 2010	General Dynamics Reception at FCO
June 2010	Corus
May 2010	Technium Optic
May 2010	GE Aviation with the Prime Minister

January 2012

ISBN 978-0-215-04185-2

PEFC

PEFC/16-33-622